The Covenant Of Grace And The People Of God

The Covenant Of Grace
And The People Of God

George M. Ella

Go publications

Go Publications
Gibb Hill Farm, Ponsonby, Cumbria, CA20 1BX, ENGLAND.

© Go Publications 2020

British Library Cataloguing in Publication Data available

ISBN 978-1-908475-15-2

Cover photograph: Seascale Foreshore (Fiona Birks)

Publisher's Preface

This is a fine defence of the integrity of the pan-Biblical covenant and the faithful and consistent testimony of God to His church and people in every age. I particularly found Dr Ella's thoughts concerning the international nature of God's covenant promises in the Old Testament helpful and refreshing. I enjoyed, too, his thoughts on how a singular view of Jewish covenant applicability is too narrow.

It has struck me for a long time how frequently the Lord was pleased to send the gospel outside of Israel's borders. Did not Joseph take the gospel to Egypt? Naaman certainly carried the gospel back to Syria where there was already at least one believer in Damascus, a little servant girl who evangelised her peers. Mordecai and Esther's greatness in the court of the Medes and Persians was immense and we are told many believed because of them. Daniel's influence was considerable in Babylon and Nebuchadnezzar had wonderful revelations of God's glory. The history of Balaam and Balak betrays a keen awareness amongst surrounding nations of God's covenant dealings with His people. These things were not hid. Jonah's testimony in Nineveh was powerful and if we may take the scripture testimony at face value, and we should, many, many believed God. This was a huge, huge city of antiquity and the vast majority must surely have been Gentiles.

Wise men came from the east seeking the King of the Jews. Even the Lord's dealings with the Syrophenician woman who by the Saviour's own testimony possessed great and genuine faith shows covenant grace was never restricted to a single race. She was a Canaanite by birth and abode, but was truly one of the lost sheep of the

5

house of Israel whom the Lord had come to seek and to save. Gentiles knew grace and were blessed in the Covenant of Peace long before the gospel was sent more fully to the Gentiles in the great commission.

This volume goes forth with the prayer and sure confidence that the same grace that always saved sinners by bringing them to a knowledge of the truth will be instrumental in opening the eyes of God's elect till the last lost sheep is gathered and the fulness of the truth as it is in Jesus is known the world over. Then the earth shall be full of the knowledge of the Lord, as the waters cover the sea.

Peter L. Meney

Table of Contents

Foreword

Having the enormous privilege of reading a pre-publication of Dr George Ella's book, *The Covenant of Grace And The People of God*, I am thrilled to commend his work to the public. This is a true treasure trove of historical, theological, and most importantly, biblical expositions. This volume will edify God's People, and in many instances, educate even seasoned scholars.

Statements such as 'There is one golden thread through all these messages from God seen in the pan-biblical Covenant of Grace' will surely ruffle the feathers of many, including dispensationalists, New Covenant Theology advocates (Ella says, 'the NCT should call itself BCT – Broken Covenant Theology!') and some reformed covenant proponents. On New Covenant advocates, Ella surmises: 'They preach only half of the Covenant of Grace which then becomes a covenant of error. Furthermore, they make the new covenant preached by Jeremiah merely appear as a book of magic rules which only they can decipher.' They will not like this, but say what they will, Ella has done a masterful job in showing that the eternal Covenant of Grace is one from eternity to eternity. As Ella declares, 'Thus both testaments with one accord serve as pointers to God's covenant promise that He is always choosing out a People for Himself to be cleansed of their sin by Jesus Christ, their Saviour and Messiah.'

His chapters on Gill and Durie were extremely enlightening and Ella takes no prisoners when interacting with so-called experts. He challenges the false notion of 'free or well-meant offer' as the covenant is not made with equals, man and God on the same footing, and not even with man and God on an uneven footing, where the condition is slight but fulfilled by man, nonetheless. Ella shows from careful insight into the book of Hebrews that the Covenant was made between the Perfect God and the Perfect Man in the divine council, and that Jesus

Christ is the perfect Man, who alone fulfils the covenant stipulations on behalf of His elect People. This will not only enlighten the reader it will cause him to pause and to praise the Lord for such unsearchable wisdom. George Ella aptly summarizes Gill: that not only was the Covenant of Grace contrived and planned from eternity, but it was always fixed and settled there as an essential factor in God's eternal nature, choosing out a Covenant People. Our God is a Covenant God and a God of Grace in His very nature. He created the world to fulfil His desire.

Ella's insight into the fulfilling of time and how Christ is the Saviour from eternity is surely Gillesque. This was a blessing to unravel through various interjections throughout this volume. It is this understanding of eternal redemption that allows Ella to appeal to the text about Christ *being slain before the foundation of the world*. As Ella puts matters: "Gill, however, teaches that grace comes to the elect 'in time' and this is 'to eternity'. In other words, the elect are chosen in time for eternity. Gill goes deeper into this question elsewhere where he distinguishes, as did the old Reformers and (some) Puritans between 'eternity' and 'aevi-eternity'. The former meaning eternal per se, which can only be used properly of God, and the latter, that which is created in time for eternity.

Later, Ella sums up: 'As Christ is the Lamb slain before the foundation of the world, His Testatorship works both backwards and forwards in time, securing all God's elect from condemnation and reconciling them to God.' This succinct and memorable phrase says it all. It is in line with Ella's definition of the Covenant of Grace: it is 'God's plan of choosing out a People for Himself'.

There are numerous helpful expressions throughout the book. Here are a few select pieces that made a mark on me: 'I wish to show that the Covenant of Grace was to all nations from the beginning of time and how its scope spread with the spreading of the nations world-wide. As Paul argues, the Jews had profited as a people by God's covenant revelations but this gave them a greater responsibility before God and was no profit to them when disbelieved.' Also, this fascinating insight: 'I would also like to further this pan-Biblical study by exploring how God chose a People for Himself out of mankind and point out how the efficacy of Christ's atoning death for His Church stretches back to the beginning of time and forwards to the end of time and the gateway to eternal peace with God.' Finally, a challenge, via an historical insight, to those in the avant-garde: ' … since the early sixties, the evangelical scene has radically changed. That enemy of the covenant gospel which, for want of a better name, we must call 'Fullerism' has revived with a vengeance as a religion of alleged 'pure reason'. It has begun once again to follow its fanatical bent of minimizing God's grace, His law and even God Himself whilst spreading the myth of a maximising of man's abilities and capacities over the sovereignty of the Father, the Love of the Son and the comfort of the Holy Spirit.'

I have very few books that I have marked up so much as this one. I found myself nodding my head frequently, and only once or twice found myself proverbially scratching my head. There is so much to learn from George Ella. I have found his works illuminating and always instructive. Not only this, but I sense a warmth and devotion to Jesus Christ that marks one of the true children of God, as John Durie would have described. Which brings me to the section on Durie and the Appendices. They buck conventional wisdom and challenge long-held beliefs or legends one might say about Puritanism and the Westminster Assembly. No doubt, there are controversial elements here, but what a joy in seeing historical scholarship scale heights that few dare to reach. For example, Ella challenges aspects of Hetherington's well-known and widely accepted account: 'This Presbyterian misuse of power explains why so often in the writings of the Westminster Assembly members, and the 17th Century Puritans, we find doctrines and political theories based on a natural theology shunned by our Reformers.'

'The Presbyterian Rutherford lobbyists at the Assembly', claims Ella, 'though they had no vote, were allowed a powerful voice in most debates. During the meetings, Scriptural doctrines were only introduced positively if they were found to be according to either natural law or the light of nature. The Westminster Confession even claims that the light of nature and natural law are the initial incentives behind setting apart a time of worship and keeping the Sabbath.'

These and other historical nuggets are part of the reason one simply must engage Ella. Also, in contradistinction to 'Naturalistic Enlightenment notions' that guided men such as Rutherford, consider this insight from elsewhere in the book: 'Sinners are in total darkness unless true Enlightenment comes through the Holy Spirit. This blindness to nature's glories is seen by Paul as a judgment of God. The

11

Westminster Confession, however, sees man as still possessing the natural ability to know God's will in nature which leads to natural worship. As the *Westminster Standards* were never finished due to Pride's Purge and other setbacks for the Presbyterians and Cromwell became too low on funds to encourage and to finance John Durie and Adoniram Byfield's continuing work on the Confession, the *Westminster Standards* reveal a most jumbled theology as they were mere bits and pieces still to be synergized. This unfinished symphony has been played by the Presbyterians ever since as if it were the orthodox faith. In my debates with Presbyterians I find few argue from Scripture, but they argue either for or against my views of the covenant and man's nature from the same *Confession* which lends itself to different interpretations.' Still on this question, Ella observes, 'It is interesting to note that Cromwell wisely denied the Scottish contingent the right to vote at the Assembly, always suspicious of their strategies. He made an exception in the case of Scotsman John Durie who represented the old but proven Reformed paths.'

There is much more that could be said. Time fails me to speak of the People of God as God defines them; the historical significance of the Law and Grace, and their theological intertwining; the characteristics of the One Mediator; the various jabs at the Hyper-Calvinist police, such as the curt (pun intended) responses to Curt Daniel, Sam Waldron and others of their ilk, including Andrew Fuller, their hero; the errors of dispensationalism and 'Christian' Zionism; and more, much more!

Do not miss this book. It is highly and heartily recommended!

Theodore Zachariades
Manchester, TN
May 2019

Introduction

No Covenant, No Gospel

The golden thread throughout the Bible

In the ministry of every faithful pastor or preacher comes a time when the man of God feels he is not preaching in a true gospel manner. He stresses faithfully this and that detail which the scriptures show clearly lead to salvation but finds he is still limiting his care of souls to teaching what he feels are 'the basic needs' of a life in Christ but he has no general framework or overall doctrine in which to place it. 'It must all belong together somehow', he often thinks but also 'How do I know I am truly teaching the essential factors that will lead my congregation to Christ and build them up in the faith?' He finds expository preaching preferable to topical preaching as, when one waits long enough, all the doctrines of grace will somehow be covered but he still would like to put his entire ministry under one heading which discloses all God's provisions for making saints out of sinners and prepares them best for meeting their Lord in glory. In other words, he wishes to have full insight into the gospel he preaches before passing it on to others.

All who are called to build up others in the faith, and fellowship with them in all earthly and heavenly matters would so often like to know more about what God in Christ has done for our salvation and what priorities the Holy Spirit has set in giving us the Word of God. Over the last thirty years or so, this author has realised more and more that he has left out of his ministry the clear teaching of scripture on the Covenant of Grace which gives the reason and structure of salvation and the time line which leads to the gathering in of the elect throughout all ages until the end of time and the Christian's entering in to glory.

In a former work *The Covenant of Grace and Christian Baptism,*[1] I explored how important the doctrine of baptism was as an audio-visual help in pointing to the Covenant of Grace which is God's plan of choosing out a People for Himself. Obviously most of these studies were in the New Testament but I trust I also displayed how important the Old Testament is in understanding the New Testament from Matthew to Revelation and the purposes of both circumcision and baptism in illustrating the divine plan of salvation in God's choosing out a People as the apple of His eye. My purpose was also to demonstrate the great importance of the New Testament from Matthew to Revelation in understanding the Old Testament from Genesis to Malachi. There is one golden thread through all these messages from God seen in the pan-biblical Covenant of Grace.

Neither the Old nor the New Testament are 'stand-alones'
In preparing this book, I have used essays, letters and notes made on the subject of the Covenant over the years, many published by *New Focus Magazine*. I have used my contributions to The *English Churchman*, besides a number of my essays published as student material by the Martin Bucer Seminary, Bonn. Then I have consulted three of my papers published by Reformed Heritage Books and one article each published by *Churchman* and the Berlin newspaper *Die Gemeinde* my latest publication being '*Henry Bullinger (1504-1575): Vater und Hirte der Reformation*' published by the *Zeitschrift für Theologie und Gesellschaft* at the beginning of this year. Then there are my books *Henry Bullinger: Shepherd of the Churches*; *John Gill and the Cause of God and Truth* and *John Gill and Justification from Eternity* published by Go Publications. I have also used my works *The Covenant of Grace and Christian Baptism* and *The Practical Divinity of Universal Learning* published by the Verlag für Kultur und Wissenschaft and have

---

[1]Theologisches Lehr-und Studienmaterial (Martin Bucer Seminar) Band 25, Verlag für Kultur und Wissenschaft, Bonn, 2007.

added much unpublished and much newly written material besides reading through the works listed in my bibliography which reflect only some of my reading during the last decade. In these writings, and especially in this present publication, I have emphasised the pan-biblical teaching concerning the central theme of the scriptures which is the Covenant of Grace. In doing so, I demonstrate how neither the Old Testament nor the New Testament can stand as separate works because both give a continued witness to the everlasting Covenant from Genesis to Revelation. Those who break this Covenant revelation by rejecting the Old Testament witness break their part in the Covenant of Grace. Thus the modern Marcionite idea that God's Covenant is a New Testament matter only is severely challenged in this book. The veracity of the New Testament stands or falls with the veracity of the Old Testament because both Testaments depict the same way of salvation through the Father's everlasting Covenant with His Son presented to everyman through the testimony of the Spirit in the written and preached Word. This is the one Gospel that depicts the only way of salvation. If we cannot accept this Covenant, we have thus no Gospel.

Christ is choosing out a People for Himself since creation
The Covenant story shows how a special People of God are chosen out from fallen mankind through the outworking of Christ's vicarious and redeeming death for them which is efficacious from creation to the Resurrection, so enabling that People to enter eternity to be ever with their Lord. Thus, through the long history of the world, Christ has always been choosing a People for Himself and this will continue until all the elect have been gathered in. In other words, the Testaments are one work concerned with the one and only way of salvation for the one People of God. These Testaments are the story of God's Covenant in revelation, history and fulfilment.

I would also like to further this pan-biblical study by exploring how God chose a People for Himself out of mankind and point out how the efficacy of Christ's atoning death for His Church stretches back to the beginning of time and forwards to the end of time and the gateway to eternal peace with God. This is because Christ was always in all the scriptures, teaching His People to walk in fellowship with Him. The Old Testament saints looked forward in faith to their redemption in

15

Christ and Christians of today look back in faith to that glorious delivery from sin and death. Thus the author of the book of Hebrews can write referring to all believers in all ages: 'Now faith is the substance of things hoped for, the evidence of things not seen'[2] and he goes through the entire scriptures from the beginning of time until his day to prove what he is saying. So, too, Paul tells us 'We walk by faith and not by sight.'[3] Habakkuk, who knew this truth as well as the other great Bible prophets, preached, 'The just shall live by faith.'[4] We Christians can faithfully bring this prophetic and apostolic truth to our own day and make it an integral part in our Christian witness knowing 'The life I now live in the flesh I live by the faith of the Son of God, who loved me and gave himself for me.'[5] We notice we have no faith of ourselves but it is Christ's faith within us that binds us to Him.[6] Thus both Testaments with one accord serve as pointers to God's Covenant promise that He is always choosing out a People for Himself to be cleansed of their sin by Jesus Christ, their Saviour and Messiah.

The Covenant of Grace is not a covenant of confusion
Nowadays, amongst people who are seeking to understand the Covenant, there is much confusion as to who are exactly the People of God within that work of grace of which Christ is the Author, Keeper and Fulfiller. This question can only be answered when we understand the doctrine of God's eternal covenant with Christ concerning the People of His choice. All else *is* confusion.

Sadly, all of us see through a glass darkly, as Paul puts it, concerning scriptural revelation. Nevertheless, our loving God provides us with insights here and there which prepare us for seeing God face to face. Our understanding of scriptural theology has waxed and waned throughout the centuries as darkness followed by enlightenment has been at ebb and flood among mankind. In the 16th century, enlightenment was desperately needed concerning the covenant of the Son with the Father drawn up for our salvation through the creation of the world. Then God, once more, intervened from eternity working in

---

[2] Hebrews 11:1ff..
[3] 2 Corinthians 5:7.
[4] Habakkuk 2:4.
[5] Galatians 2:20.
[6] See also Revelation 14:12.

time to give us that special eye-opening manifestation which we call rightly 'The Reformation'. Then the truth that was found again in biblical understanding was righteousness by faith which I believe few Christians would question nowadays. However, there is not this unanimity regarding the basic and essential and, indeed, all-embracing doctrine of the Covenant of Grace which shows why man has been granted righteousness and faith in the first place. Indeed, the Covenant of Grace seems to have been dropped from modern preaching in these days of dumbing down doctrine to the point that we hear preachers saying, 'Jesus loves you. What are you going to do about it?'

The ups and downs of the doctrine of grace in Christian doctrine
Now turned eighty, I have been in Christ for a little over sixty-three years but had many precious moments recognizing the Lord's goodness from my third year on. During this long time, now coming to an end, I have seen Christ's Covenant People go through many ups and downs and there has been much suffering but also much triumphing in the Churches. However, in the fifties and early sixties there seemed to be something of a consensus amongst Christians as to what the doctrines of grace were. Christians knew and experienced how God applied these doctrinal blessings to the sinners He had drawn to Himself through Christ's self-offering righteous life and atoning death. They believed in Christ's glorious resurrection as the Firstling to prepare the way to a like resurrection in a New Jerusalem populated by the People of God. One could stand up wherever one was in my home town of Bradford and preach the gospel. Liberalism and Modernism were shunned and the opposition to Reformed theology came mostly from the Arminians, Dispensationalists and those who speculated in eschatological fantasies, all who claimed allegiance to the Bible, unversed as they were in their understanding of it.

Amongst these groups of professing Christians, struggling to comprehend the doctrines of the Bible, there were those who were obviously also Children of God. I used to put their failings down to pastors who needed pastoral care themselves and thought of Christ's words 'Father, forgive them for they know not what they do.'[7]

---

[7] Luke 23:34.

The Covenant of Grace rationalized away

Now, thinking of Bunyan's task as a Pilgrim having to clean out dirty stables, I note that the modern faithful evangelist is faced with even more cleansing work before establishing the true Covenant of God so it can be made palatable for all people. Gospel teaching, on the whole, has become so shallow and threadbare we might rightly say 'If the righteous scarcely be saved, where shall the ungodly and the sinner appear.'[8] This is because since the early sixties, the evangelical scene has changed radically. That enemy of the Covenant gospel which, for want of a better name, we must call 'Fullerism' has revived with a vengeance as a religion of alleged 'pure reason'. It has begun once again to follow its fanatical bent of minimizing God's Grace, His Law and even God Himself whilst spreading the myth of a maximising of man's abilities and capacities over the sovereignty of the Father, the Love of the Son and the comfort of the Holy Spirit. For this reason, I feel it is my Christian duty to devote two chapters in this book on the faith-killing, Covenant-of-Grace-denying rationalism of this ever-spreading rot.

What is scholarly, learned and intellectual?

Another dire development I have seen, especially as one familiar with the inside of six universities as student, lecturer and Chairman examiner besides having taken graduate and post-graduate Senior Service Examinations in the administration of Education, is the secularizing of the evangelical, Reformed faith by a false view of what is 'scholarly' and 'learned' and 'intellectually acceptable'. Once one spoke of ministers who knew 'a little Latin and less Greek' and this was true but nowadays, one hears pulpit-thumpers with no Latin and no Greek telling us what the Hebrew says here and what the Greek says there, trusting their faith in a few popular commentaries rather than prayerful study of God's Word in a language they understand. I remember my rejecting the 'academic titles' offered by a London Bible College who wanted badly to be regarded as a university who nevertheless warned me against going to a 'secular' university and gaining professional knowledge of the biblical languages and told me that Christians 'lost

---

[8] 1 Peter 4:18.

18

their faith' there. I knew several who 'lost their faith' at Bible Colleges, too. On arriving at a real university, because this was the sole way of following my calling in education, I came under the glorious ministry of my mentor Professor Canon James Atkinson. In his first lecture he told us that we as budding theologians probably felt that we should stand over the Word of God and judge it. There was to be none of that in his courses. His students were told to put themselves under the Word of God and let it judge them. My Bible College had been too busy 'bashing' the universities whilst imitating their pseudo-academic side and had never spoken as clearly to me regarding the Faith as did that precious man of God, James Atkinson. When I continued my Greek, Hebrew and Aramaic studies at Uppsala, I was safe in the hands of professors who loved the Lord reflected in the teaching they undertook. So I shall be looking in this book into the efforts of several of such pseudo-learned 'linguists' to bamboozle us with a false rendering of Greek and Hebrew and even dare to tell us that they are correcting not only the Greek and Hebrew understanding of the best Bible translators ever but also such scholars' renderings on scripture in their mother tongues. These relatively uneducated critics use their own dumbing-down of language as their measuring rod.

Old pre-Law Covenant teaching broken
One of the greatest onslaughts against the Reformed faith has come in the last few decades from professing Christians who lay claim to the whole truth and nothing but the truth but 'edit' the Bible more than the old 'demythologisers' such as Bultmann would ever have dreamed possible. Indeed, their claim to follow the scriptures of their choice leaves them with little scripture to follow. Here I refer to modern so-called New Covenant Theologians who are sadly still playing the role of those Jews of the Exodus who broke their covenant with God before the coming of the Mosaic Law which was added to the Covenant with Abraham especially because of their transgressions. They preach only half of the Covenant of Grace which then becomes a Covenant of Error. Furthermore, they make the New Covenant preached by Jeremiah merely appear as a book of magic rules which only they can decipher. They reject the written Law and substitute for it a Law which they claim they have from the Spirit which they have never striven to write out and

be judged by the scriptures from Genesis to Revelation. I have therefore spent three chapters dealing with their 'criticism with a penknife', a complaint levelled in the Early Church at Marcion, the founder of the original NCT.

Jews and Greeks and the Covenant of Grace

In debunking false myths concerning the Covenant of Grace and the People of God, I have felt I must deal with the Christian-Zionists who provide us with their science-fiction idea of a War To End All Wars at the end of time and their belief that 'all Jews will be saved' whether they believe in Christ or not. I wish to show that the Covenant of Grace was to all nations from the beginning of time and how its scope spread with the spreading of the nations world-wide. As Paul argues, the Jews had profited as a people by God's Covenant revelations but this gave them a greater responsibility before God and was no profit to them when disbelieved. Paul showed how his Jewish background had been both a curse and a blessing to him in Galatians 1:13, 14 where he says:

> For ye have heard of my conversation in time past in the Jews' religion, how that beyond measure I persecuted the church of God and wasted it: And profited in the Jews' religion above many my equals in mine own nation, been more exceedingly zealous for the traditions of my fathers.

This ended, however, as we read in v. 16 when God revealed His Son to Paul. So Paul can argue in Romans 2:25 that the religion of the Jews is no profit to them if they are not true Jews 'inwardly, circumcised in the heart, in the spirit, and not in the letter; whose praise is not of men, but of God.' This is why almost all the books of the Old Testament stress that only a faithful remnant of Jews shall be saved. This goes, of course, for Gentiles, too.

The NCT might note that this was the Christian testimony of the Old Testament through the witness of David and the Prophets which was not annulled and changed in the New Testament. I have therefore devoted three chapters to the modern Jewish situation against the background of the everlasting gospel and the eternal Covenant of Grace. I may appear to give a *criticism of* rather than an *admonition to* the present Jewish minority state of Israel, which I find more political than religious and the religious side is far from the religion of the Old Testament which points to Christ. There is, however, as the Prophets promised us, a remnant of the true New Jerusalem within the Jewish background as also amongst the Gentiles.

Slaughtering and Dissecting the Gospel Bird of Paradise
Into the evangelical Reformed faith has now come a cold pseudo-academic movement mustering under the false name of 'Puritans'. These are analytical, systematic preachers who cut the gospel into bits and pieces and cut up and out what they feel are gospel 'titbits' as real doctrines thus making unpalatable dogmas out of wholesome truths. Accepting such cut-down 'doctrines' has become the denominational idea of what is the 'Reformed norm'. One has a baptism banner, another a Lord's Supper banner, then there are those with 'tithing' banners and also those with eschatological banners and free-will banners followed by those with their 'moderate' or 'hyper-Calvinist' banners. Each denomination picks out a piece of their special choice to serve as their 'Banner of Truth' without true regard to the wholeness of the gospel. Their 'badge' determines their club rules and even *ordo salutis*, the latter meaning 'order of salvation' in which salvation is ensured to those following their denominational programme. I have a good deal to say about these false roads to Heaven.

Allied to these are many who defend doctrines close to my own but in a most restricted manner. Reformed, evangelical 'Calvinists' take note! A typical example I have had to deal with in this book is the idolatry shown in the 'Tulip' method of teaching whereby the entire gospel is reduced to five deterministic dogmas that are supposed to sum up the Christian faith. All Christians ought to absorb all these Five Points but not as legalistic tenets to give the appearance of being 'Reformed' and a 'new law' because there is much, much more to the Covenant of Grace which depicts the whole everlasting gospel for the People of God which can only be taught in the full context of the Covenant. Sadly, many of my tulip loving brethren have split God's Covenant into two covenants, one of Law and one of Grace. The true Covenant teaches the Grace of the Law and the Law of Grace, which are fulfilled together in Christ on our behalf. Sadly 'tip-toeing through the tulips' has given birth to much legalism.

21

Beware then of these 'bits and pieces' denominations who have no all-round gospel to preach. When salvation through the love of Christ is not preached to the full, all 'systematic theologies' are empty. Being a five-point 'Calvinist' may be a good start to becoming a Christian but Calvin never wore such a narrow, restrictive doctrinal corset, nor the Canons of Dort, for that matter. Indeed, when one reads the hundreds of pages long original minutes of the Conference at Dort one wonders from where modern 'Reformed' confessors have obtained their five-point abstract. Anyway, the large collection of over fifty Reformed confessions before the Canons of Dort and the Westminster Confession came on the scene are healthily 'Protestant', wholesomely 'Reformed and almost free from politics. I wonder if this is why they are all forgotten today?

Covenant views of choice Reformers
Any historical and exegetical overview of the Covenant of Grace and the Practical Divinity based on it would be deficient without dealing in this volume with the pioneer writer on the subject, Heinrich Bullinger and the extensive work of Scotsman John Durie (c.1599-c.1680). The latter undertook the task of propagating the then almost lost doctrine from 1528 to his death in his German exile. In his day, this now almost forgotten Reformer commanded the attention and cooperation of four Archbishops and led a distinguish team of international co-workers which included Richard Baxter, George Calixtus, John Davenant, John Forbes, Johannes Matthiae, Gerhard Molanus, John Owen, David Pareus, Edward Stillingfleet, Cornelius Burges, Daniel Featley, Thomas Goodwin, William Gouge, Joseph Hall, Samuel Hartlib, Joachim Hübner, Philip Nye, Richard Sibbs, Sidrach Simpson, John Stoughton, William Twisse, Henry Oldenburg, John Downam[9] and James Ussher, to mention but some of those known to the English speaking public of the day and who looked to Durie for leadership.[10] Samuel Hartlib, Philip Nye and Henry Oldenburg[11] acted as Durie's special envoys and contact-men in Britain. Most of these men remained true to Durie's cause throughout their lives and formed what Tom

---

[9] Variously spelt Downame, Downham.
[10] See Webster, Part 4 for names of lesser known men.
[11] First Secretary of the Royal Society and Durie's son-in-law.

Webster of Edinburgh University in his *Godly Clergy in Early Stuart England* calls Durie's 'steering committee'.[12] Even Hugo Grotius was positively influenced by Durie's work.

I have thus devoted five chapters to three main Reformers, Bullinger, Durie and Gill, representing the 16th, 17th and 18th centuries, who made divine truths comforting and palatable and allowed the head to communicate with the heart in outlining the Covenant of God for the People of God. They expounded what John Bale calls the 'Everlasting Gospel of the Everlasting Covenant.' Though Bale brought me early to Covenant teaching, I reserve discussion of his wonderful expositions of the New Jerusalem for my last chapter which is about the entry of the People of God into their eternal Heavenly Home.

Scholarly and devotional Bible studies belong together
It will become evident when reading this book that I have not separated scholarly work from its devotional and spiritual home in the Word of God. This endeavour is not of my own invention but is the wisdom of our Reformers which I gratefully follow. Only here do we find our God-only-Wise who has used His divine wisdom to labour for the salvation of His Covenant children. Sad to say, the reasoning of the would-be scholar often dims his eye of faith. On the other hand the humble poor with less education are continually telling me that the Bible is a closed book to them. Given all the contradictory theologies represented by dubious modern translations, this is obviously not their fault. Thus I have striven to write a biblical overview for the intellectual, the person of average and less intelligence, the poor and the rich. I pray that the Father will make His purpose known to them in the story of His wonderful Covenant with His Son, explained in the scriptures by the Holy Spirit who always makes the gospel plain to those who sincerely seek it in Christ's Name. I know some of my evangelical friends will say that this work, like all other works from my pen, falls between two stools so I should distinguish between the scholarly and the devotional and put aside either the one or the other. I find no such necessity or distinction in teaching the whole synergized truth revealed to us in God's Word and trust that all my readers will recognize that there are

---

[12] Webster, p. 257.

23

indeed two major stools depicted in the Bible, which are the Throne of Grace and the Judgment Seat of God. The Covenant of Grace teaches us how to 'sit with Jesus' around His Throne. I trust that I have at least demonstrated that in the Covenant of Grace God's People experience that God's Mercy always determines His Justice and there is no condemnation to them which are in Christ Jesus, who walk not after the flesh, but after the Spirit.[13]

The place of Law in Grace
This truth leads me to deal in the book very much with the Law in its application within the Covenant of Grace, showing that it is not a separate covenant but an essential factor in the Covenant's distinction between the letter and the Spirit. The Law was added to the eternal Covenant with Abraham because of man's transgressions and was also a handbook to promote an understanding of the righteousness which is of faith. Sadly, those who go the way of all flesh and abolish the Law for themselves, have failed to understand the tenor and purport of Law as a guide to understanding God's Grace, His righteousness and His means of Salvation. Thus those who abolish the Law abolish God's Grace.

Repetitions needed
I am aware of the many repetitions of important points in this book and they are intentional. I have been a teacher all my adult life and learnt the value of repetition in applying learned truths to new problems. Thus when I repeatedly emphasise the unity of scripture, it is in places where this unity is variously challenged and must be applied variously. When I show how the Covenant is broken, it is to illustrate how the Covenant is broken in many individual cases throughout a varied history. Each rupture must be treated with the same healing application. When I complain that not all professing Jews represent the New Jerusalem and not all professing Christians either, it is because many Jewish and Christian sectarians reserved the New Jerusalem for their own petty clique alone and one must be challenged on the ground one stands on. This was so in Old Testament days, was the same in New Testament

---

[13] Romans 8:1.

days and is the same today. Note how often Isaiah said the same thing but applied to new problems of unbelief.

My thanks
I would like to take the opportunity here of thanking my dear friend and brother Dr Theodore Zachariades, a man gifted by God as his name indicates, to make Divine truths palatable and combine the academic with the devotional and spiritual. He has kindly read through my manuscript and spotted my 'scribal errors'. Dr Zachariades is also responsible for the *Foreword* which adorns my book.

One of the main purposes of writing a book is not merely the joy it affords the author in counting God's blessings but also the joy in believing that he trusts readers will gain from his labour of love. Thus, almost as important as the book itself is the fact that a sympathetic Publisher must be found. I have no need to look far for such a man. Peter Meney my trusted friend and brother in the Lord of many years standing has kindly published the bulk of my work since the late eighties either in the *New Focus Magazine* or through the *Evangelical Times*, *Evangelical Press* and *Go-Publications* so I look upon all our publications as our joint testimony to promote the Cause of God and Truth.

Chapter 1

The Covenant of Grace and 17th Century 'Enlightenment' Theology

Fallen Man has no Agency within the Covenant

There is much said today in Christian circles about man's agency in adapting himself to God's provisions of salvation within His Covenant. The general tone seems to be that though man is theoretically considered dead to a life in Christ, there is still something reasonable in him which longs to be right with God. Furthermore, we are told, man on hearing the Gospel knows he has a duty to believe it. They call this 'duty faith'. However, Christ's work as Mediator and Author and Finisher of the Covenant as also the Author and Finisher of the Christian faith can only be an acceptable doctrine to those who believe that man, because of his fall, is by nature outside of the Covenant of Grace until our triune God brings him in. The way in is through the only Door available to man, through Christ Himself. Until Christ enters a sinner's life, spiritually understood, he is but a heap of bones in the Valley of the Dead.[14] Only the voice of God can command people who are dead in trespasses and sins to live as both Testaments make clear. Any doctrine which thus speaks of any innate ability in man to assist or

---

[14] Ezekiel 37:1ff.

even cooperate in his own call to a life more abundant is a doctrine which rejects God's Covenant of Grace.

A brief overview of how the downgrading of the Gospel began
This sound Covenant theology, outlined from Genesis to Revelation was rejected by many revolutionary Divines in the seventeenth century. Indeed, the modern idea that the 17th century was an age of greater spirituality and theological acumen than ever former times had produced is a hypothetical bubble quickly burst. It has been propagated intensely since the late fifties by a handful of modern 'enlightened' publishing houses which have set themselves up as modern champions of a new kind of 'Puritanism' based on Andrew Fuller's humanistic view of man's capacities, and taken over from 17th and 18th century ideas of maximizing man's part in salvation. This downgrading of true religion started in Commonwealth times when both State and Church were crumbling. True, there was a high number of Christian individuals in the turbulent years of the 17th century as will be shown in this work but these were mostly solitary watchmen and side-liners who were persecuted by powerful members of the Commonwealth government and its politico-theological Assemblies.

Vox populi, vox Dei
This was the time when God was thought to have retired as a Deity from the world scene and all was left to man to reform man. Leaders of a man-made 'Puritanism' such as Scotland's Samuel Rutherford preached *vox populi, vox Dei*; the people's voice is the voice of God. By 1643/4, every member of the Westminster Assembly was given a copy of Rutherford's seditious and highly revolutionary political publication, *Lex Rex* as his spiritual guide. This was the first major rationalist and so-called Enlightenment work to be mass-distributed in Britain. Rutherford argued that 'nature's light', 'nature's instinct', 'nature's law', 'the covenant of nature' and even a common human 'law of nations' was the Divine power in the people. He came up with the idea, influenced by French Jesuit and early Humanist thinking that the powers-that-be are only of God if they behave according to Rutherford's strongly rationalistic Neo-Presbyterian view of nature. He and his followers developed the 'New Age' idea of a man-God covenant which they imposed on Britain, virtually splitting the Covenant of

28

Grace into two quite separate covenants. If monarchies and governments did not act according to Rutherford's stern Rationalism, he argued that the people must claim the natural right, led by their natural light, to use violence against them. According to Rutherford, a Christian may even take the law into his own hands and kill a neighbour if he does so 'without malice or appetite of revenge', and if he may do it out of this principle, 'Thou shalt love thy neighbour as thyself', because a man is obliged more to love his own flesh than his neighbour's.'[15] This wrong and rather senseless thinking is the natural outcome, it seems, when one deifies Reason. It is interesting to note the Scottish contingent of commissioners demanded the right to speak at the Westminster Assembly but refused to be part of it and accept membership. Oliver Cromwell, always suspicious of their strategies, thus prevented them from voting. He made an exception in the case of Scotsman John Durie who represented the old but proven Reformed paths.

The Neo-Presbyterians[16] had sought to dethrone James I under Andrew Melville and strove to end the old Scottish Presbyterian system which had rejected rule by monarchical elders for which Melville fought. They then campaigned against both Charles I and Cromwell to gain great power in Parliament and Cromwell had to agree to working closely with them until he found ways to oust them as he had ousted the Church of England. When the Neo-Presbyterians realised they were losing ground under Cromwell, though they had campaigned with him to have Charles I's head cut off, they now abandoned the 'Protector' and bargained with Charles II. They offered the Second Charles their allegiance if he would give them their parliamentary seats back. It is often forgotten that Charles II was crowned King first by Scottish Presbyterians. At first the rebel government had great success in putting down reformation strivings, outlawing those who stuck to Reformation paths but the Presbyterians lost their power after 1648, chiefly because of their policy to re-establish the Monarch under their heel. Their

---

[15] *Lex Rex*, p. 163ff. See also Questions II, IX, XI, XIV, XXXI, XXXVII, XXVII and passim.
[16] The term 'Neo-Presbyterians' applies to those divines who rejected the Scottish Reformation pioneered by the Lollards and Patrick Hamilton and introduced Jesuitical and French humanistic theories sponsored by John, George Buchanan, John Knox and Andrew Melville and carried on by Samuel Rutherford.

politico-religious philosophy became outdated. This was never a popular policy so the Independents, fierce critics of the Presbyterians, began to take over and even more chaos ensued. However, unlike the Presbyterians, the Independents showed they could learn from their mistakes. The point was that in the bitter 'Engagement Controversy', most of the churches in no less than sixteen counties throughout England, Wales and Ireland settled for a joint Protestant Church independent of a King, who had been executed, and the House of Lords, which had been abolished. Neither Cromwell nor the Presbyterians were willing to support this idea though most of those who signed the *Engagement* supported Cromwell, believing the powers-that-be are ordained of God. Western Christianity has never recovered from this Century of Chaos which brought with it a radical downgrading in Reformed theology.

The chaos spelt out
Looking back over the mythical hedge that modern pseudo 'Puritans' have planted around the Commonwealth period, we see that under the stern but soon trembling hand of Cromwell, the British public, government and churches experienced military and moral rebellion, a great down-grading and a national back-sliding in religion in all the four countries once united by James I. This was accompanied by fierce religio-political intolerance, anarchy in politics, an upsurge of Rationalism, massacres in Ireland and Scotland, a bawdy press, women's demands for large pieces of pastoral pies, the growth of denominationalism through church-splitting over minute externals and opposition from universities and colleges to the authority of both scripture and traditional Christianity. Preaching began to fall out of vogue and secular music and play-acting was more popular than ever. It was bawdy ballads for the proletarian populace, and the latest Sir William Davenant operas, enhanced with sets built by Inigo Jones, for the Puritan gentry. Cromwell encouraged this movement by supporting and patronising the first opera ever to be composed in England. Though Charles I had angered the populace enough for supporting an orchestra of some 47 musicians, under Cromwell 'mixed dancing' was allowed in Whitehall with a one-hundred-man-strong orchestra trumpeting and banging drums all through nights of celebrations.

'Christian' astrology common in the Cromwellian era

The Protector also decided to increase his funds by plundering and piracy, thus causing the wrath of his Protestant Continental allies such as Holland, Sweden and Denmark who suffered the most, leaving France and Spain laughing. He fell into apocalyptical, astrological dreams under the influence of 'Christian' astrologer William Lilly. Few in the middle of the seventeenth century could escape the impact of astronomy into the Christian faith, especially after Lilly produced his best-selling *Christian Astrologer*. Reformed university Professors, for instance, demanded the day and the hour of their students' births so they could work out their horoscopes. A pioneer in this superstition was Philip Melanchthon who started the day by consulting the constellations and working out his student's 'horror-scopes' against which true Reformer Henry Bullinger complained. However, in Cromwell's days many sects arose which combined the language of Sion with the occult fables of Nostradamus. Female dissenting clergy skilled in dukkerin pestered the 1653 Saints' Parliament with prophetic petitions signed by over 6,000 sisters and ex-Leveller John Cadbury consulted the planets for the Royalists whilst William Lilly star-gazed for the Republicans. In many ways, the Civil War was a Star War. Indeed, when Professor Gunnar Westin, a Baptist, lectured at Uppsala University on the foreign politics of the European Churches, he entitled his section on England 'Apokalyptiken och England' and then, in contrast, devoted the next section to Durie's sane and sober 'friendly unionism', believing that the English of that day (fully knowing that Durie was a Scotsman) could not tell the difference between fiction and reality.[17]

This author has read letters from Cromwell preserved in the Royal Archives of Sweden, apparently unknown to Carlyle who collected and edited Cromwell's correspondence. They were so full of eschatological phantasies as to shame any sober biblical exegete. Prestwich mentions how Cromwell's musicians took part in Cromwell's mock funeral procession, as alleged mourners. Such insiders, supernumeraries and walkers-on were set up and lined up to fool the public as Cromwell had already been quickly buried. The Cromwell that had lain in state for real

---

[17] Apocalypse and England, *Den Europeiska Konfessionspolitikens Upplösning 1654-1600*, p. 83ff. See also section on 'Kretsen kring Cromwell och apokalyptiken'.

mourners was a mere wax effigy which, after the procession, was placed in Westminster Abbey without any religious ceremony. Sadly, much of Commonwealth religion remained an effigy of the true faith.

The Rationalism of the Westminster Confession

This Presbyterian misuse of power explains why so often in the writings of the Westminster Assembly members, and the 17th century Puritans, we find doctrines and political theories based on a natural theology shunned by our Reformers. The Presbyterian Rutherford lobbyists at the Assembly, though they had no vote, were allowed a powerful voice in most debates. During the meetings, scriptural doctrines were only introduced positively if they were found to be according to either natural law or the light of nature. The Westminster Confession even claims that the light of nature and natural law are the initial incentives behind setting apart a time of worship and keeping the Sabbath.[18] So we are told:

The light of nature showeth that there is a God, who hath lordship and sovereignty over all: is good, and doeth good unto all; and is therefore to be feared, loved, praised, called upon, trusted in, and served with all the heart and with all the soul, and with all the might[19]

I must admit that until Christ came into my life I was quite unaware of all that. Yet the seventh paragraph starts with the words:

As it is of the law of nature that, in general, a due proportion of time be set apart for the worship of God ...

I personally was a lover of nature before I became a lover of God and nature never commanded me to set 'a due portion of time' for the 'worship of God'. I think most other 'strangers to the Commonwealth of Israel' would have thought the same before they were introduced to

---

[18] *Westminster Confession*, especially Chapter XXIII. Mankind is addressed as if he were not fallen and was 'neutral' in his tendencies to do good or evil (Chapter XI: *Of Free Will*). Note, too, how later additions to the Confession go further and emphasise duty-faith and the universality of God's saving love (Chapters IX , X, XXIII George S Hendry, SCM edition).
[19] XXIII,1. This was the real start of 'Duty Faith' teaching.

God's Covenant. It is thus no wonder there is so much opposition to the Presbyterian 'Sabbath' today!

Such rationalistic theologies, though patched up somewhat in later editions, disregard the fact that sinners are either unaware of God in nature or blind to any real function that nature has as a handmaid to the gospel. Thus they are condemned by scripture as being without understanding, without natural affections and thus without excuse.[20] Sinners are in total darkness unless true Enlightenment comes through the Holy Spirit. This blindness to nature's glories is seen by Paul as a judgment of God. The *Westminster Confession*, however, sees man as still possessing the natural ability to know God's will in nature which leads to natural worship. As the *Westminster Standards* were never finished due to Pride's Purge and other setbacks for the Presbyterians and Cromwell became too low on funds to encourage and to finance John Durie[21] and Adoniram Byfield's[22] continuing work on the Confession, the *Westminster Standards* reveal a most jumbled theology as they were mere bits and pieces still to be synergized. This unfinished symphony has been played by the Presbyterians ever since as if it were the orthodox faith. In my debates with Presbyterians I find few argue from scripture, but they argue either for or against my views of the Covenant and man's nature from the same *Confession* which lends itself to different interpretations. One might say this is the same with scripture but arguing from scripture is to be preferred to arguing from rational denominational precepts.

The mixed theologies of the Westminster delegates

So, too, as Warfield has pointed out in his writings on the Assembly, the so-called 'Standards' were penned and collected by ministers, politicians and military men of widely diverging theologies and political ideas. Indeed, we only have to read William Prynne's pamphlets to see what a battle there was between the so-called 'Old Puritans' and 'Old Protestants' in the fierce controversies of the time.

---

[20] See Paul's teaching in Romans 1, 2.
[21] The only Church of England member at the Assembly.
[22] One of the milder English Presbyterians whom Cromwell said was the only Presbyterian he trusted.

Here, the Presbyterians defended themselves against the charge of being Puritans, calling themselves 'Protestants'. Nowadays very many Puritans praised by the Presbyterians were real men of God but in those days the Presbyterians caused them 'drunkards, malignants and Episcopalians'. Cromwell reacted to Prynne as Charles I had done and had him imprisoned for treachery. It is to be noted that modern Presbyterians criticize Charles for punishing forger Prynne, though Prynne himself as a lawyer felt he had come off much lighter than he had deserved. Yet the same Presbyterians soft-pedal on Cromwell's punishment of Prynne who refused to recognize Cromwell's power. Why they do this, I do not know as Cromwell was no friend of the Presbyterians.

The totalitarian manifesto of the *Solemn League and Covenant*
The Scottish Presbyterians furthermore, through their *Solemn League and Covenant*, which Milton rightly called 'sad and ominous,' sought to enforce a reign of terror and totalitarianism on the British people which was fully akin to Marian Roman Catholic terrors in the century before. They preached and passed through Parliament that the mighty Scottish armies, fresh from the Continental Thirty Years' War, were an essential element in forcing the English to accept the Word of God and absolute Presbyterian control. These armies were not paid but relied on plunder for their upkeep. Private armies of British noblemen were also employed in forcing Britain's citizens to adopt the new religion which was nothing but an abandoning of God's covenant for a man-made pact with God. It is all in the Westminster Assembly minutes safely recorded by Byfield so one can quickly read up on this if such facts are queried. Even irenic men of God such as Philip Nye, Thomas Goodwin, John Owen and John Durie were called 'malignants' and 'Episcopalians' because they sought the unity of all Protestants on biblical Covenant lines. Presbyterian fanatics such as Englishman William Prynne, through publishing his forgeries of other men's works and, using all his skills as a lawyer, sought to rule any man of Christian tolerance out of court. Protestants throughout the Continent were astonished that Cromwell was prepared to ally with Roman Catholic countries such as Spain rather than with Britain's old Protestant allies. Though Cromwell strove to curb the press allowing only one newspaper to appear in

London, a great pamphlet war ensued which condemned the irreligiosity of the Government.

Whitelocke's great blunder

Powerful Sweden, champion and governor of the German Protestant states in the Thirty Years' War, was surprised to find that Cromwell's senior ambassador to their country was more keen on teaching the court ladies to dance than cementing diplomatic ties with England and called Bulstrode Whitelocke a 'Cavalier'[23] for his love of dancing. Whitelocke annoyed the Swedes because though not of noble birth and appearing in the name of farmer Cromwell, he arrived with a great royal contingent and a hundred horses to carry his own personal regalia and courtly attire. Whitelocke wished to impress Christina with the magnificence of Cromwell's court but the Queen kept him waiting for a month before greeting him, saying that royal ambassadors were dealt with before commoners. This is said to be the reason why Cromwell had himself 'crowned' as 'His Highness' to gain more international respect for his status. Posters concerning the occasion depicted Cromwell wearing the three crowns of England, Ireland and Scotland like the tiara of the pope.

Both the Queen and Uppsala University had asked for Durie who had cemented good relationships in Sweden through close contact with Gustav II Adolf, Queen Christina, many of the leading Swedish clergy and the Uppsala Professors. Those authors who rely on Wikipedia for their research and insist that Durie accompanied Whitelocke to Sweden err. Durie's own correspondence shows conclusively that Durie did not visit Sweden on this occasion. In a letter to Richard Baxter dated 27 October, 1653, Durie says that he had helped to prepare Whitelocke's visit but could not accompany him because of illness.[24] Anyway, Durie would have gained immediate access to Christiana and her academics though he was only a 'commoner'.

---

[23] Of course this was a deep insult said of one of Cromwell's men who 'on paper' denounced the Cavaliers.
[24] *Calendar of the Correspondence of Richard Baxter*, Keeble/Nuttall, Vol. 1, 1638-1660, OUP, 2002, p. 114.

Cromwell did not delay the diplomatic mission because of Durie's sickness as he needed him in Holland, Germany and Switzerland, thinking he already had a sure treaty with Sweden in his hand through Durie's spade work which only needed to be signed by the Queen. Furthermore Ambassador Lisle who was first chosen to lead a delegation to Sweden a second time assisted by Durie complained that his assistant had been given priority over himself by the Swedish court and refused point blank to go as Durie's shadow. Whitelocke was Cromwell's Plan B.[25]

Lord Chancellor Whitelocke, the highest paid man in England, having obviously no idea of international diplomacy, made a mess of things and all Durie's irenic work was brought to an end. After his unaccomplished mission, Christiana forced Whitelocke to board a Swedish ship bound for Hamburg. There, Richard Bradshaw, the British Resident in Hamburg, decided that he had better go to Sweden to bend things back to normal and remembering his correspondence with Durie during his 1652 visit to Sweden, he wrote to State Secretary Thurloe on 24 March 1656 to say that he was planning to visit Sweden as a mediator and wanted a multi-lingual diplomat to accompany him. This could only mean Durie. He goes on to write:

The council of state were pleased to send mr. Durie with mr. Lisle to Sweden: I should be glad of such a friend and companion, if he would undertake it, being now in London, as I heare he is. He is one whom I love and honour for his eminent parts and good affection; but if he cannot be prevailed with, then to have some other gentleman suitably qualified.[26]

However, Durie was now serving Cromwell in the Netherlands and Germany where he stayed another year and Cromwell dropped the idea. This must be stressed here because our modern 'puritans' praise Cromwell for his international diplomatic skills. Actually, Cromwell blockaded international sea routes and confiscated all the gold and goods transported between Britain and the Continent, thus angering many countries. Queen Christina strove to right this British wrong and

---

[25] See *Förlorarnas Historia*, Magnus Nyman, pp. 263-271.
[26] Thurloe's *State Papers*, Vol. vi. pp. 138, 139.

condemned British government organized piracy and forced Whitelocke to stop confiscating Swedish gold transports. From then on all Cromwell's transactions with Sweden were to Sweden's advantage and Christina proved she was the better diplomat.

The modern chaos of the cults has a 17th century basis

Rutherford argued from Aristotle, Plato and even Cicero to this anarchistic, deistic, secular theory of man's divine dignity and a retired God. Sadly, these pagan philosophers are still viewed as Apostles in much modern allegedly Reformed theology. Thus, not only Charles I, Oliver Cromwell and Charles II are to be blamed in different ways for spreading the chaos and the downgrading of religion, politics and society in the troubled years of the seventeenth century. The churches, on the whole, were even guiltier and their sinning during the 17th century gave rise to the myriads of denominations we have today and the chaos of the cults.

This Presbyterian Enlightenment philosophy, found fitting soil in Oxford University and then spread throughout the country before being re-exported abroad through the pen of Tom Paine.

Tom Paine (1736-1809) and the Age of Reason

Tom Paine, a Norfolk rope-maker, built further on 17th century 'Christian' rationalism and brought out his revolutionary, populistic multi-volume work *The Age of Reason: Being an Investigation of True and Fabulous Theology*, arguing that reason was a surer guide than revelation in governing man's life. Fearing opposition in England because of British opposition to the French Revolution which voiced similar ideas, Paine fled to the New World where his works, for a time, were best-sellers. Arguing that natural religion was a surer basis of faith than Christianity, Paine argued like Andrew Fuller after him that even God must give up his arbitrary use of revelation and the Mosaic Law and place Himself under the Laws of Nature. This idea was enthusiastically accepted by the Colonialists as a reason for denouncing British rights over American citizens. Thus Paine's *Age of Reason*, *The Rights of Man* and especially his *Common Sense* are said to have persuaded the Colonies to proclaim themselves a Republic and separate from the British monarchy. After Independence was gained, the new republic forgot how they had been infused with Paine's thoughts to accomplish it and proclaimed it was a work of God and denounced Paine in their new politico-religious fervour. His works were no longer allowed to be printed and he, having held high political offices in America, was now denied the right to vote. He became a stranger with no rights in a land he had inspired with his *Rights of Man*. Only six people, including a family he had supported and two slaves he had freed attended his funeral.

Lessing and the Holy Spirit of Reason
The French, through René Descartes were continuing along the Rationalistic line but in Germany, the movement became particularly strong. Hermann Samuel Reimarus (1694-1768), a Professor of Oriental Languages, had spent decades working out a Theology of Reason (Vernunft) earning for him the dubious title of 'Father of Modern Theology'. Gotthold Ephraim Lessing (1729-1781) published fragments from Reimarus' work under the name of 'Anonymous'. It was thus some time before the world knew that these ideas of a religion of reason were not Lessing's own. Building on Reimarus, Lessing taught that when Christ said He would depart but the Spirit would come, He was speaking of the spirit of Reason which was now mankind's schoolmaster to bring human beings (homo sapiens = man of reason) to true knowledge of the Reason behind all things.[27] Lessing is, however, dangerous in another way, too; he is such a gripping writer, so communicative and has so very many uplifting thoughts so his readers are easily persuaded that he must be right. Even I must admit that I enjoy reading Lessing and wrote my Uppsala 3-Betyg thesis on his rationalistic theology in the light of scripture.

Kant and his 'categorical imperative'
Another Enlightenment philosopher Immanuel Kant (1724-1804) is in quite a different category with his harsh, unbending dogmatic theories which have influenced our modern (or modernistic) evangelical

---

[27] In order to understand the heart of the then modernistic Liberalism, this author made a special study of Higher and Lower Text Criticism as well as Lessing's theology of reason at Uppsala University. His thesis was entitled *Gott, Offenbarung und Mensch in Lessings, Nathan dem Weisen*. His comparative textual studies gave him a sure trust in God's Word.

theology so much. Kant's motto was *Sapere aude* - Listen to your reason. He introduced his so-called 'categorical imperative' in his *Grundgesetz der reinen praktischen Vernunft* which was, 'Handle so, dass die Maxime deines Willens jederzeit zugleich als Prinzip einer allgemeinen Gesetzgebung gelten könne!' which being translated means 'Act so that the precept of your will could at any time be also acceptable as a general rule of law.' Many of my students have found Kant impossible to understand which was probably not a bad thing. He had the gift of putting trite ideas into high-faluting terms. Kant argued that moral duties are derived from moral rules and moral obligations applicable to all human beings. The guiding principle here is the person's own reason which tells him all such moral obligations are right, i.e. if they are for the common good. All such actions for the common good are moral and one is thus duty-bound to perform them. Now, according to Kant, if the moral law commands that we ought to be better human beings, it inescapably follows that we must be capable of being better human beings. I am using Kant's *Religion Within the Boundaries of Mere Reason* here. With this dubious theory, Kant thought he had built a logical basis for arguing that if a person felt he ought out of pure duty to the common good perform an action, then he must be quite capable of performing that action. This was later further simplified by those who sought to understand Kant by the slogan, 'I ought, therefore I can.'

Meanwhile, the Kantian view of man's natural abilities and the law of reason had hit the churches in the USA and given rise to what was termed 'New Divinity', featuring the work of Joseph Bellamy and Timothy Dwight who used their 'natural religion' to campaign for armed revolt, like Rutherford before them. They believed that though man was fallen in will, he was not fallen as a natural creation of God but he was on probation so that he might find God through willing aright. All this, of course, was theorizing in the face of God's Covenant of Grace which showed the true way to 'enlightenment'.

Summing Up

Modern theories concerning God's provisions and man's agency and duty in salvation are mostly contra-productive to the Gospel of salvation contained in the doctrine of the Covenant of Grace found in scripture. It appears the doctrine that man is dead in trespasses and sins plays little part in much modern evangelical preaching. This can be chiefly traced back to the downgrading of Covenant teaching in the 17th century propagated by politico-humanists in the Christian fold who strove to stamp out all opposition whether from the Church of England or the Independent remnant of Reformed believers.

The voice of reason was seen by the followers of Samuel Rutherford as the voice of God and Christianity was found acceptable merely if it met the rational criteria of fallen man's mind. The perpetrators of these new Enlightenment errors caused a century of chaos and political turmoil and since then peace has scarcely ever reigned in the Christian churches with brother warring with brother. The Reformation received nigh irreparable damage. True, a number such as John Durie believed that the powers that be are ordained of God and a Christian should take everything as 'normal' which they received from God's hand. This helped them to suffer humiliation, banishment and financial ruin, if they were not massacred or executed. However, with the Engagement Controversy[28], the Solemn League and Covenant, Pride's Purge, a Christian Press forbidden and a reduction of Parliament to an ever changing handful of Cromwell's lackeys alongside Cromwell's many idiosyncrasies and a powerless Charles I and Charles II, the 17th Century was truly a century of chaos giving traditional evangelical Reformed believers hard times indeed. The growth of scores of denominations made sure the battle flags continued to fly.

Soon all Europe from France to Scandinavia was revelling in the New Learning taught through Paine's popularizing reason above God's revelation and Lessing's gentle and friendly but dogmatic teaching that Reason was the Holy Spirit in Man. Then came Kant's harsher and more uncompromising insistence on a Utopia formed by every man following his own will to the common good. Soon British and German

---

[28] The 'Protestants' under Prynne refused to sign this document but the 'Puritans' under Durie did. It stated: 'I declare and Promise, That I will be True and Faithful to the Commonwealth of England, as the same is now Established Without King or House of Lords.' Former Church of England minsters such as Baxter and Durie encouraged signatories to form a national church free of the political influence of a monarchical or Presbyterian rule. This is why the Presbyterians refused to sign the Engagement. The Baptists were divided on the issue but it was a Baptist who led the petitioners to beg Charles II to return from Holland and take up the Crown. It is symptomatic of the tactical changes in denominationalism that today's Presbyterians boast of their 'Puritan' background yet they called such Puritans 'Malignants and Drunkards' in Cromwellian times.

Rationalism entered the very churches in the New World who had first welcomed, then rejected Paine and were now re-welcoming these ideas through the so-called New Divinity (alias Old Rationalism) teaching which has dominated much Christian thought there and in Britain until the present time.

Chapter 2

Modern Evangelical Thought Still
Burdened By Old Rationalism

Andrew Fuller and his 'reason and fitness of things'

Whilst Andrew Fuller (1754-1815) was preparing his would-be intellectual lectures for his 'Further Education' students, the theological academic world was ablaze with this New Learning now sandwiching British theology between the New United States revolutionary moral theology and the non-revolutionary Germany version. Fuller grasped at this moral and political philosophy calling it 'The Gospel Worthy of All Acceptation', which he described in terms of 'right reason'. He thus argues in his essay entitled *The Principle of Church Discipline*[29]:

> The form and order of the Christian church, much more than that of the Jewish church, are founded on *the reason and fitness of things*. Under the former dispensation, the duties of religion were mostly *positive*;[30] and were of course prescribed with the nicest precision, and in the most exact minuteness. Under the gospel they are chiefly *moral*, and consequently, require only the

---

[29] *Works*, Vol. 3, p. 452.
[30] Fuller's euphemism for 'legal' in the sense of 'legalistic'.

suggestion of general principles. In conforming to the one, it was necessary that men should keep their eye incessantly upon the rule; but, in complying with the other, there is more occasion for fixing it upon the *end*.[31]

Here Fuller is emphasizing his two Covenant theory whereby in the Old Testament rule was by law but in the New a common moral code motivates all those who use right reason. Andrew Fuller's teaching is extra beguiling to a right understanding of Christianity because, though on the surface he uses scripture for his evangelistic goal and writes often in 'the language of Zion', his background theology is a mixture of Paine, Lessing and Kant. The only difference being that Lessing internalized the work of 'Right Reason' in man on the pattern of the Holy Spirit but Fuller divided the internal work of Reason from the external work of the Spirit on Man. This position helps Fuller to argue that there is a difference between a moral fall, and a total fall of all man's natural and spiritual capacities. To him the Fall is 'wholly of the moral, and therefore of the criminal kind'.

This fall, he teaches, is not total because man is not 'totally unable' or 'unable in every respect' to believe in Christ,[32] he has still an internal awareness of 'the reason and fitness of things'. Fuller and his modern followers indeed tend to take the doctrine of man's total fall and total inability to understand spiritual things as the doctrine of Antinomians because they feel this is a mere excuse for Christians not to live according to their inner light.[33] Fuller was never sure in his own mind what role the Covenant Law plays in Christian theology and changed his mind repeatedly, and eventually dropped the debate and argued for a mere moral understanding of sin and grace. Andrew Gunten Fuller, Andrew Fuller's son, taking up the scriptural teaching that man is totally unable to respond to God, protests against it, taking his father's side and argues that this would take away the universal obligation to

---

[31] Fuller's emphasis. See John Gill's refutation of this philosophy in favour of 'the superior force and evidence of divine revelation' in his The Moral Nature and Fitness of Things Considered, occasioned by some passages in the Rev. Mr. Samuel Chandler's Sermon, Lately preached to the Societies for the Reformation of Manners, *Sermons and Tracts*, Vol. 3, p. 463ff.
[32] See *Works*, Vol. 2 p. 438, Reply to Mr. Button.
[33]Ibid, Vol. 2, p. 745. Modern Fullerite criticism is met in my Chapter 'A Saint is Slandered', *John Gill and the Cause of God and Truth*.

exercise faith in Christ, thus the idea that man cannot do anything to save himself just cannot be true. He further claims that his father shows: 'this inability is in no way represented in scripture as of a *proper* or *physical*, but of a *figurative* or *moral* kind'.[34] Anxious that the reader will understand the true significance of these words, he adds in a footnote words of his father which claim, 'All such terms as *necessary*, *cannot*, *impossible*, &c., when applied to these subjects, are used improperly.' The word 'improperly' being Fuller's pet-name for 'figuratively'. We have thus figurative sins, figurative debts, a figurative sin-bearer and a figurative fall. Indeed, Fuller tells us in a footnote that his gospel:

> ... represents man as not only possessing great advantages, but *as able to comply with everything that God requires at his hand*; and that all his misery arises from his *voluntary* abuse of mercy, and his *wilful* rebellion against God. It is not want of *ability*, but of *inclination*, that proves his ruin.[35]

Thus Fuller takes up Kant's 'categorical imperative' and tells us that fallen man could believe but his only weakness is he does not want to. Thinking of the old adage 'Where there's a will there's a way', we can only comment that as man has no will to be saved there is no way for him to be saved of himself, so why all this argumentation about man's abilities which are obviously non-existent? This is why Arthur Kirkby, who was particularly helpful to me on this matter both in his doctor's thesis and personal correspondence and phone calls summed up Andrew Fuller's doctrine of man and the fall succinctly in the sentence 'He could if he would'[36]. I feel this is a correct analysis as Fuller argues that the image of God in man is of two kinds: the natural and the moral. The former, consists of man's reason, conscience, natural freedom and immortality[37] and is not fallen. He is only morally fallen. Right reason,

---

[34]Memoir of Mr. Fuller, *Works*, Vol. 1, p. 38. A. G. Fuller's emphasis.

[35] *Works*, Vol.1, Memoir p. 38, 3rd London Edition, 1845.

[36]See Arthur Kirkby's PhD thesis, *The Theology of Andrew Fuller and its relation to Calvinism*, Edin., 1956, p. 160.

[37]*Works*, Vol. 3, p. 38. See also *The Image of God*, E. Clipsham, *Andrew Fuller and Fullerism*, 3, BQ, p. 218.

Fuller tells us, 'is perfect and immutable, remaining always the same'. 'No Divine truth can disagree' with it. So, for Fuller, the practical use of right reason distinguishes New Testament teaching from the Old which was law-bound.[38]

Even man's moral powers are seen as not truly fallen
However, Fuller goes further in his reasoning and stresses that as the moral fall was only of a figurative kind, it in no way took away man's 'proper' moral abilities as his proper moral duty to believe never left him. This idea took some time for me to digest but it seems as man is only figuratively fallen in his morals, according to Fuller, he is still able, 'properly speaking' to act as an agent in his own salvation. Fuller thus holds that exercising faith in Christ is a proper moral duty for fallen sinners who are aware of their moral duties and obligations to Christ. By their very nature they can see the fitness of things because 'man has the same power, strictly speaking, before they are wrought upon by the Holy Spirit, as after; and before conversion as after; that the work of the Spirit endows us with no rational powers, nor any powers that are necessary to moral agency'[39]. He goes further and argues in his *The Gospel Worthy of All Acceptation*:

> Or if the inability of sinners to believe in Christ were of the same nature as that of a dead body in a grave to rise up and walk, it were absurd to suppose that they would on this account fall under the Divine censure. No man is reproved for not doing that which is naturally impossible; but sinners are reproved for not believing, and given to understand that it is solely owing to their criminal ignorance, pride, dishonesty of heart, and aversion from God.[40]

The figurative fall then to Fuller is not physical and spiritual death, nor even moral inability, but merely an 'unwillingness to believe'. The *real* fall, according to Fuller, comes when Christ is rejected on hearing

---

[38] *Works*, Vol. 3, p. 452.
[39] The Reality an Efficacy of Divine Grace, *Works*, Vol. 2, pp. 546, 547.
[40] *Works*, Vol. 2, p. 355.

the gospel because man then refuses to use his inherent capabilities to believe in Christ savingly.

Rutherford's, Paine's, Lessing's, Kant's, New Divinity and Fuller's 'gospel' stands in absolute opposition to the Covenant of Grace on behalf of God's People

This sober fact is illustrated by recent (2018) discussions between Sam Waldron and Curt Daniel in an exchange with Daniel on Waldron's web-site. Here, Daniel argues that the synonyms of responsibility have remained constant since before the Fall. These are: accountability, obedience, duty, liability, obligation, morality and what he calls 'oughtness'. These terms according to Daniel depict the natural obligations or responsibilities of man towards God which man has always had. In these matters man as a natural agent has always had the freedom to say 'yes' or 'no' to God. This is because, Daniel believes, no man is neutral in his response to God. If man were neutral in his relationship to God, he would have ceased to be man. Thus, even though he is now fallen and lost, man has kept his awareness of who God is and what his obligations to Him are.[41] This alleged never-lost guide in fallen man, making him continually aware of God is the basis of duty-faith. When the gospel comes, man is thus duty-bound to accept it. This is surely a great misuse of the term 'duty'. Furthermore how can one postulate, given the biblical evidence, that if a fallen man were not aware of his duties to God, he would be 'neutral' in the whole matter? The truth is that fallen man is at enmity with God and has always been so since the Fall. He has never been 'neutral'. This Paul makes clear in Romans 8:6-8:

> For to be carnally minded is death; but to be spiritually minded is life and peace. Because the carnal mind is enmity against God: for he is not subject to the law of God, neither indeed can be. So then they that are in the flesh cannot please God.

---

[41] Listen to Daniel's website talk on Divine Sovereignty and Human Responsibility and what he calls the 'paradoxes', 'dilemmas' and 'tensions' between them.

Since when were God's enemies 'neutral'? This enmity, Paul further argues in Ephesians 2:15, 16, has been done away with in His Bride by Christ's vicarious sacrifice made known to her through His Spirit. There is no second chance of an access to Christ in the Spirit through any duty of man; otherwise God's Word would have taken this into account.

As a Lifeboy[42] in the late forties, I was inspired by Horatio Nelson's appeal to the British fleet from H.M.S. Victory on October 21st, 1805 when Napoleon was threatening to crush England. The message was 'England expects that every man will do his duty'. This war duty, of course, was a British, not just English, duty to protect both the Mother Country and the growing Commonwealth of Nations under the British Sovereign. Foreigners outside the realms of Britain were not counted here. The duties were for insiders. Thus those who are 'without Christ, being aliens from the commonwealth of Israel, and strangers from the covenants of promise, having no hope and without God in the world,'[43] cannot possibly behave as if they were fellow-citizens with the saints, nor can they be expected to perform Christian duties.

Daniel believes otherwise and positions himself as a preacher of a free 'well-meant' offer based on duty-faith. In taking this stance, he defines such words as 'responsibility' and 'duty' quite incorrectly and errs in his list of his other supposed synonyms. For instance, he confuses 'morality' with 'obedience' and 'liability'. They may have in certain cases a relationship to one another but they are not the same thing. Bad theology in many cases is due to the dumbing down of language which some preachers pioneer.

Daniel's gospel is no good news for sinners
Daniel, followed by Waldron who seemingly agrees with him, is also severely mistaken about man's relationship to God and God's relationship to man as revealed in scripture. Daniel's gospel is, in fact, no good news for sinners at all because he rejects the basic condemnation of man after the Fall and the hopeless condition he is now in until God undertakes to save him through His Covenant mercies. Daniel has only a Gospel for the 'duty-bound' who must all be already

---

[42] We all wore sailors' hats and marine jerseys and our badge was a brass representation of a life buoy. I have lost trace of the movement since around 1951.
[43] Ephesians 2:12

in Christ's fold otherwise they could not have duties to their Christ-given faith. If one does not understand fallen man's problem, one can hardly chose a remedy for it. This remedy is not to be found in a 'free offer' based on 'duty-faith', or at least not with the contents these modern radicals put into these terms.

Both Waldron and Daniel confuse duties with responsibilities. What man has done wrong is condemned by God and man is alone responsible for his breaking the Covenant. This is the broken responsibility which man can never remedy of himself. Daniel believes, however, that man has an innate non-fallen awareness which declares to him that he must follow certain duties to attain faith. If one denies this, one is denounced as a Hyper-Calvinist who does not believe in preaching the gospel to the lost.

Daniel argues in his thesis *Hyper-Calvinism and John Gill*, p. 90, that:

> The Reformed doctrine of the revealed will of God is that there is a sense in which God certainly *does* will the salvation of all who hear the Gospel, just as He wills all who hear the Law to obey. He has no pleasure in the death of the one who rejects either Law or Gospel. True Reformed theology keeps the balance between the secret will (election) and the revealed will (Gospel), but Hyperism over-emphasizes the secret will. Similarly, special grace reflects election and the secret will, but there is also common grace for all men as creatures in the revealed will.

To this one can only say that for God to will the salvation of all means that all will be saved. If God willed all to obey the Law then all would obey it. This doctrine would be quite the opposite to the biblical doctrine of the Covenant of Grace where mankind is not able to follow the law and God saves the ungodly irrespective of the curse of the Law. Daniel, again, is being careless with language here. This becomes plain to see when we read what Daniel says further on in page 410 of his doctoral thesis:

> 'Free offer' was the debated term in mainstream Hyper-Calvinism, but 'well-meant offer' has been the debated phrase

within the Hoeksema school. In essence, however, they are one and the same. The first simply brings out the aspect that God wishes to give something without cost, while the second points to God's willingness that it be accepted.

Now just as Daniel confuses responsibility with moral ability, he also confuses God's will with 'wishful thinking'. To will something into being is a long, long way from wishing something to come to being. The idea that God wishes something but does not will it is not the same as God wills something and therefore wishes it. To say that God is willing that salvation be accepted is too weak for words as the Bible clearly teaches that God wills the salvation of Christ's Bride and thus saves her. God's will is always one of action and His Word never returns to him void.

Here Daniel is at fault by speaking of revealed and secret will, he being for the former and 'Hypers', he maintains, for the latter. This author has read all the 'Hypers' Daniel denigrates but has not met up with one who feels he has personal insight into any secret will of God. 'Who hath known the mind of the Lord?'[44] Yet Daniel goes beyond revelation and warrants salvation for all men should they exercise duty-faith, believing all men can exercise duty-faith if they would. Daniel must be claiming access to some alleged 'secret will' of God here as such a doctrine does not occur in God's will as revealed in scripture. The revealed Christian religion teaches man will not exercise faith dutifully because he has no faith to exercise. I have exchanged correspondence with David Engelsma in the past on his faulty presentation of Gill in the *Standard Bearer* but when he reviewed Daniel's thesis on the *Common Grace: Deliberations* web-site, I was certainly one mind with him when he wrote of two complaints he had concerning Daniel:

> The first is that Daniel does not distinguish 'offer' as the promiscuous preaching of Christ as Saviour with its command to all hearers to repent and believe on Jesus for salvation, from 'offer' as the declaration to all hearers that God loves them, Christ died for them, and God is now giving them the chance to

---

[44] Romans 11:34.

be saved by believing. This distinction is both biblical and confessionally Reformed. 'Offer' as promiscuous preaching with a summons to all to believe in Christ is the external call of the gospel as taught in Matthew 22:1-14 and in the *Canons*, II, 5. 'Offer' as a declaration of universal love and atonement dependent on the sinner's will is the Arminian heresy that the Reformed and Presbyterian churches condemned at Dordt and Westminster on the basis of the apostle's doctrine in Romans 9:16.

By failing to make this fundamental distinction, Daniel labels all who deny the 'offer' as hyper-Calvinists, regardless of what specific doctrine of the offer they have in mind. The result is that those whose rejection of the 'offer' consists of a denial of universal love dependent on the will of the sinner are tarred with Daniel's broad brush of hyper-Calvinism, even though they preach to all and call all to believe in Jesus Christ.

The second fault is gross. Daniel argues that genuine Calvinism is the doctrine of a saving love of God and a death of Jesus Christ for all without exception. On this basis, the proper 'offer' is, in fact, the 'bold declaration' to all who hear the gospel, 'God loves you, Christ died for you, and now God pleads with you to believe so that you may be saved' (p. 459). Accompanying this offer is 'a sufficient common grace' that enables all to accept the offer, if only they will (pp. 161, 162).

It is Daniel's basic thesis that hyper-Calvinism began to develop when, after Calvin, the Reformed faith adopted limited atonement. This jeopardized the offer. What is necessary for the warding off of hyper-Calvinism is the embrace of universal atonement. This involves repudiating the decree of reprobation.

This is the remedy for hyper-Calvinism! This exotic mixture of Arminianism and Amyraldianism, Daniel calls, with a kind of fetching modesty, 'Low Calvinism'. It is, indeed, low—very low. It is abased and debased 'Calvinism'. The glory of salvation in this gospel belongs to the sinner. Using his 'sufficient common grace' rightly, he not only saves himself by accepting the offer but also makes the death of Christ atoning and the love of God successful.

There is an important warning here. Those professing Calvinists who insist on an 'offer' expressing God's love for all and desire to save all cannot escape universal atonement. When universal atonement is adopted, the eternal, double decree of predestination is rejected.

Minimising and maximising man

Joining Waldron and Daniel, we have also David Mark Rathel who complains that John Gill, whose doctrine of the Covenant will be dealt with in Chapter Twelve and Thirteen, not only 'radically minimized human *agency* in the reception of salvation'[45] but also that 'Gill constructed a soteriology that minimized human *responsibility* in the reception of salvation'.[46] In these essays, Rathel presents 'duty-faith' as the traditional gospel teaching throughout all time, and claims Gill, as also his biographer George Ella, have introduced a novel teaching. Thus Rathel turns the tables in favour of gospel offers attached to duty-faith requirements. Nowhere, however does Rathel demonstrate that all his anti-Gill statements fit. Instead, he picks out two writers on Gill, Tom Nettles and myself who have argued that Gill was no Hyper and in debunking us to his own undocumented satisfaction concludes thus that Gill was indeed, a Hyper-Calvinist. He argues that Nettles sits on the fence and that I am on Gill's Hyper-Calvinistic side but 'do(es) not convincingly demonstrate the contrary' to Rathel's views. This is a strange argumentation as Rathel was neither around to refute me in the nineteen eighties and nineties when I wrote the bulk of my works on Gill. Nor was he around so that I could refute his 'contrary argument'. It is, however, obvious that Rathel wishes to affirm his position against mine in the pages of the *Baptist Quarterly* which had published my long essay 'John Gill and the Charge of Hyper-Calvinism' in the October, 1995 edition, which, to use Rathel's exaggerated words, made me 'very visible'. He thought I had been given a pedestal there which I had not deserved. However, at the time, I was complimented by the BQ editors

---

[45] *Exploring Gill's Doctrine of the Covenant of Redemption*, Journal of Reformed Theology, 2017
[46] My emphasis. *Was Gill a Hyper-Calvinist?: Determining Gill's Theological Identity*, BQ, Vol. 48, 2017, Issue 1. Also interesting in the development of Rathel's self-given mission to 'determine' and 'settle' opinions on Gill is Rathel's essay *Innovating the Covenant of Redemption – John Gill and the History of Redemption as Mere Shadow*, Evangelical Theological Society, 2016.

for being at the forefront of research on Gill. Since then, time has not stood still and I have deepened my studies of Gill but find that Rathel comes up with old ideas long since refuted. The BQ publication Rathel challenges came after various other publications from my pen on Gill during Rathel's childhood. Though Rathel claims I did not prove my case in that article, his evidence shows he has overlooked what 'my case' was. Nor did my BQ article come alone as in the same year I also published my *John Gill and the Cause of God and Truth* (365 pages) and three years afterwards my Tercentenary appreciation *John Gill and Justification from Eternity* (332 pages). Here, too, Rathel fails to pick up my biblical arguments as he comes from a completely different perspective with his own preconceived ideas and a very personal axe to grind. Up to the present date (2018), Rathel has published only a few small essays but has merely ignored all that has been written by those who cannot accept his rational explanation of duty-faith as being spiritually biblical and the norm for entering into Christ's Covenant.

There is no life to be offered in the gospel of rationalism
Gill was never burdened by this unscriptural dead-weight. The scriptures clearly teach man is totally incapable of aiding and abetting in the process of salvation and we find no talk there of minimizing man's agency. The long list of biblical passages which speaks against Rathel is common knowledge amongst Christians but for strangers to the Covenant of Grace, the gospel in them has still to be spelt out. There is no life to be offered in the gospel of rationalism. Ephesians 2:1-5, for instance, clearly outlines what is entailed by being spiritually dead and being quickened by Christ. The first verse tells us: 'And you hath he quickened, who were dead in trespasses and sins.' Here, Christ is the only agent mentioned in making the dead to live. In verses 4, 5, we read, 'But God, who is rich in mercy, for his great love wherewith he loved us, even when we were dead in sins, hath quickened us together with Christ, (by grace ye are saved). Paul then goes on to declare in verse 8, 'For by grace are ye saved through faith; and that is not of yourselves; it is the gift of God.'

In footnote 34 of his BQ article, Rathel mentions that I teach that the duty-faith warranty of salvation is 'highly liberal'. This is correct but Rathel neither gives evidence against my view nor does he give biblical evidence to support his own view, but merely provides dogmatic conclusions that he himself has somehow made or he feels others have made. He then decides he has thus both 'determined' and 'settled' the issue (Rathel's own words). Furthermore, Rathel's handling of Gill's teaching on the Spirit's work in making sinners sensible to the Gospel is again, dumbing down the meaning of the term and merely an attempt to pick out bits and pieces here and there and give them a new shape. He accuses Gill of not synergizing his theology, which I believe Gill does remarkably well, but Rathel merely hammers out fragments from Gill's well-defined wholes. Any student of knowledge-engineering would prefer Gill's method of synergism rather than Rathel's off-the-point, analysis of his scrapings and scratchings from Gill. I feel that Rathel also needs to take note of what others have wisely seen.

John Hazleton, in his great little book *Hold Fast: A Sketch of Covenant Truth and Witnesses* says:

> It is the fashion now to sneer at Gill, and this unworthy attitude is adopted mostly by those who have forsaken the truths he so powerfully defended and who are destitute of a tithe of the massive scholarship of one of the noblest ministers of the Particular and Strict Baptist denomination.

So, too, Rathel's handling of Gill on the issue of time and eternity sounds nicely philosophical but he has still failed to understand Gill's biblical doctrine of justification from eternity in time which is for eternity as also his teaching on aevi-eternity. What he says about Gill here is mere misunderstanding based on a far too narrow amount of information. Until Rathel, or David Gay, or Curt Daniel, or any other critic of Gill's doctrine of the relation between time and eternity, is able to define Gill's doctrine aright, they are in no position to challenge it. Rathel needs to study these issues historically and biblically and not take a party stand. This, he also combines with a denominational stand which merely determines and settles his own very strict and narrow party line to suit his own taste. The truth is that Rathel has an entirely different soteriology and ecclesiology to Gill's but he refuses to get under Gill's skin and understand what he means.[47]

Man has no duty-bound abilities to open Covenant doors

True Covenant of Grace theology denies that man has any duty-bound abilities or any capacities to believe at all. Our Reformers, followed by many Puritans, then Gill, Huntington, Brine, Crisp, Romaine, Hervey, Toplady, Trail and many more, held to a doctrine of man which found its fulfilment, perfection and salvation in Christ who performed as Righteous Man all the conditions regarding salvation that man was blind to since the Fall. Man fulfilled all for man. Sadly, this doctrine does not appear in the theology of our accusers who thus minimize the work of Christ as Redeemer.

Man is responsible for not believing but not responsible for believing

I suppose no Christian would deny that Man is truly responsible for not believing. Given the scriptural documentation, however, one would think that it can never be concluded that man was responsible for believing. Faith is God's precious gift. Here we see Daniel's and Rathel's false view of man and their false view of God which reflects false Enlightenment theories. God has made it His self-given task or duty to save sinners. It is not fallen man's duty to save himself. A duty is a task to be done. This task can only be done by Christ. Responsibility can never be in the case of man a synonym for 'duty'. He must carry the consequences of his irresponsibility which cannot be remedied by any duty to a faith which he does not have. In the Son of Man it is quite different as Christ the God-Man always keeps to both his duties and responsibilities. Man has failed in his duties to the Law and failed in his responsibilities. So he can never be like Christ, the True Man, in his fallen self. It is thus ridiculous to speak of 'duty-faith' to a man who does not even understand duty to the law and will always be incapable of knowing what duties to faith are until he finds himself in Christ. Rathel accuses Gill of not viewing man's responsibilities correctly. But

---

[47] See Rathel's 'Baptists and the Emerging Church Movement: A Baptistic Assessment of Four Themes of Emerging Church Ecclesiology'.

the boot is on the other foot. Gill sees man as totally responsible for a total fall whereas Rathel sees man as being partly responsible for a part fall. To substitute the gospel with duty-faith rationalism is irresponsible.

All man's responsibilities point to his fallen nature
Man's fallen responsibilities are thus all on the negative side. He is responsible for everything he has done wrong and still does wrong. Though Daniel equates duty wrongly with a natural obligation to accept grace and exercise faith, the very Bible passage he gives as proof points in quite a different direction. He builds his duty-faith emphasis on Ecclesiastes 12:13 which says: 'Fear God, and keep his commandments: for this is the whole duty of man'. We accept this as a divine truth but keeping commandments according to the Bible is the responsibility of all sinners and is not an entrance to grace as no man can keep God's commandments, not even Adam, and God's commandments merely show up man's inability to keep them. Daniel sees keeping commandments as obeying a moral law only. But there is a difference in striving to keep the so-called 'moral law' and being saved. You can tell a person not to steal or not to lie but you cannot say 'sinner save yourself'. It cannot thus be said that man has duties to a faith he has never been given, has never earned, and which he has never owned.

Curt Daniel, and other advocates of these notions such a Erroll Hulse, and the editors and various contributors to *Banner Of Truth* magazine and *Founders Journal* tell us they can get around this difficulty by giving fallen man a so-called 'well meant' offer which brings with it a 'warranty' or 'warrant'[48] of salvation. This well-meant offer, they say, when seen for what it is by the sinner, appeals to his duty-faith. The only warrant for our salvation is Christ who has fulfilled all obligations for the salvation of His Bride. We do not know who is and who is not of His Bride. No matter how 'well-meaning' we are, our task is not to warrant, that is guarantee, salvation, but to preach it allowing the Holy Spirit to do His work which is not ours. Thus the

---

[48] In the sense of authorizing the offer and promising success. Today the word 'warranty' is often used to describe a 'guarantee' for a product purchased.

'well-meant' gospel of man given to man as a 'warranty' of salvation based on duty-faith is a gospel of deceit.

Even if we perform all duties, we are still unprofitable servants
The fond idea of duty-faith preachers that, on hearing the gospel, all men receive a 'warranty' or guarantee to enable them to repent and believe is quite false. All men are not 'authorized' to believe and 'justified' to believe which is the meaning of being warranted, on hearing the gospel. He who has been given ears to hear and a heart to respond receives this warranty. Man can only have a duty to faith when he has it. To appeal to a non-existent duty-faith is to try to fool both man and God.

Man has, nonetheless, duties to the Law but fails to keep them. That is why he needs an act of grace from God or he perishes. Indeed Jesus made it clear in Luke 17 that even if we have done all our duties, we would still be unprofitable servants as it is only by grace and not via natural duties we are saved. The status 'good and faithful servants' (Matthew 25:21) is only given to those to whom God grants faith. Man is fully unaware of any such faith in himself before that faith is given to him. This is because faith does not exist in fallen man. Responsibility for the anti-pseudo-hypers mentioned above is the duty to grasp faith. This is wrong: responsibility means that man is responsible for his rebellion against God. Belief can never be a reward for performing duties nor ever attained through human responsibilities as it is a free gift of God. With the gift comes the authorization and justification to use it as God's children and not the children of false shepherds. God, however, has bound Himself dutifully to foster and maintain that belief in His chosen children.

Redeemed man's duties to that belief for which God alone is responsible are outlined to him and given him solely as a belief-carrier or believer and not as an agent of sin. Such duties are God given and are not inherent or innate in fallen man at all. Nevertheless, the call of mercy goes out to all to repent and believe, coming as a savour of death unto death to some and a savour of life unto life for others as the evangelistic work of harvesting goes on. Though fallen man's responsibilities, obligations, liabilities etc. are all on the negative side, he being responsible for what he has done against God's Holy Law, duties concerning what God has done in rescuing sinners from their plight through an act of grace are all on the positive side. Just as there is no sin in God and He thus never acts as a sinner; there is no belief in natural man so he can never act as a believer. Daniel is merely flogging a dead slave-to-the-law and believes he can raise the corpses in the valley of bones by declaring his well-meant intentions so that those dead will rise. This is the message of the Council of Trent which was rightly condemned by our Reformers, though not by our duty-faith enthusiasts. Their gospel is useless and if morality is the same as responsibility as Daniel says, it is thus highly immoral. Only God can awaken the dead. He alone makes former slaves to sin dead to sin and alive in Christ.

Christ shoulders all duties
Man is never duty-bound to save himself whether he hears the gospel or not. If he failed in his duties to the Law how can he be yet under a duty to faith in his fallen foolish state in which he says 'There is no God'? Christ alone has shouldered the whole duty of saving sinners and the sinner only receives saving faith when it is given him. Only then can one speak of duties to faith. Thus the teaching of duty-faith rationalisers that not the fall but the gospel is where the disobedient trip over their own misunderstanding of duties is clearly wrong. All men are condemned for falling in Adam but the gospel brings life to those who are already fallen so they might be lifted up. Duties have nothing to do with it. Man has failed in both his duties and responsibilities and can be given faith only from God's hand. It is obvious not all men are given faith, although, according to Daniel, all men stand equal in their duties to faith. Daniel merely gets over this problem by saying it is a 'paradox' or a 'tension' and we must leave it at that. Daniel, however, has not left it 'at that' but given us the rational answer that some men say 'no' to God and some say 'yes'. Some recognize their duties, others do not. He will not accept that all men say 'no' and cannot say 'yes' until God changes them.

Fuller's faith is based on his denial of total depravity
Writing under the caption 'Faith Being a Duty', Fuller claims that if man were truly dead in trespasses and sins, 'it were absurd to suppose

that they would on this account fall under the Divine censure.'[49] Fuller forgets here that man has already fallen under the divine censure and this has resulted in his damnation because man has disobeyed God and always does when left to himself. Fuller thought that man was not yet under final damnation and was still on probation, like Adam. Indeed, Fuller saw sinners after the Fall as being more privileged than Adam as they only received damnation if they rejected Christ. Otherwise sinners could not be agents of their own salvation which Fuller believes they are. His motto was God's provisions must harmonise with man's agency and man is not yet fully condemned as thus God could not exercise what Fuller called 'the divine censure' if he were. This seems to be what Rathel calls 'Minimising' man's duties in salvation if we do not follow Fuller. It is this view which is theologically absurd.

All men, according to Fuller, like Adam once was, are still on probation despite the Fall. For Fuller, it is as if the Fall had not happened. Indeed Fullerites forget the story of Adam and maintain man is on probation until he rejects Christ. In this spirit, Fuller continues by writing:

> No man is reproved (by God) for not doing that which is naturally impossible; but sinners are reproved for not believing, and given to understand that it is solely owing to their criminal ignorance, pride, dishonesty of heart, and aversion from God.[50]

Fuller does not understand that belief is impossible with fallen man but nothing is impossible with God. Fuller, however, has an easy remedy for man's 'aversion' which maximizes his agency in salvation. Sinners need only love God, he says, 'the same as if they had never apostatised'.[51] He appears to believe also that this is what God expects of fallen men, that is, that man should pull his own socks up and is indeed commanded to do so. Hence duty-faith! This is where Fuller gets it wrong again believing that commands from God are proof that fallen man must be still aware of his saving duties. This was true of

---

[49] *The Gospel Worthy of All Acceptation*, Philadelphia, 1805, p. 61.
[50] *Works*, Vol. 2, p. 355.
[51] *Works*, Vol. 2, p. 375, 376.

probationer Adam before he sinned but it is not true of condemned man after he sinned.

The fall of man is thus to Fuller and his followers merely a neglect in man's mastering his own 'oughtness' or 'duty' though he could if he wished. In this capacity of freedom of choice man has not changed since before the Fall. This might suit Kant, Fuller, Waldron, Daniel and sadly so many others but it certainly does not suit the Christian's walk with God which is by grace and not by an in-built sense of duty supported by natural capacities to love God and attacks of amnesia regarding the Fall. When God commands 'repentance', He refers to needs not duties. When He says 'believe', He also refers to needs and not duties. Neither the need is known nor any duty known until the Holy Spirit opens the sinner's eyes. This is what our fathers in the faith called being 'made sensible' to one's plight.

The will that allegedly moves mountains

Fuller, following Enlightenment theology, was adamant we could move mountains if we only willed it, that is, we could if we would but we will not. However, those who say I 'ought' therefore I 'can', therefore I 'will' are self-deceivers. Fancy telling a pauper in debt that he ought to pay off what he owed and could do so if he only counted it his duty and thus willed it! This is the Fullerite 'free offer' of the gospel based on 'duty-faith'.

The late Erroll Hulse, who called me publicly an 'ignoramus' for sticking to the doctrine of the total depravity of man, agreed with Fuller's boast that all fallen man's rational and moral powers are intact and only need to be implemented in salvation by man's willingness and tells us:

> There is nothing to hinder him (the fallen sinner) from being spiritual except his indisposition, his rebellion, his sin, his unwillingness. He is absolutely free to do good, to be spiritual, to repent, to believe. That is, he is a free agent.[52]

Hence, these people who find fallen man is 'absolutely free' to do good, provide him with what they call 'the free offer' based on so-called

---

[52] *The Great Invitation*, p. 60.

duty-faith to have him perform that good and accept Christ as being 'the whole duty of man'. However, if God says that man is 'carnal and sold under sin' (Romans 7:14) and can only be free from this bondage by an act of God as outlined in Romans 8, how can he be a free agent in his fallen state?

In the thirties of last century, the 'probation theory' based on man's alleged free will pervaded all the denominations and there is little evidence it has left them. Writing in 1935 on *The Atonement*, published by Hodder and Stoughton, Bishop Arthur Headlam claimed that though Adam failed, God still appeals to his offspring to use their wills in turning back to Him saying:

> Just then, as the purpose of creation was that man should freely, of his own will, fulfil God's will, so his method of Redemption was not to force or compel acquiescence in his will, but to appeal to man's own conscience, that by his own will he may strive to fulfil God's will.[53]

The idea that despite being dead in trespasses and sins man's free will lives on is, it seems, part of the Zombie mentality of a wide range of professing Christians.

A return to the Covenant of Grace is an Absolute Necessity
In their *History of the Church of God*, the Hassells argue:

> Andrew Fuller becomes a wonderful standard. He takes repentance and faith out of the Covenant of Grace, and puts them under the law, in the sense that he makes them man's duty, and not gifts of grace.[54]

This criticism must hold as Fuller argues that the law provides us with all the obligations necessary to believe in Christ savingly and the gospel merely brings with it the encouragement to perform them.

---

[53] Pp. 178, 179.
[54] P. 310.

It is highly detrimental to the preaching of the Gospel that modern evangelical, Reformed expositors insist on going back to ancient Greek rationalistic thinking concerning the so-called 'moral law'. This action on the part of the 'well-meant offer' enthusiasts can hardly be claimed to be 'moral' because they tell sinners that Christ has died for them without any biblical warranty to back them up. All they have is their own conviction that they are 'well-meaning' in their 'let's go fishing' evangelism. They are, however, commanded to cast the net out for whomsoever the Lord draws in. The warranty, guarantee or success of the evangelical venture is not in the net-casting but in the way Christ fills the net.

The evangelisers need evangelizing
Thus we are faced with the fact that modern so-called evangelical Reformed people are marching along the broad and steep track of Rationalism, trodden hard by such as Rutherford, Lessing, Kant, Fuller and such men as Waldron, Daniel, Rathel and Walter Chantry[55] who provide us with a 'moral law' and a 'gospel' of man's abilities in lieu of the biblical Covenant of Grace for God's People. These evangelisers need evangelising in order that they may join us in the true work of a gospel fisherman.

Summing Up
Andrew Fuller propagated the idea of a Christianity of 'right reason' and the basic fallen man's ability to see 'the fitness of things', based on his faulty understanding of a double covenant of Old Testament Law obligation and New Testament moral obligation. Unlike Lessing who saw the work of the Holy Spirit in 'right reason', Fuller saw 'right reason' as a natural attribute of man should he wish to employ it. Man's Fall into sin was not actual and total but only 'figurative' and 'moral'. If man so wills he can comply with all God's demands on him. Right reason is immutable and everlasting so man has not lost the power to follow God as he is his own moral agent. The difference between the Testaments is that in the Old man was chained to a legal codex from which he is now freed by reason's enlightenment. The Holy Spirit cannot enlighten sinful man more than he is already enlightened.

---

[55] E.g. in his book *God's Righteous Kingdom* published by Banner Of Truth.

17th and 18th Century Enlightenment theories of the idea that if one ought, one can, are echoed today by such as Curt Daniel who argues that man has ever had the capacity to say either 'yes' or 'no' to God despite the Fall. However, Romans 8:6-8 tells us, 'they that are in the flesh cannot please God'. They have no hope whatsoever in themselves. They have said 'no' to God and are thus lost should God's grace not intervene. This is the revealed will of God. Daniel claims that all who deny that the universal love of God in salvation is dependent on the will of the sinner are 'Hypers' though they, unlike Daniel, preach the whole Gospel as revealed and not worked out by any rational indicatives or knowledge of some 'secret will'. There a no sufficiency of common grace enabling fallen sinners to turn to Christ as our 'duty-faithers' wrongly argue. Saving enlightenment is the work of the Law and Grace enabled through the Holy Spirit motivated by Christ's love for His Bride.

Rathel's plea for maximizing man's agency in salvation is contrary to revealed Christianity. Ephesians 2:1-5 makes it quite clear that fallen man is dead in trespasses and sins.' One cannot minimize him more than that! Christ is shown as the only agent who can make the dead live. To deny this is to minimize Christ.

Daniel props up his ideas of a 'well-meant offer' and 'duty faith' on a Babel of misunderstandings concerning the meaning of words such as 'responsibility', 'obligation', duty', 'liability' 'obedience' and 'oughtness'. The only duty-faith sheep in Christ's fold are those to whom He has given faith to believe. All outsiders are totally lost until found by Christ. Ecclesiastes 12:13 does not point to duty-faith but to duty-law. As man has failed in such duties, he is in need of God's free gift of Faith. However, even if man could perform his law duties correctly, he would still be an unprofitable servant faith-wise. Here, too, Erroll Hulse's idea that there is nothing naturally in man to prevent him believing must be weighed and found wanting. It is high time Reformed evangelicals put back repentance and faith under Grace and stopped dabbling with moral rationalism and legalism which is, according to the Bible, immoral, irrational and illegal. These 'well-meant' people seriously need evangelizing themselves before they can do the true work of an evangelist.

Chapter 3

Moral And Legal Interpretations
In False Covenant Thinking

Two different Covenant Theologies clash over biblical 'Morals'
In modern times, the thrust of evangelical, Reformed teaching has shifted from an emphasis on the grace of God to the abilities and capacities of man as an agent in salvation. There is little talk of spirituality but much about morality. They are not synonyms. I have before me a work concerning a recent debate between a representative of the Banner of Truth Trust, Walter Chantry, and two New Covenant Theology (NCT) proponents, John Reisinger and Randy Seiver who represent different covenantal theories. Under the title *God's Righteous Kingdom Unrighteously Defended: A Review of Walter Chantry's God's Righteous Kingdom*, Reisinger and Seiver refute Chantry's moral view of the covenants and would replace it with their own moral view which is even more radical than Chantry's. They state dogmatically that the choice open to Christians can only lie between these two highly contradictory but quite un-biblical views.

I have corresponded with all three of these authors all of whom have rebuked me for my opposition to their New Divinity and New Covenant teaching which obviously have a joint basis. My opposition is three-fold: they challenge the biblical doctrine of the Covenant of Grace.

They also challenge the biblical doctrine of the People of God according to the Covenant of Grace. They also reject the biblical revelation of a single Covenant of Grace including the Law which is central to the teaching of both the Old and New Testaments.

What I find totally unacceptable from a Bible-believing, evangelical and Reformed stand point is that all three authors have erased the gospel story of the Covenant of Grace from their theology and argue solely in terms of moral law and the narrow question of what moral laws a Christian ought to recognize and practise as his rule of life. This reminds me of Jeremiah's rebuke of the old unbelieving Children of Israel for their infidelity regarding God's Covenant through rejecting the spirit within it and their trust in self-motivated moral and legal rules of life. This is the difference between man-kept old Covenants and God's Christ-kept ever-new Covenant. Such man-kept covenanters were, according to Jeremiah and the Prophets, Covenant-breakers. The lengthy review which Reisinger and Seiver have written deals both with the modern emphasis propagated by former Reformed leaders on the 'moral law' as the sole rule of behaviour for a Christian and also their own equally unscriptural dogma which reduced Old Testament believers' faith to two tablets of stone, seen merely morally and legally by those who have stony hearts. So they interpret the theology of the Old Testament by its misuse and not its right use. Both sides thus fail to present the everlasting Gospel of the everlasting Covenant of Grace.

Arguments over what is moral rather than revealed truths

Both sides agree in their moral rationalism that there is a 'covenant' of sorts to be seen in the two Testaments but they stand in strong disagreement as to what the underlining 'moral' issues are which might or might not join the Old with the New. Nevertheless, Seiver, listing what he believes are areas of agreement claims that both sides hold that the moral law of 'righteous requirements' continues in force today. When I read of this 'agreement', presented by Seiver, I placed a large question mark in the margin. However, Seiver tells his readers immediately afterwards that he disagrees with Chantry because he understands 'righteous requirements' differently.

It would seem to a Bible-believing onlooker here that there is no possibility of a Godly understanding of the Gospel where one renders everything down to 'moral issues' and then quarrels over what they are.

Reisinger and Seiver claim there are only nine moral commandments, whereas Chantry believes there are ten. Seiver thinks the commandment to keep the Sabbath is a ceremonial commandment which is no longer valid and thus not 'moral' any more. Seiver does not go into detail here which I believe would be necessary. Those who give sources for this idea usually quote Augustine in his *Reply to Januarius* which our Reformers often discussed. Modern critics of a 'Christian Sabbath' also quote Clement and Barnabas as the sources of their argument. However, Augustine in his *Reply to Januarius* is claiming that the Third Commandment is a Type of our eternal rest with God which is everlasting. He does not argue that 'the Type' is abolished as we have yet to enter into our eternal Sabbath rest, a fact which Augustine clearly points out. Here Bullinger shows more discernment than those who merely look on the Sabbath as ceremonial by saying:

> For so far forth as the outward worship of God requireth a certain appointed time to be exercised in, and carrieth with it the sacrifices of the law, so far, I say, it is ceremonial; but in respect that it teacheth to meet in holy assemblies to worship God, to pray, to preach, to be partakers of the sacraments, and to offer spiritual sacrifices, therein it is eternal and not ceremonial.[56]

Chantry believes that the Sabbath commandment is still 'moral' and thus 'binding'. Indeed, he appears to toe the then popular BOT line that the Ten Moral Commandments were the sole rule of the Christian life. This writer holds both these positions to be wrong and does not see what is 'ceremonial' about keeping the Sabbath or what is merely 'moral' about the others and what this has to do with the biblical doctrine of the Covenant of Grace. He would also condemn strongly the reduction of the vast Covenant teaching of the Bible in both Testaments to a mere question of morals, or to a mere Nine or Ten Commandments.

Though obviously socially important, morals of whatever kind are relative things and they are neither spiritual, nor doctrinal, nor theological in themselves and are thus no criteria for judging the Bible.

---

[56] *Third Decade*, Sermon VIII. Bullinger has a full sermon on the Sabbath in the *Second Decade*, Sermon iv.

Nor are they the underlining factors and driving force on which God has built His Covenant of Salvation. However, Reisinger says on the back cover of this moral discussion concerning his book *Tablets of Stone*:

> This is a careful examination of the place and function of the Ten Commandments in the history of redemption. Few people realize that the Ten Commandments were the actually (sic) terms of the Old Covenant.

This will come as a surprise to Bible scholars as, according to Jeremiah 31:31ff, the 'Old Covenant' was broken before the Children of Israel had received the Mosaic revelation because of man's sinfulness. The Ten Commandments came after that breakage and were obviously part of God's plan to put covenant-breakers back on the right track. They dotted each 'i' and crossed each 't' of the Covenant with Abraham. Furthermore, it is obvious in their review booklet that Reisinger and Seiver are arguing for what they call a Jewish 'National Covenant' based solely on the Ten Commandments which is, to say the least, a very radical way of boiling down the Old Testament's entire testimony to the Covenant of Grace to ten moral rules, one of which the NCT people say they have abandoned.

What is merely 'national' about the Covenant of Grace?
This writer is also at a loss to know what Seiver means by calling the Covenant in the Old Testament 'national'?[57] Which 'nation' has he in mind? Of the two thousand years of God's Covenant with Christ relating to pre-Davidic days, of which nation is Seiver thinking? After the brief forty years or so of Davidic reign over a very loosely united nation of Israel which included non-Jewish tribes or proselytes (for instance Edom), what happened to Seiver's 'National Covenant' after Israel ceased to exist as a short term single nation? Where is such a 'National Covenant' in the artificial modern state of Israel with its minority of the world's Jewish citizens? How would such a 'National Covenant' apply to the Jews of the Diaspora?

---

[57] *God's Righteous Kingdom Unrighteously Defended*, p. 33.

I wish to show in this book that the Covenant of Grace in the Old Testament was for all time and it thus continues in our days, too. No one is, no one ever was, within the Covenant because of his 'nationality', whether in Old Testament times or in the present time. Indeed, all nations were put under the promises of the Covenant even in Abraham's day. When Abraham was chosen to be the father of all nations in the faith, he was chosen as a father of the entire Bride of Christ. There is hardly a biblical prophet who does not emphasise the world wide nature of the Covenant and their allegiance to the faith of Abraham which was Christ-given.

Using wrong 'blueprints'
Seiver says he agrees with Chantry that 'The Mosaic Law was not a blueprint for social, political, or economic reconstruction in the present'.[58] This is surely not an issue anywhere amongst Christians. The point which Seiver ignores here is that the Old Testament Covenant of Grace, of which God's Law was an essential part, was also never a mere social, political and economic pact in the past. Nor were the Ten Commandments if Seiver insists on isolating these from the rest of the Covenant of Grace and viewing them as a fictive, purely legal 'National Covenant'. Old Testament writers never strip the Ten Commandments of their place in the entire Covenant which is a corner-stone on which to build the salvation of God's People in New Testament times. Here Seiver fully ignores the entire testimony of Moses, the Psalms, the Prophets and the 'Writings' of the Old Testament. One cannot possibly separate the Ten Commandments from all this gospel teaching and say the Jews knew only of a 'National' contract of Ten Commandments which ended as a covenant at the coming of Christ. Moses' five books all beg to differ!

Unbalanced language used for an unbalanced theology
It is also strange, for one who has read both Seiver's and Chantry's works to read that Seiver denounces Chantry's 'vitriol spirit, monstrous caricatures of his opponents' positions, and an outright misrepresentation of their beliefs'. What an exaggeration! However, in

---

[58] Ibid, p. 32.

69

his own publications Seiver calls those who disagree with him on very good grounds, (especially when he is on his own ground in his blogsite *Truth Unchanging*), 'clowns' and 'loons'. He ridicules their academic status and complains they must either be on drugs or should take psycho-pharmaceuticals. Yet here he complains that Chanty's party are guilty not only of 'false witness' but of being 'thieves', 'haters of God's righteousness', 'haters of God' and even 'murderers'. Furthermore Seiver's examples of harsh punishment for those who would accept the biblical Sabbath teaching in a more liberal way than Seiver would allow 'if he were them' merely displays the self-righteousness of a very partial judge.[59]

I would thus think it obvious that Reisinger and Seiver cannot be taken seriously in their effort, also outlined on their back cover, that one must choose between their radically cut down and misguided New Covenant solution, backed by uncontrolled language, or the Banner of Truth's rendering of Covenant Theology as if Seiver believed this was the only alternative. Such false alternatives are numerous both in Seiver's and Reisinger's works where they often, to strengthen their arguments present two false views and demand their readers take either the one or the other. The scriptures, history and the testimony of the Church in all ages prove Seiver quite wrong in his narrow myopic view of the Covenant of Grace and the 'alternative' understanding he demands concerning it. Indeed, the Covenant of Grace is a far bigger Gospel that either the NCT or the BOT have imagined.

A Review of NCT teaching
I recently found an article termed 'A Review of NCT Teaching' on the net and thought the author Randy Seiver would at give us at last an overview of what he believes as he has often scolded me for lumping his views with those of other NCT adherents. However, I discovered that Randy Seiver was not reviewing his own NCT teaching but dealing with a review of mine on a book by Tom Wells and Fred Zaspel entitled *New Covenant Theology*, which the *New Focus Magazine* had kindly published. In my review of this work, I did not deal with the whole scope of NCT teaching which I find is continually changing and outdating itself but solely with the matters arising from the book which

---

[59] Ibid, pp. 36, 37 and (sadly) passim.

Seiver purports to give verbatim followed by his comments. I felt this move was safer as I am also constantly rebuked by NCT writers for not taking their own personal NCT teaching as standard for all other NCT contenders. However Seiver presents a mangled and cut down version of what he calls my review as evidence showing 'how prodigiously those who rail against New Covenant Theology can misrepresent our position'. In his review of my review Seiver dwells only on what he feels contradict *his* views, leaving out my handling of Wells' and Zaspel's views which had been my purpose. In his retort, Seiver not only misrepresents my position but also that of the *New Focus* editor whom he also attacks. If Seiver had kindly reproduced my review as I had written it and commented on that review 'as written' and not as a most personal 'cut and pasted' version leaving out my main criticisms, readers would have been able to decide for themselves if I had 'railed' and misrepresented the NCT position as given by Wells and Zaspel. Seiver overlooked, for instance, my mentioning of Wells' rebuke of Paul for being in error when handling Timothy's faith. This is a fundamental NCT argument. Wells obviously thought that as Timothy was not brought up on New Testament doctrines but on supposed Old Testament anachronisms, he could not have a 'Christian faith'. So when we read in Second Timothy that the scriptures are Spirit-breathed,[60] are we to suppose that Wells and Zaspel are referring to the New Testament only which was not written when Timothy came to faith, nor Paul either, nor any of the Apostles? We know that when 'the prophets' are mention as the basis of the Church, the NCT tell us that there is no such 'basement' (their word) in the Church and that the prophets mentioned were anonymous N.T. prophets. We must also ask what scriptures our Lord was reared on and used in His preaching. Christ obviously believed, for instance in the Gospel of Isaiah whose Gospel He fulfilled![61] So, too, in his first letter to Timothy, Paul outlines how the Mosaic Law is positive in the hands of Christians and negative in the hands of unbelievers relating to Paul's Covenant teaching continued from the Old Testament.[62] Are we to suppose that Paul was in error,

---

[60] 2 Timothy 3:16.
[61] Luke 4:17-21 and passim.
[62] 1 Timothy 1: whole chapter.

here, too? I repeatedly hear from professing NCT people that Paul became a Jew to the Jews in modifying his gospel to suit them and a Gentile to the Gentiles when stressing the abolition of the Law of Moses.

Seiver did not take up these vital issues for the Church of the Lord Jesus Christ which demand an answer from the NCT but merely used my work as an excuse for his further outbursts against those he feels 'rail' against the NCT. Paul was called as the Apostle to the Gentiles and firmly declared in Romans 15:18, 'For I will not dare to speak of any of those things which Christ hath not wrought by me, to make the Gentiles obedient, by word and deed.' Paul boldly started his letter to the Romans by stating that he was 'called to be an Apostle, separated unto the gospel of God which he (God) had promised afore by his prophets in the holy scriptures.' Peter tells us in his first letter, chapter 1:11 that it was the Spirit of Christ who was in the Prophets testifying to the sufferings of Christ and the glory which should follow and in 2 Peter 1:21 he tells us 'the prophesy came not in old time by the will of man: but holy men of God spake as they were moved by the Holy Ghost'. And yet the NCT says there is no covenant continuation between the Testaments! William Fischer states with biblical confidence in the Introduction to his work *The Old Testament's Witness to Christ*:

> The Christian Church stands or falls on its recognition of both Testaments. A 'Church' which discredits the value of the Old Testament as compared to the New, disbelieves the crucial factor in the Apostles' message and stops being 'Christian'. The main factor in the Apostolic Gospel is simply that Jesus is the Christ of the Old Testament.[63]

Seiver's ten questions on the Ten Commandments

In the New Covenant Forum web-site under the heading *Questions that Demand an Answer*, Seiver asks ten questions which he partly answers himself but also opens up for others to answer, indicating that he is offering an over-view of NCT thinking concerning what they believe

---

[63] My translation. I am grateful to Blanke and Leuschner for these thoughts.

and do not believe. I shall quote these ten questions in full and comment on them all so as not to reap Seiver's previous strong complaint that I misrepresent him. Here are then the 10 questions concerning Seiver's theology of a broken covenant that really do demand an answer:

1. *Do the scriptures describe the 10 Commandments as a covenant, namely, the national covenant God made with Israel? (Exo. 34:28).*

My Answer: In the Bible words translated as 'covenant' have many meanings from a mere command to the Covenant of Grace, Peace and Mercy made between the Father and the Son on behalf of fallen man. I take the two uses of the usual term for Covenant in the wider, spiritual sense (berit) and in Exodus 34:27, 28 to be a common example of Hebrew repetition for the sake of emphasis. For clarity's sake, Seiver ought to have quoted both passages here, not one (Exodus 34:27, 28) and fitted them into the whole context which contradicts Seiver. Exodus 34:27, 28 reads:

> And the Lord said unto Moses, Write out these words: for after the tenor of these words I have made a covenant with thee and with Israel. And he was there with the Lord forty days and forty nights; he did neither eat bread, nor drink water. And he wrote upon the tables the words of the covenant, the ten commandments ... [64]

It is clear here that God is speaking of a covenant already made and now He is giving the 'tenor' of God's revelation within the Covenant of Grace which was never to be understood merely legally. Indeed, the Hebrew word 'al' in verse 27 translated 'tenor' refers to keeping to what has already been covenanted which is clearly and faithfully represented in the grammar of the A.V. text. God is saying that one must interpret the purpose and character of the written word and not merely stick to its letter.

Seiver also makes an automatic stop in v. 28 as if God was merely speaking of ten commandments bar their 'tenor' and contextualisation.

---

[64] My dots represent the fact that the revelation to Moses goes on and on.

The entire context and the following chapters make it clear that Moses had a great deal more to say concerning what the Lord had told him on the mountain (vv. 31-35). This was all part of the Covenant teaching God gave to Moses. So, too, it was obviously God's Law that Moses received and not 'Moses Law' in any other sense than Moses was the vehicle of revelation as one who was 'God's friend'.

We also note as in Chapter 35:29 that those who understood the 'tenor' were those who had a willing heart to bring forward a willing offering. We read further in Chapter 36 of those wise-hearted people who were such because it was God who had given them a wise heart. This is emphasized again and again. These people, like David after them, loved the Law as they understood its tenor, the purpose and the character of the Law which was the hope to which it pointed. It is obvious that this is Jeremiah's teaching in chapter 31 and following, where he sees the old covenant as that of the legalism and letter-beliefs of certain Jews and the New Covenant as that of those who understand the 'tenor' and know that the just shall live by faith and not with hearts made stony because of their fossilized legalism.

Again, Seiver's term 'National Covenant' must be scrutinised carefully as the Israel of the twelve tribes, (as opposed to Israel as the people of God) was not yet a nation and had not yet reached by very many years the Promise Land where after a further long time the Davidic kingdom of Israel was grounded but ended after a few decades. The teaching of the everlasting Covenant with Abraham was, however, well-known at the time even by the surrounding nations and in Moses' dealings with God concerning the Sinai revelations, Moses insisted that he could only understand his part in extending the Covenant within that already signed, sealed and delivered by God to his Fathers as Deuteronomy and Exodus make clear. Thus the great revelation given to Moses was a further development of the Covenant with Abraham already made. This was a Covenant promised to all nations. This fact led John Bale in 1645 to write:

In the land of Moab, Moses was commanded by the Lord to make a Covenant with the Children of Israel, beside the covenant which he made with them in Horeb. This Covenant they entered into was the same that God made with them upon Mount Sinai, even the same that did contain the blessings and cursors[65] before pronounced. But this Covenant was a Covenant of Grace, not of works: for God never commanded his people, that he might set them on high above all people of the earth, and that they might be unholy people unto him to avouch him to be their God by Covenant of works: Moses would never have exhorted the people by oath to bind themselves unto the Lord in a Covenant of works: for that had been to bind themselves unto the most dreadful cursors, whereas they were to enter into this covenant that they might prosper in all that they do. That Covenant is of Grace, wherein the good things promised are all free and gracious: but it was of Grace that God had promised to be the God of Israel: and therefore the Lord, when he keepeth Covenant with Israel, is said to keep the Mercy which he swore unto their fathers, and when he established them for a people unto himself, and is their God, he is said to perform the oath, which he swore unto their Fathers, to Abraham, to Isaac, and to Jacob.[66]

Bale goes on to point out that as God promised forgiveness, the Covenant after transgression could be renewed and the people receive the Law written on their hearts which facts point to a Covenant of Grace.

That God chose out Moses to continue the Abrahamic Covenant is obvious from Exodus 3:6 where we read of Moses' first contact with the Divine revelation. He is told that it is the God of Abraham who is speaking to him. This is emphasized throughout the Pentateuch. Moses is seen as continuing in Abraham's footsteps, hand in hand with God. Indeed, we find Moses in Exodus 32:13 pleading with God to allow him to carry on Abraham's work, in spite of the disbelief of the covenant-breakers. This is repeated in even more detail in Deuteronomy chapter nine.

At this time, we note the wayward Children of Israel who were already a mixed nation and were continually absorbing other tribes, had to be told by foreigners what the Abrahamic Covenant really meant and

---

[65] Curses
[66] *A Treatise of the Covenant of Grace*, p. 107.

that a Sceptre in Israel would be raised up and a Star out of Jacob. Indeed, it appeared at times that those people who eventually merged into Israel from outside such as the countries Balaam (and his donkey) represented knew more of the Messiah than the forgetful Jews. God's Covenant of Grace was international and pan-biblical from the start. Indeed when the descendants of Joseph and his brethren left Egypt, they took many with them who were not of the tribes and gathered thousands on their long march. The Covenant has always been missionary-minded. Job was most likely pre-Moses but he knew that his Redeemer was alive and at work. Indeed the Messianic faith of the Old Testament saints was pre-Israelite.

That the Ten Commandments should sum up the Old Testament's total teaching on righteousness and for some the only rule of conduct for Christians is an idea quite foreign to the Bible. Those who separate Law from Grace in either Testament are splitting the scriptures down the middle. Here Seiver loses contact with the biblical timing and historical overview. He emphasizes the defects of the 'old covenant', which he at times calls 'the first covenant' and complains, by using a most odd translation of parts of Hebrews 8, with altered vocabulary and tenses, which seems to be his own, that there was something wrong with it.[67] When I challenged Seiver both personally and through the pages of *New Focus* concerning what he had written, Seiver called me 'a clown' and a 'loon' in his various published attacks and he answered in the New Covenant Theology Web-site:

> Oh! By the way, George, why don't we tell the folks what I actually did write about the Law (Old Covenant). Please notice I didn't even use the word, 'wrong'.

This was followed by the two quips 'George, I know the truth doesn't matter to you, but maybe someone reading this will care.' And 'I guess I just have to keep reminding myself that things are different in Ella world.' Though I sent Seiver exact details of where and in what context he had used the word 'wrong', the author of the word still denied he had written it. He also denied that other NCT men had written the quotes I gave from their books although hinting that he had not read

---

[67] *In These Last Days*, p. 123.

them. Indeed, Seiver gave his readers a false page in his own book for the source of my challenge where, he claimed, the word 'wrong' did not occur. He was correct but wrong in not giving his readers the right page where it did occur and which I had pointed out to him before he produced the 'wrong page'.

Seiver gives the wrong meaning to 'Covenant'

It is obvious through any discussion with Randy Seiver that he rarely really agrees with the biblical quotes he gives, as they stand. He interprets them quite differently to their original and true meaning. Seiver, when looking into Jeremiah and using the word 'covenant' is referring to the Old Testament and when he uses the term New Covenant, he is referring to the New Testament. Jeremiah in Chapter 31, whom the author to the Hebrews quotes correctly, is referring to the broken covenant of the Jews *before* receiving the stone tablets. The New Covenant is that which is already inaugurated and goes on for all time. However, instead of following Jeremiah here who speaks there and then of the revealed New Covenant which is the true Covenant, Seiver equates the useless covenant of the unfaithful Children of Israel as if it were the entire Old Testament Covenant which is thus also annulled. The Hebrew word for 'covenant' can also mean a cutting into two parts signifying the responsibilities of two parties, here the Father and the Son. Here Seiver 'cuts' the Covenant story, but not into two parts. He cuts it out altogether from where it belongs. But it is this very New Covenant which is recommended by the Prophets as being superior to the 'old' in that it teaches righteousness through faith. This is the New Covenant teaching which certain Jews, who were heavily punished for their impiety, either did not understand or did not want. Yet Seiver has merely interpreted the Ten Commandments by the letter without paying due heed to the 'tenor' which they point to concerning their being kept in Covenantal faith in hearts of flesh and not stone.

The author of the Hebrews refers to this tenor in Chapter 9:20 where he quotes Moses reference to 'the blood of the Covenant'. This mention of 'blood' is surely, as the Hebrews' author claims, a reference to the shedding of Christ's blood in the everlasting covenant in Chapter 13:20. Yet when Seiver refers to this mention of the blood of the everlasting covenant, which in both cases points to Christ's shed covenant blood, he quotes Hebrews 9:20 as referring to 'the blood of the (old) covenant', the insert being his, thus robbing the Covenant of its lasting nature and forcing his own faulty interpretation onto his readers.[68] This is highly misleading as the reference is to Christ's blood which Seiver also points out but he looks on it as part of an old, annulled covenant prior to the New Covenant. Here is one of the many incongruous features of NCT faith which leave their doctrines all with loose ends. Where they have clear proof of the everlasting Covenant signed and sealed by Christ's blood, they nevertheless choose to reject it as Old Testament legalism.

2. To what does the Apostle Paul refer when he writes about the "ministry of death engraven in stones" (2 Corinthians 3:7)?

3. Does he seem to suggest that the new covenant of which he is a minister is inferior or superior to that ministry of death written in stones?

Answer: Both questions refer to 2 Corinthians 3:7-18. Here Paul in context is continuing his advice to fellow-believers in linking up with his Old Testament Fathers in condemning those who do not follow the spirit of the law but only the letter. These have not hearts of flesh but hearts of stones. They have not been given, as Jeremiah preaches, a heart to know God.[69] Or as Ezekiel teaches, God replaces rebellious stony hearts with hearts of flesh.[70] This was the doctrine of both the Prophets and the Apostles following them. This biblical, Covenantal truth is the doctrine of the entire scriptures in which God lifts the judgment of condemnation and replaces it with Grace. One might even venture to say that this doctrine is repeated and emphasized more in the Old Testament than in the New as illustrated by the Prophets and the fact that New Testament writers use the Old Testament to back up their doctrine as they find New Testament truths in it. The Old Testament scriptures are also much larger than the New and were the Bible of Christ and His Apostles. Death engraven in stone points to those who think merely in terms of laws chiselled in stone without due application

---

[68] *In These Last Days*, p. 129.
[69] Jeremiah 24:7.
[70] Ezekiel 11:19.

to God's revelations of grace which is the tenor of the Law in the heart. Stony hearts, we read, rob Moses of his glory and title of being God's friend and deny Christ's title of being the Covenant Author and Keeper of the covenant of Grace, Mercy and Peace of which the Law was a natural part. This Covenant was made with all the Old Testament saints before and after Moses and continues today. Paul, referring to the actuality of the Law in New Testament times, was quick to point out as in 1 Timothy 1:8 that the law was good when used lawfully as an agent of grace, but condemning in the hands of stony hearts. So here, it is clear that Paul is saying that the misuse of the law leads to condemnation. There is no indication in scripture that this function of the Law has ceased. Seiver only recognizes an Old Testament Law for stony hearts.

The NCT would also have us believe that the vail (letter of the law in stone for stony hearts which covered the faces of unbelievers) was abolished at some uncertain time during the life of Christ but Paul firmly affirms here that this vail is still on all unbelievers. When Christ enters sinners' hearts, the legal vail under which they are in darkness is removed. What was a bad thing for them in their own hands becomes a good thing for them in the Hands of Christ.[71] When David said he loved God's commandments, it was God's grace in them he was referring to and not to the bare letter. Naturally, therefore David meant far more than the Ten Commandments when loving God's Covenant. He was expressing his love for God Himself. A study of the Covenant with the law included in David's faith ought to be compulsory reading for the NCT. Loving the law means loving God in Christ the Lawmaker, Keeper and Fulfiller. Loving a 'moral code' or a 'national Covenant' does not help at all salvation-wise.

Seiver is here obviously striving to influence the person prepared to answer this question via the NCT's narrow view of biblical law as being merely a letter law. Here, Paul is not dealing with a new Covenant in the New Testament but with the Old Testament which was Paul's scripture and in which the New Covenant was taught. The pan-Old Testament Covenant of Grace was renewed and extended because of strong opposition from unbelieving parties all through the Old

---

[71] 2 Corinthians 3:13, 14.

Testament period. The apostolic preaching in the New Testament continues this task. NCT opposition to this Covenant carries on the old unbelieving Jew's self-righteous misunderstanding. All talk of a renewed, refreshed new Covenant and the way Jeremiah describes this renewal refers to the fact that unbelieving Jews rejected the balance of Law and Grace within the Covenant. This is why the Covenant was renewed not only from the beginning but kept fresh in all the preaching of Moses and the Prophets. The NCT, however, misunderstands the preaching and prophesying of the Old Testament as being riddles solved hundreds of years after their revelation by their own NCT 'prophets'. Prophesy was preaching forth to a people who were to build their faith on the message given to them when they needed it in their day and age. The Covenant was not *renewed* in Christ but *established* in Christ for all ages. Thus Paul is not comparing a past situation with a present but referring to the everlasting Covenant of God which always abolishes the curse of the Law in those who have received righteous hearts through Christ's righteousness.

We must ask, however, what the NCT mean by the term 'righteousness'. We find, that just like their unwillingness to state what their 'New Law' and 'New Age' are, they are also unwilling to declare what Christ's righteousness means to them. David Gay takes a most dubious approach in defining the righteousness which is imputed to us by faith. In his book *Eternal Justification* Gay deals with righteousness in purely legal terms, even Christ's righteousness, and finds that righteousness imputed to us is merely a legal declaration of our new status before God. He tells us that in salvation we do not encounter Christ's intrinsic righteousness, but merely what Christ has done in legally acquitting us from the wages of sin. Happily we have the scriptures and the testimony of true saints which teach us better things from the Covenant of Grace. John Davenant in his *Treatise of Justification* tells us:

> We openly affirm that the righteous God justifies no one, that is, absolves him from guilt, declares him just, and accepts him to life eternal, which is the reward of righteousness, unless by the intervention of a true and perfect righteousness, which also becomes truly the righteousness of the justified person himself … no one is justified, but he upon whom God has bestowed a

righteousness so complete and perfect, that God in beholding him cannot but regard as righteous the person upon whom the same is bestowed.[72]

It is interesting to note that the NCT people profess to accept only doctrines mentioned in the N.T. but their whole interpretation of their new covenant is based on a misunderstanding of Jeremiah and all the other O.T. authors concerning the Covenant and the Lord Our Righteousness,[73] two of Jeremiah's main themes. In other words, they are embedded and bogged down in the wrong understanding of the law, making the same mistake as they claim the Jews made as an alleged 'nation'. Here we have a direct comparison between the true enlightening ministration of the spirit as opposed to the darkness gained in striving to follow the mere letter of the Law.

4. What does Paul say is happening to that ministry of death/national covenant made with Israel?

Answer: Again, a strange question as the Covenant of Grace was not made with a nation but was established outside of Judaism hundreds of years before the nation of Israel came into being. It was always revealed to chosen individuals. Even that part of the Covenant which we call the Ten Commandments was first revealed to the individual Moses. This Covenant was widely known in the Near East as the witness of Job and many others show but enlarged and explained as the need arose. The Covenant made with Abraham was broadcast far and wide long before and much farther than the much later Jewish short-term State.

The law is a ministry of death for unbelievers but our job is to rescue unbelievers from such a death through our Christian witness. The law in the hands of Christ has brought us life.

5. Is the covenant God made with Israel identical with the Old Testament scriptures? If the two are not identical (and they are not) is

---

[72] *Treatise of Justification.* p. 159, London 1844.
[73] Jeremiah 23:6; 34:16.

it not possible to live under a New Covenant without denying the value and validity of the Old Testament scriptures?

Answer: This is really two questions. Seiver's first question avoids the entire issue of the Covenant of Grace and the mixed interest the Children of Israel gave it. When Seiver uses the term 'covenant' regarding Israel, he invariably means the Ten Commandments which, of course, are not according to the letter identical with the entire Old Testament witness which is far more comprehensive and glorious, to use Paul's word in 2 Corinthians 3:7ff.. It also avoids the fact that the witness of the New Testament centres around and commentates on the entire Covenant of Grace as given in all the scriptures, starting with the Old Testament. The Old Testament believers, especially the prophets, spent their lives striving to win unbelievers for the Covenant of Grace but this was so in New Testament times also where believers in Christ and especially the Apostles spent their lives preaching the same Covenant.

Concerning Seiver's second question here, it is also unclearly worded. What does Seiver mean by a 'New Covenant' which he also wrongly dates? He obviously means something far different from the biblical fact. He is talking about a phantom covenant. What does Seiver mean by 'the value and validity of the Old Testament scriptures'? Here, again, Seiver does not take the biblical stand concerning these valid values and would rob them of both the continuing Covenant of Grace and the continuing Law. Such 'tongue in the cheek' dodgy questions are therefore unhelpful in Christian debate. Seiver must make it clear whether he is speaking of the attitude of all believers to the Covenant of Grace, which includes the Law, or the attitude of Jews, some of whom by God's grace understood the 'tenor' of the Law and some did not. He appears, however, never to refer to the remnant of Jewish believers but judges the entire Old Testament scripture through the practice of unbelieving Jews. The question of Jews or Gentiles is irrelevant here as God's Covenant embraces not all Jews and all Gentiles but *all believers*. And the evangelical command goes out to them to seek out those who are in other folds. The 'Fold' of Christ is not an earthly nation but it is a heavenly Kingdom where He reigns.

There is no new, different Covenant of Grace but an ever-new one. Luke begins his Epistle by affirming the continuation of the Covenant as did Abraham, Job, Moses, David and all the prophets up to Malachi before him. Malachi's teaching is continued in the next book Matthew who establishes this teaching in the Old Testament. Mark, Luke, and John also start with the Old Testament and show how it is continued in the New. There is no discontinuation between the Testaments. Those who teach so deny the value and validity of the whole of scripture.

6. Where is the passage in the New Testament scriptures that gives the slightest indication that the New Covenant believer is to look to the Ten Commandments as his standard of sanctification? It would be helpful in proving your contention if only the Apostle had written, 'He who loves his fellowman WILL FULFILL the law (Romans 8:13)'. The problem is he didn't. He wrote, 'He who loves. . . HAS FULFILLED THE LAW.' The New Testament scriptures do a superb job of defining for us what it is like to love our fellowman, thus preventing us from turning love into lust and licentiousness.

Answer: Again, this question has a faulty basis. Those few who taught that the Ten Commandments are the sole rule of life for the Christian are now either in the NCT or near to it. Look, for instance, at those once almost fanatically engaged in defending this erroneous doctrine in the *Banner Of Truth, Founders Journal, Reformation Today* and other Neonomian bodies. The NCT has sadly come to believe that all binding law as law is abolished but they have a non-binding 'New Law' which they never spell out. However, they find at least nine commandments in it, identical to the Law given on Sinai. Yet they say this Law is for NCT believers only so what is the fate of sinners if there is no Law to condemn them?

Praise God, Christ has fulfilled and satisfied the law so that it has become good in the hands of Christians who have Christ's faith in their hearts but it is still a stumbling block for unrepentant and unbelieving sinners. Obviously pre-Jewish Abraham looked to His Messiah Christ in faith to fulfil the Law for him, otherwise Christ would never have said that Adam's faith was accounted, or imputed, as righteousness. To limit the fulfilment of the Law in Christ to New Testament-only historical events contradicts the Christ of All Ages.

7. If a person believes New Covenant believers are under the law of Christ and that Christ's law expresses the same eternal, and immutable righteous standard as that reflected in the 10 Commandments, he can't really be considered as being against law (antinomian) can he?

Answer: This question is so unclearly expressed that I can only make a reasoned guess at what Seiver is hoping we might understand. One cannot reject the Ten Commandments as being the sole pattern for the moral conduct of Christians (what a strange idea, anyway!) and then say 'Christ's law says the same thing'. Is Seiver thinking only of NCT people here or all Christians, or all sinners? Besides, what does Seiver mean by 'the Law of Christ' and who here is accusing whom of Antinomianism? As the NCT rule out God's use of His law in New Testament times for unbelievers and believers alike, is it thus not legitimate to call them 'Antinomians'. My NCT friends tell me that they serve a New Law so that they cannot be called 'Antinomians'. This is doubly dodging the issue. First: they are obviously Antinomian in regards to the Covenant Mosaic Law but as they still have no Law for the unsaved, whether moral, or spiritual or whatever, they are still Antinomian in this respect. Second: as they say their New Law is not binding, then they are Antinomian in their own understanding of their own 'New Law' whether they see this as being a mere moral law or not. David knew how to combine Grace and Law and understood what righteousness really was so he wrote in Psalm 119:142 'Thy righteousness is an everlasting righteousness, and thy law is the truth.' The NCT not only denies the perpetual nature of the Covenant but also the perpetual, immutable nature of God's righteousness and the everlastingness of God's Law. David also tells us that God's Old Testament testimonies are also everlasting (v. 144).

8. Is the ministry of the Holy Spirit in the believer's life sufficiently effective to accomplish the work of sanctification according to the New Testament standard?

Answer: I believe so, but would not add the word 'standard' as does Seiver. He argues, alongside Reisinger, that the N.T. has new moral and ethical standards, rules, regulations and commandments which the O.T. did not have. What has this to do with the Gospel story? Laws do not save us but Grace. NCT law-bound thinking is not New Testament thinking. Furthermore, as God's righteousness and the sanctification of believers was firmly established, preached and often believed in the Old Testament, we cannot isolate the Testaments in our definition of 'sanctification'. So, too, the NCT has still to come up with a biblically acceptable definition of 'sanctification'. I suggest that this is impossible without adding the teaching of the Old Testament to the New.

9. If the Sabbath observance is the sign of the covenant God made with Israel (see-Exodus 31:17), would it not be temporally coextensive with the covenant of which it was the sign? In other words, would not the Sabbath observance endure only as long as the covenant endured? Now, if that covenant has become antiquated by the establishment of the new and everlasting covenant, and the New Testament scriptures provide abundant evidence that it has now been thus replaced, would it not make sense that God's new covenant people are not now under the sign of a covenant that does not belong to them?

Answer: This, again, is unhelpful reasoning as it compares ifs with ifs and mixes up the chronology of the scriptures. The Sabbath commandment was pre-Sinai and was re-affirmed after the breaking of the old covenant which was no covenant. One cannot erase God's Sabbath rest from the history of creation. Let us be concrete. As the Day of Rest was a sign of the fact that God rested on the Seventh Day, it always has that function. God has not cancelled the truths of Genesis or any other scripture. Surely this is what Exodus 31:17 is teaching. However, the Sabbath here depicted does not cover, though it overlaps, the Covenant of Grace but it is a sign to say that God made Heaven and Earth in six days and on the seventh God rested and was refreshed. What has Seiver against such signs? Seiver is of course frightened that we would demand that the NCT should say 'Go thou and do likewise' as the NCT has rejected that part of the Covenant which they call 'Old Testament Law' and profess not to keep the Sabbath holy. Indeed, they profess not to keep any of the Law at all! Not even its 'tenor'.

However, is this not a piece of biblical common sense with God acting as our Divine Instructor? What is wrong with keeping a day of rest once in a week? Why ban it? The NCT makes such a palaver about the Sabbath as if the common-sense Sabbath were an idol. The NCT would forbid it but they say they rest on the Lord's Day. O. K. They rest one day in seven, though they find the idea antiquated. What is the difference? Though they tell us that the Lord's Day is different from God's Day of Rest after creation, their evidence is unconvincing. Here Seiver is splitting God into parts. Who was it who was active in creating the world according to John 1? It was God in Christ and the work of the Spirit. Without Christ nothing was made that was made. The fact that the Godhead rested in His triune function of Creation on the seventh Day was also the rest of Father, Son and Holy Ghost. It was the first Lord's Day as we know that without Christ nothing was created which is created. 'Lord' is the common term throughout the scriptures not only for God but also Christ. So the creation Sabbath was the first Lord's Day, the Day of Christ's rest. This heavenly rest is the rest all believers shall share in the calling up of the New Jerusalem. Why abolish this wonderful gospel? So, too, the re-creation of man after the Fall is the work of the Holy Trinity and we merge both Days into one because they refer to a rest after an accomplished creation and re-creation. Forgetting the O.T. commandments of God, the NCT claim they keep the Lord's Day out of choice. Fair enough! I would say that this act is a command of God, kept by Christ, and we obey it because we are in Christ and follow Him whether referring to His actions in the Old Testament or the New. Thus it is a choice which enables us to say, 'as for me and my house, we follow the Lord.' However, the NCT tells us that they are bound by no law. Then why do they keep the Sabbath, albeit in their new interpretation of the new everlasting law in Christ shown in keeping the Lord's Day? Is not the Lord's Day the whole Gospel from creation to Christ's resurrection and thus our resurrection in Him what the Lord's Day is all about?

The obvious NCT's answer must be that they find a Lord's Day rest somehow practical for those who wish to rest as they say their New Laws are not binding. They thus keep their Seventh Day holy by choice. Again, fair enough! Believing Jews regarded the everlasting sign of the Sabbath rest as a guide to faith but they also kept it by choice. Surely, the NCT must accept that this freedom is still open to all believers? Yet they tell silly stories of Sabbath-keepers and ridicule them in their works and show absolute scoffing intolerance concerning their beliefs and deny them the right to observe the Sabbath. This is again one of the many instances of the NCT wishing to eat their cake and keep it.

Anyway, how does the NCT know that their Lord's Day was actually the Day of Christ's resurrection? At least three different calendars were in operation at the time and the six day week was in competition with the seven and eight day week. Is it not legalistic and perhaps superstitious to pin down one day in the week in our celebration of the Lord's resurrection when it might have been a Saturday, Sunday, Monday or Tuesday? This is the same with Christmas, Easter, Whitsuntide etc.. Here we take the Church Fathers, such as Augustine, Clement and Barnabas as witnesses who claimed that the Lord's Day was on the eighth day. They argued that the final seventh day Saturday night Sabbath would continue into the Lord's Day and signified a blessed period that would never end. So they were eight day Sabbatarians. Augustine in his Confessions tells us clearly that the Sabbath was the sign of the Christian's entry into eternal life. Why abolish such a testimony? Where is this eighth day in Seiver's calendar? No, we place the Lord's Day on the Sunday out of utility thinking and convention and because we cannot forget these pillars of our Christian heritage. They are there with a purpose 'lest we forget'. Even today we are undecided whether we should call Sunday the last day of the week or the first. In our fishing club's hut our service calendar ends the week on a Sunday. Monday starts it. In our home the calendar starts the week with a Sunday. My Russian friends tell me they have quite a different calendar as have also traditional Jews, the Chinese etc.. In biblical times it was, however, far more confusing as different calendars were used even in very limited area.

Furthermore, if Seiver wishes to throw out the Decalogue and the Sabbath ruling with it, then he throws out also the nine 'moral commandments' which he professes to follow.

10. Are today's believers under the old covenant or the new covenant? If under the old covenant, why does the Apostle Paul write that he is a minister of the new covenant (2 Corinthians 3:6). If the covenant Paul is talking about is the ministry of death/condemnation written on tablets of stone, the 10 commandments, what does that tell us about the believer's relationship to the 10 commandments?

Answer: We are under the one Covenant of Grace as all believers past, present and future. 2 Corinthians 3:6 refers to the state of the ministers of the Covenant of Grace in New Testament times. We are declared to be ministers of the epistle of Christ written in our hearts not via anything written in ink or engraved in stone. Just as in the Old Testament believers looked forward to Christ in spirit not merely in letter, so Paul tells New Testament ministers that they are also called to live by the spirit and not by the letter. They are ministers of the ever new covenant as was Jeremiah. The spiritual understanding of the New Testament is life but living by the letter is death. Here, Paul demonstrates the continuity of the renewed Covenant as believed in the Old Testament. Paul explains in 2 Corinthians 3:14, 15 twice that the vail on the Mosaic revelation exists still in his day unless taken away by Christ. We read:

> But their minds were blinded: for until this day remaineth the same vail untaken away in the reading of the old testament; which vail is done away in Christ. But even unto this day when Moses is read, the vail is upon their heart. Nevertheless when it shall turn to the Lord, the vail shall be taken away.

Surely this is also today's situation in the realms of both Jews and Gentiles. When Paul writes this to Corinthian believers and says in verse 18, 'But we all with open face beholding as in a glass the glory of the Lord, Are changed into the same image from glory to glory, even as by the Spirit of the Lord', he is not thinking merely of Jews (as some NCT people tell me), but of all who are in Christ whether Jews or Gentiles.

I am open to discussion on these points and I know I have not even covered the ground to my own satisfaction but I wish to show Brother Randy and his NCT brethren how fragile others might view their position.

Summing Up
Modern evangelical theology, chiefly through the erroneous teaching of several 'Reformed' publishing houses, has altered the spiritual course of Covenant preaching towards a moral understanding of the gospel. Here we include also the NCT who profess to be evangelical

and reformed. These modern enthusiasts even reduce Christianity to a discussion concerning the moral requirements of the Ten Commandments as if the entire Covenant of Grace was according to moral and legal jurisdiction chiselled into two tablets of stone. They reject biblical teaching that here was a further act of Grace on God's part, sealing His Covenant with Abraham concerning the just who shall live by faith, not works. Sadly, many of these moral preachers break their own moral rules by forging new translations and interpretations of scripture and strive to minimize the great Work of Christ as our Covenant Head.

With his ten questions on the Covenant of Grace, Randy Seiver shows he views the New Covenant believed in by the Prophets merely as a legal, politically national covenant of a people who, on the whole, were rapidly departing from God's true Covenant of Grace which offered them redemption. This time of redemptive Grace Seiver only recognizes in the New Testament, seemingly oblivious to the fact that the New Testament continues Old Testament teaching, leaning fully on it and which in no way breaks with it. So, too, it is obvious from scripture that God's Covenant was known amongst the Gentiles before, parallel to and after the Jewish national state came and was soon gone. Seiver errs because of his fundamental theory that the Old Testament Jews (forgetting non-Jews such as Job who knew his Redeemer lived) merely followed a 'Letter Law' carved in stone for stony hearts. That David and the Prophets rejected such a faulty interpretation in their days means nothing to Seiver who moves all their teaching into New Testament times as if the Old Testament saints were unaware of what they were talking about and experiencing. Though Seiver speaks of 'the value and validity' of the Old Testament scriptures, he, nevertheless, robs them of their main value and validity. The New Law of Christ which he would substitute for the Old Law of Christ is never spelt out by Seiver who gives Moses all the responsibility for the 'Old Law' and not Christ who is in all the scriptures as the Covenant Maker and Keeper. NCT spokesmen confuse the issue even further by arguing that their (undefined) New Law is not binding.

It is also difficult to know what Seiver means by the NCT doctrine of sanctification 'according to the New Testament standard'. A 'standard' is a rule but the NCT tells us that Christ's rules are not binding. He also argues vainly that this 'New Testament standard' was unknown to the Old Testament.

Concerning abolishing Sabbath keeping, Seiver is never so unclear as on this subject and gives quite the wrong reasons for either keeping it or abolishing it. Yet he does set one day in seven apart for the Lord!

In his tenth question Seiver asks if we are under the old or new covenant, showing that Paul was a minister of the New Covenant. He does not relate that Paul took his cue from the Old Testament where the New Covenant, interpreted as a Covenant of Grace was widely preached by Jeremiah and his true fellow-prophets.

Chapter 4

New Covenant Theology On Law And Grace

Our never changing God

As demonstrated in the previous chapter, one of the main contenders for abolishing the biblical doctrine of the Covenant of Grace is the so-called New Covenant Theology movement (NCT). It is a small movement in itself and still having teething troubles and a difficulty in establishing a theological basis for all those who reject the idea of a Covenant of Grace. It has arisen, however, at a time when many other denominations are leaving the gospel path for a more modernistic, rational view of God's once and for all time revelation in the scriptures. Whereas the one will of God in salvation through Christ was the corner stone of evangelical, Reformed theology, it has now become commonplace that even evangelical teachers and pastors preach rationalistic speculation to their flocks concerning the alleged changing wills of God and supposed contradictions in the testimony of scripture. Suddenly, God is being presented to us in a minimalised form but man in a maximalised form and God's word is seen as a collection of contrary documents awaiting to be clarified by further rationalism. This author therefore looks on the NCT as part of the present degrading and dumbing down of religion which, under new names, has come and gone throughout the world since creation. The Bible tells us, however, that we can still look forward to great revivals to come in the days of the New Jerusalem.

When and where truth is preached error is not far away
The gospel news of a Covenant of Grace from eternity covering the whole of time has been severely challenged recently by these Dispensationist-Neo-Covenant campaigners with their cut-down theology who are quite out of date with their views mainly built on heretical teaching spread by the Marcionites at the beginning of the world-wide Christian outreach and the Catabaptists at the beginning of the Reformation era.[74] It appears thus that where truth has to be preached, it is because error is not far away. The views of the NCT seek to destroy the seed, root and branches of the Covenant of Grace which pervades throughout all the scriptures.

We still find NCT people extolling Christ as Lord and this convinces many that they are orthodox. However, they have altered the traditional meaning of many theological expressions, cut out much of the gospel in both Testaments and introduced their own NewSpeak to explain away the gospel truths to which they pay lip-service. They separate law from grace in Christ's Covenant, and rid the Saviour of many of His eternal attributes, thus making Him no Saviour at all. Above all, they split the Bible into multiple parts in Dispensationalist fashion seeing no continuity of revelation from Genesis to Revelation. They also teach that the God of the Old Testament had a lower standard of righteousness than the God of the New Testament. Indeed, they argue that God's revelations of grace on Mt. Sinai 'smited' and 'imprisoned' sinners, hiding them from faith through grace instead of turning them to God for his mercy.

This movement has combined the Marcionite and Catabaptist heretical views of the Old Testament with their New Age, New Covenant, New Order and New Law eschatological thinking. They started off by teaching that we are in the Endzeit of 'realized eschatology' but in recent years they sweep what they cannot explain

---

[74] The New Covenant was the teaching of both the greater and lesser prophets and believed by the Old Testament saints. NCT teaches that the New Covenant was first preached and believed after Christ's resurrection. When the N.T. testify to the 'Prophets' knowing the New Covenant, NCT contenders say New Testament Prophets only were meant but they do not specify which.

under the carpet of a further New Order after the present NCT Covenant and tell us that it will all be revealed at some future date. The Old Testament had opened all this out before them and one must look backwards to move forwards in revelation but the NCT have cut off their Old Testament foundation and thus their own future.

The NCT's dissipated progress
In modern times the so-called New Covenant Theology (NCT) argues for two separate Covenants, the one having come after the other since the resurrection of Christ.[75] They rightly reject the Presbyterian idea of a separate Covenant of Law (or Works) running parallel with a Covenant of Grace but not merging with it. They, however wrench the Law within the Covenant of Grace out of its biblical usage and effectual work and replace it with an entirely 'New Covenant' which has brought in a 'New Law' rendering the supposed 'Old Law' and 'Old Covenant'[76] obsolete and thus abolished. Obviously the law has no condemning power over believers but it still speaks to the unconverted. The NCT thus often speak of their 'New Law' as a synonym for their 'New Covenant' so following the Old Testament Scribes and Pharisees whom Christ corrected by teaching the grace of the Law and the Law's purpose in grace. One can, indeed, use the law unlawfully as well as one can misuse the doctrine of grace. The Catabaptists saw the Jews as being the People of the Old Covenant (within their understanding of the term) but claimed that this Covenant is no longer valid with reference to the Gentile churches. New Covenant Theology holds to a similar belief but its followers are prepared to accept certain parts of the O.T. which fit their system, a system which, however, is being developed and altered continually as we see in their eschatology and their former emphasis on what they termed 'the moral law' is now changing. Their Ten Commandments have become Nine but these, they often say, are not obligatory for believers as none of their 'New Law' appertaining to their 'New Order' are. The movement is at sixes and sevens concerning

---

[75] Here the NCTs are of different opinions as to when the New Covenant took over. Older contenders thought the Sermon on the Mount was the turning point, recent NCT authors say Christ's death and resurrection.
[76] They do not mean the 'old Covenant' as per the Prophets but the entire Old Testament.

what else to accept out of the Old Testament. Indeed, their teaching on law and grace is so cut-down that they offer us far less of the gospel than the Old Testament does and reduce the gospel in the New Testament so radically that the Covenant of Grace is hardly recognizable. They are not even of one mind concerning when their 'New Covenant' began. Though they at first propagated 'Realised Eschatology', they now speak of 'A New Age' and a 'New Epoch' but appear to have moved the 'Final Days' forward to an 'unrealised' future.

The error of basing Christianity on a reduced law
The NCT have certainly been led astray here by a small group of protagonists who claimed to be 'Calvinistic' whom I have combatted in my writings since the eighties. Then, at least three of these 'Modified or Moderate Calvinists', denigrated me for objecting to their watering down of Reformed principles as I not only denied that the Ten so-called Moral Commandments were the sole rule of life for Christians but also showed they were never the sole rule of life for the Jews either. Now some of these 10 point Calvinists have come out for NCT's 9 point Calvinism and are now watering down both Covenant and Law.

The so-called 'Reformed' or 'Moderate' Calvinists, led by the Banner of Truth school, began to base Christianity on the Ten Commandments which they called 'the moral law' in the late eighties which shocked many. A few, still mixed up through what they had experienced, eventually attached themselves to New Covenant Theology.[77] It is thus the theological weakness of these so-called Calvinists which has proved an impetus in founding the NC movement.[78] The NCT contenders say they have also rejected Dispensationalism but most of their critics, including myself, see Dispensationalism still strongly evident in New Covenant Theology,

---

[77] See my writings against this Neonomianism, especially within the Banner of Truth fellowship, from which several prominent NCT men have separated themselves. Many Christians who honoured the Law that exhibits God's righteousness, including myself, were labelled 'Antinomians' by the BOT because they would not accept their watered down 'mini version' of the Law. Now the New Covenant people have dropped the Law altogether and become a law unto themselves.

[78] I have published several essays on the BOT's misuse of the law on my website.

now wrapped up in a new NCT jargon. A rose by any other name would still be a rose but one can say the same of a thistle.

A Covenant of Law with no Grace

Some Presbyterians differ from holders of New Covenant Theology in seeing the Jews as a people representing the Old Testament Church. This is a most dubious position. The NCT people teach that the Old Testament Covenant, or what they call the 'Sinaitic Covenant' or 'Mosaic Economy', was one of law only and not grace and this has been succeeded by the New Testament under a New Law. This position is even worse as it robs both the Old Testament and the New of the one gospel and destroys the Father's Covenant from eternity with His Son on behalf of man. As both the Old Testament and the New Testament clearly distinguish between believing Jews and Jews with no faith, it is strange how the idea of a Church of all Jews, as if all Jews were believers in the Messiah's salvation, entered Presbyterian heads. It is also very strange that, though the New Covenant was widely preached and believed in the Old Testament by Moses and the Prophets, the NCT deny this fact but, oddly enough, base their utterances on Old Testament texts which they claim, nevertheless, are redundant. It is well that the NCT profess they are still working on their system – it is most a most urgent necessity and they, as yet, are only half-way to discovering the full gospel message of the Bible. Our prayer must be that all Christians should keep on expanding their knowledge of the scriptures, not reducing it, because in them we find Words of Eternal Life.

Blurred Christianity

The dividing line between biblical Christianity and the NCT seems to be blurred by them these days. Some NCT people who have recently left other equally questionable 'positions' as they term it, such as ex-BOT man David Gay,[79] testify that they feel at home amongst the Anabaptists. The outcome of NCT scepticism against the Old Testament is that they will only accept what they feel are biblical truths if they are stated in the New Testament. However, they have yet to discover the bulk of Old Testament truths which God has revealed to

---

[79] See his YouTube 'Testimony'.

mankind and also the New Testament's witness to its effectual guiding of Christians. So it is no wonder that many biblical truths have not yet found access into so-called New Covenant Theology with its radical break between the Testaments.

The modern highly restricted view the NCT has of the Old Testament is totally unconvincing as the New Testament affirms the veracity of the Old from start to finish and builds mostly on truths already revealed in the Old Testament. Furthermore, when modern NCT adherents, such as John Reisinger and Peter Ditzel argue that NCT is a solid Baptist position, this is far from the truth. Some former Fullerite Baptists in league with Presbyterian and Congregationalist counterparts have lost several men to the NCT but the Old Particular Baptists of the John Gill kind are united against these Catabaptists and are once again standing up to be counted. Sufficient be it to say here that John Gill's work on the Covenant of Grace is the very best of Baptist teaching and is fully in line with the very best of Reformed thought. I differ from Gill only in eschatology and in my integrated view of circumcision and baptism within the Covenant of Grace as pointers to God in Christ choosing out Christ's Bride, the only true Church.

The Banner Of Truth Trust are going through a troubled period at present after leaving their former mainly Presbyterian position, and taking a more Wesleyan, Dispensational and Fullerite-Baptist stance. Today, this is challenged by their ex-Banner friends such as Tom Wells and David Gay who now emphasise that the Law and the Covenant in the New Testament are totally different from the Law and the Covenant in the Old.[80] It seemed for some time that Walter Chantry, then the editor of the Banner of Truth Magazine, would join the NCT but David Gay complains in his YouTube 'Testimony' that he had second (better) thoughts. It is good to see that a number of former Banner Of Truth friends on both sides of the Atlantic and the Australian Continent are now sweeping the dangerous dust of NCT-ism from their clothing and skins. May the Lord bless their work!

---

[80] See Adam T. Calvert's excellent review of Wells' and Zaspel's book *New Covenant Theology* on his blog site *Lord of Life*, 11.11.2014. One might also consult Thomas R. Schreiner's review in the Ryan Center for Biblical Studies Journal for July 15, 2004 and also Richard C. Barcellos' review on the website 'The Reformed reader' undated. There is also my own review of Wells' and Zaspel's book published in '*New Focus Magazine*' Dec. 26, 2006.

Flogging the 'Moral Law' horse unsaddles many

When I corresponded with Walter Chantry, he was obviously in his 'I do not know what to think' position. A BOT editorial featured, at David Gay's prompting, an article claiming I was a Hyper-Calvinist and did not believe in preaching the Gospel to sinners.[81] Maurice Roberts called me a Hyper-Calvinist and an Antinomian, though all my publications show how much I abhor such positions. Though he denied ever calling me such, Roberts did not remove his accusations from his internet sermons as requested. When I gave Chantry old BOT definitions of an 'Antinomian' and showed they certainly did not apply to me, he answered that there were different kinds of Antinomianism but refrained from telling me under which he felt I suffered. I explained to him that my theology had not changed since the BOT welcomed my articles in the eighties at Iain Murray's prompting and great encouragement, but sadly theirs had. My correspondence with Chantry was when the Banner was flogging the dead horse of the 'Moral Law' as the Christian sole rule of life. This was Antinomianism at its height but the BOT reserved the 'theological swear word' (so John Legg) for those who were not satisfied by this unlawful reduction of the Covenant of Grace. Legalism, according to the scripture view of law, is always illegal.

The BOT's peep into Dispensationalism

Happily, the younger BOT appear to be coming back to the old paths now save an occasional squint at Dispensationalism. John MacArthur, Iain Murray's new banner-carrier, views Jews as an ethnic, national, political and religious unity (which they never really were) under one kind of salvation and the Gentiles who are in Christ under another. MacArthur is still unclear about what will happen to unbelieving Jews who have already died as such. He believes God will finally forgive all Jews living at the end of time. No one would welcome that more than I but would this include all Jews past and now present? His peculiar idea is that the Jews as an ethnic-religious group will be automatically saved without going through the Gentile process of repentance and faith in

---

[81] BOT, February, Issue 497, 2005, p. 9.

Christ, the latter view leaving many Gentiles outside Christ's Fold. This is a clear refutation of John 1:11-13:

> He came unto his own, and his own received him not. But as many as received him, to them gave the power to become the sons of God, even to them that believe on his name: which were born, not of blood, nor of the will of the flesh, nor of the will of man, but of God.

The gospel transforms both Jews who believe and Gentiles who believe and there is no question of ethnic or cultural preference. However, all must go through the same Door of our Lord Jesus Christ. MacArthur's views would abolish the function of both law and grace as radically as does the theology of the NCT. Is the cut-down Christianity of MacArthur and the NCT thus a mere Gentile religion? It appears that in our once relatively orthodox evangelical circles we are now finding teaching regarding two peoples of God, two ways of salvation which have been termed 'by sight' and 'by faith' and two contrary Covenants one of Grace and one of Law. These views really indicate a belief in two 'gods' as the Marcionites taught or at least one god of two totally different characters providing two different ways of salvation. The NCT's exclusion of the Old Testament Jews is purely political and anti-Semitic and has nothing whatsoever to do with evangelical and biblical theology.

NCT Christianity is Neonomianism
Our New Covenant Theology friends, on the whole, do not see a Covenant of Grace in the Old Testament and view their idea of the New Covenant in terms of new legislation laid down by the Lord Jesus Christ. They now claim they have an easier law which is not binding. Exactly what this New Law is supposed to be, I have never understood from the scanty and contradictory information culled from NCT books and my personal talks and correspondence with professing NCT holders. They preach a law which they never spell out, so what use is such preaching to sinners? The NCT's Nine Commandments will, most likely, never save them but we must always be open to God's grace in salvation.

Looking for clarity in NCT teaching

Many reviewers of NCT books have complained of this lack of clarity. In order to hear what NCT writers are saying on Law many years ago, I consulted John Reisinger's booklet *Christ: Lord and Lawgiver over the Church*. This lecture, as the Introduction shows, was addressed to Baptists whom Reisinger sees as being at the height of Reformed Theology and only need to take on his NCT re-construction to become perfect in their teaching.[82] Sound Baptists will laugh at this affront. David Gay professes to be a Baptist but the church 'pedigree' he gives us bears no relationship to that of traditional Baptist doctrines. So, too, he always mixed with 'outsiders'. It appears he has 'fellowshipped' with a good number of deviations most Baptist churches would seek to avoid. Yet is Reisinger preaching the whole gospel when he emphasises a New Lordship and a New Lawgiver only? Is he really exalting the Lord of Righteousness as so often emphasized in the Old Testament? I miss very much the 'repent and believe' of Christ's ministry with its combination of Law and Grace. The Old Testament people were often admonished to repent and believe as also those born after Christ's first Advent so why is this not an essential part of the NCT ministry?

The NCT say they base their faith on the laws of the New Testament only but the New Testament clearly teaches the continual call to repent and believe taken over from the Old Testament. One can only repent if one has been shown that one has broken God's Law which is valid in both Testaments. The NCT is all about Law for saints who, they stress, are not obliged to keep them, but what about Law for sinners which condemns them? Are the wages of sin no longer death? True, Reisinger's subject is law in the Church and not the Law which condemns sinners but I miss the emphasis on soul-winning in all NCT works. Reisinger and his NCT followers, like Marcion, belittle the righteousness demanded by their Old Testament 'God'. Arguing from page 14 on that the Old Testament Law under the Old Covenant was not stringent enough to combat sin, Reisinger sees this as proof we need a much higher standard of Law which he finds in New Covenant Theology. On page 18 he claims concerning the Two Testaments:

---

[82] See pages 8-10 (especially 9); and 19.

There are two different canons of conduct even as there are two distinctly different covenants – and in both cases the one *replaces* the other.

NCT writers need to confess what their New-Law-Faith is

I would like to know what kind of a 'New Covenant' Reisinger and his followers really have and what their New Law is but they do not reveal their ideas hidden under their NewSpeak.[83] Both the Old Testament and the New are quite in unison regarding God's righteousness. Indeed, when the New Testament speaks of God's righteous nature, it leans very much on the Old Testament in doing so. Not only Isaiah and Jeremiah spoke of the Lord being their righteousness but we find this truth engraved in the Old Testament from start to finish. Paul said, 'What sayeth the scriptures?' clearly meaning the Old Testament scriptures, and gives the answer himself, 'Abraham believed God, and it was counted unto him for righteousness'.[84] God has not a different righteousness in the New Testament from the righteousness He demanded in the Old as NCT leaders claim. We have noted that John Gill, when speaking about the Covenant of Grace took at least half of his proof-texts from the Old Testament. Good, so, because that is where the gospel of redemption began.

This writer takes the position that the Covenant of Grace is not only an essential ingredient of Reformed doctrine but it is the central doctrine of the Christian Church whether we are thinking of former Jews or former Gentiles. God's righteousness is so great that Two Testaments were needed to extol it. The old 'Wall of Partition' has been done away with in Christ. Christ's salvation is complete for all His Church and is as timeless as His own righteous Person. I mean by that, Christ has been the Author and Finisher of His Covenant from the foundation of the World and since then He has been calling out a People for Himself throughout both Testament times.

---

[83] The horrific political language of the Government which was not intended to be understood outside that ruling body as outlined in George Orwell's book *1984*.

[84] Romans 4:3. Here, Paul is relying on the testimony of Genesis 15:6 for his gospel teaching, showing that from the beginning of the Bible on, the just lived by faith as Habakkuk still describes in chapter 2:4 at the end of the Old Testament. Look what a vision of Christ Habakkuk had. He was welcoming Christ with open arms!

Peter Ditzel's dubious New Laws

Peter Ditzel like most Neonomians is very sensitive about Antinomian charges against the NCT and complains that he does not enforce new laws as 'Law is not for the righteous'. This is a misuse of Timothy's words in 1 Timothy 1:8, 9, which reads:

> But we know that the law is good, if a man use it lawfully; knowing this that the law is not made for a righteous man, but for the lawless and disobedient, for the ungodly and for sinners, for unholy and profane, for murderers of fathers and murderers of mothers, for manslayers etc.

Here Paul is speaking of the one law which was revealed in Old Testament times which is good in the hands of believers but horrible in unbelieving hands until grace comes into their lives as Paul witnessed himself. Under the heading 'Law is not for the righteous', Ditzel addresses a man who had challenged his view of rejecting the fourth commandment, wondering if Ditzel would reject the others as being irrelevant for a Christian. Ditzel replied, calling the man 'unrighteous' because he challenged Ditzel's understanding of the Commandments, saying:

> So, do I believe that it is okay to murder, commit adultery, steal, lie, and covet, and so forth? No, I do not. But I do not believe this because the Ten Commandments that were written on stone and given to the carnal Israelites prohibit these things. I believe this because the Holy Spirit working in me tells me so.[85]

The point seems to be here that Ditzel ignores the Old Testament biblical expression of righteousness, written in words breathed out by the Holy Spirit, yet declares that his decision not to murder, commit adultery etc. comes directly from the Holy Spirit telling him not to murder, commit adultery etc.. Why then reject the same message simply because it was given in Old Testament times and claim incongruously

---

[85] Wordofhisgrace.org website 27th January, 2017.

that the Spirit is now telling him the very same thing? This is certainly trying to keep one's cake and eat it.

Furthermore, from where has Ditzel obtained the idea that the Mosaic Law was only for 'carnal Israelites'? Who said that Moses and his fellow believers understood the Covenant merely in a carnal manner? Moses and the Prophets pointed to the tenor of faith and not the letter of the Law. Was God carnal because He gave mankind a righteous Law? Furthermore, it would seem pointless for Ditzel to reject the Spirit's words in the Old Testament, as the Spirit, he claims, confirms these very words in his own heart. What about all those people who did and still do understand the spiritual tenor of the law and its place in the Covenant of Grace? Was David thus carnal because he loved the Law in its right context? What about Isaiah and Jeremiah and all the other Old Testament writers? Were they all carnal and without hope? If the origin is carnal, then so must Ditzel's idea of confirmation be. Though he called the man who asked him a difficult question 'unrighteous' for asking it, is not Ditzel really saying that he has no biblical grounding for his faith? I have heard too many fanatics who tell me that they can dispense with the Word because the Spirit talks to them directly to be convinced of the validity of Ditzel's claim. Surely, the Spirit through Christ tells us not to go a step beyond scripture. Ditzel has his own Hot Line to the Spirit but the Spirit acts according to His Word.

Furthermore, one would think it obvious that Christ fulfilled the Law for the very purpose of making people righteous. He never rejected the Law but said that not a jot or tittle of it would pass away. He clearly taught with His Apostles that the Law is good for the redeemed but bad for those still in their sins. There is no New Law here. However, Ditzel, in spite of his misquote of Paul's teaching to Timothy, wishes to usher in a New Law which is binding, oddly enough, neither for sinners nor saints. He gives Christ the responsibility for this! I would have expected him to come up with a definition of what this law entails as a condemning factor, but sinners are left out of his scope. He opens his lecture entitled *New Covenant Theology: Must We Obey a New Law?*[86] by stating: 'New Covenant Theology teaches that Jesus Christ fulfilled

---

[86] Wordofhisgrace.org website, 30th January, 2017.

the law, and that by fulfilling it, He ended it.' And goes on to say under the heading 'New Laws':

> One of the reasons New Covenant Theologians are accused of being neonomian is simply because we teach that Jesus Christ did, indeed, give us new laws. Our detractors believe that the New Covenant is merely a new administration of the Old Covenant, and that, instead of giving new laws, Jesus only corrected the Pharisees' misinterpretation of the Old Covenant law. Their position is a curious one, since we can find where Jesus quoted the Old Covenant law and then said, 'But I tell you.' Plainly, Jesus was giving new law, new commandments (see 'The Sermon on the Mount'). In John 13:34, Jesus explicitly states, 'A new commandment I give to you, that you love one another. Just as I have loved you, you also love one another.' Since Jesus said this, it is bizarre for someone to criticize me for repeating it.

No one, we trust, would criticise a person for quoting Christ but they might criticise him, as I do, for taking Christ's words in summing up the correct tenor of the ever-new Law like the Prophets did to mean the abolishing of the Law. Moses must have abolished the Law before it got underway and the Prophets were preaching anachronistically as they used Christian interpretations of Law and Grace. We must remember that Neonomianism is not only believing that Christians have new laws but it is believing that these new laws are necessary for the Christian faith. Here, again, NCT wishes to keep its cake and eat it by postulating that their new laws are not binding. This makes them doubly Antinomian as they reject the Law which condemns sinners but reject their New Covenant Law as binding for unbelievers and believers alike.

Ditzel's odd idea NCT people are not obliged to keep his New Law
So Ditzel is arguing in naïve self-contradiction that though Christ placed believers under new laws, which is the normal meaning of Neonomianism, Ditzel is not a Neonomian in believing this. He also argues that we are not required to believe the new laws for our salvation. Again, we must ask but why then preach, like the Old Testament and

New Testament believers 'repent and believe'? What 'New Law' has Ditzel for sinners if neither the Old Law is for him, nor the New Law? Present day NCT have scolded me in their early development for not emphasizing the evangelical pan-biblical command 'Repent and believe' enough, though it was in all my books, articles and sermons. I now see that their idea of 'repentance' and 'belief' is totally different from mine. They criticize such as myself for preaching repentance and faith because they feel we are under the Old Law seeing repentance and faith as law-bound duties. This, Ditzel says, would be preaching that we are saved by law. He can only argue this because he denies that law is an integral and essential part of the Covenant of Grace. However, though Ditzel believes that salvation through the law is the position of his critics, I have only come across this view in NCT literature as a mockery of their 'detractors' as they call them. Ditzel comes very near to saying that it is Christ's New Law that saves. Nevertheless, and in contradiction to other strong statements which come from him, Ditzel's new gospel appears to be that the NCT has a New Law but their adherents are not obliged to keep it. New Law-keeping is for Christ only. Again, this ignores the perilous plight of sinners and the onus of 'repent and believe' is taken from them. Likewise, he argues that his 'detractors' believe they are merely under 'a new administration of the Old Covenant'. What he means by that I really do not know. I always thought we had one Covenant continually administrated by Christ. Within this Covenant the law still plays its part in comforting, condemning and leading. I would think introducing two administrations would be the same as introducing two laws and two Covenants which the NCT appears to favour and then we have no Covenant of Grace at all. This is also my criticism of the *Westminster Confession* which has split up the one faith into different case-studies without merging them back into the one whole truth.

Furthermore, Christ in the Sermon on the Mount expounds the One Law as He meant it to be and His sayings are part of the continuing testimony of the Covenant. Christ is not merely a Lawgiver and Fulfiller in the New Testament but the Old Testament clearly testified to this, too, as Christ so often explains. True, Jesus sums up the Law, which summing up somehow the NCT takes for a new law, but it was the Mosaic Law, that is Christ's own law that He was summing up. We must stick to Christ's interpretation of the Law, not Ditzel's. John Ball puts this well when he says:

> For wherein Moses mediated, it was by the power of Christ, but Christ was that one Mediator, who mediated from his own authority and immediate power.

For the NCT Christ's Old Testament work as Mediator and Messiah is all A.D. and 'New' because they have rejected the first revelations concerning the position of the Mediator and Messiah in the Covenant and Christ's use of the Law. They look upon the law as an evil 'imprisonment' as we shall see when we consider David Gay's new-fangled ideas, thus challenging God's integrity as well as His righteousness. I must ask why the NCT paint the Father's and the Son's gracious law in such dark colours as if it were meant merely as an evil to enslave sinners and not as Christ's well-meant instrument of grace. This is also Marcionism resurrected. I have also often wondered why the NCT misunderstands the entire gospel in Christ's Sermon on the Mount, including the Beatitudes and speak only of 'Law' there where Christ points out the Way of Grace.

David Gay's pilgrim's progress

I have again, after writing the above paragraph, listened to new NCT convert David Gay's explanations in a series of YouTube talks concerning why he has once again changed his theological position in his quest, as he says, of recognizing that God's Word is true and everyone else a liar. Gay starts off by erecting straw arguments which he says represent non-NCT believers. This is chiefly the idea that the so-called 'Moral Law' is the sole rule of life for Christians. We see that Gay has a BOT hangover here which is spoiling his vision. What Gay says is certainly not the stance of the vast majority of Christians but was indeed the very stance the NCT took in their early years. They have now rejected what the vast body of Christians never held, apart from a few modern so-called 'Reformed' men of the Fullerite school, some of whom, like Gay, have now gone the whole hog and embraced NCT teaching. Fuller had one foot in biblical theology as he had witnessed God's grace in Christ deeply but his head quarrelled with his heart and he had his right foot in rationalism and a trust in Natural Law. He was a great springboard in effecting the NCT's leap in the dark. It appears that Gay has only researched the Reformed view of the Covenant within this narrow group of Neonomians and was rightly appalled by their teaching but when I tackled Gay on the subject of his shallow view of the Reformed faith a good number of years ago, he reacted by writing two books against me and parts of other books which showed that he had researched my theology as little as he had researched Reformed Theology. At that time, Gay was deeply into Fuller as were most of the BOT people with whom he affiliated himself in the eighties and nineties right into the new Millennium. There are a number of great weaknesses in Fuller's system which have paved the way for so-called New Covenant Theology as did Dispensationalism. Fuller is most hazy on the Covenant and rejects God's revealed Law as a permanent display of God's character, regarding it as being arbitrary and of a temporary nature. Fuller went further than the NCT are prepared to go today as he argued that all God's revealed law would disappear and all, starting with God, will eventually bow to Natural Law as if this were something outside of God. However, who knows what the NCT will be doing tomorrow?

Old Testament law according to Gay

After much argumentation concerning the Mosaic Law, Gay outlines his new faith in his 'Testimony' and then tells us that there is another law, other than the 'Jewish' one, but leaves this confession merely in the air. In further YouTube lectures on the subject termed 'New Covenant Theology Simply Explained', Gay comes back to this 'other law' and then links Moses with what he calls 'the pagan philosophers. He then mentions as a further example Francis Bacon but gives no proof of his ever reading Bacon. This rather surprised me as Bacon was most orthodox and fervent in his faith, a faith which Gay has obviously as little researched as Moses' faith. I have found Bacon's books and essays a delight and strength to my soul as he synergises scripture and does not tear it apart by Roman Catholic Aristotelianism. Naturally, Bacon clothed much of what he said with references to ancient Greek philosophers and strange cultures but it was the required method of scholars in those days.

Gay and his 'Mosaic Economy'

In his lecture in this YouTube series on Colossians 2:11-14, Gay deals with the verses completely void of their context and makes them a criticism of the Old Testament 'shadows' and what he calls the 'Mosaic economy' but does not see Paul is addressing both former Jews and Gentiles here with his reference to circumcision and baptism showing that both Old Testament circumcision and New Testament baptism pointed forward to faith in the Messiah, Christ, so he could tell both parties that if they were in Christ, they were 'complete in Him'. Gay splits this passage into a Jews and Gentiles debate on what he sees as a conflict between the Old Testament and the New but Paul is writing to people whose former nationalities or religions were irrelevant to his purpose and opens his epistle with the salutation, 'To the saints and faithful brethren in Christ which are at Colosse'.

Gay sows seeds of division even between the Testaments where absolute harmony is depicted. In his YouTube series expounding Matthew 5:17-20 Gay makes glaring errors in his personal rendering of the Greek. He quotes Christ's clear statement 'Think not that I am come to destroy the law or the prophets: I am not come to destroy but to fulfil.' Gay then tells us rightly that Christ completed the Law, though he seems to be uncertain as to what Law it was that Christ completed. Gay tells us that the N.T. uses 'Law' without the article but with the article when it is used for 'the law of Rome' and 'the law of faith'. However, here, 'law' is used with the article though Gay cannot possibly be referring to 'the law of faith' and certainly not to the 'law of Rome' but to the Law outlined in scripture as depicting God's righteousness. This is called *the* Law which is a definite, specific Law '*ton nomon*'. This 'Law', (but not *the* Law as written') Gay tells us, was not abolished but fulfilled and completed. So far, so good, but Gay goes on to say 'fulfilled' means 'rendered obsolete'. Now the five or six Greek dictionaries on my table, usually consulted by Greek scholars all look upon 'destroy' as the opposite of 'fulfil' but Gay sees the words for destroy and fulfil (*katalusai* and *pleroosai*) as synonyms! In being fulfilled in Christ, Gay tells us, the Law is done away with. So Christ, according to Gay, first completes the Law and then tells us it was all a part of 'the Mosaic economy' and not part of the Christian life within the Covenant. Why does Gay insult Christ in this way and have Him

107

put Himself under a useless law of whipping and imprisonment (so Gay)? Furthermore, what is now the situation of sinners who were, according to Gay, once under the Law but now are freed from it as the Law has been abolished for sinners and saints alike? Gay seems to teach that they are all set free as there is no Law to condemn them. How sinners would rejoice if this were true!

The discontinuous development of many NCT leaders exemplified
To show how he has come to entertain his so-called New-Covenant teaching, Gay tells us of his progress through some nine or ten 'positions', as he calls them. Most of these 'positions' mentioned refer not to sound biblical theology or a sound biblical faith, nor a home in a true Christian church but to highly speculative eschatological fantasies and narrow denominational extremes through which our pilgrim made his 'progress'. We are told how Gay has moved from a secret rapture 'position' to a pre-millennial 'position', then to an a-millennial 'position' and now he is in the 'realised-eschatology' of the NCT-ites 'New Age'.[87] He has tried out Anabaptists, Plymouth Brethren, Strict Baptists, Reformed Baptists, Sabbatarians, Anti-Sabbatarians, Fullerism, a misunderstood Puritanism, a faultily defined Calvinism and Banner-of-Truthism. One would think it impossible to develop a sound theological understanding of the scriptures on this basis. It seems like 'ever learning and never able to come to the knowledge of the truth'.[88] It appears that Gay has never been a member of a body of sound Christians in deep fellowship with one another. Gay tells us, however, that he felt most at home with the Anabaptist position but does not explain what he means. Having followed Gay's journey into sensationalism for some three decades, read several of his books and corresponded with him, I found him as extremely certain of himself now in the NCT fold as he was then in his former self-confessed errors. He still, for instance, tells us repeatedly that we must let God be true and every man a liar, as he did in his former enthusiasm for other 'positions'. All I can say is where will Gay land up next? Being even

---

[87] See *In These Last Days* by Randy Seiver. See especially his chapter 'The New Age has Come'. Seiver's comment on the abolition of the Covenant as outlined in the O.T. is 'When the ends for which God gave it had been realized, it had outlived its usefulness and was ready to pass away (p. 22).'
[88] 2 Timothy 3:7.

older than elderly Brother Gay, I have seen so many NCT-ites come and go through various 'positions', each with his own additions. All have scolded me, including Gay, for not accepting their notions, but I still do not find their multi-Covenants, multi-Laws, multi ways of salvation, multi views of righteousness, multi-views of God, multi-peoples of God, multi-economies (whatever they mean by that) and a Bible split down the middle in the Bible and can only conclude with the global churches represented by Marcion's critics, that the NCT people cut the Bible up with their Marcionite pen-knife.[89] The discontinuity; 'tensions'; anomalies and abolishments which they see in the scriptures are entirely of their own making.

Gay's NCT version of Galatians Chapter Three
The biblical continuity of the Covenant of Grace is clearly expressed throughout Galatians chapter three, as in Galatians as a whole. There we are told that Abraham believed God, and it was accounted to him for righteousness' (v. 6) and 'They which are of the faith, the same are the children of Abraham' (v. 7). Then we are told that the Spirit preached the gospel to Abraham telling him that God would justify the heathen also through faith so that in Abraham (who believed the gospel) would all nations be blessed. It is understood in the text that these then heathens must go the way Abraham went in believing. So that, as the scriptures repeatedly teach in the Old Testament, 'the just shall live by faith' (v. 8, 9). Then Paul takes up this gospel and clarifies the matter of the relationship between law and grace in God's Covenant for his readers in the following verses, especially vv. 19-29. This has caused the NCT in recent years to challenge the traditional interpretation which quite refutes their theology strongly by isolating parts of verses 19-25 from the entire text dealing with Abraham, and the relation between law and grace in the Covenant. This cut-down and reinterpreted version of Paul's entire argument in Galatians has become a NCT mantra. If ever 'criticism with a penknife' was practised, it must be here in Galatians Chapter 3 in an attempt to erase Christ's and the Spirit's testimony to the Old Testament. I shall quote all the verses under scrutiny from v. 19 to 25 in the A.V. text which comes under heavy fire from David Gay,

---

[89] Marcion was accused, when denounced as a heretic, of 'Criticism with a penknife'.

pondering on why NCT exegetes leave out so much that clearly refutes them, including much that supports the A.V. translation which is heavily challenged.

> Wherefore then *serveth* the law? It was added because of transgressions, till the seed should come to whom the promise was made; *and it was* ordained by angels in the hand of a mediator. Now a mediator is not *a mediator* of one, but God is one. *Is* the law then against the promises of God? God forbid: for if there had been a law given which could have given life, verily righteousness should have been by the law. But the scripture hath concluded all under sin, that the promise by faith of Jesus Christ might be given to them that believe. But before faith came, we were kept under the law, shut up unto the faith which should afterwards be revealed. Wherefore the law was our schoolmaster *to bring us* unto Christ, that we might be justified by faith. But after that faith is come, we are no longer under a schoolmaster. For ye are all the children of God by faith in Christ Jesus. For as many of you as have been baptized into Christ have put on Christ. There is neither Jew nor Greek, there is neither bond nor free, there is neither male nor female: for ye are all one in Christ Jesus. And if ye *be* Christ's, then are ye Abraham's seed, and heirs according to the promise. (223 words)

Galatians 3:19-25 made 'simple'

In his internet video on the text, 'New Covenant Theology Made Simple', Gay uses Galatians 3:19-25 to demonstrate how 'simple' he can make it sound after it has been made complicated by *millions* who have misled both sinners and saints. He adds that no passage of scripture has suffered so grievously at the hand of translators than this section in Galatians but he will render it exactly as Paul wrote it. I thought of my renowned teacher Henry Oakley who coached me through the B.D. so professionally and graciously and that great Bible translator Prof. Harold Riesenfeldt who strengthen my faith in the Lord deeply through his Greek exegesis. One expects such a definitive and highly skilled authority in New Testament Greek behind Gay's words which his CV does not provide. It is true that several of the A.V. terms have suffered from the modern dumbing down of language but a good pastor is there to teach his flock and these terms, sadly grown out of use, are all explained in less than minutes, so improving the vocabulary of his fold. Gay, however, wishes to rewrite this passage according to the NCT position and asks to be allowed to give his own '*fair translation and a proper translation*' of Galatians 3:19-25. He tells us that if we cannot take his word for granted we must read the Greek New Testament for ourselves. This, I have done.

I was very sceptical about Gay's dogmatic statement concerning his 'proper translation' because almost everywhere where Gay appeals to the Greek in his books and articles, he dabbles in speculative mysteries. Where the harmony of the Covenant is stressed and where progression, fulfilment and continuation are emphasized in both Testaments, Gay sees a total break with the past and a new look at the future after Christ's advent to redeem all His elect past, present and future. He speaks only of 'Two Epochs' or 'Two Ages' as being as different as cheese and chalk. I thus approached Brother Gay's 'translation' with much doubt about his abilities to understand New Testament Greek.

Gay's alleged 'fair and proper' translation
In his 'fair and proper' new translation, Gay deals with the text completely out of context which is Paul's introducing of the Law and the Abrahamic Covenant to the Gentiles. He then erases whole sentences from the original Greek so that his 'new meaning' not only destroys the A.V. translations but also alters the old, original meaning which pervades through the original language.

Gay's 'translation' of the six verses quoted reads as follows in his 'New Age' Version:

The Law was added because of transgressions until the offspring should come to whom the promise had been made. Before the faith came we were made captive under the law, imprisoned until faith would be revealed. So then the law was our guardian or pedagogue until Christ came in order that we might be justified by faith but now that the faith has come, we are no longer under the guardian' (71 words including Gays double re-translation of 'schoolmaster').

Now, we must ask, has this version which leaves out whole passages of Paul's exegesis and plays about with the original Greek text proved better for our understanding of the entire text in its pan-biblical context? Our answer must be in the negative as Gay, even in his cut-down version does not follow the original grammatical and lexical structures and gives a different time-line to that of the Bible, departing radically from the original text.

What purpose has the Law?

To start with, Gay leaves Paul's introductory question 'Wherefore then serveth the law?' concerning the being of the law in verse 19 out, though he tells us repeatedly that he has translated it. 'Translation' often means 'omission' for Gay who then gives a weak part-answer to an unraised question he appears only to have assumed. This speaks volumes to this writer as the NCT never, ever, either pose or answer questions referring to the true nature of the law which is irrelevant to their New Covenant teaching. The Law has been done away with in their antinomian dogmas. The wording and grammar of Paul's answer to his own question is, however, essential to the meaning both of the question and the answer and the tenses Paul has chosen which follow. If the question is erased, an answer is anyone's guess, so Gay attempts a guess. If one gets the start wrong, one is sure to flounder. We notice that Paul does not ask what purpose the Law had but what purpose it has and this is the question Gay faces but will not answer. Paul also starts by saying that the Law was 'added' to the Covenant, not taken away from it.

However, the opening question in verse 19 which Gay leaves out is answered using the 1st aorist bearing the meaning of 'add'. This is followed by a 2nd aorist bearing the meaning 'come' before arriving at the tense-carrying verb concerning God's promise given or made. These aorists or aspects are 'imperfect', not in the tense sense but in the sense that they need a governing tense to explain when the action takes place. The passive verb governing the application of the promise is in the original text a *present perfect tense* indicating an action *started in the past and which continues up to or into the present*. Not agreeing with this biblical timing because it spoils his New Covenant Break-with-the-Past Theology, Gay claims that we must alter the original tense to a *pluperfect* which refers to an action in the distant past before another past event occurred. It is used of things which have come and are long gone in the 'past before the past'. Thus, for Gay the Law was added then subtracted. This is not what Paul says. Thus Gay changes what is still going on to what once was but is now, he claims, obsolete. The promise to him 'had been given', that is, it is no longer there. This is a falsification of God's word, to say the least. God's covenantal provisions regarding the law have not come and gone, they are still added. So, unhappily for Gay, the would-be translator, Paul's clear words say exactly the opposite to his rendering as does the entire N.T. text. Paul's argument directly before and directly after Galatians 3 is on the relationship between Law and Grace in the Covenant and its application to both sinners and saints. It is not an argument saying that there is no law for sinners but only Grace for saints.[90]

Wrenching the Law from its Covenant position
So all along Gay will have the reader believe that the text is only concerned with a law which has been abolished. This is quite wrong. The context is dealing with the Covenant of Grace in which law and grace each have their divine-initiated places, implemented as one gospel. Furthermore, the text is not dealing with a break and discontinuity in this Covenant but demonstrating from the beginning of the chapter on that from ancient Old Testament times, believers have always found their salvation within the Covenant of Grace, in particular as made with Abraham who was pronounced righteous because he believed in Christ.

Gay does follow Paul, as the A.V., by saying, 'It was added because of transgressions', but Galatians 3 gives us further information so that we might understand the text perfectly. Gay withholds this evidence from us and does not tell us when and how this 'addition' took place and what it entails. This is outlined in detail in the context which Gay erases. We have thus NCT dogma based on altering the Greek grammar with no biblical explanation which would, of course, have refuted Gay. There are none so blind as those who will not see.

---

[90] Read Galatians Chapter Two and Galatians Chapter Five.

The meaning of 'add'

The first aorist in verse 19 translated 'added' given its full meaning indicates being placing side by side or adjoining. Now we must ask, added to or adjoined to what? Gay leaves this question unanswered. Paul, however, is speaking of the Covenant of Grace to which the Law has been adjoined as part of it, not in opposition to it. The original Greek text, before Gay messed about with it, teaches that the Law part of the Covenant is to make man aware of His transgressions and the grace part is to offer him forgiveness in Christ. Furthermore, Christ, in fulfilling what man has failed to do, has combined all the elements of the Covenant in Himself and for His people. Gay eradicates this blessed merger by a make-believe process of cancelling the Law for all mankind, sinners and saints alike, so creating a new Covenant which caters for grace for the saved, but not for the Law under which unbelievers are still placed. Gay interprets 'added' as something which is now taken away though the text says nothing of the kind. In this point I am much indebted to Edward Fisher in his *Marrow of Modern Divinity* with notes by Thomas Boston. Fisher records a conversation between a seeker and an evangelist on the issue and writes:

Question: Then, sir, it should seem that the covenant of works was added to the Covenant of Grace, to make it more complete?

Answer: O no! you are not so to understand the apostle, as though it were added by way of ingrediency as a part of the Covenant of Grace, as if that covenant had been incomplete without the covenant of works; for then the same covenant should have consisted of contradictory materials, and so it should have overthrown itself; for, says the apostle, 'If it be by grace, then it is no more of works; otherwise grace is no more grace: but if it be of works, then it is no more of grace; otherwise work is no more work,' Romans xi. 6. But it was added by way of subserviency and attendance, the better to advance and make effectual the Covenant of Grace; so that although the same covenant that was made with Adam was renewed on Mount Sinai, yet I say still, it was not for the same purpose. For this was it that God aimed at, in making the covenant of works with man in innocency, to have that which was his due from man: but God made it with the Israelites for no other end, than that man being thereby convinced of his weakness, might flee to Christ. So that it was renewed only to help forward and introduce another and a better covenant; and so to be a manuduction unto Christ, viz. to discover sin, to waken the conscience, and to convince them of their own impotency, and so drive them out of themselves to Christ.[91]

Joel, the preacher of repentance and forgiveness, obviously knew what he was talking about from experience when he spoke of the Grace of God in the work of the law. He tells his fellow-countrymen who have broken God's Law:

Rend your heart and not your garments, and turn unto the Lord your God: for he is gracious and merciful, slow to anger and of great kindness.[92]

This was the state of salvation in Joel's time and was not reserved for the New Age of New Covenant Theology, so-called.

It is interesting to note that at a time when the Banner Of Truth were rightly praising the Marrow Men, they were also criticizing severely William Huntington and myself, who had written a biography on him, for not believing in a 'free offer' outside of the Covenant of Grace. They had overlooked the fact that both Huntington, and myself, his pupil, saw offers of Grace being given within the Covenant of Grace where they belonged and from where the Banner Of Truth had wrenched it. This is exactly what the Marrow Men taught and Huntington followed them in his preaching. Of course, they were following Joel and all the Old Testament Prophets who knew the oneness of Law and Grace, long before the NCT divided them and thus rejected God's Covenant with Christ on behalf of such as the NCT.

---

[91] *Marrow of Modern Divinity*, 1837 edition, chapter 2, p. 43.
[92] Joel 2:13.

Juggling with tenses to rob the Bible of its continuity

We see this error manifested in the theology of doubt represented by David Gay. We read on in verse 19, 'till the seed should come to whom the promise was made.' Gay's action in falsely replacing the original meaning with a pluperfect would kill off not just the meaning of the promise but also of the seed which, I presume, Gay would not wish for himself personally though this is the crux of the current NCT faith. However, Gay misunderstands Paul's use of the word 'seed' and thus uses the term quite wrongly. The 'seed' are the perpetual promise-carriers. The term takes us back to the opening sentences which Gay, however, leaves out of his 'translation'. Here we see that the promise is fulfilled in Abraham's seed but the harvest is going on until Kingdom come. It is by no means a 'had been', or even a 'has been' but a continuous process until all the Elect are gathered in. Gay as a NCT man would argue un-biblically that 'the seed' refers solely to Christ who has come in Person and thus all the great Old Testament teaching (which the NCT see as mere prophesyings of the future) regarding His Coming in relation to the Law have been fulfilled by their abolishment. This is, of course, not what the text says. The text is dealing with Christ as Mediator and the promises are to those who believe in Christ vs 19-22. Christ is not only the Mediator of the Covenant but He represents all that believe in Him. Here we have John 1:11, 12 again. Believers are thus taken up in the 'seed' mentioned. Gay has left all this out of his NCT 'translation'. He maintains that the promises to the 'seed' have been abolished. What a sad state the Bride of Christ would be in if this were true! In abolishing the promises and the seed who believed them, Gay abolishes Christ's Bride, the Church!

Gay skips over passages uncomfortable for him

Having badly translated the first part of verse 19 and skipped over the essential meaning embedded in it, Gay now jumps suddenly to verse 23, leaving out the important teaching in the verses between in his 'translation'. Now, the 'translator' goes into much complaining detail because the A. V. and other good translations speak of 'But before faith came.' We must read 'the faith', Gay claims and although he has not noticed the bulk of the Greek text in verses 19-25, he has spotted a definite article in the Greek. Yes, it is there in the Greek but abstract nouns in English do not take a definite article because they are self-defining. In English, we say 'Through courage he gained honour'. We do not say 'Through *the* courage he gained *the* honour.' In the early decades of the 20th century, pupils still learnt to write all abstract nouns beginning with a capital so that they would remember that they did not carry an article. A pity this method is not used today. Old letters from my parents still testify to this wise usage.

So we note that the A.V. uses abstract nouns where no article is needed but when they translate abstract nouns which need to be defined further as something special and particular, they do so as in Galatians 3:23, 'But before faith came, we were kept under *the* law, shut up unto *the* faith which should afterwards be revealed'. Concentrating so much on trying to understand the Greek in vain, Gay quite loses his English in this verse, which he renders, 'Before the faith came we were made captive under the law, imprisoned until faith would be revealed.' What is strange here is that Gay has omitted the article before the word 'faith' in the second instance where an article is, however, needed because it is defined by a present participle (mellousan) referring to 'the faith near at hand' to be revealed. The A.V. has 'afterwards' instead of 'near at hand' but both mean that it has not happened yet but will shortly. Gay just erases the word, which does not fit his altered timing, but, in doing so, he removes words which are essential to the meaning!

Nowadays it is common for people to mix up 'shall' and 'will' and their imperfect and conditional forms 'should' and 'would', yet here the word translated 'reveal' is a first aorist infinitive passive form guided by the 'faith near at hand' clause. The revelation thus seems to be in the certain immediate future so the use of 'should', as the A.V. has it, would appear less conditional than 'would'. To alter 'should' to 'would' is obviously merely to stress that Gay is paraphrasing independently. Gay does not explain why he has opted for 'would'. Then, moved more by his faulty understanding of the Covenant than what the text says, Gay speaks about being imprisoned by the law. This misinterpretation is obviously not what Paul is writing about.

Having lived most of my life away from Britain in Sweden, Germany and other countries, my Bible has not been the A.V. for many decades, though I still find it the best English translation going. I was converted in Sweden aged 17 and the gist of my Swedish versions of verse 23 is 'But before faith came, we were under the oversight of the law, kept until the revelation of the expected faith.'[93] The gist of my German versions is, 'Before this faith could come we were under the oversight of the law and were kept in its care until the coming revelation of faith.'[94] These translations all look upon the law positively as a Guardian who kept us especially with a view to the reception of faith from ancient times on (see context). Thus Gay's words in his alleged translation of Galatians 3:23 'we were made captive under the law, imprisoned until faith would be revealed' is certainly incorrect. For the record, the original seventeenth century meaning of the A.V.'s 'shut up' before the English language was dumbed down was 'enclosed'; 'guarded'; 'kept secure'; 'restrained'; 'looked after'. This is the exact meaning of the word Paul uses but which Gay has not understood. Gay, too, should have read on to Galatians 5 where Paul is still applying the Law which Gay feels is abolished, to those who do not walk in the Spirit.[95]

Guardian and Pedagogue

Gay criticizes harshly the use of the term 'schoolmaster' which he says is 'utterly foreign to the text' and wishes to substitute it by 'Guardian' or 'Pedagogue'. He also denies that the law could 'lead us to Christ', complaining of the words 'bring to' and 'lead to' used in translations not made by himself, as faulty 'insertions and interjections' in the text. What he means by this criticism is difficult to guess. We must look at Gay's new-fangled approach to God's Word a little closer to see what his intentions are. Gay goes on to tell us frightening and imaginative tales of Greek guardians and pedagogues. He feels the term 'schoolmaster' is too kind and the guardians mentioned were those who whipped their boys to their goal (school/faith) but when their pupils came to faith, the Guardian (the Law) was made 'redundant and

---

[93] See the 1903 translation (my favourite) and 1917 (for me the most accurate). A new translation came out in the late sixties which my professors at Uppsala undertook. I thought it was excellent but I do not have it at hand.

[94] I use mostly the 1964 Luther Bible and the older Zürich Bible versions before they were messed up by modern 'paraphrasers' but a more 'word for word' translation is found in the Mülheimer Ausgabe (my copy from 1968). The latter is the one Harald Riesenfeld, my Greek professor at Uppsala, used and recommended that all his students buy it.

[95] Read verse 15 to the end. I am grateful to Dr Zachariades for pointing this out to me.

sacked'.[96] The reference refers to harsh disciplinarians, not teachers, Gay tells us.

Such disciplinarians, Gay emphasises, were smiters of boys, going behind them with a whip, signifying how the law imprisons us. However, the term 'guardian' which Gay suggests is a better translation for these boy-smiters than 'schoolmaster' has none of the evil connotations which Gay gives the term. Furthermore, if Gay uses the word 'pedagogue', he is immediately in difficulties. This is not a common word in normal parlance and does not contain the meaning Gay gives it at all. Anyone unfamiliar with teaching methods will be forgiven for looking up the word in the dictionary. He will invariably find that the meaning is given as 'schoolmaster' and/or 'teacher'. Gay, in his linguistic disabilities has thrown out a good old English word as 'utterly foreign' and replaced it with a 'foreign' Greek synonym which means exactly the same. So what has Gay gained by torturing the text? Nothing whatsoever!

I love reading John Ball's *Treatise on the Covenant of Grace*. He foresaw Gay's acute mistake and wrote of Christ:

> He is not the end of the Law, if the Law did not direct to him, and require faith in him. He is the end of the Law, as the Law leadeth and driveth us out of ourselves, and from all confidence in any works of the Law, that by faith in Christ we might obtain righteousness. It is not the property of a schoolmaster to beat and strike, and not to direct or teach.[97]

Gay has a 'translator's surprise' up his sleeve

Furthermore, Gay will have no translation which refers to the law bringing or leading anyone to Christ, as stated in the original text, yet the word used in the Greek which the A.V. translates as 'schoolteacher' and which Gay now uses oblivious to its meaning, indicates one who *leads* boys or *brings* boys to (eis) Christ. Here the term 'pedagogue' is used which Gay has used unwittingly in self-contradiction. So how does

---

[96] Americans use the word 'fired' which is also good English.
[97] Ball's *Treatise*, p. 109, Peter and Rachel Reynold's 2012 edition.

Gay get out of this difficulty exegetically? In his lecture on making Galatians 3 simple, Gay comes up with his big surprise. He tells us that the entire passage has *nothing to do* with bringing people to Christ at all. It means that the 'epoch' or 'age' of the law ends and the 'epoch' or 'ages' of Christ begins. 'Law' signifies the Old Testament 'Epoch' and New Law the New Testament 'Age' and never the twain shall meet. This is a most extreme form of Dispensationalism.

Yet, apparently where the text speaks of 'faith' which is the substance of things hoped for, according to Hebrews 11:1, Gay reads 'New Law'. So, how can Gay alter a chapter so radically where Paul describes faith within the Covenant God made with Abraham embracing all peoples throughout all times? Abraham believed and this made him righteous. It does not say 'Abraham believed a New Law' and this made him righteous. Faith does not come by the Law but through our place in the Covenant of Grace, which is with our father Abraham in the bosom of Christ! We were enabled to believe in the same Christ as Abraham, our Father in the faith, because Christ is the same, yesterday, today and forever.

Gay's statements are thus astonishingly un-scriptural and makes one wonder that the NCT are so imprisoned by their own system that they can ignore entire chapters of holy writ in the search for a line or part line here or there which might be bent to New Age NCT specifications. I do not charge them with conscious dupery but they are so lost in their new-fangled system that they think it entitles them to play havoc with the scriptures. If ever a chapter had to do with individual Christians who did not know where they stood regarding salvation by grace given faith or through law-works then Galatians 3 must be it, yet Gay claims here that it has nothing to do with individual sinners coming to faith but with the entrance into the New Age Epoch of the NCT's invention, which I presume, from Gay's testimony, will be a legal 'New Faith' with a 'New scripture' under a dormant, inactive 'New Law'.

The fact is that hardly any other text in the Bible emphasizes the continuing work of the Law in leading sinners to Christ than Galatians Chapter Three. In verse 10, after criticising his readers for neglecting the clear gospel teaching of both Law and Grace in the Old Testament, Paul says that faith is not of the Law but of faith. I quite agree that faith is not of the Law for the Christian. But what relation do the unsaved have to the Law? Paul gives the only biblical answer possible:

For as many as are of the works of the law are under the curse: for it is written, Cursed is every one that continueth not in all things which are written in the book of the Law to do them.

Here, Paul is building on similar sayings from the Torah, through the Prophets and Wisdom Literature and continued throughout the New Testament. Paul thus concludes from this pan-biblical truth for all time that as 'no man is justified by the law in the sight of God, it is evident that the just shall live by faith'. This truth is revealed clearly in the Old Testament but clearer still in the New. However, the fact that those who are still under the law shall be judged by the Law is a covenantal truth ignored by so-called New Covenant Theology. This robs them of their incentive to rescue perishing sinners. They boast of their gospel being engraved on their hearts but have developed hardly any theology of mercy and grace for those who have no heart for God. They cannot meet the sinner with the gospel of grace and lead him to Christ as they have abolished the Law and fired the schoolmaster.

New Covenant Theology is over four thousand years out of date
The widespread biblical New Covenant teaching (in stark contrast to the NCT greatly altered, manipulated and cut-down version) from Genesis to Revelation and beyond shows how thoroughly out of date the NCT people are with their understanding of New Covenant literature to the tune of some four thousand years. The whole Bible teaches that the New Covenant was ever there since the old covenant with man failed because he could not keep it. Fallen man was revealed as not of the right upright stature to enter into a pact with God. The ever-new Covenant refers to the Covenant with Christ which came into being to show man that though he was powerless to keep any Covenant with God, God would faithfully keep it. The first Covenant between God and man was continually broken by Adam's and fallen man's sin. The ever New-Covenant between The Father and the Son cannot be broken. The New Covenant with Christ was not a post-lapsarian thought with God as He acts from eternity where the New Covenant was, so-to-say, written down, signed, sealed and delivered. This is why Hosea and Jeremiah could cry out in righteous anger against Israel because they

had altered God's Covenant of Grace and knowledge of God and followed symbols and shadows and not the reality to which they testified.[98] Just as Adam, they wished to interpret God's commands, advice and promises as they willed, not God.

The NCT understand the Law only in its abused state

Thus our NCT 'prophets' see the Law only in its abused state and how the ancient peoples lost out on God's provisions. It is true that many Old Testament unbelievers, like those in New Testament times, did not see that God was using His revelations in the Old Testament to bring them to Himself but misused God's ordinances as a kind of magic as if making sacrifices etc. automatically brought forgiveness by the very act. Thus we hear Hosea preaching to the Israelites in Chapter 6:6 that God 'desired mercy, and not sacrifice; and the knowledge of God more than burnt offerings'. This was an Old Testament truth and not a truth which was first revealed many hundreds of years later to the recently emerged NCT. The broken Covenant was an ancient affair even in the days before Moses but the NCT knows of no other and judges the entire Old Testament as if it revealed only a history of covenant-breakers to be replaced by their 'New Age', 'New Epoch' and 'New Law'. Hosea saw centuries before Christ that this 'letter faith' and not 'spirit faith' was a breaking of the Covenant of Grace whereby sinners dealt treacherously with God. Right at the start of His ministry, Jesus pointed the Pharisees back to Hosea to show that He still gave such mercy both then but also now.[99]

So when I read what the NCT says of the Old Testament being ruled by a letter-law it appears they have taken this abuse as the Covenant itself and thus followed the path of the unbelieving Israelites. They belittle Moses by reducing his message merely to a law covenant and they belittle Christ by making him merely the Lawgiver of a New, post-Old Testament Covenant for Christians only. They forget that Moses in his pleadings with God wished to place the law within the Covenant with Abraham where it would be merged with grace. This the O.T. saints always believed as do true followers of the New Testament.

---

[98] Hosea 6:4-7.
[99] Matthew 9:13. For good measure Jesus repeats this in Matthew 12:7.

Invalid claims of a 'new discovery' leading to a 'new covenantal order' of salvation

The New Covenant of mercy, grace and peace is made with Christ from eternity and is always at work. It was not made *with* sinners but made *for* them. They rejected it at their peril. So, all the ideas the NCT people have concerning what they call the 'New Covenant' are taken out of the Old Testament where they were general knowledge from Adam on. The NCT brings nothing new as it was all arranged from eternity as Christ's design in choosing out a People for Himself from all ages. The NCT react to this clear teaching by saying that if true this would make the New Testament superfluous. They can only say this because they reject the continuity of the Testaments. The Covenant of Grace is upheld and sealed in the whole Bible and if one rejects either the Old Testament or the New one has only half of God's revelation in one's hand. The two Testaments stand together as one. This we see in the way the Old Testament prepares us for the New. In rejecting the Old, the NCT people are in the same category as those unbelieving Jews who reject the New. They break the Covenant. Thus we neglect either part at our peril.

The Covenant of Life, Grace and Peace was known in O.T. times

Revelation concerning the Covenant of life, grace and peace was emphasised more and more through great reforms and further revelation in God's mercy in the Old Testament as the bulk of mankind still would not live by faith. It is odd that the NCT believes in progressive revelation in New Testament times but not in Old Testament times though Christ always speaks throughout all times. The NCT get their timing of creation and new creation all wrong as they do not see Christ working from eternity in time all the time. This is why the Old Testament writers and believing prophets denounced the Old Testament peoples more and more sternly for rejecting the Hand that was feeding them. The prophets gave their false pastors most of the blame. It is the same today. All NCT talk about their new discovery that one will find a way to have the law written on one's heart through their ministry as if it had never happened before, is taken from the O.T. prophets who were familiar with the doctrine and certainly preached it and applied it in a more New Testament way than the NCT does. They did not have

123

the NCT's cut-down, non-binding, neonomian law-faith to hinder them. Indeed, the New Testament writers take this Old Testament doctrine up to show how it points to Christ and is fulfilled in Him and shows His work in history. Isaiah preached these truths as did Jeremiah a hundred years later. They were clear on this point as would be many of their hearers though they preached so many hundreds of years before Christ, showing sinners that they could have these covenant truths written on their hearts.

New Covenant preaching was believed in the Old Testament
Surely we must accept that many in Israel believed this gospel as it was preached by all the major and minor prophets who eternalized their preaching in written form. True, in Jeremiah's case his hearers were first shocked at the news of their covenant-breaking sin and wanted to kill him but Jeremiah stood firm in his preaching and finally, though the wicked priests and false prophets still wanted his death, the princes and the people said, 'This man is not worthy to die: for he hath spoken to us in the name of the Lord our God.' Thus the idea that all Jeremiah's hearers either refused to believe this revelation from God or ticked it off for the benefit of future generations only is absurd.[100] Our Christ is the same yesterday, today and forever!

Summing Up
The NCT is a modern spokesman for the downgrading in doctrine which is sadly pervading our modern Christian society. They break the Covenant of Grace into two at the Incarnation, though the purpose of Christ's intervention in history was to atone for the sins in time of His Bride in that glorious 'Fulness of Time' which embraces all time. Though they extol Christ as Lord, to them He is only really Lord of a Half-Covenant and thus not the full Covenant Lord of the whole Bible. In splitting up the Covenant into two, they are following in the footsteps of Marcionism, Dispensionalism and the legal view of the Covenant as taught by 17th Century Neo-Presbyterianism. Their understanding of the Law which God in His revelations as Father, Son and Holy Ghost added

---

[100] Read the exciting story of New Covenant preaching in Jeremiah chapters 26, 31, and 36. The idea that the New Covenant is in the distant future contradicts Jeremiah's word as he says this New Covenant is to replace that not kept when the twelve tribes and their associates left Egypt.

to the Covenant of Abraham owing to the transgressions of the Jews is that of the unbelieving Jews who also did not understand God's Covenant purpose. However, the NCT is an ever-changing body, ever working at their 'multi-culti' doctrines to suit new rational theories in their dumbing down of the Christian faith. I have seen several of their persuasions who have learned from their mistakes and adopted a more biblical stand. Not all NCT errors have grown on NCT soil and it is symptomatic of their breach in doctrine that such dumbing down now prevails over many religious institutions which invariably need a 'new doctrine' to establish their 'right' to split up the Church. As it is, the NCT will only accept truths in their cut-down Old Testament if they reappear in their cut-down New Testament. Both Old Testament and New Testament teaching, however, show the folly of the NCT position.

Symptomatic for this modern disdain of biblical doctrine is the entirely superfluous debate on what is and what is not a 'moral law'. It takes the gospel light from the more needy discussion concerning who the People of God are. They are certainly not first and foremost 'moral' enthusiasts but people of God's Covenant of Grace who preach repentance, forgiveness of sins and faith in Jesus.

The NCT is very sensitive about not being seen as Antinomians or Neonomians. Most seem to have come from a legally minded background which has moved them to be suspicious of laws. They reject what they call a 'National Covenant' of law in the Old Testament and say that their undefined New Law for their 'New Age' is not binding so such as Reisinger and Ditzel certainly need better arguments than they give to prove that they are not Antinomians.

Furthermore, NCT followers are very adamant in teaching that the righteousness of New Testament believers, including our present age, is more righteous than that of Abraham and all the Old Testament believers in God's Covenant of Grace. They associate Old Testament righteousness merely with their legal understanding of the Covenant revealed in the Old Testament and call it the righteousness of 'carnal Israelites', leaving God's own declaration of His own righteousness quite out of the picture. Ditzel appears to believe that he can dispense with Old Testament revelation of God's immutable righteousness, claiming that he has the Holy Spirit guiding Him. Since when does the

Holy Spirit misguide believers so that they reject His own Old Testament revelation?

David Gay has rightly put those who build on a mere moral faith behind him, though obviously he has not rejected his former Fullerism concerning the Divine Law. He sees no unity of address in the New Testament debate on the purpose of the Law but sees such as Paul arguing with the Jews on a different basis to how he handles unbelieving Gentiles whom Gay insist have no responsibility to the Law and have no laws. Why then are they considered law-breakers in scripture?

Gay's 'exposition' of Galatians chapter 3 is one of many examples of how the NCT strive to dumb-down scripture to their own level of unbelief and make it appear that God's Word says the opposite of what it clearly says. We remember Marcion's 'criticism with a pen-knife' and Isaiah's complaint that unbelievers are those who turn everything up-side down.[101] Least said, soonest mended! We must note, however, that Gay wrenches the Law out of its sure place in God's covenant with Abraham. Typical also of NCT thinking, Gay tells us that the passage has nothing to do with the conversion of sinners but is a statement concerning a New Age or New Epoch under a New Law. All this leads to my comment that NCT is at least four thousand years out of date and all that they say concerning the alleged New Age was known by all the major and minor Prophets.

---

[101] Isaiah 29:16.

Chapter 5

Further New Covenant Theology Methods Of Translating And Expounding Scripture Queried

Dabbling in New Testament Greek and Hebrew

In my correspondence with David Gay, he has never presumed to know Greek though he often dabbles in it but Randy Seiver tells me he is in the privileged position of knowing the language. In his works such as *In these Last Days* on the Covenant, Seiver quotes scripture with huge passages removed like Gay but at least he gives lines of dots to show that he is leaving out much of the essential scriptural message instead of 'translating' like Gay as if the large omissions were never there. Like Gay, Seiver deals with the New Covenant as explained by Jeremiah, apparently not having tackled Jeremiah's Hebrew, and the author to the Hebrews and without mentioning the historical scriptural facts on which both Jeremiah and Hebrews build their conclusions. The situation commented on in Jeremiah and Hebrews was that the covenant which God made with the children of Israel on the day they left Egypt was immediately broken by them and God thus forbade them to enter the Promised Land just as Adam and Eve broke their Covenant with God and were banned from Eden. The scandal concerning the Golden Calf and the broken law tablets besides the misuse of the 'types' give the passage meaning here. Jeremiah then gave the Israelites, *as had many before him*, the true gist of God's Covenant with mankind which the author to the Hebrews takes up. The word '*covenant*' is often not in the original Greek of Hebrews where the A.V. uses it. The A.V. translators wisely put it in to remind the readers that they were talking about a covenant given when the pilgrims started off from Egypt. This was during the time of the setting up of the Tabernacle whilst Moses was on the Mount. The Book of Hebrews, when commenting on Jeremiah's example of an old covenant which was never ratified, uses the word *amemptos* which means 'not faultless' 'not without defect', 'not perfect' or 'needing completion'. Of course any covenant at any time is imperfect when it is imperfectly understood and imperfectly implemented and not even ratified by the parties concerned. Jeremiah pointed this out to his hearers hundreds of years before Christ. It was the unbelieving Jews, however, whom he was correcting and not God's Word. The stains, spots, blemishes, blots, taints, flaws, defects and faults referred to referred to man's misuse. Man's actions were at fault, not God's provisions. The Covenant was to put man right.

The covenant that was broken and made obsolete was pre-Sinai
The failed and broken covenant to which Jeremiah is referring as opposed to the ever-new Covenant was rendered useless and obsolete because the holders of it failed to see the mediating role of the Messiah in it. They strove to fulfil both sides of the Covenant contract by themselves, rejecting the role of the Godhead in it. They did not live by faith in God. It was only possible to keep the Covenant by faith in God which alone could make them just. The covenant-breakers had only faith in themselves. The NCTs are carrying on this misuse by arguing that Jeremiah is condemning Old Testament revelation in general and God's revelation to Moses in particular. Exodus mentions repeatedly that the Lord used his servant Moses in establishing the Old Testament Covenant and Moses argued that he would only act in conjunction with the Covenant of Grace given to Abraham. New Testament usages of the Law are always appended to teaching on the whole Covenant of Grace. This was also Moses' desire when pleading with God to keep the Covenant. Sadly, Moses' positive thinking in seeing law as an integral part of the Covenant does not receive the NCT's blessing!

Seiver thinks Jeremiah's preaching merely refers to eschatological events foreign to the people to whom he preached

Randy Seiver claims that the subject of Jeremiah's preaching referred to some indefinite 'new' time to come. However, Jeremiah is obviously not talking about a distant *future* but about the *past* and his contemporary situation with his God-given solution for it which he outlines in several chapters, sadly, rarely studied and quoted in any contextualized depth. We notice that both Jeremiah and Hebrews blame the people for this misuse and not God and do not leave their preaching to be explained by some NCT follower several thousands of years later. They preached to the people of their day so that the people of their day would believe and live within the Covenant.

Playing with the Greek text

Seiver quotes Hebrews[102] as saying 'the time is coming', whereas The A.V. gives 'the days come', using the 3rd person plural *present indicative* of the verb ερχομαι, which means in its infinitive form either 'to come', 'to go' or 'to pass'. So we do not have a future reference, referring to a far off future from Jeremiah's preached word as Seiver teaches but a reference to the then present time and how it can be made better than the time before. Indeed, it appears that this verb ερχομαι is never used in the form Seiver gives it in the whole New Testament. Jesus is referred to in Matthew 11:3 as the ερχομενος (nom. sing. masc. part. pres.) or 'the Coming One', that is not One who is to come but the One who is always coming'. Christ as Covenant Keeper is always there. I see, too, that the Bibles in five other languages I have consulted, all treat the term in Hebrews as a present form and not a future form. Thus Seiver is wrong from the start with his 'New Covenant' prognosis. So we may ask, 'Why does Seiver deliberately alter the scriptural timing?' It is because as scripture stands, it contradicts Seiver's NCT faith. Seiver is doubting both Jeremiah's and Hebrews' words in his preference to the NCT version. He is suggesting that Hebrews backs him up in re-dating the New Covenant. Jeremiah's own dating must be our final court of appeal concerning this NCT misunderstanding as we cannot possibly profess to know better than Jeremiah as the NCT

---

[102] Hebrews 8:8. See *In These Last Days*, p. 123.

teaches. In Jeremiah 31:31, Jeremiah uses the word באים, which means in context that the days of the New Covenant (are) come. The days of the New Testament Covenant were already there in Jeremiah's time, and had come to stay. I admit there is a slight problem here in judging the following tenses which are placed in the future tense in A.V. English. Biblical Hebrew has only an 'already happened' tense and a 'yet to be finished' tense, as it is a matter not yet completed. The latter is often rendered as a future tense in English to emphasise the unfinished nature. I read Jeremiah 31 as pointing to a renewing of the Covenant in keeping with Genesis 17:7:

> And I will establish my covenant between me and thee and thy seed after thee in their generations for an everlasting covenant, to be a God unto thee, and to thy seed after thee.

Here we see again that the A.V. use of the future refers to what has now been established and will continue. Thus when studying Hebrew I was taught the 'future tense' can be translated with the present perfect referring to what has happened and is continuing. On checking with Hebrew experts, I find this usage perfectly acceptable today.[103] This is why I say the NCT men are centuries out of date with their timing.

Renewing the Covenant
Next Seiver refers to Jeremiah's words quoted by Hebrews 'when I will make a new covenant', again taking them from their ancient context and placing them in New Testament times. Here Jeremiah's gospel preaching shows how threadbare is the cloth out of which the whole structure of the NCT is woven. This appears to be the only source in the Bible for the term translated 'new covenant' and this is taken up twice by the author of the Hebrews in Hebrews chapter 8, 9 and chapter 12:24 which follows the author's assertion that New Testament saints are witnessed to by the Old Testament saints and should follow their example. Paul, in accordance with the author of Hebrews takes up the term translated 'new testament' by the A.V. in 2 Corinthians 3:6

---

[103] It is usually agreed the use of 'will' and 'shall' was not standardised until the Great Vowel Shift of the 15th Century occurred and continued throughout Britain. However, the Great Vowel Shift is still continuing and there is still a great deal of debate concerning the usage of these auxiliaries.

obviously with reference to Jeremiah as his gospel is also taken up by Paul.

Apart from in Jeremiah 31:31 where the term 'new covenant' is used and all New Testament descriptions refer back to this one mention, there is no other reference to a 'new' covenant in the Old Testament but there are many references as we shall see to the constant newness of Covenant revelation. Similar words are used for 'new' such as 'reformed', in both Testaments but Seiver also rejects those meanings. Yet Jeremiah is certainly, in context, using the Hebrew for 'new' in its sense of 'renewing, refreshing and reforming' as the term is used throughout the Old Testament. There is no other comment on a 'new' covenant' in the New Testament but there is much about it being repeatedly renewed and renewing man, which is the same thing. Indeed, when Hebrews speaks about the Covenant in Chapter 10:29, he refers to the 'blood of the Covenant' referring to Christ's sacrificial death. In Chapter 13:20, he writes of 'the blood of the everlasting covenant', a phrase also used often in the Old Testament. Christ is obviously referring to the one Covenant of Grace which is obviously the 'new' Covenant Jeremiah is preaching, though NCT writers claim that the Old Testament Covenant was a temporary one and 'everlasting' does not mean 'everlasting'. However the NCT might curb the meaning of 'everlasting', it is obvious that 'everlasting' means 'eternal', however one denies the eternity of Christ's office. Perhaps it is thus a waste of good time to demolish the vast claims NCT place on their superstructure when it can be so easily shown that their foundation is based on faulty theology, faulty representation of the Old Testament, faulty exegesis, faulty linguistics, faulty logic and faulty common-sense. Thus other references to a 'New Covenant' or 'New Order' will be shown to be mere inventions of the NCT.

The law written on hearts is an Old Testament truth.
That the NCT faultily present the testimony of the Old Testament in this multiple way can be clearly seen from the way they treat Jeremiah 31 and Hebrews 8:8-12. Jeremiah is talking about how the Israelites disobeyed God from the beginning of the Exodus out of Egypt onwards. This was no new declaration as most of the previous Old Testament writers emphasise this fact. So, too, the fact that God would write the

law on believers' hearts is repeated in various forms (to make it stick) throughout the Old Testament. In Deuteronomy 29:4, we read how with the advent of the renewing and extending of the Covenant under Moses, God had given the people a heart to perceive and eyes to see, and ears to hear'. This is especially the gospel which Jeremiah preached as in Chapter 24:7 and Ezekiel as in Chapter 11:19. These prophets preached a gospel that the NCT ignores and the emphasis in the original utterances is constantly on God's giving believers a 'new' heart there and then and not merely in times to come. The Covenant which was new to them brought them the Gospel of a new heart. In fact, one might easily say that this theme is far more common in the Old Testament than in the new, bearing in mind also the size of the Old Testament and the perhaps two thousand years it covers. This goes also for the many descriptions of God's righteousness in the Old Testament on which the New relies. So, too, when the New Testament writers speak of a new heart given to believers, they quote the Old Testament as their authority. As we have seen the letter-law was never meant to make inward faith obsolete but it was the idea of letter-law which was made obsolete with the knowledge of the Covenant of Grace. The NCT cannot or will not distinguish between the letter law and the Spirit-filled law. Besides, the Old Testament continually affirms that a remnant of the Israelites have not bowed their knees to strange gods and a misusing of Law and Grace. Such people, for the NCT believers could only exist in post-Old Testament times as before Christ they were 'carnal'.

Challenging NCT expertise

Exegetically, it is very dangerous to build a new theology on one text when there are literally hundreds of parallel texts in the Old Testament which emphasise, like Jeremiah, what the true Covenant is. This is the advice the NCT gives its critics but we say 'Physician, heal thyself'. A number of other enlightening O.T. texts have been mentioned above but I advise NCT 'scholars' to do their own homework and study the use of the term 'new' and also the use of the term 'covenant' in the Old Testament. I have become rather weary of NCT correspondents who tell me what the Greek and Hebrew say with the absolute authority of the NCT behind them but they could not tell a participle or aorist from a main verb and mixed up the Greek imperfect tense with the present perfect and pluperfect. Their Hebrew exegesis is even worse. Their etymologies of words seemed to be pure wishful thinking. I am not saying that the NCT people are absolutely void of Hebrew and Greek scholars but it is clear that most have not yet reached that goal yet profess to be at home in those languages. Gay who seems to have little knowledge of Greek and seemingly less of Hebrew yet believes he can correct all the Bible Scholars who have gone before him with his new translations. How does he know that the world's greatest New Testament scholars have mistranslated the passages he queries, not having had Gay's linguistic know-how? I must honestly say, I laughed aloud when I heard Gay triumphantly proclaiming this error in his judgment as a fact. My recent criticisms of Seiver's handling of the Greek moved him to stress that he 'knew Greek'. If so, he must show it. Such people remind me of the two so-called Jehovah's witnesses who came to my door in my village of Saarn. One was the contact man and the other the Bible 'expert'. He told me he was fluent in Greek. The latter began at once to inform me of what the Greek said about Jesus so I took out my *Novum* to follow his argument. I was, however, not able to follow him very far, though I knew where he was going, so I asked him kindly to explain from the Greek Testament what he meant as he had promised. On handing him my *Novum* the poor fellow looked crestfallen at a text he perhaps saw for the first time in his life but suddenly, he smiled again and said it was his mistake, what he wanted to explain was in the Hebrew. Having my Kittel at hand, I gave the Hebrew Testament to the JW and asked the gentleman to point out to me from the Old Testament what he wished to say. The bluffer browsed through the O.T. the wrong way round, looked at me and said, 'We are wasting our time with you.' They surely were! But what shall we say to NCT purveyors who bluff in the same way? Sadly, they have not the training, the politeness and discipline of the JWs and usually tell me that I am a moron, a sick man, a loon and a garbage-speaking clown as their publications show. However, all the NCT men I have dealt with, like the JWs, have made a pretence at knowing Greek and many claim they know Hebrew just as well.

Deniers of the times of reformation in Old Testament days
I have challenged several leading NCT men on this issue who believe that they are qualified to re-translate huge passages of scripture which

do not fit their categories. One told me with pride that he had a degree in 'Ministries', another said he had studied mathematics but carried no title, another had an M.A. in American Football and another leading NCT man when challenged concerning his public condemnation of my theology confessed that he had never read me. I have pointed out several of Seiver's guesses at what the Greek and Hebrew teaches and will mention more. Seiver quotes Hebrews 9:10 where the author follows the prophets and speaks of 'the time of reformation'. This was Jeremiah's 'New Covenant'. Seiver begs to differ. He tells us that though the words could refer to a time of 'setting straight, a restoration of that which is out of line, an improvement, a reformation' the words καιρου διορθωσεωσ really mean 'the time of the new order',[104] thinking in terms of his version of the New Covenant and perhaps David Gay's 'New Epoch'. Of course, the word 'reformation' fits into Jeremiah's testimony like a hand in a glove of the right size. My French Bible also reads 'une époque de réformation', not a 'new epoch'. Seiver's translation is incorrect. Διορθωσεωσ may be used for putting order into something, which Jeremiah strove to do but this is a long way from forming a 'new order' as if this were a clean break with divine revelation hitherto and with some sort of new ranking and abrupt cancelling of the past.

Then there is Seiver's most strange 'howler' in his translation of Hebrews 9:26 where we read 'επι συντελεια των αιωνων which the A.V. translators render 'in the end of the world', (lit. in the end of ages'). Seiver claims these words are not as they stand in Hebrews 9:26 but should be substituted in transcribed form by 'scintilla ton aeonian' and goes on to say how 'scintilla is characteristic of Jewish apocalyptic literature'. This might seem very scintillating, but all three words Seiver substitutes for the original are quite incorrect, given the Greek text. 'Scintilla' is neither found in the text nor the critical apparatus. Besides, the word is Latin and means a spark, a speck of dust or a crumb. It is true that the term is used in Latin apocalyptic texts but only to describe a spark or flash of fire.[105] I have consulted my Latin versions of the

---

[104] See the section under the title 'The Time of the New Order' on page 20 of Seiver's *In These Last Days*.

[105] See, for instance, *The Fate of the Dead: Studies in the Jewish and Christian Apocalypses*, R.B. Bauckham, Brill, 1998.

Bible and Latin commentaries on the text but seen no trace of a 'scintilla' there. So, too, Seiver's 'ton' is an accusative article in Greek but Hebrews uses των which is a Greek masculine plural article. Instead of αιωνων which is a genitive plural noun Seiver gives a transcription of the singular noun.[106] Thus it appears that Seiver had no Greek New Testament in his hand when he 'translated' this passage and must have copied it from another source which he apparently little understood.

The completely 'new' idea in NCT revisionism

But let us again refer to Seiver's theory of a non-existent 'new' covenant in the Old Testament which Reisinger, Ditzel, Wells, Zaspel, Gay and Seiver claim is a completely 'new' idea of the NCT thinkers. Their use of the term 'new' reminds me of my weaker students in a trade school where I taught translators for some 15 years alongside other educational tasks. They invariable took the first of many words listed in their dictionary as the only meaning possible and thus came up with hilarious translations. We were confronted with the word 'dumb-bell' in English. Some students confessed they were puzzled by their German translation which translated back was 'a stupid or speechless young beauty'. Thus our N.T. 'scholars' look up 'new' in the English dictionary and read 'Not existing before' and do not read on to find all the other English meanings of 'new' such as 'renewed', 'fresh', 'further', 'additional' etc. etc.. If they looked at the meaning of 'new' in school dictionaries even in these days of the dumbing down of language, they would find synonyms such as 'fresh', 'discovered anew', 'different' and 'not previously used'. The same variety of choice is given us in Hebrew and Greek dictionaries. When I looked into my English-German dictionary for a translation of 'new', using the same procedure as the NCT writers, i.e. picking the first word, it said 'frisch' which is 'fresh'. If the NCT writers would examine Middle English, Elizabethan and Jacobean usage, i.e. the language of the A.V., they would be surprised what additional meanings were used such as the term 'additional' itself. But we are not dealing here with the NCT dumbing down of English but the Hebrew word 'chadash'. Stop, the NCT people tells us. 'Old' can only mean 'done away with' and 'New'

---

[106] *In These Last Days*, p. 22.

means 'never before in existence'. This is not so. 'chadash' in the Old Testament means 'refreshed', 'renovated', 'rejuvinated,' 'repaired' or even 're-applied' and has many by-meanings such as 'sweet' and 'refreshing' and 'reforming', the latter in the sense of making better. It is getting back to the roots and the original intended meaning. In the New Testament 'palaios' (old) means also 'In existence for a long time.' 'Neo' means 'ever fresh' and 'kainos' used in Hebrews for the Covenant has just the same meaning as chadash used in Jeremiah 31 for the same Covenant.

Our old-time, eternal Gospel is ever new, fresh and reforming and brings renewal with it like the morning dew. It only makes sense, however, to renewed and restored sinners. A golden rule here in translation work is that:

> If we can safely say there was no knowledge of the matter before that which was 'chadash', we can use 'new' as meaning 'never before'. If there was something of the kind already in existence, we can translate 'chadash' as 'renewed' or 'restored'. If we are referring to something refreshing or sweet, we can translate 'chadash' as meaning such.

I cannot go into the background of all the references to 'covenant' in the Old Testament in this book but the NCT must do the research others have done and where the cap fits, wear it. Our Reformers, however, were adamant in claiming the unity of both Testaments in this matter. God's Word is ever 'new' just as we sing 'New every morning is His love'. Indeed, Moses referred to his own service to God within the Covenant as the introduction of 'a NEW thing', looking back to the Covenant with Abraham.[107] So we see that Moses was a real New Covenant Theologian and Reformer thousands of years before the NCT who have cut themselves off from the biblical Covenant! All those who had destroyed the former Covenant in unbelief were tilled from the ground. This is surely what Jeremiah is referring to throughout his chapters. In Lamentations 3:23 he tells us that God's mercies are new (renewed) every day, so is His Covenant. We declare with Lamentations; Great is His faithfulness!

---

[107] See Numbers 16:28-30. My emphasis.

God forgave sins in the past as also in present times

Now, let us take a brief look at the supposed novelty of Jeremiah's covenant teaching. Jeremiah says the covenant he preached replaces the one God promised to the Jews on leaving Egypt. Now, of course this was rendered null and void because all those Jews broke the Covenant and none reached the Promise Land. Indeed, the initial Covenant-breakers who could not wait for the covenant to be ratified and abused it, perished on the spot of their treachery. They preferred to interpret God's promise as referring to graven images. Jeremiah in Chapter 31 is merely freshly touching on his detailed account of Israel's rejection of the Covenant in chapter 11:3ff. not mentioned by Seiver. This was a truth Jeremiah preached openly to the people of his day, because they kept forgetting it and kept on losing touch with the Covenant. This is a dire warning to the NCT to trust in God's Covenant mercy.

The Mosaic Covenant is not mentioned negatively in Jeremiah at all but the prophet insists on correcting misunderstandings referring to God's dealings with man. So we have clear reiterated evidence from the Settlement onwards to the one, true Covenant of Grace not only through the wonderful evidence of David at the founding of the Jewish Kingship when God again confirmed the Covenant for eternity (long before Jeremiah). David and a remnant of His people did not say all this was 'pie in the sky' but they believed it as a remnant of Jews did from the resettlement on. They could say with Jeremiah and almost every book of the Old Testament, that God was willing to forgive and forget their sins.

So, too the idea that the Law should be written on the hearts of believers was not new to the earlier O.T. writers and greater and lesser Prophets (see the five hundred or so citations in Alexander Cruden's Concordance) and David testifies 'I delight to do the will of God. Yea, thy law is within my heart'.[108] David combined the will of God in His covenant with the knowledge of the law in his heart. A study of David on the Covenant and his heart's godly experiences is most profitable as I found when tracing all that David has to say about the Covenant in the Hebrew in preparation for my Dr Theol. finals. Never was hard work more rewarding!

---

[108] Psalm 40:8.

The truth also that God would forgive sins and remember them no more which Jeremiah affirmed adorned the entire Old Testament Covenant, as a quick search with a good concordance will soon show.[109] One of the first texts I learned of by heart as a tiny tot in the Bradford Home Mission Sunday School was Micah 7:19, 'He will turn again, he will have compassion upon us; he will subdue all our infirmities: and thou wilt cast all their sins into the depths of the sea.' Is not this a renewal of God's Covenant? There are dozens of such new (renewed, refreshed) references to the Covenant in the O.T.. Naturally, my Sunday School teacher, Mr Lee, well versed in God's ways in God's Kingdom but a lavatory-cleaner during his pilgrimage on this earth told us that on the banks of that sea, there was a sign saying 'No Fishing'. It is an old joke of long standing but ever new.

Old Job knew the New Covenant

This morning my wife and I were discussing Handel's 'Messiah'. My wife in her lovely voice began to sing 'I know that my Redeemer Liveth' in German, Handel's mother-tongue. She then exclaimed, 'What a wonderful New Testament Truth that is' and I agreed. But who first said those words? Well, one of the oldest parts the Bible is the Book of Job whose story was most probably written down before the time of Moses. The early affairs of Israel in the Mosaic period are not mentioned in the book which could mean that Job lived before Moses or lived far away from the events of the Exodus. There is no indication in the book at all that Job was a Jew but some claim that he was because he expresses his faith in a similar way to later believing Jews. The oldest MSS containing the Book of Job are in Aramaic as are also parts of Genesis. Personally, it would appear to me that Job was not a Jew. Talmud texts refer to him as an ancient Gentile. The textual evidence could point to Edom as his place of residence. This was one of the first countries to join in with the Children of Israel and one of the first to leave Israel at the breakup of the Kingship. We are only told that he

---

[109] I write this to encourage readers to search the scriptures where the quotes are many. I have received letters from NCT writers denying what I have resaid above and demanding to know where their New Covenant utterances are common knowledge in the Old Testament. This was because they just do not know the Testament that they would render 'obsolete' for faulty reasons, mostly because of plain ignorance. They feel they have the truth before studying what righteous faith is throughout all the scriptures.

lived in the East and was 'the greatest Man in the East'. If Job lived before Moses, then he would certainly be pre-Jewish, if he had witnessed the founding of Israel and were a strong believer in God and of that nation, it is strange that he never mentions their exploits or anything remotely related to the Mosaic system. Many date Job's testimony from 1,500 years before Christ and some back into the 'Ice Age', whenever that was. However, Job does refer to snow and ice conditions more than any other Old Testament author.

What interests us here is that Job was in Covenant with God at a very early stage in the spread of godly truths in the Near East. He testifies to hearing about God but then seeing Him face to face. Yet this man of faith understood divine truths which the NCT people have yet to discover. In the face of ruthless opposition to his standing with God, he could yet declare:

> I know that my redeemer liveth, and that he shall stand at the latter day upon the earth; and though after my skin worms destroy this body, yet in my flesh shall I see God: whom I shall see for myself and my eyes shall behold, and not another: though my reins be consumed within me.[110]

A closer look at Jeremiah 31

So let us re-examine Jeremiah 31:31 in the light of Jeremiah's context and the testimonies of God's People who lived before him such as Job, David and Isaiah. It is perhaps strange that though Jeremiah is one of the longest books in the Bible he is only referred to some four times in the New Testament. Isaiah, however, who pioneered the Great Prophets a hundred years before Jeremiah is mentioned about fifty-five times in the New Testament (My rough count, though some say ninety). So, too, Isaiah preached the same truth as Jeremiah a hundred years before him and Isaiah referred constantly back to doctrines long believed before

---

[110] Job 19:25-27, but read to the end of the chapter. That this most ancient text is difficult to translate can be seen from the italic words added by the translators for clarity's sake but the meaning is very clear. More than one NCT man has told me that such a testimony can only be given in their so-called 'New Order', 'New Covenant' and 'New Law'.

him. Why then is Jeremiah given this preeminence amongst the NCT? It appears to be merely because they think that Jeremiah lends himself best, when taken out of context, to the NCT view of a New Order and a New Law after Christ came which the O.T. saints knew about but supposedly ignored in their time as if it were too good to believe. Jeremiah uses the word 'new' with relationship to the Covenant so that is reason enough for the NCT to build their superstructure on it.

Jeremiah preached nothing new
I learnt in my first Greek lessons in 1959 at London Bible College under the tutorship of that dear, wise man of God H. C. Oakley that when a Greek word has obviously several meanings, we should try to merge all those meanings together instead of cutting them apart. This was also John Gill's method. But a hundred years before Jeremiah, Isaiah refers to God's ever-renewed, everlasting Covenant many, many more times than Jeremiah and has a more detailed Messianic thrust in what he says. The idea of a renewed Covenant is prevalent throughout the Old Testament scriptures. Thus Jeremiah, also walking in Abraham's and David's footsteps, held to the everlasting nature of the covenant as he explains in Chapter Thirty-One and the following chapters, as did his predecessors in the faith. The NCTs start and stop in the study of the lasting Covenant with Chapter Jeremiah Thirty-One taken completely out of its context as their 'proof-text', a task for which it is useless outside of its context. They have found what they want in their misunderstood little word 'new'. Any way, if we read the whole story of Jeremiah's re-emphasising of the Covenant, we see, as Hebrews hints at, that the people of the covenant that never came into being according to Jeremiah were at fault in their part of it but God was not at fault in His part. The Covenant to which Jeremiah particularly quotes as having decayed is given as the story of the Golden Calf and the breaking of the first tablets and cutting of a calf in two and passing through it to which Jeremiah refers but seemingly never the NCT. Jeremiah says that this was not done to God's specifications so that He did not accept such disobedience. In other words, this covenant never actually took place as

intended and was never ratified.[111] The idea that Jeremiah was referring to the annulling of the entire Covenant of Grace or the Law here or the supposed 'Old Testament Dispensation' is absurd as Jeremiah immediately outlines the true Covenant of Grace for his contemporaries. Furthermore, the events recorded by Jeremiah refer to the time immediately before the presentation of the renewed Covenant by Moses. Then the Siniatic Covenant was newly introduced after the punishment of the Covenant breakers. Jeremiah had already cried out against Israel's and Judah's covenant-breaking in chapter 11:1ff.:

> The word that came to Jeremiah from the LORD saying, Hear ye the words of this covenant, and speak unto the men of Judah, and to the inhabitants of Jerusalem; And say thou unto them, Thus saith the LORD God of Israel; Cursed be the man that obeyeth not the words of this covenant, Which I commanded your fathers in the day that I brought them forth out of the land of Egypt, from the iron furnace, saying, Obey my voice, and do them, according to all which I command you: so shall ye be my people, and I will be your God: That I may perform the oath which I have sworn unto your fathers, to give them a land flowing with milk and honey, as it is this day. Then answered I, and said, So be it, O LORD. Then the LORD said unto me, Proclaim all these words in the cities of Judah, and in the streets of Jerusalem, saying, Hear ye the words of this covenant, and do them. For I earnestly protested unto your fathers in the day that I brought them up out of the land of Egypt, even unto this day, rising early and protesting, saying, Obey my voice. Yet they obeyed not, nor inclined their ear, but walked every one in the imagination of their evil heart: therefore I will bring upon them all the words of this covenant, which I commanded them to do: but they did them not. And the LORD said unto me, A conspiracy is found among the men of Judah, and among the inhabitants of Jerusalem. They are turned back to the iniquities of their forefathers, which

---

[111] It would be better to read all Jeremiah's arguments in his book but the heart of the matter which led to Jeremiah's correction is found in Chapter 34:18-20. So, too, one should read Exodus so as to fit Jeremiah's remarks into their historical context.

refused to hear my words; and they went after other gods to serve them: the house of Israel and the house of Judah have broken my covenant which I made with their fathers. Therefore thus saith the LORD, Behold, I will bring evil upon them, which they shall not be able to escape; and though they shall cry unto me, I will not hearken unto them. Then shall the cities of Judah and inhabitants of Jerusalem go, and cry unto the gods unto whom they offer incense: but they shall not save them at all in the time of their trouble.

This is Jeremiah's death-toll to covenant-breakers throughout his book and not just one verse of warning twisted out and taken from its multi-chaptered context. If the original covenant-breakers fared so horribly before the Law was added to the Covenant, what will be the fate of those who reject Jeremiah's teaching on the real thing? However, the Holy Spirit's Word, our scripture, is full of mercy to those within the Covenant as Isaiah tells us throughout chapter 55 and the following chapters. This is no new covenant for the future only as David, Isaiah and Jeremiah and countless others knew all about it in their life-times. It was the gospel of the Holy One of Israel to whom the entire scriptures point.

Hebrews follows Jeremiah closely

So Hebrews follows Jeremiah 11 and 31 and other chapters in the book in understanding that the agreement with Israel at the start of the Exodus failed because so many Children of Israel did not follow it. It had to be renewed – by God, not man. The same Covenant had to be renewed time and time again because Israel repeatedly broke it, not keeping it through spiritual faith but through letter-obedience which was also too much for them. The author of Hebrews is affirming that whereas Jeremiah and the other prophets he quotes unnamed looked forward to the Messiah in faith, That Messiah had now come bodily. He assures us that the Old Testament saints witnessed true faith by spending a whole chapter telling us that these are our mentors in the faith. He mentions many details, reaping his facts from the Old Testament to show that Christ was the One looked forward to by the believing prophets. We know there were many unbelieving prophets and priests in the Old Testament whom the later prophets dealt with fiercely, foretelling the end of earthly Jerusalem where they had their headquarters but faithful men such as Isaiah and Jeremiah were both prophets and priests. Referring back to the 'new Covenant' again in Hebrews Chapter 12, the author reaffirms that the Old Testament saints believed what had come to pass in their day. Just as we today still, two thousand and more years after Christ's glorious death and resurrection believe in him by faith.

The main argument of Hebrews is that what the Old Testament knew, we know 'much more'[112] today. But this is exactly what the prophets said would happen and this caused them to admonish the people to start believing it there and then. Thus later believers could understand much more of the Old Testament as they had been spoon-fed by it. However, the O.T. saints were honoured as pioneers in the faith because their faith took in future substantiations. So the author to the Hebrews praises them in setting such a marvellous example before us in chapters 11 and 12), ending with those wonderful words:

> Wherefore seeing we also are compassed about with so great a cloud (crowd) of witnesses, let us lay aside every weight, and the sin which so easily beset us, and let us run with patience the race that is set before us, Looking unto Jesus the author and finisher of our faith.

If the truth were to be said, Old Testament believers seem to have fared better on their more meagre revelation than many today who ought to know 'better'. This is why Hebrews recommends that we join them in their strong faith rather than the other way round as the NCT teaches.

NCT theology is no 'new discovery' but old gospel teaching wrenched from its biblical context and robbed of its Christo-centric contents

The New Covenant of mercy, grace and peace is made with Christ in eternity and is always at work. It was not made *with* the Jews but made *for* them and the countries which gained the good news *before* them,

---

[112] Hebrews 9:14. Was this not what the prophets said would happen and admonished the people to believe it?

from them and *after* them. They rejected it at their peril. So, all the ideas the NCT people have concerning the New Covenant are taken out of the Old Testament where they were general knowledge from Adam on that the just shall live by faith. This was intensified more and more up to the time of Malachi as the bulk of mankind would not live by faith for which they reaped the prophets rebuke as salvation by grace-given faith was freely preached to them. So we see there is something radically wrong with Seiver's cut down translation of Hebrews 8:7-13 which he renders:

> For if there had been nothing wrong with the first covenant, no place would have been sought for another. But God found fault with the people and said 'The time is coming, declares the Lord, when I will make a new covenant.

Here Seiver then erases part of verse 8 and verses 9-12 which gives the biblical interpretation and source of verses 7 and 8 and continues:

> By calling this covenant 'new', he has made the first one obsolete; and what is obsolete and aging will soon disappear (86 words in the whole 'translation').[113]

What the author to the Hebrews actually writes is:

> For if that first covenant had been faultless, then should no place have been sought for the second. For finding fault with them, he saith, Behold, the days come, saith the Lord, when I will make a new covenant with the house of Israel and with the house of Judah. Not according to the covenant that I made with their fathers in the day when I took them by the hand to lead them out of the land of Egypt; because they continued not in my covenant, and I regarded them not, saith the Lord. For this is the covenant that I will make with the house of Israel after those days, saith the Lord; I will put my laws into their mind, and write them in their hearts: and I will be to them a God, and they shall be to me a people: And they shall not teach every man his neighbour, and

---

[113] *In These last Days*, p. 123.

every man his brother, saying, Know the Lord: for all shall know me, from the least to the greatest. For I will be merciful to their unrighteousness, and their sins and their iniquities will I remember no more. In that he saith, A new covenant, he hath made the first old. Now that which decayeth and waxeth old is ready to vanish away (216 words).

Here Hebrews is obviously referring back to the truths preached by Jeremiah concerning the time before the Law was given and to the Old Testament writers teaching concerning God writing His laws in the minds and hearts of believers. This is continued into the present and is a valid truth for all time. It is not the true covenant of God's laws written on minds and hearts which is at stake but a covenant which denies this. The old covenant of rebellion, we are told in Hebrews when the new is there is thus shown to be out of date, grown old or rendered inactive (πεπαλαιωκεν an active perfect indicative). It does not work as a rule by letter. This does not mean that the Old Testament Mosaic Law is 'obsolete' as it still stands as a command of God which causes God's anger when it is misemployed and misapplied. We learn from 1 Timothy that the law is good when used lawfully but bad when used unlawfully. Rightly applied, the Law is a very good thing, even 'glorious' as we are told in 2 Corinthians 3:7. Romans 7:12 tells us, 'Wherefore the law is holy, and the commandment just, and good.'

I believe this is also Hebrews and Jeremiah's conclusion. Furthermore, Hebrews tell us that even the Tabernacle was put up for divine service because all these rituals were pointers to Christ. This is also part of the Old Testament teaching which, I believe, all points to Christ. However, the misuse of all these gospel opportunities culminated in Aaron's fall and led to Moses breaking the tablets of stone. This end to a covenant of man's failure cannot be erased from the Bible's witness as it an essential part of scripture teaching us the history of Christ's salvation. Jesus so often cited Old Testament history when teaching his disciples about Himself. The NCT, especially Tom Wells, have belittled the importance of what they feel is Timothy's testimony as a Jew for his love for the law. They look upon this as a mere remnant of Jewish belief, now rendered obsolete. However, Tiny Tim, so well cared for by his parents and grandparents as a testimony to all parents and grandparents nowadays, is not the author of the two books bearing his name but it is Big Paul, also a Jew but the apostle to the Gentiles who declares that the law is good when used lawfully, that is within the Covenant of God's Grace through a life in Christ. It appears, however, that the NCT would erase all teaching concerning the continuation of the Covenant of Grace, including the part Law plays in it from their scriptures.

A solution offered to the NCT

I therefore put forward as a solution to the NCT problem that Jeremiah's first Covenant was the misused rites prior to the second writing of the Tablets. This was, however, all prior to the law given at Sinai and when Hebrews 9:19 arrives and we read of Moses part in the Covenant, we find God emphasising its importance in prophesying Christ. We have thus Christ's life, sufferings and testimony to His Covenant responsibilities in both Old and New Testament times, radiating out to all times and Christ said that not a jot or tittle of the law would pass away. God's standard remains even today and was never rendered obsolete. It is symptomatic of NCT exegesis that when the New Covenant is displayed throughout scriptures from Genesis to Revelation, they pick out only that which, in the artificial context they give it, can be used to explain that all the blessings of the Covenant of Grace started after the close of the Old Testament. However, the Old Testament was never closed but ran seamless over into the New which continued and built on its teaching.

New Covenant Theology in the Old Testament

One of the most often used group of words in the Old Testament is that referring to the Covenant (without an epithet); the making of the Covenant; the keeping of the Covenant, the Book of the Covenant, the Everlasting Covenant and also the New Covenant. Sad to say, there are also many references to forgetting and transgressing the Covenant. This abundance of information on the Covenant led me to try to work through the numerous usages of the term for my *rigorosum* in O.T. exegesis at Marburg University under Prof. Dr Christl Meier who chaired the Examination Board. I was quite astonished at what I discovered and had never realized how closely the Old Testament teaching on the Covenant merged with New Testament teaching.

Indeed, the step-over from the Old Testament to the New was so well prepared by the Old Testament prophets that when reading through from the Greater to the Lesser Prophets up to Malachi, one was not at all surprised when Matthew turned up as the very next book. John Reisinger questions whether 'everlasting' could be truthfully applied to the Covenant, perhaps thinking of Noah where the everlasting Covenant not to flood the whole world again made with him by God was for the whole duration of creation. Reisinger, and those following his teaching, would say, here is proof that 'everlasting' does not really mean 'everlasting'. However, the Covenant of the rainbow was really not with Noah but with creation[114] and it is too speculative to try to define how long creation will last. For a person who lives only a few decades on this earth, creation would seem to be of infinite duration and then what about the Renewed Creation? Even the everlasting nature of the covenant expressed through God's dealings with Abraham cannot be said to be at fault in their infinite application.[115] Circumcision, for instance, as baptism, is nowhere said to be an eternal necessity but they were designed to point to God's eternal purpose in choosing a People for Himself, who will be His for ever and ever. Or does not Reisinger believe in life everlasting? The everlasting nature of the Old Testament is that it points to the everlasting nature and purpose of Christ.

It was interesting to note, for instance, that from the very start, the Book of the Covenant was associated with the shedding of blood, thus paving the way for belief in the Messiah by whose stripes we are healed.[116] We also read in 2 Kings how a great revival in religion followed the neglected reading of the Book of the Covenant. We note, too, how far the priests had transgressed the Covenant but King Josiah 'turned to the Lord with all his heart and soul and with all his might'.[117] There were many periods of reformation and refreshment in the Old Testament, may we pray that such will not cease today when many churches are breaking the Covenant. The NCT would do the world a favour if instead of ripping the pages of the Book of the Covenant out,

---

[114] Genesis 9:13.
[115] Genesis 17:7.
[116] Exodus 24:7, 8.
[117] 2 Kings 23:25.

they would open God's Book which they have neglected and preach the whole truth concerning it, and nothing but the truth that sinners might 'turn to the Lord with all their hearts and souls and with all their might'.

Bible teaches continuity in Covenant Theology in both Testaments
Contrary to Gay and Co., we must now closely examine the introductory passages in the New Testament which explain how God's Covenant, outlined in the Old Testament, is now being continued in the New. In the first chapter of Luke's epistle to Theophilus, the author repeatedly looks back at the Covenant promises and states that these are 'those things which are surely believed among us'.[118] We do not have a Jew speaking here but a Greek Physician. In this declaration, the Gentile Luke tells us he is relying on eye-witnesses who were there from the beginning of the New Testament era and minsters of the Word. His words refer to writers who start off their theology with the occurrences of the Old Testament and in the Spirit base their belief on the testimony of the Old Testament. He affirms this in his opening words to Theophilus in Acts, claiming as did the Old Testament prophets that God's Covenant promises are for Jerusalem, Judea, Samaria and for 'the uttermost parts of the earth'. In Luke's epistle, the author emphasises the continuation of the Covenant by introducing his readers to the Jewish priest Zacharias and his wife Elizabeth who became the parents of John the Baptist. Both, we are told, were blameless in the eyes of the Law. However, Zacharias though not lacking in his understanding of *law* still lacked *faith*. Zacharias disbelieved the heavenly revelation that his old wife should conceive through him and bear a child. This seems all the more astonishing as Zacharias had prayed for a son and now doubted that his prayers would be fulfilled. Soon, however, not without Gabriel's assistance and that of his faithful wife, Zacharias recognised God's grace with thanksgiving and joined his wife in her faith. An interesting comparison arises here between Zacharias and Elizabeth at the beginning of the New Testament and Adam and Eve at the beginning of the Old. In the Old Testament, Adam followed his wife into breaking God's Law. In the New Testament, Zacharias followed his wife in believing through Grace.[119] We also note

---

[118] Luke 1:1.
[119] See Luke 1:50, 72.

148

that Gabriel, who appeared to Zacharias and Elizabeth as also to Mary, said that many of the Children of Israel would turn to God. He did not say 'all'. The very fact that Gabriel, the angel who appeared in the Old Testament to Daniel, now appeared at the commencement of the New Testament, must be seen as evidence of the continuity between the Testaments.

The revelation of this vision of judgment and grace and the angel Gabriel's explanation is very significant concerning the one doctrine of the Covenant which pervades through the entire Bible. In Daniel chapters 8 and 9 Gabriel tells the prophet that the Messiah will come at a certain time, and now, in Luke Chapter One, here is Gabriel again explaining that this great and holy occasion has arrived. Here we have the same Covenant with the same heavenly ambassador overbridging the times with his good news. If this is not continuation, what is? Furthermore, the New Testament pioneer, John the Baptist, was at once likened to Elias, having the same spirit and power. There is no sign here of the completely new start to the Covenant that the NCT-ites claim is a New Testament fact. Indeed, Zacharias, now full of the Holy Spirit, saw all this as the fulfilment of the mercy performing Covenant which had been given to his fathers and the holy prophets.[120]

All Scripture is given on inspiration of God
In our defence of the correct New Testament understanding of the Old, we must return to Timothy of whom Paul affirms that he was brought up as a child by his family who were Jews and could say of the Old Testament:

> All scripture is given on inspiration of God and is profitable for doctrine, for reproof, for correction, for instruction in righteousness: That the man of God may be perfect, thoroughly furnished unto all good works.[121]

Tom Wells challenges this clear testimony of Paul's to the efficacy of God's Word in 2 Timothy 3:14-17 with reference to Timothy's

---

[120] Luke 1:68-80
[121] 2 Timothy 3:15-17

149

upbringing,[122] arguing that O.T. scripture such as Moses' Law was merely for a specific people for a specific time but is now redundant so we cannot take Paul's account of Timothy literally. 'No Christian believes 2 Timothy 3:16, 17', he says in unbelief. However, Paul's testimony stays firm in Holy Writ, telling him 'from a child thou hast known the holy scriptures, which are able to make thee wise unto salvation through faith which is in Christ Jesus.' Paul is speaking of the Bible of Christ and the Apostles and the Early Church's inheritance. This was the Old Testament from which they preached New Covenant salvation. Wells, however, cannot accept a New Testament salvation preached from the Old Testament. The New Testament reveals that God's Covenant is at work throughout all times and thus we pray, 'Unto him be glory *in the church* by Christ Jesus *throughout all ages*, world without end. Amen.'[123]

The fact is that it is no use appealing to the saving vision of Abraham and the other Patriarchs of the Old Testament when witnessing to the NCT people who have only half a Bible in their hands. Tom Wells, Fred Zaspel and Randy Seiver tell us that Old Testament references to believing patriarchs are merely figurative and whenever the testimony of 'prophets' is given in speaking on the foundation of the Church, they tell us we must read 'New Testament prophets only'.[124] So the Church, for these people has no Old Testament because God's Covenant in that dispensation was only applied to temporary land promises. They thus ban both Jews and non-Jews from salvation in the O.T., claiming pre-Jewish Patriarchs were merely physical pointers to spiritual things to come in a post-Jewish era. Thus the Jewish prophets predicted a salvation which neither they nor their hearers could understand and believe, so Christ had no saving function for them. I have often asked NCT people if they thought there were no members of Christ's Bride in the Old Testament. Older NCT men told me that Christ went to Hades and preached to the Old Testament people after His crucifixion and the Elect were chosen out then. Modern NCT men indicate honestly that they have not settled that problem unanimously yet.

---

[122] *New Covenant Theology*, pp. 85, 201.
[123] Ephesians 3:21.
[124] *New Covenant Theology*, Wells and Zaspel, pp. 52, 53.

On the road to Emmaus

It is refreshing to look at Luke 24:13 for an account of Christ's words on our subject. Gentile Luke who has found he is one in the faith with believing Jews begins with his teaching of a continuous Covenant of Mercy and Grace, linking up with Isaiah and Malachi and ends by re-establishing the importance of the Old Testament testimony to a graceful law and a rule of grace. It was a testimony that even Christians were beginning to forget. So the Spirit-led author begins his work by showing believers in Him how the New Testament is a continuation of the Old and ends it in the same vein. When the disciples tell Jesus their woeful tale, He responds with emotion and cries 'O fools, and slow of heart to believe all that the prophets have spoken.' Naturally here Christ is not speaking of New Testament prophets, as NCT leaders would have us believe, but of Job, Moses, David, Isaiah, Jeremiah and all the other Old Testament writers who believed in Christ. Our Saviour, after rebuking the disciples for still doubting, says, 'Ought not Christ to have suffered these things, and to enter into his glory?' Then we read, 'And beginning at Moses and the prophets, he expounded unto them in all the scriptures the things concerning himself.' What happened to these doubting disciples? The Bible tells us that 'There eyes were opened'. My heartfelt prayers go out to the NCT that they will follow the Lord's road to Emmaus, harken to Him and experience what His disciples at last found true so that their eyes too might be opened.

Summing Up

Another attempt to out-translate the Greek New Testament is to be found in Seiver's book *In These Last Days* in which the author gives his own truncated and highly edited version of what the Greek can be bent to mean. In his efforts to make Hebrews and Jeremiah conform to NCT specifications, Seiver, like Gay, stands the scriptures on its head ignoring the context and purpose of the passages he 'translates'. Most of this chopping and changing of the original text, as in Gay's case, comes via changing the message of the Old Testament which is timeless to that of a time before a time which is not relevant for today. That Christ was always the Founder and Keeper of His Covenant in both Testaments and the Author and Finisher of faith in Him in both Testaments is avoided and ignored. Throughout his appeal to Jeremiah

151

and Hebrews commentary on him, Seiver writes as if Jeremiah's preaching had no reference to the needs of Jeremiah's time. All Seiver's emphasis on the law written on New Testament hearts of flesh as if all Old Testament hearts were hearts of stone is completely foreign to the everlasting gospel of the everlasting Covenant in both Testaments. What Seiver is doing is denying there were ever times of Reformation and spiritual renewal in the Old Testament which, contrary to Seiver's insistence, emphasizes time and time again that the righteous are given hearts of flesh and the just shall live by faith.

Also typical of Seiver and his NCT friends is that there is no 'New Covenant' in the Old Testament, meaning that all the Old Testament preaching on the Covenant was meaningless to the hearers and believers in the gospel as preached by Christ's faithful men of old. Indeed, it becomes clear to the readers that the only ones who Seiver believes understood Jeremiah's true message are present day NCT believers. Even Moses, long before Jeremiah introduced the additions to the Covenant because of the Jewish transgressions as a 'New Thing' because, in the interpretation of the original preachers of the Covenant, it was always 'new' just as we still sing today 'New every morning is His love'. The everlasting newness of the gospel is lost to the NCT dealers in a dead and abolished Old Testament past yet God in Christ was very active and forgiving sins and blotting out all remembrance of them on His part in the Old Testament as in the New and writing His law into the hearts of believers. Even non-Jew Job, before ever Seiver's 'National Covenant' was there to be torn apart by the NCT, had been given the faith to know that his Redeemer was alive and working out His purpose in Job's life and testimony.

Seiver's exposition of Jeremiah 31 without his Old Testament background but highlighted in an NCT setting, would reveal, one would think, the folly of such scriptural mishandling. The whole of the Old Testament and the New must be studied to put Jeremiah in his correct background as a preacher of Covenant righteousness. Hebrews does not go into much unnecessary detail concerning Jeremiah's chapter-long preaching on the subject but Seiver fills in the alleged breaks with his NCT re-writing of the original text, so destroying the original meaning of both Jeremiah and Hebrews utterly. He misunderstands what was wrong with the old covenant mentioned, and continues his faulty idea of identifying this pre-Sinai unratified covenant with the legislation added to the Abrahamic Covenant because of the Jewish covenant-breakers' sins. The truth that it was Christ's blood which sealed the all-time Covenant Seiver seems to delegate to his annulled Covenant, which illustrates the jumble in which the NCT theology has snared itself.

The Bible clearly teaches the continuity of the Covenant teaching of the Old Testament into the New which even Gentile Christian writers, as Luke, were quick to point out at the very beginning of their gospels. And no less a personage than the Angel Gabriel himself links up the Old and the New Testament together. Tom Wells and other NCT co-contenders are suspicious of New Testament references to the faith of Jews but the scriptures affirm this and where Wells uses his criticism with a pen-knife, Paul is talking about ALL scripture being inspired by the Holy Spirit. Here we see the great difference in the scriptures own testimony and the 'I know better' attitude of the NCT.

On the road to Emmaus we find our Saviour, no NCT enthusiast by any means, opening the scriptures at the Books of Moses, going through the testimonies of all their blessed writings showing how they all testified to Him. They were all gospel-witnesses to salvation in Christ which is the all-being of the Covenant of Grace. We notice that here 'the scriptures' refer solely to the Old Testament which Christ, as Paul believed could make us 'wise to salvation'. Here we see the truth of Bullinger's belief that the New Testament is a commentary on the Old.

Chapter 6

Moses Guides The Exiles Out Of Egypt

The international setting of the twelve tribes

The subsequent witness of both Testaments demonstrates how these early Covenant promises mentioned in the previous chapters were fulfilled on an international basis. When Moses was first chosen to lead Israel out of Egypt, a very important country in the history of the Messiah, he was reminded they would spend much time in the countries or territories where the older peoples of the Canaanites, the Hittites, the Amorites, the Perizzites, the Hivites and the Jebusites already lived[125] and were to accept foreigners into their fold under certain conditions only. These conditions were invariably broken and mass integration from other tribes ensued. A strip of land on the west coast was provided for the Philistines and was not part of the land given to the 'Children of Israel'. Today only a small part of this small land remains independent of modern Israel and that is cut off from life-bringing trade with other nations by Israel's sea-blocking policy to starve out their brother Palestinians. Furthermore, Moses not only led six hundred thousand of 'Children of Israel' out of Egypt but also 'a mixed multitude' of people who were not descendants of Joseph and his brethren.[126] The basis of

---

[125] Exodus 3:8.
[126] Exodus 12:37, 38.

the future state of Israel was thus international and provided a home for many who were in no way related ethnically to Joseph and his brethren. They professed to be ready, however, to take on the same covenantal conditions which the Children of Israel professed they would accept and thus became 'Children of Israel' themselves. They were drawn from all parts of the commonwealth of Egypt. Without God's work amongst the diverse ethnic peoples in Egypt and control over affairs there and on the way to the Promised Land, the twelve tribes could never have been able to start or finish their wanderings. Indeed, these well-to-do Egyptians under God's sovereign hand funded the initial Exodus from Egypt by providing Moses and his followers with the 'traveller's cheques' of the age; gold, silver and precious stones. We must also face up to the truth that as all these initial hundreds of thousands of emigrants of mixed nations rejected God's grace, they never reached the 'Promised Land' which remained only for future believers and their kin. So those who eventually were privileged to people the land God promised them were different peoples to those who left Egypt and far more variant in their ethnic and national attributes. In other words, those who reached their goal cannot possibly be described as 'ethnic Jews'. It was religion that bound them together and that only from time to time according to how they interpreted God's promises.

Biblical Hebrew was not the mother-tongue of the exiles

Furthermore, these peoples represented a large number of language speakers who spoke not only other Semitic dialect than the yet to develop biblical Hebrew but also Indo-Germanic languages and other languages little known today. The modern idea that the Twelve Tribes spoke biblical Hebrew as their mother tongue before, during and coming out of Egypt has no evidence to back it up. It only gradually became a standard language for recording the history not only of revelation but also of the multiple peoples who formed later Israel. Something like Latin used by the Roman Catholic Church for centuries. Hebrew as we know it from the scriptures appears to have functioned like the modern kind of 'High German' or the English 'Received Pronunciation', which still have not driven out the major and minor dialects spoken in Germany and Britain. Indeed, local dialects in both countries are now encouraged and the 'Queen's English' of my youth seems to be a dying language, especially in the British Royal Family. I love to hear the old recordings of John Snagge, the newsreader whose English must be something of an embarrassment to modern reporters and TV journalists because of the beauty of his pronunciation and vocabulary.

The exiles, however, were a literate people
These early Palestinian peoples also had different scripts and kinds of writing. So they were a literate people as we know from the records gathered and written down, not only by Moses but also by his soldiers and spies. Even pre-Mosaic Job wished for a book to be written concerning his experiences with God and Moses used several earlier written records as he tells us and written records were kept throughout the 70 years' wanderings. However, it is no exaggeration to say that at the time of the Exodus the 'Children of Israel' reflected the languages of the countries of the known world. We are talking about post-Babel times here. The Hittites of Palestine alone influenced not only the areas of the seventy years wanderings of the future Jewish nation but Turkey, Syria and Egypt and countries beyond, in particular the Greek islands. They have even been associated with the Scandinavia and German peoples as their early kings were thought to be blond or golden-haired. Indeed, contemporary pictures of the Israelites show quite distinct ethnic types. It cannot be denied that the Hittite influence in the areas of the 12 tribes and far beyond Palestine was enormous. I am not confusing the Hittites here with the Hivites as so often is the case but even the Hivites were widely spread as a people and language group. It was the time of the great Migration of Nations similar to what we may be experiencing again today.

The Children of Israel were part of a multi-racial setting
The point I am seeking to make here is that the early, multi-racial Children of Israel were thrust into an international setting to live out God's international Covenant and their witness as ambassadors of the Truth to the nations around them. To be a true People of God was always a matter of faith and not DNA and gene factors. God's Covenant of Grace was always multi-racial as it was for believers only and not for people of one nation or language. Abraham was not the genetic root of the People of God but his faith was. His genes were also inherited by

Ishmael and his descendants, many of whom profess the Muslim religion today. This is why the Early Church and our Reformers spoke of the Covenant of Grace as being always Christian from its very start and that Jerusalem, founded much later than Abraham, served as a type of the Christian New Jerusalem to come.

The early proto-Jews, as a body, failed to keep God's Covenant

History shows that these early Proto-Jews were not equal to the Covenantal call and at times had to be reminded of this by the foreigners amongst whom they dwelt who often understood the Covenant better than they did. We also see, however, that the Gentiles of the Covenant alongside and within the budding Jewish system also miserably failed to keep it. Like the Jewish failures, Gentile failures were commented on time and time again by the Jewish Prophets and the New Testament writers. As covenant breakers, there was no difference between Jews and Gentiles but it could be said that the former had the more responsibility as they had more revelation, a fact Paul points out. From the earliest times, however, it was clear to those who had eyes to see and ears to hear that the People of the Covenant were those who, like Enoch, Abraham and Job who were not Jews, trusted in God. God's Covenant was to Jews 'and also' Gentiles.[127] It is interesting to note that the English words 'and also' are an emphatic 'and', representing 'kai' in the Greek. We are thus talking about the same gospel for Jews and Gentiles. Paul is here speaking of the fact that 'there is no respect of persons with God.' He takes up the same theme in Romans 10 where he talks of the potter's power over the clay. Here he claims that the 'vessels of mercy' he has created are 'even us, whom he hath called, not of the Jews only but also of the Gentiles'.[128] The expressions 'of the Jews' and 'of the Gentiles' do not mean 'all the Jews' and 'all the Gentiles' but that God has chosen His 'vessels' out of the Jews and out of the Gentiles. It cannot have escaped the attention of the NCT contenders either that Paul's argument is set in a Pan-Testament context.

---

[127] Romans 2:9, 10.
[128] Romans 9:24.

Palestine seen from a Historical Perspective

Nowadays the distinctions drawn between the area occupied by the nation of Israel (as if this were not part of Palestine) and areas occupied by Palestinians (as if they did not overlap with areas claimed by Israel) are clearly historically and politically artificial. So, too, as far as biblical history and eschatology goes, they have no validity whatsoever. However, groundless theories concerning present political Israel are not merely found in the Dispensational and Premillennial Christian camps but also among various ancient Jewish sects many of which came into being as late as the seventeenth century. Indeed, it is clear these views of the Diaspora influenced the politics and religion in British thinking and it was Britain who held the mandate for Palestine until the founding of the two states Israel and Palestine whilst Jewish Zionists and land prospectors were at war with Palestinian inhabitants who had never fled their countries.

Multi-cultural Palestine

Historically Palestine is the name used for that part of the Middle East which was formerly populated by a large number of peoples of whom the Philistines appear to have been prominent. Indeed, the term 'Palestine' is merely an English translation of 'Philistine'. Historically Palestine sheltered not only various peoples who spoke and wrote Semitic languages but also a large number of peoples who spoke languages from other linguistic families in Palestinian kingdoms, principalities, dukedoms and confederate states hundreds of years before ever David united the Jewish tribes under his own Kingship and before ever Christians and Muslims arose in those lands. Subsequently, and throughout history, it became a joint home for ancient, pre-Jewish religions, Christians, Jews and Muslims alike as was foretold repeatedly in the Old Testament. So Palestine was never solely a Semitic area. Indeed, even today modern political Israel is a multi-national state and over 30 different languages are spoken there. Russian is, however, growing as a means of communication. My old Hebrew Professor Helmer Ringgren at Uppsala University told us students about his latest visit to Israel in preparation for which he had taken night school classes

159

in Ivrit,[129] he had greeted passers-by, shopkeepers and newspaper salespeople first in Hebrew, then in Ivrit but they had invariably answered in Russian. Hebrew is also becoming a dead language in German synagogues in two of which locally I found only Russian spoken and not even 'Ivrit'.

Modern Ivrit is not the language of the Torah

It is commonly thought amongst linguistic scholars that the Philistinians originally spoke an Indo-European language. Indeed, a number of words borrowed by the early Children of Israel during their encounters with Philistinians and Phoenicians belong to the Indo-Germanic language groups. Nowadays, 'loan words' in the Ivrit language greatly outnumber those derived from Hebrew roots. This has caused committees of purists to be set up to base modern Ivrit more on ancient Hebrew, giving the old words more flexibility in meaning. It is as if English speakers would strive to get back to Old Anglo-Saxon. The Norwegians tried this after they became independent from Denmark and Sweden but it caused a Babel of confusion. The modern effort to make Ivrit more antiquated will probably not work out either as no one knows what 'Ancient Semitic Hebrew' was really like and the very limited vocabulary of biblical Hebrew words preserved in the Old Testament and other ancient documents cannot express the thoughts of a modern language of many thousands of words. Old Anglo-Saxon has only developed into the tongues of the English, Germans and Dutch by absorbing a majority of loan-words from any different international sources. This is the only way to go for Ivrit.

I have had first-hand experience through many years of watching the modern development of Norwegian which has sought to go back to Old Norse to make it free of Danish and Swedish influence. Rather than signifying a resurrection of old words, it has led to a complete linguistic reconstruction and a great instability in both the written and spoken languages isolated one population group from another. In my time of speaking and reading Norwegian Bokmål and reading Nynorsk (mainly poetry) since the 1950s both languages have changed radically and local

---

[129] I attended the beginning of these lectures, hoping that it would help my fluency in Biblical Hebrew, but quickly realized that Ivrit taught by the citizen of Israel was further off from the language of the Bible than Dutch is from German.

dialects seem to have sprung up as variations throughout the country. Where I heard and used three words for 'not' (inte, ikke, ej) in the fifties, to give one example, there are now at least ten words to express the one English term. When I mention this to Norwegian friends, they merely say 'Ord kommer og går'[130] and tell me that each Norwegian speaks his own language. I see this being the linguistic future of Israel. Babel is still in progress. A worse case is that of the Swedish Lapps. When I taught scripture at a Samë (the then word for the Lapp People) Nomad School, the children spoke at least four different Samë languages and children in the North spoke two more. Since my time trying to learn the original languages with over 28 cases, the Scandinavian governments have forced a new Same language on the Samë people (now called 'Sami') which is a Babel and 'dumbing down' of all the other Lapp languages mixed up. This has cut off the Lapps from their old literature and culture. Let us trust that Ivrit will not go the same way! Modern Israel badly needs the ancient Torah in the original language.

No word so misused as 'Semitic'
However, there is hardly a word as misused as 'Semitic' in modern political jargon. The term technically refers to the family of languages and dialects including Arabic, Hebrew, Aramaic, Amharic, Tigrinya, Syriac, and even Maltese though the latter is now in Latin script. We must also include many ancient Palestinian languages such as chronologically parallel Ugaritic without going into problems of which were the older languages. It does appear that peoples, like the Jews, who took on Semitic languages most likely had used other languages before they became Semitic speakers. There is much evidence of this both in the Old and New Testaments. Most modern older Israelis of today had not Ivrit as their native mother tongue. The Babylonian Exile and Greek and Roman occupations have also naturally altered the ancient language of the Jews, not to mention the music and terms for instruments. Since the founding of modern Palestinian Israel, English, French and especially Russian have influenced Ivrit immensely and taken over Hebrew terms.

---

[130] Words come and go.

161

Many modern Jews know neither Hebrew nor Ivrit

On a recent visit to the grave of Professor Fried, my old Jewish instructor in Linguistics at Duisburg University, I found his grave surrounded by Russian-speaking Jews donned in praying scarves and scull caps. When they saw me studying the Hebrew inscription, they asked me if I could kindly translate the words for them as they knew no Hebrew. I then visited a synagogue in Berlin which displayed old vocalized texts and newer unvocalized ones. On being encouraged to ask questions concerning the artefacts displayed by the synagogue guide, apparently the only German speaker employed by the synagogue in the middle of Berlin, I asked in German for an explanation why recent texts were unvocalized though older forms in the exhibition were vocalized. The lady confessed that her congregation only spoke Russian and only a few spoke German or English but none knew Hebrew. She confessed to not understanding the texts she presented to us for study at all! I treasure the Jewish heritage both in language and religion but many German synagogues are run as social clubs for 'Jews' who use the name but not the linguistic traditions. This means they cannot read the Torah. How did they manage their Bar Mitzvah?

Muslims are branded as 'Anti-Semitic' in the Western world

So, too, throughout history, there have been numerous languages which have used a Semitic script but belonged to other language groups. A more modern example is Turkish which has changed its script several times. English, too, has so changed that most people cannot even read Middle English today, let alone the language of the Doomsday Book. In other words, modern allegations of Anti-Semitism amongst Muslims need to be explained more carefully as they probably refer to an anti-Israel or anti-Jewish position but are certainly not anti-Semitic. A large percent of today's Muslims are Semitic and some Semitic peoples ruled in Palestine long before the Jews were established as a nation. The situation has become most precarious here in Germany where people who criticize some of the policies of the present Israeli regime, like this writer, are immediately branded 'Anti-Semitic'. I have no respect for people who are anti-Jewish but I am, at times in disagreement concerning modern Israel's land-policies. Their building of double roads with a wall between for on the one side Jewish and on the other side Muslim cars and their policies in Hebron are cases in point. I do not equate modern Israel with ancient Israel apart from the fact that some of their territories overlap with the Israel of forty years under David's precarious rule. To say this in certain present-day German circles, one is branded as a 'Nazi'. Indeed, I have been called a Nazi by a number of English, American and Australian Zionistic Christian 'friends' for claiming that the Jewish faith is not a matter of ethnic background.

Hebrew is not the oldest language of the world
It is usually thought amongst Christians that Hebrew is the oldest language in the world and was spoken from Adam's days on. Egyptian, Arabic and Aramaic are demonstrably older than Hebrew and possibly Ugaritic. We must therefore allow for the strong likelihood that most of these peoples and nations, including those who became 'Children of Israel' took on Semitic languages as second languages or kept to their own languages. Some of the oldest Old Testament texts are in languages which are probably older than Hebrew. Thus, neither Jewish people in general nor citizens of the present state of Israel can claim a monopoly on the title 'Semitic'. This goes also for non-Jewish Palestinians and Muslims. Nevertheless, the quirks of politics are often without logic or reason and in present day politics behind much pseudo-religious ardour we find prominent statesmen and the media limiting the meaning of 'Semitic' to those speaking Ivrit in Israel or Jews in general and we find Semitic Muslims having to protest that they are not 'Anti-Semitic'. This fact, however, is changing the meaning of 'Anti-Semitic' in Germany. As the German solidarity with Jews is immense, and I believe rightly so, Islam is given the entire blame for being 'Anti-Semitic' which I feel is exaggerated, but politicians in the last few weeks before my writing are complaining of 'Muslim Bashing' (New German) and are now saying there is Anti-Semitism in Germany which has nothing to do with the Jews. However, most Muslims I have spoken to profess it is not Jews they hate but the present government of Israel which will not accept that Palestinians are also 'Semitic' and that they are also under the land promises of God.

When is a Jew not a Jew?

We must also take into consideration that there is no commonly accepted definition of who a 'Jew' is, not only in the world at large but also in modern Israel. Today's *Jüdische Allgemeine*[131] features an article explaining that the present State of Israel disagrees with the Diaspora as to who a Jew is. In recent times Jewish Tigrinya speakers have had great difficulty in finding acceptance in Israel and the status of Spanish, Russian and Yemeni Jews in Israel has even given rise to inter-Jewish racism. We now hear of Israeli politicians who claim Israel is a nation of 'white Jews'. They do not believe as Solomon's maid told the King that 'black is beautiful'![132]

The Algerian Jews and other North African ancient Jewish peoples can also be used as examples. These Jews who have fled their country in recent years are numbered at 25,000.[133] Of these, the vast majority have been refused a home in Israel but have been accepted by France and are supported there by grants from other European countries, including Germany who has a special debt to Jews world-wide and supports individual Jews and Jewish institutions with millions of Euros per year. One would think this is the least they can do given Germany's horrible past but it must be realized that almost none of the German tax-payers living today had anything whatsoever to do with the Shoah[134] but still feel they must place a protective hand over the Jews. Indeed, international funding of international Jews is way higher than Israel's funding of international Jewry. It is interesting to note that literally thousands of once-German Jews who for very good reasons took on British nationality are now, under the Brexit threat, seeking German citizenship again.

Defining who is a Jew is made difficult by post-Torah sects

The difficulty in defining what entails being a Jew has been caused by post-Torah rabbis in their liberal tendencies to place Jewish and Babylonian 'oral traditions' above the Torah. They use the Halacha[135] method whereby 613 commandments have been drawn up to regulate

---

[131] 06.02.2018, The organ of the Jewish community in Germany.
[132] Song of Solomon 1:5.
[133] WAZ, Tuesday, 6. Feb. 2018.
[134] Alternative spelling 'Schoa' another term for the Holocaust.
[135] Alternative spelling 'Halakhah' meaning 'law'.

the life of their Jewish followers. It cannot be denied that the Talmud which they use as a basis for their interpretations diverges greatly from the text of the Torah. It was these interpretations with which Jesus had to cope in his Sermon on the Mount. The so-called New-Covenant theologians claim Jesus is arguing against Moses here and introducing a new Law but Jesus is pointing out, rather, the folly of rabbinical interpretations leading away from the plain text of the Torah. This was the same argument found in the preparatory prophetical books in the Old Testament and Jesus verified their statements and showed where the Old Testament peoples had erred. Indeed, many of these Halacha interpretations have been used as a basis of further interpretations as if the first interpretations were not clear enough, each interpretation departing further from the Word of God.

Vaterjude and Mutterjude

One of these rabbinical traditions is that Jews must trace their ancestry through their mothers but even female rabbis tell me they agree there is no evidence for this in the Torah, nor can they place their finger on any firm historical basis apart from the fact someone started up with the idea at one time or another in the Diaspora. Of the various Talmuds in circulation since around the fifth century A.D., the Babylonian Talmud is the most popular amongst modern rabbis of this school and their followers are encouraged to study a page a day. This is strongly influenced by the philosophy of the Persian Zarathustra and the Persian Kabbalah.

Recently a most interesting film[136] has been made by a 32 year-old so-called 'Vaterjude' by the name of Dmitrij Kapitelman who has been rejected as a Jew because his mother was not a Jew though his father was. His Leipzig Jewish community has decided to follow the Halacha and keep to the 613 commandments as opposed to the Mosaic Law. Of course, the Old Testament as the New traces the descent of the Jews through the male line, though the female line is also used. The young 'Vaterjude' who by Providence was not born a 'Mutterjude' has shown all the difficulties people of the Jewish faith have in being recognized

---

[136] Meschugge oder was? Meschugge is Yiddish for 'crazy' or 'cracked' thus the title translated would be 'Crazy or what? The word is also used in German for 'mixed up' or 'confused'.

as Jewish and shows how Judaism is split into different sects which stand in stark opposition to one another. One lady Mr Kapitalman interviewed had, out of her passion for the Jewish faith, adorned herself with a modest David Star tattoo, only to be told that such a sign was forbidden to Jews and she, too, was struggling to receive recognition but would not have her star removed protesting that her star was her sign of being a Jew.

Political forces from abroad are putting strong pressure on German Jews to follow the Halacha, which is causing a world-wide struggle for Jews. If the Halacha wins, this could mean the end of the traditional, Old Testament, Jewish religion and a purging of Israeli Jews until only a legal new Babylonian captivity is left and Mosaic, Davidic Jews are extinguished.

The Karaite Jews

On the other hand, there still are the Karaite Jews who rely solely on the Torah for their religious views and therefore hold to a patrilineal descent for all Jews with the exception of proselytes. It is interesting to note that when, in the 17th century, John Durie and Samuel Hartlib, supported by many Anglicans, Independents, scientists and men of letters, formulated their exegetical cooperation with Jewish peoples, they put forward the Karaite Jews as a people willing to cooperate with them in searching the scriptures in their plans to set up a Department of Hebrew Studies in their planned University of London.[137]

The Samaritan Jews

Many citizens of modern Israel claim that especially the Samaritan Jews, who have peopled Palestine since long before the Babylonian Exile, are not true Jews, ethnically or according to their religion. Yet the Samaritans have claimed to be Jews for almost three thousand years and feel they are free from the alleged religious pollutions which other Jews underwent during the Babylonian exile. They are obviously a mixed people ethnically but it is hardly fair when modern Israelis of mixed blood look down their noses at them. It is their Halacha that is

---

[137] See my book *The Practical Divinity of Universal Learning: John Durie's Educational Pansophism*. See Chapter Five: 'The Place of the Jews in Durie's Quest for Universal Learning' and passim.

destroying Israel not the mixed blood of the Samaritans. We know from Jesus' words that there are 'Good Samaritans' and Jesus faced criticism by the over-conservatives in emphasizing this.

As far as the 'land rights' of people to a settlement in Palestine are concerned, the Samaritans have far stronger rights than the European Jews. Indeed, the Zionists who claimed they had a 3,000 year right to Palestine, based their claims on Samaritan occupation to prove that Jewish rights to Palestine were ancient. Now modern Israel, taking advantage of the Ugaritic Ras Shamra fable texts, claim that the Apiru people mentioned there is a reference to a nation of Jews in Palestine hundreds of years before Abraham. They however, reject most other poetic interpretations of Palestinian history recorded in these cuneiform poetical texts of uncertain history picking out what they feel strengthens their claims on wider Palestinian territories.

There is no one definition of a Jew
The fact is that there is no one definition of a Jew, or even an Israeli citizen. So, too, in states outside of Israel there are also many contradictory and conflicting theories concerning what genetically a 'Jew' is. Like the ancient Picts, some trace their Jewish lineage through their mothers, others through their fathers. As in the case of the Native Americans, many ethnologists discuss what percentage of blood makes an ethnic Jew just as they think in terms of half and quarter bloods etc., when speaking about the American Indians. It is also to be noted that Ivrit, the enforced language of the modern state of Israel is less a Semitic language than is either ancient or modern Arabic (with its many dialects) and is a modern, artificial language which has left many of its linguistic Hebrew roots, and even these may not have been originally Hebrew.

It is clear, however, that Jewry today has no common genetic factor to back it up ethnically. It is solely a group of religions using certain broad categories which are still not commonly agreed upon. They have nothing like the Covenant of Grace for God's People anchored in Christ's work of salvation. Since the Diaspora began forty years after the founding of the Jewish Kingship under David, there has been no one Jewish religion but a host of sects have sprung up similar to those within Christianity. On the surface, the Jews are not as split-up as the

Christians but their numbers are far, far less. So Jewry is neither an ethnic unity nor a religious whole.

Modern Israel cannot speak for world Jewry

It is interesting to note that though Israel, or rather her democratically elected politicians, often claim to represent world Jewry,[138] they have no rights whatsoever to such a bold claim. I can only refer my readers again to the most interesting article on world Jewry in the *Jüdische Allgemeine* referred to above which I have before me. The article points out there has been a growth of 8% amongst Jews in the last ten years. So rapidly are the Jews growing in numbers they now almost equal the number of Jews before the Shoah. This is amazing news considering the massive slaughter of Jews by the Nazis throughout the hideous Second World War. But where exactly are these Jews now?

There are an estimated 5.7 million Jews in the U.S.A.; 475,000 in France, 385,000 in Canada; 290,000 in the U.K.; 200,000 in Germany and 180,000 in Russia. There are also Jews in many other countries of which I have no reliable statistics. So here we have a Jewish population outside of Israel which is far more numerous than the 6.1 million Jews registered in Palestinian Israel. So, too, with the present Israeli state wishing to cancel Israeli citizenship for those they claim are non-Jews, the population will surely shrink. So how can that small, artificial Palestinian state claim to represent the Jews? Furthermore, there are several Jewish political parties in Israel who do not accept their present Prime Minister's view of what 'Israel' entails. Even Benjamin Netanyahu's own Likud party disagrees with his stance concerning a two state compromise between Jews and the other Palestinians. Indeed, the Israeli government has been warned recently by the European Union's foreign ministers and representatives that 'the present Israeli government is not Israel, though she likes to claim this.'[139]

Anti-Israel is neither anti-Jewish nor anti-Semitic

Nor is Anti-Israel the same as Anti-Jewish. In my teens I helped out in a Jewish hospital in Leeds, England, and two Jewish boys were my best friends. They were attached to the Progressive Synagogue near Busby's

---

[138] Depending on which party is in power.
[139] WAZ, Thursday, 1. Feb., 2018. 'Halbherzige Annäherung'.

in Bradford where many members were strongly opposed to the setting up of the artificial state of Israel. They protested that the Zionists had given up their Messiah and were putting their hope in horses, chariots and political demi-gods instead. Those 'strict Jews' under the leadership of Rabbi Jacobs who came into Yorkshire in my early teens, mostly from Eastern Europe spoke of a Messiah Israel which they wished to found. For them an Israeli state was the Messiah and certainly not Jesus. This is obviously not the traditional Jewish religion. However, because of the slump in the textile trade nearly all the Jewish families I knew in Yorkshire up to my adulthood left Leeds and Bradford, not for Israel but for America. America was their 'Promised Land' as it was in the seventeenth century for many. I noticed this exodus of the Jews also as a student in London. Wigmore Hall, where I occasionally attended concerts, was once almost a Jewish Concert Hall but gradually new-rich 'Christians' took over as the Jews left for America.

Summing Up
The 'Children of Israel' led by Moses out of Egypt were already of mixed origin before their period of social acceptability and then slavery in Egypt. After generations, those who were culled from the North, South, East and West of Egypt, as David relates, left that vast country in company with a large contingent of Egyptians. These exiles were told to cross many borders where they often, mostly against God's Covenant commands, married foreigners of other religions and had children by them. Some nations, such as the Philistines on the Gaza coastal area were not included in the land promises though present Israel now occupies most of their country. As the original mixed nationalities of exiles died out during the Seventy Years of trials, the idea of twelve tribes had become a mere matter of organization and administration such as the early Scottish clans. Exactly what language or dialect the early settlers spoke is not certain. Some of the peoples whom they absorbed spoke Indo-Germanic languages. What is certain is that the language spoken and written by the Exiles was different to that of our Hebrew Bibles. So, too, the Covenant of Grace which was revealed before, during and after the Exiles' wanderings, was to all peoples as God had promised Abraham. It was always a Christian Covenant as it

169

pointed to faith in the Messiah which was far older than the establishment of Israel as a nation and was always for both 'Jews' and 'Greeks' alias Gentiles.

Nowadays, the territories claimed by the State of Israel as their biblical right have no biblical, historical, or political foundation. The country in which the Children of Israel settled had also been settled by other children of Abraham for hundreds of years before them. What we now call Palestine, including the relatively new state of Israel was always an international territory with a number of languages spoken, several being also Semitic so to limit the terms 'Semitic' or 'Anti-Semitic' to citizens of Israel or Jews in general has neither a political or linguistic basis. So, too, the modern ever-changing linguistic structure called 'Ivrit' was, of course, never spoken in Palestine, nor developed until after the founding of the present state of Israel. This new language has already lost a number of linguistic factors common to traditional Semitic languages, even given that they, too, are always changing.

Though it is possible to roughly define what a Semitic language is, defining who a 'Jew' is becomes much more difficult. Here modern Israel, which represents a minority of world-wide Jews is in strong disagreement with the Jewish Diaspora, though Israel claims to speak for all Jews, forgetting the Non-Jews amongst them. Modern pronouncements from official Israeli sources concerning colour and countries of origin of many professing Jews would be deemed racist and *apartheid* in the countries of the West as leading European politicians such as Foreign Minister Sigmar Gabriel have pointed out.

So, too, much modern Jewish thinking is based on the Babylonian Talmuds and other extra-biblical sources so that those Jews who keep to the Torah have a different religion to those who keep to the Halacha, the latter being outside the tenor of the Covenant of Grace. The result is that many so-called Jews have now placed themselves outside of the eternal promises made to Abraham and Moses. This had already become evident whilst Jesus was on the Mount and had to distinguish between what Moses said and meant and what certain scribes said and meant. Thus Dispensationalist and Christian Zionist statements referring to the hope that 'all Jews shall be saved' do not distinguish between the Mosaic Law which was added to the Covenant promises to Abraham and the 615 laws of the Babylonian sect which pay only lip-service to the Jewish faith and Old Testament understanding of the Covenant of Grace.

To be anti-Israel because of disagreements with their politics has thus little to do with being anti-Jewish which far, far fewer are. Israel's present propaganda claiming that criticism of them is criticism of the Diaspora often places Jews in other countries in a situation of being misunderstood. Indeed, the majority of Jews are still looking for a peaceful home outside of Israel and many have indeed found it in the Diaspora until they hear of the Messiah's approach.

Chapter 7

Historical And Political Ideas Of A 'Promised Land'

The search for an eternal Jewish Home

The idea of a geographical Promised Land has remained with the Jews since long before the Christian era. Surprisingly, however, this was not related specifically to the Near East until relatively modern times. Indeed, even today not all Jews by any means are united about how their imaginary or expected Promised Land could be constituted. I agree thoroughly with many Jews of the Diaspora when they object to the rulers of Palestinian Israel speaking as if they represent world Jewry. Many Jews outside of modern Israel look on that state as a mere part of the Diaspora as there is nothing of the spirituality of the Davidic kingdom to give it any truly Jewish identification. The majority of the Jews of the Diaspora have thus not followed the political call to populate that part of Palestine now claimed contrary to history and God's Covenant with old Israel as 'Israel Regained'. Indeed, I often think it more the idea of would-be Christians, especially those in the United States of America who wish to see a new Temple built in Jerusalem and the suppression of both Mohammedans and even Christians as all the world becomes Jewish. This is not what the Prophets claimed New Jerusalem would be like. The big puzzle also about modern Israel is that so many international Jews are not accepted in Israel today so how can modern political Israel be said to be the Kingdom of the Jews?

England was once thought to be the Jewish 'Promised Land'
The early Zionism of the seventeenth century looked to many other areas in the world where they might set up a kingdom in a free country where peace, mercy and justice for all reigned. Menasseh Ben Israel in the seventeenth century saw England as 'The Promised Land', not Israel, as did many Puritans and people of the Great Awakening. Still today, in their 'National Hymn' British people often sing Blake's early 19th century words:

> I will not cease from mental fight,
> Nor shall my sword sleep in my hand
> Till we have built Jerusalem
> In England's green and pleasant land.

Indeed, it was quite common at one time for both Christians and Jews to call Britain 'The New Jerusalem' and Blake's words have become something of a national hymn today. Menasseh Ben Israel claimed the English kingship was Davidic agreeing with many Welsh Christians and he even believed Cromwell might possibly be the expected Messiah. Many Jews in Germany rested their eschatological hopes on the state of Hessen, the first German state to become Reformed and set up a Reformed University at Marburg where the Professor for Hebrew Studies examined me on David's view of the Covenant for my Doctorate in Divinity. Indeed, Christian sects in Saxony claimed that Saxons were 'Isaac's sons' and the British Israelites found their roots in that movement.

When it was reported in 1649 that the 'ten lost tribes' were gathering in America, Menasseh and his followers thought America might be the promised land after all. Reading letters to editors in American Jewish newspapers has convinced me that such people exist even today, looking to the Native Americans as the alleged 'Lost Tribes'. Indeed, Jews in the seventeenth century from all over Europe were examining possible countries for re-settlement amongst the Chinese, Tartars, Cumanians, Scythians, the Welsh and the Irish. Some even campaigned to apply to 'The Queen of the Amazons' so they might gather together as one people in South America. None of these Jewish Messianic movements considered a state for Jews only but merely a state where religious freedom was maintained and it was the English Millennialists, not the 17th century Jews, who thought of deporting the Jews back to troubled Israel so they would not trouble England.

This writer's lengthy studies of Jewish Messianic movements in the 17th century convinced him most of these Jews were not fanatics but scholarly representatives of internationalism and religious tolerance. Many of their writings were hardly distinguishable from biblical, Christian works from the same period. There was also a common interest amongst them to join the Christians in 'searching the scriptures'. This led John Durie and Samuel Hartlib to argue for the setting up of a 'Jewish' College as part of a planned London University. All the colleges were to be open to all and students were expected to move freely from college to college in search of 'Universal Learning'. Durie was confident that Christian exegesis would be vastly improved by listening to Jewish Hebrew scholars in preparation to educating the world to be ready for Christ's Second Advent and the restitution of all things. My own interest in Hebrew was greatly fostered by most loveable Rabbis in Yorkshire and London who were strongly against the setting up of a militant Israeli State in Palestine where war and not peace reigned.

Re-settlement of Jews in a favourable country was an English idea
In 17th century Britain, some 'Christian' churchmen and politicians believed that Jews could help the British economy and thus should be allowed citizenship providing they paid double taxes as so many international Jews saw Britain as their 'Promised Land', anyway. They were thought of as second-class citizens who might help the Commonwealth budget. Jews who visited England were told, however, that if they were given permission to settle, their legal rights would be curbed and they would not be able to appear as witnesses in court or take on state appointments. The official state-church of Cromwell, firmly under military hand, voted against giving the Jews a New Eden in Britain. It is thus often forgotten that most of the pioneers for re-settling persecuted Jews in Palestine were not Jews but professing

'Christians' who were against them settling in Great Britain. Even proto-Baptist Henry Jessey, for instance, one of my theological heroes, thought mostly how the Jews might profit the British economy and eventually gave up the idea and collected large sums of money to send Jews to Palestine. Unlike his friend John Durie who urged a Jewish settlement in England on German lines, Jessey became finally averse to them settling in Britain. The mass transport of Jews to Palestine after the Second World War was a development of this British project as Palestine was under British rule.

Seventeenth century attitudes to Jews were mainly Millennial
Most of the ideas for a 'Promised Land' propagated by British Christians showed very strong but also very divers and contradictory views concerning eschatology. Indeed, discussion concerning a home for the Jews became a millennium controversy and sparked off a number of eschatological theories based on the philosophies of the 17th century and not primarily on scripture. Most Christian support for Israel today seems still to be mainly of an eschatological character. John Durie, who invited Menasseh to England in the first place, condemned his brethren in the English churches for neglecting the present material and spiritual needs of Jews in order to enforce their own eschatological policies. Cromwell, at last followed Durie's advice, and became open to Jewish settlement and his Parliament finally approved of giving Jews the right to citizenship in Britain but the churches would not hear of it as the Protectorate, they claimed, was for 'Christians only'. So we cannot be too hard on modern Israel for arguing for a Jewish-only nation. However, the Cromwellian Church had a very narrow idea of what was 'Christian', just as many leading Israeli politicians have a very narrow idea of a 'white' Israel. Indeed, those Christians who were for religious freedom, mostly Anglicans and Independents, were criticized[140] by their hardliner brethren from so-called 'Presbyterian' parties. At present Israeli citizenship is open to Christians under quite complicated conditions. But, quite contrary to Israel's 1948 Declaration of Independence, the present Prime Minister of Israel is now threatening to drive through a bill to give national rights to Jewish citizens only. At present there are at least 20-25 per cent of Israeli citizens who are not

---

[140] Branded 'malignants and drunkards'.

'Jewish'. This number is growing as more and more secular Russians seek a home in Israel.

Palestine always international, multi-religious and multi-cultural
The fact is over the last four thousand years or so, Palestine has been internationally settled by scores of different peoples of different nationalities and religions. In modern times we can mention Turkey and Britain. Even hundreds of years before Christ, Palestine was an international centre of trade to the occident, orient, septentrion and meridian[141] with sea and land routes radiating out to the four corners of the known earth. Peoples like the Philistines and Phoenicians traded with the British Isles and it appears Greece, Italy and Turkey were founded by invaders and settlers from Palestine as also were most likely the ancient Etruscans. Indeed, years before the coming of Christ, tin, lead, chalk, Fuller's earth, cattle and even dogs from Britain were traded throughout Europe, Asia and Africa by dwellers in Palestine. So, too, the languages of Palestine spread throughout the known world. Languages using a Greek alphabet are as ancient as those using a Semitic alphabet in the Palestinian regions. The Philistines themselves are said to have spoken a kind of Proto-Greek. We know that many kingdoms and confederation of states existed in Palestine over 1500 years before Christ and 1 Chronicles chapter 1 provides us with a long list of kingdoms, principalities and dukedoms before ever the Jews set up a kingdom under Saul and David.

Yet there has never been a lasting definition of how large or small the Palestinian area was supposed to be and in exactly what area they were in or how great their populations were. We know from scripture that dukedoms such as Edom, after the proto-Jewish Exodus from Egypt were at times part of the league of nations which were to become Davidic but left that confederacy after a short time. We must also not forget that in the pre-New Testament era there was a great wandering of peoples from countries surrounding Palestine, especially from the North to the South. Indeed, Israel itself was really a UN of twelve nations which we call the Amphictyonic League. The only rule that kept

---

[141] The last two terms for 'north' and 'south' are now going out of fashion but the terms 'orient' and 'occident' are not following them. This is one of the many whims of language development.

these twelve tribes together was that of a Covenant which united them off and on until the end of David's material Kingship and before their separation into Israel and Judea. During this time, there were many prophesies of an eternal Davidic Kingdom but which had little to do with material Israel and much to do with the lasting spiritual Israel of God. Old Jerusalem of the unbelieving priesthood was condemned as a 'dead covenant' and the New International Jerusalem was again placed in its stead. All this was, however, many hundreds of years before the birth of Christ. This fact will be taken up in more detail in my last chapter as it has to do with the glorious future of the People of God.

Israel has no valid historical or religious claim to sole possession of Palestine or any parts of it
Thus modern claims concerning an alleged historic ownership of any of the territory from either the present day state of Israel or those people now called Palestinians must be examined most critically. What is historically, geographically and politically true is that Israelis are as much Palestinians as are the so-called Palestinians though each side has difficulties in acknowledging the truth of this statement concerning the other side. Indeed, most of present day Jews in Israel are of European stock who immigrated to Palestine from the end of the 19th century onwards, initially through the Zionistic movement, though this came in drops rather than as an inrushing torrent. It was not until 1947/8 that a United Nations edict opened up mass deportation and emigration to a part of Palestine for the Jews. Though this has been seen as an act of God as God rules over history, it was also an attempt by the war-torn nations to rid Europe of a most difficult problem.

Artificial Israel was then given the same rights as the Palestinian Muslims and various other peoples and religions and three separate states were planned dividing Palestine largely into an Arab State, a Jewish State and the City State of Jerusalem. The Kingdom of Jordan, also part of ancient Palestine, agreed to this transaction. At least, that is what our school history books tell us. Jerusalem, therefore, was an explicit exception within this land participation. It was to be a 'No Man's Land' or rather an 'Everybody's Land' and was to remain an international centre for Christians, Jews and Muslims. This was coming very near to the Prophets preaching concerning the New Jerusalem after they had written off the Old.

The settlement of the Jews in Palestine was bound to cause trouble
Neither the Jews nor the Arabs were satisfied with this arrangement.
The Jews wanted more land, the Arabs did not want to give up parts of
their own land and both groups wanted Jerusalem. Recently, there was
a flood of protest caused by an American unilateral breech of this UN
mandate, followed quickly by Israel who has often played the part of a
'yes man' to the North Americans. It was declared by a country proud
of acting independently that Jerusalem should be taken over as the
capital of Israel and seat of the U.S. Embassy. There was a world-wide
negative reaction to be seen in the headings of many articles and Letters
to the Editor in most European newspapers and many TV news
programmes. The common feeling was that 'Jerusalem belongs to us
all'. These reactions were based on the clear United Nations mandate
given to the new Palestinian Jewish state and to the other Palestinians.
This mandate has now been broken.

The reasons for the UN's settling the Jews in Palestine did not please
all members in 1947/8 but the reaction of the UN to the United States
political blunder this year[142] was quite unanimous. Jerusalem must
remain a free and holy city for Christians, Jews and Muslims alike and
a centre for world peace. We remember that Melchizedek was likened
to the Son of God and was not only King of Righteousness but also
King of Peace and King of Jerusalem. Here was a clear Messianic
prophecy. This was proclaimed hundreds of years before Jerusalem
passed into Amphyctionic possession and Israel was founded.[143]
Western interference has long dictated what policies Israel ought to
have and both this dominance over Israel and Israel's private
interpretation of it has caused many Near East troubles. We should all
follow David's example who kept up the Covenant though with major
failings: 'Pray for the peace of Jerusalem: they shall prosper that love
thee.'[144]

---

[142] 2018.
[143] Hebrews 7:1ff.
[144] Psalm 122:6.

Modern Israel claims to occupation rights over Palestine

The displaced Jews entering Palestine after the Second World War named their new host-country at first 'Judah', thinking of the great and ancient Jewish tribe from which the Messiah, the 'Lion of Judah' would come. However, Zionistic Messianic thinking soon gave way to nationalism, patriotism and political dissatisfaction leading to warfare and land-grabbing. These were some of the reasons why the name 'Israel' was finally agreed on. This name was formerly given to Jacob indicating that he had 'wrestled with God'. Israel was now to take up this battle. 'Israel' had formerly been the name of David's kingdom which soon lost tribes through internal disagreement. Even David's sons quarrelled with David and with one another and after a mere forty years a group calling themselves 'Judah' and one claiming the name of 'Israel' formed two separate Jewish states. Jerusalem, however, was in Judah and not Israel. The name 'Israel' was finally chosen for the 1947/8 deported Jews because Israel had been larger than Judah and there was a strong urge present to set up again the Kingdom of David within the boundaries he had conquered during his long reign but which were quickly lost.

A 'Promised Land' of unkept promises

Modern Israel apparently wishes to outdo even David and has turned Israel from being a Promised Land into becoming a highly armoured warrior nation. Israel's modern claims, too, go far beyond what God gave the Children of Israel at the end of their decades-long wanderings. The fact that this kingdom disintegrated after a few decades apparently interested few but it became a peg on which to hang further land-claims. Similarly I have met British, Dutch, French, Canadians, Chinese and Germans who still think they hold rights to their lost colonies!

A longing for allegedly lost power and rights

Much of these old biblical territories, however, were in the hands of the old Palestinians and, in anticipation of the Declaration of Independence, Jewish forces were fighting Palestinians in order to gain more territory before the settlement was even sanctioned by the UN. Egypt entered then into the inner-Palestine disputes by attacking Israel from the air on the very first evening of the new state. However, Israel stubbornly entered a war of expansion which was far from merely defensive, occupying Palestinian territories. This occupation continues and is constantly spreading and has led to Israel's action being called 'the lengthiest military occupation in modern times'. Israel has not learnt from her own past when she was the underdog. Many former imperialistic UN states such as Britain, France, Germany and Holland were to lose great areas once belonging to them or colonized by them but not having learnt from their own blundering histories of their risings and fallings, they gave Israel a free hand to spread such old imperialism. There was no universal protest at the folly of the Jews as the world had shown enough folly themselves throughout the Second World War. It is certain, however, that though the blame for a troubled Palestine is placed at the feet of either Jewish Israel or Arab Palestine, much of the blame must rest on the Western world for thrusting on the Jews and Arabs alike a yoke which neither the one nor the other could carry. For a foreign power to create three new artificial states in an area where war was predominant must have been the worst diplomatic act of the 20th Century and a blunder unlikely to be put right before the Lord comes.

Looking back to Father Abraham

Looking back into the origins of the Palestinian situation, it is surely of great interest to note that the three peoples representing the three religions Christian, Islamic and Jewish, in order of present size, all trace their descent to one man who was technically and historically neither a Jew, a Christian nor a Muslim. This was Abraham whose God-given name means 'Father of Nations'. Many take the term 'nations' to mean political states but many Christians believe that true descent from Abraham is to be considered spiritually rather than nationally and politically because through the same faith which Abraham had according to the Bible, one becomes a member of the People of God. The present political understanding represented by Israel at this time appears to be purely secular and is not based on a bilateral interpretation of God's Covenant with a faithful Israel, nor indeed with the Messiah. So Abraham can be called the *first Christian* to be named in scripture as he foresaw and believed in Christ and solely for this reason was called 'righteous' and the patriarch of the People of God.[145] It was thus

---

[145] Galatians 3:6.

181

obvious from the start that all peoples would be called the People of God who followed His God-given Covenant with Abraham. This Covenant was not merely a land covenant promising prosperity under certain conditions but a means of God choosing out a People for Himself. These conditions were admittedly impossible for fallen man to fulfil but we Christians believe that our Messiah, Jesus Christ, laid these conditions on Himself on our behalf and He was always the Keeper of the Covenant in place of His people from whatever colour, class or creed they might have belonged to formerly. As I shall seek to show, the same conditions were applicable to both Jews and Gentiles as we read clearly in both Testaments. The People of God were always those who trusted in the Messiah and found their salvation in Him.

Are there true Jews in Palestinian Israel?
Now one may argue that the Jews have the same claim as Christians on Abraham as their father, at least those Jews who are still looking for a Messiah who descends through his spiritual seed. There are such Jews in Israel today but they certainly do not make up the majority of Israel's citizens. They are a remnant. The Israeli system is clearly, at present, anti-Christian. I say 'at present', because I believe that God will work wonders amongst the Jews as the Elect are gathered in from whatever nation. Whilst learning Hebrew in Bradford and London, I was aided by Jewish Rabbis who loved their Messiah. They were very suspicious of UN leaders who stove to rid themselves of the 'Jewish' problem through their mass deportation from Western countries. The only difference between those Messianic Jews and me in our love for the Old Testament was that my Messiah had graciously come to me and I could only hope and pray that He would come to them. This is all the more urgently necessary as present non-Messianic Israel, a child of the mainly secular Western world, is facing the threat of war sponsored and financed more from without the realm rather than from within. The rot of Harold Lindseyism amongst so-called Christians is not called 'Political Zionism' for nothing.

Many churches are forbidding the evangelization of the Jews
It has sadly now become the practice of European churches to forbid the evangelization of the Jews. It appears they feel that any pressure on the Jews to turn to their Messiah would be 'Anti-Semitic'. Jewish

evangelism is banned in my country and our politicians wish to ban also the evangelisation of the Muslims and want a politically controlled pulpit, just like Hitler did. Many Muslims are coming to Christ in Germany at the present time. Most are converted in the State Churches but quickly move to the Free Churches for political and eschatological reasons, besides religious ones.

Unlike the old Christian missions to the Jews, which grew out of a genuine evangelistic desire to see the saving gospel preached to all men and women, the modern benevolent attitude to Jews from those who consider their welfare is often based on speculative pseudo-Christian eschatological and political grounds rather than biblical arguments, theological understanding and plain common sense. So, too, present Israel's claims that they are Abraham's successors and heirs of land rights allegedly promised to him unconditionally are national and political rather than Biblical, spiritual or even religious. On the other hand, few Christians have land claims on Israel today, though they possessed parts of the land for very many hundreds of years. Their claims are eschatological focused on the time of Christ's return when He comes to judge the quick and the dead. These claims, it is believed, they will share with believing Jews in an international world-wide revival of true religion. Many Christians hold this to be an event which will start initially in Palestine and end before God's Heavenly throne. To them, Israel is seeking to ban Millennium fulfilments. My position is that the New Jerusalem which will meet Jesus at His Second Coming, is a description of all true believers everywhere and always was. This is fully in accordance with the preaching of the Prophets who speak of an international New Jerusalem of believers from all over the world. This will be looked into further at the end of this book when I write of the Great Harvest.

Christian Zionists want no peace in Jerusalem
It is also clear to see that Christian Zionists have also dropped the idea of peace coming to Jerusalem and actually have the effrontery to rejoice when they feel Israel and the Muslims are about to wage war over Jerusalem. They expect Christ to come with conquering armies with massive bloodshed just as did those whom Christ disappointed at His

First Coming.[146] Christ's emphasis that His Kingdom is not of this world[147] still falls on many deaf ears. In my long Christian life, I have met scores, if not hundreds, of Christians who seem to have a quarrel with God because they are not born Jews but are merely born-again Christians. They do not believe that the boundary line between Jews and Gentiles is annulled in Christ through His Messianic Covenant with True Israel and the New Jerusalem with its City of God, true Sion. They actually believe that secular Jews are superior in redeemed status to born-again Messianic covenant-keepers and Christ will give them special privileges denied to 'Christians'. This, of course is the zealous political Jewish thinking of the seventeenth century East European and Dutch sects and not biblical and experimental thinking.

Summing Up

The Jews have always been called a restless people because of their permanent hope that a Promised Land would one day be theirs. Traditionally, after the Temple was destroyed and earthly Jerusalem sacked the Jews looked for their Promised Land here, there and everywhere. Over the centuries hope has been raised in Jewish hearts for such a land of peace and security in Asia, Europe, the New World and South America only to end in disappointment. Some would have settled for a political state offering them maximum protection, others looked around the world for the signs of a Davidic state. In the seventeenth century there was general revival of this hope, coupled with eschatological fantasies amongst both professing Jews and professing Christians. These theories which were neither biblically nor traditionally Jewish, nor biblically and traditionally Christian, still hinder our conception of the New Jerusalem as outlined throughout the Old and New Testaments. Gradually, false millennial hopes of Christion Zionists encouraged the Western world to campaign for a re-settlement of the Jews in Palestine as the European States began to show them less and less tolerance. Sadly, England led the way insisting she must remain 'Christian'. This is similar to modern Israeli behaviour in insisting that Israel is for Jews only.

---

[146] This author realises that there are many other theories.
[147] John 18:36.

However, unlike most of the Western world at the time, Palestine was almost always a territory of tolerance and openness to other peoples with other religions. It was also always a multi-national area. So, too, the Jews had lost the emphasis on the Covenant of Grace for all peoples and the responsibility of preaching this to the nations so they were ill-equipped from the start to be artificially placed in a new homeland to which they had no historical, biblical or political claim. Furthermore, those peoples who had traditionally sought peace and waged wars with their neighbours whom they had known for centuries were now invaded by a warring mixture of Jews from many countries who were total strangers to the mentality of the area but united by religious and political ideas that now they had come into their traditional 'rights'. However, they soon extended even these dubious 'rights' in their land-grabbing mentality and turned what ought to have been the people of the Prince of Peace into a warrior nation.

In these quarrels to 'win back' what they thought had always been unconditionally theirs, the new settlers forgot that according to their own Torah other peoples had land rights which were to be respected and other peoples could trace their natural lineage back to Abraham as well as they. Furthermore Jewish land rights had always been conditional on their keeping the Covenant but the lands given to the Ishmaelites and related tribes were totally free of such conditions. The promise of God all along was that the Messiah, Christ His Son, would fulfil all the conditions for all believers in His Covenant. This truth is still rejected by the modern state of Israel. That spiritual blindness is still on Israel might appear obvious to many but Paul tells us this is only in part.[148] But what shall we say of the total blindness shown by a large body of so-called Christians to the Jewish people? All who reject the Covenant of Grace whether Jew or Gentile are sadly still spiritually blind. But Western European churches, such as ours in Germany have forbidden the evangelization of the Jews and especially North America is investing great sums in Israel to revive their old religion which the Prophets condemned. They are even working to set up a new Jewish Temple of types and shadows. This is a blatant rejection of the true tenor of its symbolic teaching that the Church herself is the Temple of

---

[148] Romans 11:25.

the Holy Spirit to which the Old Temple pointed. How can the Jews ever hope for salvation when it is denied them by so many Harold-Linseyites and so-called Christian eschatological dukkering steeped in secular and pagan millennial myths?

Chapter 8

Modern Israel Is Not The Sion Of The Bible

Deportation of Jews to Palestine in 1947/8 was neither a Palestinian nor a Jewish initiative

It must be said repeatedly that the partitioning of Palestine was not a decision made by the dwellers in Palestine concerning their own future but enforced upon them by Colonial powers. The Turks had occupied large parts of Palestine for most questionable reasons and the British had ousted the Turks on equally dubious grounds. International organisations who represented mostly Western interests decided that in order to bring peace to the West, those Jews in Europe not murdered by Nazi rule should be given freedom elsewhere; thus using the Jews as pawns in the Western strategic game of chess. Britain realized that colonizing Palestine with its mixed peoples was too big for their boots, so took the opportunity to pass the buck on to the U. N. and Jews of the Diaspora to see what good they could bring the area. Europe may have gained some peace this way but certainly not Palestine. However, the Christian British soldiers on leave from Palestine who spoke in the Bradford churches and youth clubs I attended around 1947/8 certainly believed the British solution for deporting Jews to Palestine was of eschatological value to both Jews and Christians. Indeed, the soldiers spoke of Messianic ideas which I later found out were originally propagated by European Messianic Jews in the seventeenth century and did not arise from the Bible or the Christian faith. The Muslims were never mentioned but much was said about all Israel now having a chance to be 'saved' and led by Christ against the rest of the world. Muslims did not interest them. The idea scared me at the time and still does. After the Second World War this Harold Lindseyism, featuring dispensational Zionism, became popular in reducing the Bible to an Old Moore's Almanac which prophesied an end to the Peace of Jerusalem.

The claims of Muslims on Palestine
Now we must look at the claims of Muslims to possess the land of Palestine. They are based both on firm historical grounds of thousands of years of settlement in Palestine but also, as in the case of the Jews, on their alleged physical descent from Abraham. A religious connection, as we shall see, is offered but this lacks sure historical verification as do Jewish claims. The 'Christian' West has been most unfair to the Muslims in that though the Jews clearly trace the evolution and development of themselves back to Abraham which is accepted by many Christians, Muslims who bring up the same claims are not taken seriously by either Jews or Christians. We must not forget, however, that Abraham lived 450-480 years before the short-lived Jewish nation came on the scene and over a thousand years before Islam became an established religion. Still, it is strange that Christians have traditionally been sympathetic to Jewish claims but antagonistic to land claims from Muslims. Both Israeli Jews and those Palestinians living within and without Israel would both be really surprised if they allowed themselves to be ruled by what scripture actually says about their predicament. Muslim claims are the least respected in our Christian circles and sadly not respected at all within modern nationalistic, patriotic Israeli politics. This is obvious when one examines present Israeli-US diplomacy.

Ishmael and the Muslims
Many Muslim land claims in Palestine are centred on the figure of Ishmael, Abraham's first-born via Sarah's Egyptian maidservant Hagar. Modern Muslims regard Ishmael as a prophet and a forefather of Mohammed and founder of Mecca and builder of the Kaaba. In some Muslim traditions, Ishmael is confused with Isaac and it is said that Abraham wished to sacrifice Ishmael and not Isaac. This, however, does not fit in with mainline Christian, Jewish or Muslim teaching. What

most Christian, Jewish and even Muslim teachers tend to disregard is God's land promises to Ishmael according to Old Testament accounts which are also part of Jewish holy scriptures. The scriptures tell us in Genesis 16 and through into chapter 17 that Sarah had given her maid Hagar to Abraham according to the customs of the time, so she might raise a son to Abraham as Sarah was too old to have children of her own. Thus Ishmael was Abraham's firstborn. This future son, Ishmael would be 'a wild man' who would be 'against every man and every man's hand against him'. Afterwards, when God had told Abraham that Sarah would now bear a son to be Abraham's heir, Abraham became anxious about the fate of Ishmael as Hagar and Sarah despised each other as one can well imagine. God reassured Abraham that Ishmael was still under His blessing and would beget twelve princes and establish a great nation. It is significant to note that Ishmael was circumcised with Abraham as a sign that God was in covenant with both (Genesis 17:23-26). The covenant with Ishmael was unconditional.

Covenant with Ishmael not made null and void by the birth of Isaac
Many Christian commentators claim that God's promises to Hagar and Ishmael were made null and void by the birth of Isaac. This is not the case. When Hagar and her son, now entering into adulthood, were cast out of Abraham's household through Sarah's jealousy, they suffered terribly from this temporary banishment. However, we read in Genesis 21:18ff that when Hagar had given up her son for dead an angel from Heaven told her that God had heard her son's cries and said to her, 'Arise, lift up the lad and hold him in thine hand; for I will make of him a great nation.' God always keeps His promise. Ishmael's was a God-given inheritance whether Ishmael was a wild man or not; whether later Jews and Christians accepted this or not.

Furthermore, Ishmael did not continue as a stranger but afterwards had intimate contact with Isaac and his family and married into other Abrahamic families. The nation, and then nations, promised to Ishmael were thus linked strongly with those descended from Isaac and the two half-brothers continued to have close intercourse. There was room in Palestine for both in cooperation with each other. Thus it was not in accordance with the Bible that the UN gave the Jews a home which automatically would banish the Ishmaelites. It was the Ishmaelites' home, too. Ishmael is mentioned in the Bible accounts repeatedly as being near at hand to his half-brother with whom he organized, for instance, Abraham's funeral and was present at his burial. This is recorded in Genesis 25:9ff where we are told that Ishmael lived to be a hundred and thirty-seven years old and had twelve sons who founded twelve nations with many 'towns and castles'. The fact is that Ishmael's territories always overlapped with those of Abraham's other family members and their offspring. Indeed, the reason given in scripture for all the blessings given Ishmael was because Abraham's first-born was of Abraham's seed.[149] To demonstrate the strong connections between the line of Abraham through Isaac and that of Ishmael, we note in Genesis 28:8ff. that Esau, Isaac's son, and Abraham's grandson, married a daughter of Ishmael. In 1 Chronicles 1:29ff. Abraham's, Ishmael's and Isaac's sons are mentioned under one heading and Ishmael's twelve sons are named first, then the many sons by Abraham's concubine Keturah, whom he married after Sarah's death. Then Abraham's son by Sarah, Isaac, is mentioned. The scriptures do not suppress uncomfortable facts. We see also that Abraham was the tribal father of the Midianites who were closely attached to the Ishmaelites and seen by later Christians as enemies of the Jews. However, we cannot say that historically the Jews behaved any better than the Ishmaelites and Midianites. The Bible tells us of the unrighteous cooperation of the sons of Israel with their cousins the Ishmaelites and Midianites in selling their unloved brother Joseph to them. When Joseph's brothers planned fratricide, Reuben, the eldest suggested that they imprison Joseph in a pit, where he would be left to rot. Judah then thought of how they could be rid of their father's favourite Joseph in a way more profitable for their own pocket. When some Ishmaelites/Midianites passed on their way from Gilead to Egypt, Judah offered Joseph to them for sale. This is how Joseph came to be traded to the Egyptians as a slave.[150] It appears that the Ishmaelites were not aware of whom Joseph was and regarded him merely as a slave to be bartered according to the customs of the times. It was not a custom anywhere in Palestine for brothers to sell their own kith and kin. I have vivid memories of my Sunday School teachers, one an army officer

---

[149] Genesis 21:13.
[150] Genesis 37.

from Palestine, still wearing his uniform but hoping to be demobbed, telling me how horrible the Ishmaelites were for buying Joseph but never how horrible Reuben and Judah were for plotting to kill him and eventually selling him off.

The International Covenant after Isaac's Birth

We must now look at God's promises to Abraham and Sarah after the birth of Isaac. In Genesis 17 we read of the covenant of God with Abraham and the repeated promise that 'he will be the father of many nations and kings'. Furthermore, Abraham was told[151] that Sarah, his wife and half-sister, 'shall be a mother of nations; kings of people shall be of her'. In Chapter 18 we read of the three men (angels unawares) who told Abraham that Sarah would bear a child and Abraham heard again that he would 'become a great and mighty nation, and all the nations of the earth shall be blessed in him'[152]. It is already obvious here that the covenant promises to Abraham were not to be understood as promises to mere genetic descendants of Abraham such as Ishmael. These covenant promises ruled out such an interpretation by adding clauses such as 'all the nations of the world shall be blessed in him'. This is emphasised by the added explanation that the covenant with Abraham which the Bible calls 'the everlasting covenant' would not be through Ishmael but through Isaac[153] (17:19) in this international framework. It is thus quite contrary to the records to believe that the Jews were Abraham's sole heirs both spiritually and genetically and that Jews were the sole recipients of the covenantal promises to Abraham as the 'Father of the Faithful' who alone represent 'The People of God'.

God's promises to Abraham and Sarah spiritual and conditional

This indicates that Covenant promises given to Isaac were not a matter of mere descent as were those to Ishmael, Midian etc.. Thus we read in Genesis 21:12ff that though Ishmael is of Abraham's 'seed', the true covenant-keeping seed would now be traced through Isaac alone.

---

[151] Genesis 17:15.
[152] Genesis 18:18.
[153] Genesis 17:19.

However, even the covenantal promises to Isaac were not to be understood merely genetically. It is clear from Genesis 18:19, 20 that the covenant through Isaac was not unconditional as was the covenant with Ishmael but conditional; the condition being that those within the everlasting covenant should 'keep the way of the Lord'. This was also a condition concerning land rights given. This is reflected, too, in God's promises to Abraham in Genesis 22:17, 18 which is related to the fact that Abraham obeyed God. It is again emphasized in Genesis 26:24 that Isaac would be blessed for the sake of Abraham as Father of the faithful. This ruled out future unbelieving Jews before there was any idea of a 'Jewish Nation'. Indeed, rather than tell Abraham he would suddenly found an Abrahamic political dynasty when still Abram, the patriarch was told 'Know of a surety that thy seed shall be stranger in a land that is not theirs and shall serve them; and they shall afflict them four hundred years.'[154] Nevertheless, the spiritual promises to Abraham continued throughout these centuries before the founding of a political Jewish state. So the conditions that placed both the Children of Israel and the strangers (foreigners) within their gates was present throughout the earliest O.T. revelations and were applied in those times worldwide.[155] Jews, like Gentiles, are thus strangers to God's covenant promises unless they become the People of God. Furthermore, it is also clear from these O.T. prophesies that the Ishmaelites, Midianites, Edomites, etc. who were true sons of God through following the Covenant, would be counted also as the true spiritual sons of Abraham. There is a story previously often told about Hudson Taylor whose heart's desire was that 'All Israel would be saved'. This hope is certainly not limited to Jews. So when Hudson Taylor sent a cheque to the Mildmay Mission to the Jews with a written remark on it saying, 'to the Jew first', the Director of the Mission, John Wilkinson thanked him and finished Hudson Taylor's biblical half-quote by adding, ' – and also to the Greeks'[156].

---

[154] Genesis 15:13.

[155] See Exodus 20:10; Deuteronomy 5:14; Leviticus 17:8ff and passim.

[156] 'Greeks' here is to be interpreted as 'Gentiles' see Romans 2:9, 10. Here we see that in the eyes of the Messianic Covenant there is no difference between Jews and Gentiles.

The 'Children of Israel' broke the Covenant repeatedly
Now, in the further revelations of God to the children of Israel regarding their future throughout the Exodus and law-giving period, we find God's conditional approach to Israel emphasized more and more as Israel broke the Covenant time and time again. So we read in Exodus 19 that God's covenant with Moses and Jacob's descendants is valid only as long as they do not break it. Verse 5 says, 'Now, therefore, if ye will obey my voice indeed, and keep my covenant, then ye shall be a peculiar treasure unto me above all people: for all the earth is mine.' Then Moses told the refugees from Egypt that God was going to put them to the test (v. 20). The children of Israel were then given a very long list of 'thou shalts' and 'thou shalt nots' which were designed to keep them in the covenant with God.

Chapter 23:20ff. makes it very clear that Moses and his followers in the wilderness wanderings would be punished if they disobeyed but be blessed if they obeyed God. Part of the blessings promised to the obedient offspring of Jacob was that God would protect them from aggression from the many states through which they would be travelling under condition they did not enter into covenants with these people or recognize their gods. They were in covenant with God alone. The entire people now promise to obey God (Exodus 24:3, 7) but the promise was soon broken. We read in Exodus 32:7 that God told Moses, 'thy people, which thou broughtest out of the land of Egypt, have corrupted themselves.' We note God here does not call them 'My people' because people who abandon God and worship golden calves are outside of God's covenant. Covenant-breakers are thus, as the Prophets such as Isaiah, Amos and Hosea preach 'Lo Ammi' and not 'Ammi'.[157] It is also usual that when it is denied in the biblical records that Covenant-breaking Israel is 'Ammi', it is explained carefully what a true People of God is, as we shall see more clearly as this chapter proceeds. Here we note that Aaron was a ringleader in this covenant breaking which shows us the best of men are but men of clay. The conditions of God's Covenant with the Messiah must be fulfilled within that Covenant by virtue of the Messiah Himself. This is the ever new Covenant as Jeremiah points out.

---

[157] *Ami*: my people; *Lo Ami*: not my people.

193

Nevertheless, Moses pleaded for the offenders and found grace in God's sight. If there is one righteous man in a people, God is prepared to hear him on behalf of others. As James 5:16 tells us, 'The effectual fervent prayer of a righteous man availeth much.'

A stranger to the Children of Israel obeys God's Covenant for them
Even Moses, however, angered God in disbelief and was not allowed to set his foot in the Promised Land. The greatest prophesy concerning the children of Israel was not permitted to come from either Moses' or Aaron's lips but from the lips of an Ishmaelite, then regarded as an 'unclean' foreigner and an enemy. He was thus a descendent of Ishmael, Abraham's first-born. God used this man to help the nations keep the Covenant the budding Jewish nation had once again broken. Indeed, the Children of Israel had sunk so low in human and spiritual status that God also used the inspired braying of an ass to put Israel back on the right path. God always uses methods suiting the occasion. Here was God's patient attempt to hammer in home truths for the future Jewish kingdom and make it clear to them that Israel's only hope of salvation was the hope destined for an international environment of believers with obedience to God being the saving feature and not nationality or birth. The idea the Ishmaelites knew nothing about God's revelation to Abraham must be refuted as the children of Isaac and Ishmael grew up together as kinsmen. Blood-ties did not separate them but life under God's Covenant was there to merge them in faith.

Balak King of the Moabites and Midianites descendants of Ishmael, had commanded a prophet from his own people to curse the children of Israel. This man, called Balaam, son of Beor, is usually seen as the first great Messianic prophet to put the children of Israel on the right Messianic path. This divine sensation would be akin to present day Assad of Syria or Abbas of Palestine helping modern Israel to get back to her roots and the destiny of the true, faithful children of God. It is now obvious that under God's hand they might well do so. God gave Balaam the courage to tell Balak and his princes that even if they offered him a house full of silver and gold, he would not curse those whom God had blessed. We are reminded of Peter's first letter to the scattered believers, saying:

For as much as ye know that ye were not redeemed with corruptible things, as silver and gold, from your vain conversation received by tradition from your fathers; but with the precious blood of Christ, as of a lamb without blemish and without spot. Who verily was foreordained before the foundation of the world, but was manifest in these last times for you, Who by him do believe in God, that raised him up from the dead, and gave him glory; that your faith and hope might be in God.[158]

Looking to the future, Balaam proclaimed the coming of One whom he said prophetically,' I shall see him, but not now: I shall behold him, but not nigh: there shall come a star out of Jacob, and a sceptre shall rise out of Israel'. Again, he said 'Out of Jacob shall come he that shall have dominion.'[159] This was no new thing to the Children of Israel but they had to be reminded of the truth which Jacob had believed long ago.[160] He gathered his sons together just before he died to tell them what would befall them in the last days. Of Judah he said:

Judah, thou art he whom thy brethren shall praise: thy hand shall be in the neck of thine enemies; thy father's children shall bow down before thee. Judah is a lion's whelp: from the prey, my son, thou art gone up: he stooped down, he couched as a lion, and as an old lion; who shall rouse him up? The sceptre shall not depart from Judah, nor a lawgiver from between his feet, until Shiloh come; and unto him shall the gathering of the people be.[161]

Shiloh was the earthly place where the congregation of the Lord used to gather and was used as a temple of worship. I would not like to thrust any foreign meaning onto this term but as we are talking about the everlasting sceptre of Judah which will one day lead to the fact that 'unto *him* shall the gathering of the people be, whatever 'Shilo' does

---

[158] 1 Peter 1:18-21.
[159] See the whole story in Numbers chapters 22-25.
[160] Genesis 49:1-33.
[161] Vv. 8-10.

mean, we are nevertheless speaking in the light of Balaam's repetition of a Messianic event.[162]

Since these predictions, many prophets in the Old Testament have spoken concerning the Messiah who will come 'out of Jacob', be 'a great light' or a 'star' and raise a 'sceptre' with which He would reign over true Israelites. This was also spoken by a man God had chosen to tell the truth who was not of the physical 'Children of Israel'. As John Gill shows in his commentary on the text, Jewish theologians have long seen Balaam's prophesy as a pointer to the coming Messiah and New Testament authors such as Peter have not hesitated to link this prophesy with Christ as the long expected Redeemer of the true sons of Abraham in the faith.[163]

It is interesting to note that Peter, who seems to be addressing the first converted Jews in the Diaspora, likens Balaam before his prophesy to those who had forsaken the right way, and are gone astray'. So Balaam was familiar with Covenant Theology. Peter tells his addressees that 'if after they have escaped the pollutions of the world through the knowledge of the Lord and Saviour Jesus Christ, they are again entangled therein, and overcome, the latter end is worse with them than the beginning.'[164] Whether Balaam, as a 'Gentile', acted on the enlightenment he had, or not, the Children of Israel at that time turned against their God. But as Balaam was given the truth again that Jacob had declared, so God grants repentance to those who confess they have broken God's Covenant. This is one of the many reasons why this writer looks on the Law as a means of Grace because repentance and faith annul the penalty of breaking it, no matter if one is a Jew or a Gentile. As the Bible repeatedly states, true Israelites are a remnant whether they come from the Gentiles or the Jews. However, Peter warns his readers not to neglect what God's holy prophets (Jew or Gentile) have told them.

To crown all this teaching, we read Christ's words in the last chapter of the last book of the Bible where Christ declares, obviously referring to Balaam's prophecy:

---

[162] This author has examined a multiple of arguments concerning the etymology of the name 'Shilo' but has not found any interpretation which is not open to question apart from the name of a place where the Lord's people gathered.

[163] 2 Peter 2:15ff.

[164] V. 20.

I Jesus have sent my angel to testify unto you these things in the churches. I am the root and the offspring of David, and the bright and morning star.[165]

Here we see the same Covenant of Grace enacted from the earliest days of the Children of Israel's flight from Egypt before Israel was established until the last trumpet call when Christ shall come to judge the quick and the dead whether Jew or Gentile, indeed, Christ emphasizes that His message deals with 'all the nations of them which are saved' (Revelation 21:24). We note that one of Bullinger's earliest works was on Revelation and John Bale[166] delighted in preaching and writing on the book. These early Reformers depicted the fruits of the Covenant in preparing the New Jerusalem for the coming of Christ which they found revealed in Revelation. Calvin did not write on Revelation and there is no evidence of his ever preaching on the book. The usual argument is that Calvin died too early to work on Revelation but this is a very weak argument as Calvin wrote profusely on other books of the Bible, leaving out a few, like Luther, which he thought were questionable or out of the range of his understanding. However, other Reformers dealt with the book in younger years seeing in it the story of the fulfilment of the Father's Covenant with His Son, explained by the Holy Spirit. My reason for Calvin's silence on Revelation is that the book obviously did not meet up with his ideas of the Covenant of Grace.

What criteria kept True Israel from becoming false?
We see that sadly, the children of Israel did exactly what they had been told by God not to do. As they were now tolerated by Moab, they could not resist whoring amongst their women and worshipped their idols and bringing pagan religion into their midst. Their betrayal of God ended in slaughter and twenty-four thousands of their number died of a dreadful plague. Thus the early history of the children of Israel was fraught with rebellion against God, disobedience to God's Law, a breaking of the

---

[165] Revelation 22:16.
[166] Not to be confused with John Ball of more than a hundred years afterwards.

Covenant of Grace given them and a preference for idols followed by severe punishment. Sadly, the entire Old Testament witnessed to the fact that the majority of the Jews were traitors to their own cause and only a remnant stood firm believing the promises of God. This remnant, the Prophets tell us, was to people the New Jerusalem.

Those men of God who believed in God's overtures of salvation and the prophets who led them, aided later by King David, concentrated on two methods. One was to emphasise the true and everlasting nature of a covenant based on faith, trust and obedience which would sift the wheat from the chaff. The other was to affirm that the Children of Israel as an institution was not the same as the People of God committed to the Messiah by faith. Thus we have the decisive declaration of the joint Testaments of the Bible that those who ranked themselves as God's people through their genetic descent from Abraham could not use that claim to prove they were the People of God'. They could not do so then and cannot do so today.

A new look at the Covenant of Grace
This move was accompanied by a new look at the Covenant of Grace designed both for the children of Israel and to all the nations of the world. 'Remember the Covenant' was now the slogan preached with renewed vigour by prophets such as David, Isaiah, Ezekiel, Jeremiah, Nehemiah, Amos and Hosea and affirmed in other O.T. writings such as Numbers and Chronicles 2. The real People of God were to populate a New Sion and a New Jerusalem. There was to be no difference between Jews and Gentiles as far as either their condemnation or redemption was concerned though the Prophets emphasized that believing Jews would be sought after by Gentiles in order to learn the faith from them. God did not annul the records of the history of the Children of Israel which was being committed to writing for both Jews and Gentiles. The great time of believing Jews was to come in the New Testament when they led thousands of Gentiles to Christ. The New Testament is full of their names with Paul to the fore. Now the Torah Covenant of Grace is seen by both Gentile Christians as a treasure for both, and a schoolmaster to teach the world the way to Christ. So the new, deeper, wider, surer look at the Covenant, though with a growing number of exceptions, remained largely in the hands of the Jews until New Testament times. The Jews were still a privileged people.

Summing Up

The 1947/48 mass immigration plans for Jews sponsored by the Western powers had little to do with the Jews' own hopes and fears and meant a most troubled future for them. Western Christians, on the whole, believed that deporting the Jews to Palestine was of immense eschatological significance and ignored the plight of those peoples and religions, represented in Palestine since the Jewish Exodus in the first century A.D., which of course had started during the Greek occupation. Those who felt this turbulence come into their country the most were the Muslims who had entered the vacuum left by the Jewish flight into the Diaspora. They, too, see themselves as descendants of Abraham through Ishmael and their claims to biblical land rights outlined in the Jewish scriptures were also ignored by the growing number of Christian Zionists. God's Covenant with Ishmael was limited to land rights only and not annulled with the birth of Isaac. God's Covenant with Isaac was for both land rights and the spiritual enjoyment of the Covenant with Abraham which were both conditional and annulled for unbelieving Jews. Furthermore, the Covenant with Abraham had an international basis as he was to be the father of many nations and we can presume that believers within a Jewish state were included in these 'many nations'.

It is thus wrong to believe that the Jews are the sole heirs of God's Covenant promises: Abraham was and is the Father of the Faithful who are the People of God which know no national boundaries. As the original Exiles failed to keep God's Covenant, God no longer called them 'my people' but gave their descendants a new chance through the intervention of Moses who promised God that he would continue the Covenant with Abraham and the laws God gave him were within this framework of Grace. Still, however, only a remnant of the new 'Jews' under a fresh Covenant start were considered within the Covenant by God and even those amongst whom the Children of Israel settled had to tell them why they had failed to keep the Covenant and remind them that following the Messiah, the Star out of Jacob, was their security within the Covenant. All this was but part of the glorious revelations of the Covenant from Genesis to Revelation. Now it was made clearer and clearer by the Prophets that only a remnant of the Children of Israel were firmly safe within God's Covenant. So the main 'preaching text' of the Prophets now became 'Remember the Covenant'.

Chapter 9

Henry Bullinger And The
Revival Of Covenant Teaching

Introductory note

I originally wrote this chapter with reference to Bullinger only whose status as the *Father of Covenant Theology*, indeed, the *Father of Reformed Theology*, I believed could not be challenged.[167] However, on finishing the chapter, I received, through browsing the web, news of Andrew A. Woolsey's *Unity and Continuity in Covenantal Thought* which relegates Bullinger's massive contribution to a few pages whilst dealing with Calvin's alleged Covenantal influence on the Westminster Confession in the bulk of the book. On obtaining this book, I realised I was compelled to rewrite the entire chapter (making it rather long) in order to defend Bullinger's challenged position against the presentation of a Covenant which is not Christo-centric but based on Zwingli's philosophy of determination as per his *The Providence of God* written in 1530, a year before his death on the battlefield. Zwingli's work departed radically from the development of Reformed Covenant theology from Apostolic times to Oecolampadius and the German and Swiss Reformers, finding its main exponent in pastor-theologian

---

[167] Blanke, Fritz and Leuschner, Immanuel, *Heinrich Bullinger: Vater der reformierten Kirche*, Theologischer Verlag Zürich, 1990.

Heinrich Bullinger.[168] Is this not why Johannes Suts, calls Bullinger 'the rescuer of the Zürich Reformation'?[169] Woolsey maintains that Calvin based his predestination orientated Covenant theology on that of Zwingli, which would mean that Calvin left biblical Covenantal thinking aside as did Zwingli.[170] This is not my position but Woolsey's.

Bullinger wrote on the Covenant in the fifteen-twenties

The earliest, most developed, comprehensive and meticulously perfected exposition of the doctrine of God's Covenant made for His people was presented to the public during the middle 1520s by teenager Heinrich Bullinger (1504-1575) of Zürich who staunchly combatted the Catabaptists' social, religious and political teaching. It was not baptism here which was the main issue but the Catabaptist rejection of a pan-biblical Covenant. They also challenged the role of the individual Christian in social engagements and in his duty to be a shining light to the unbelieving community in which he lived. This did not stop gracious Bullinger from defending the Catabaptists before the courts when they were, in turn, unjustly accused and their citizenship denied. He corrected both the establishment and over-zealous forms of radicalism wherever they occurred. He also rejected the politician-soldier status of Zwingli and after Zwingli's death, refused to follow him as a member of the Council. The Council, however, out of respect for Bullinger's wisdom, asked him to attend Council meetings at any time and put forward the desires of the Zürich Church, that is, the people under his Covenant care.

Bullinger's exposition of the Covenant remains for this writer the classical and most widely acceptable and accepted view of God's Testament for His People.

Bullinger's position recently challenged

Sadly, this conviction is not shared by some modern writers who call themselves 'Calvinists' but have not done their homework correctly and place Bullinger's laurels on his Genevan protégé's head. They argue

---

[168] French speaking Geneva was not part of Switzerland at this time.
[169] *Heinrich Bullinger: Der Retter der Züricher Reformation*, Zürich, 1915.
[170] See The Place of Predestination in Zwingli and Bucer, William Peter Stevens, *Zwingliana*, 2010, pp. 393-410.

backwards from the Westminster Assembly, saying, but not proving, that this was Calvin's Presbyterian heritage and thus most, if not all, modern Reformed doctrine concerning the Covenant of Grace came from him. However, far more scholars, not of Woolsey's persuasion, argue historically and chronologically in showing how clearly Bullinger led the Reformation and how the Westminster Confession is not a summary of Calvin's teaching. Wayne Baker, for instance, shows the influence of Bullinger's teaching in his 1980 work on *Henry Bullinger and the Covenant and the Other Reformed Tradition*. This was severely criticized by some holders of what Baker rightly calls 'High Calvinist Scholasticism', such as Andrew Woolsey. In his 1988 dissertation on the development of Calvinism in its influence on the Westminster Confession's view of the Covenant of Grace, Woolsey quite lost trace of older Covenant teaching by other pioneer Reformers. This led to further intense research on Baker's part in co-authorship with Charles S. McCoy who published their *Foundation of Federalism: Heinrich Bullinger and the Covenantal Position*. For Baker, 'the covenant was the leading persuasive conviction in Bullinger's theology' and that 'Bullinger's (Zurich) theology was the basis for the original Reformed tradition to which Calvin and the Calvinists presented a later alternative in the matter of the covenant and predestination'.[171]

On reading Baker's original work and noting that it was found 'too narrow' by several scholars, reviewers, and authors of a strict Hyper-Calvinist position, I strove in several essays published around 2000 in the United States, Britain and Germany to underline the importance of Bullinger as the 'Father of Reformed Covenant Teaching'. In 2004, I worked with Joel Beeke on the introductions to the *Reformation Heritage* reprint of Bullinger's *Decades*, to demonstrate that Bullinger was earlier, more detailed and broader in his conception of the Covenant than Calvin. Then in my book *Henry Bullinger: Shepherd of the Churches* (2007) I outlined Bullinger's work in a wider European sphere especially regarding his influence on the Reformed Church of England and the reception of his theology in Eastern Europe. Much of the work was taken up with a comparison of Bullinger's and Calvin's contribution to Reformed Theology. Then followed essays published in

---

[171] See my various references to Baker in my Bullinger biography, especially p. 339.

the *Gemeinde* (Berlin), *English Churchman* and the *Zeitschrift für Theologie und Gesselschaft* (Bonn). The output of German and Swiss scholarly works emphasizing the importance of Bullinger's Covenant teaching has been enormous since Woolsey wrote his dissertation. I have made ample use of this material. In my above mentioned book, after years of studying and writing on the subject, I claimed:

> 'Covenant Theology is widely thought today, especially amongst Presbyterians, to be a product of Calvin's genius but Bullinger's covenant teaching is far more developed, comprehensive and meticulously perfected than Calvin's and was presented to the public some fourteen years before Calvin took up the theme. As Prof. Fritz Büsser of Zürich points out, Bullinger's covenant teaching first became widely known in the mid-twenties when Zwingli and Bullinger were combating the Anabaptists and reached various other countries long before it reached Geneva. Büsser argues in his 1994 work on the subject that:

> > 'Without a doubt' it was Bullinger's teaching which Calvin took up in his 1539 and 1559 *Institutes* and that the Germans and English followed the teaching 'a long time before Calvin.'[172]

He can thus conclude concerning God's Covenant of Grace which embraces the entire Bible:

> Although this is commonly thought to be typically Calvinistic, its origin is in Zürich. It is to be found since around 1525 as a decisive term in the controversies Zwingli and Bullinger had with the Baptists (Täufern), and it was Bullinger who, in answer to a booklet of Schwenckfeld's on the Difference between the Old and New Testaments, wrote his fundamental thesis on covenant theology in his tract *De Testamento seu*

---

[172] 'Längst vor Calvin'. *Die Prophezei*, p. 215.

foedere Dei unico et aeterno (On the One and Eternal Testament or Covenant of God).[173]

I was thus rather surprised to find in 2012 that *Reformed Heritage Books* had seemingly adopted a new course by publishing Andrew A. Woolsey's old thesis entitled *Unity and Continuity in Covenantal Thought* which challenged the *unity* of contemporary Reformers around Bullinger's doctrine and broke the *continuity* by putting forward Calvin as the great pioneer teacher of the Covenant. Oddly enough this work, which has ignored the vast positive work done on Bullinger in the long years between Woolsey's writing his dissertation and publishing it, traces Calvin's Covenant teaching back to Zwingli's deterministic double-predestination doctrine rather than to the Covenant of Grace teaching of his mentor, tutor and friend Bullinger. Büsser's multi-volumed works on the subject are not so much as mentioned, though they were published between Woolsey's writing of his thesis and its delayed publication.

This most dissatisfactory and quite outdated work of Woolsey's must be dealt with here because of the most exaggerated claims it makes to its own pioneering importance. Richard Müller in his Foreword claims that:

> Woolsey's dissertation, completed in 1988, is the first (and after more than two decades), remains the only major attempt in English to present a view of the movement of Reformed thought on covenant from its Reformation origins to the more detailed formulations of the early to mid-seventeenth century.

There is some truth in this startling and surprising statement. Though much has been written before and between 1988 and 2012 and afterwards to challenge Woolsey's work, it remains 'the only major attempt' to see the history of the biblical Covenant trimmed to suit the Westminster Confession which has comparatively little to say on the Covenant of Grace. Indeed, what Woolsey presents is a complete break with the historical Calvin and his overall teaching by presenting

---

[173] Bundesbegriff in *Die Prophezei*, p. 214.

Calvin's alleged double-predestination theory supposedly taken from Zwingli as the basis for his Covenant teaching which is certainly not the position of the Westminster Confession, weak as it is on the Covenant. I take it that through this move Joel Beeke and his Publishing House were striving to give all sides on the Covenant question a fair hearing. However, Woolsey's work, in which he argues backwards from his view of the Westminster Confession to Calvin, fails to do justice to the wealth of original documents and studies on Bullinger which find most selective hearing in his book in spite of his massive reading on peripheral writings. To be fair to Woolsey, his views of Bullinger and Calvin are not mine so it is clear that his use of primary and secondary literature would not meet my approval.

Richard Müller's reading up on Bullinger is highly deficient
Alarm bells began to ring on reading Richard Müller's Foreword to Woolsey's work where he gives an all too brief and fragmentary overview of research into the covenant question. Here Müller, in mentioning Bullinger's contribution leaves out the enormous work done by such internationally-known scholars as Emidio Campi, Peter Opitz and Willem van 't Spijker (2004) and many other writers who have written profusely for the Theologischer Verlag Zürich. With his over eight volumes of editorial work on Bullinger's writings, Campi's works cannot be avoided. So, too, Campi has written widely on the relationship between Bullinger and Calvin. Fritz Büsser's two further volumes on Bullinger (2004 and 2005)[174] are a must for Covenant scholars as the author gives a very precise and concise analysis of Bullinger's major work on the Covenant in Vol.1 on pages 225-237 and in the same volume devotes 33 pages to the *Decades* (p. 265ff.), yet Woolsey has ignored them. Müller and Woolsey might also have consulted Büsser's lengthy comparison between the Zürich and Geneva schools. Here, Büsser does not exaggerate the differences as does Woolsey. Büsser puts the relationship between Bullinger and Calvin in the correct historical perspective in showing that Büllinger led the Reformation forty-four years in Zürich whereas Calvin was only twenty-six years in Geneva, leaving out the four years of his exile. So, too, we read how Zwingli and Bullinger founded the Reformation in

---

[174] *Heinrich Bullinger: Leben, Werk und Wirkung* (2 Vols).

Zürich in the early twenties whereas Calvin took over an already Reformed Geneva Church in the middle thirties after the Bernese drove out the Savoyards and turned Geneva into a Reformed bastion. We might also add that Bullinger had no opposition in Zürich, whether on the part of the Council or the Church or the other Swiss Reformers whereas Calvin found great opposition before the last few years of his ministry from the Council, Church, Swiss Reformers and the Bernese controllers of Geneva. Indeed, the Swiss Confederacy allowed Geneva to join them only after Calvin's death as they always feared he would hand over Geneva to Roman Catholic France. Spijker's Chapter on *Bullinger als Bundestheologe* in the 2007 publication of *Heinrich Bullinger: Life - Thought - Influence* edited by Campi and Opitz is also of immense value and would have been most worthy of Müller's overview. So, too, had not pro-Bullinger Joachim Staedke and his large team of Bullinger experts gone to such painstaking work collecting together their two volume Bibliography of Bullinger's works, Müller's and Woolsey's work in finding sources would have been much more difficult.

A Covenant without a scriptural, historical and salvational context
Müller believes he can belittle Bullinger's influence via his display of the alleged deficits he finds in Heinrich Heppe's work *Geschichte des Pietismus und Mystik in der Reformierten Kirche* (1879).[175] The choice of this work for criticism is most questionable. Heppe's studies in Pietism and Mysticism can hardly be used as a starter for a biblical exegesis of the Covenant.

Next, Müller takes a brief look at Gotlob Schrenk's *Gottesreich und Bund im älteren Protistantismus* (1928) which gives a most positive picture of Bullinger as the main exponent of the Reformed Covenant teaching. He complains, however, that Schrenk:

... also tended to perpetuate the view of Bullinger as the primary source of covenantal thought by stressing the path taken

---

[175] Foreword p. viii.

by Bullinger's followers – to the exclusion of followers of Calvin.[176]

This is unfair to both Calvin and Bullinger as Calvin was not around at the time of Bullinger's major work on the Covenant and beside that fact, in what way are Calvin's followers said to have bettered it? As Calvin never caught up with Bullinger's reforming work, his followers had not the impetus to dig deeper into the subject if they neglected 'Bullinger and his followers'. Furthermore, many of the *Confession's* authors could not possibly agree with Woolsey's 'Calvinism' as the compiler John Durie and chief minute-taker Adoniram Byfield certainly did not. When Durie visited Geneva in the Cromwell era, he found many kindred spirits and 'followers of Calvin' there who certainly rejected Woolsey's lop-sided view of 'Calvinism'. Indeed, these men supported Durie's work on the Covenant and Christian unity connected with it most strongly. Durie campaigned for Christian unity on the basis of a common doctrine of the Covenant of Grace in Parliament but was ridiculed by the Presbyterians.

Müller also criticises Schrenk because he supports Bullinger's teaching which provided 'a biblical, salvation – historical counter to the Scholastic dogmatics of the era'. He suggests that Calvin's and Theodore Beza's work left this path. So here we have a professing 'Calvinist, who rejects a 'Calvinism' argued from scripture and the history of salvation. We notice that Müller's measuring rod of orthodoxy is not the Bible but what he calls the '*Confession*'.[177]

Woolsey indeed, clearly rejects the biblical, salvational and church historical aspect of Bullinger's depiction of the everlasting love of Christ for His Bride and dwells on double-predestination and double-reprobation instead. This is neither Bullingerism nor Calvinism but an over-strained Zwingliism. This is all preliminary spadework for Woolsey's presentation of the 'Calvinism' of the Westminster Confession. However the *Confession* certainly does not major on Woolsey's view of the Covenant, which he claims is the 'Calvinistic' norm.

---

[176] Unity and Continuity.
[177] Westminster Confession.

Woolsey, follows Müller's disregard for an examination of a scripturally based view of the Covenant by declaring at the beginning of his Introduction that:

> The scriptural origin of the Reformed doctrine of the covenant is indisputable, so that serious research in this area has never been considered necessary. The temptation to include a section on scripture in this study has likewise been resisted, but its importance has been kept in mind throughout.[178]

This is not good enough as we do not read what Woolsey finds 'indisputable' and wish to hear what Woolsey's scriptural basis is for his theory of the Covenant. As Bullinger stressed that scripture and its gospel is the whole story of the Covenant of Grace, we must ask Woolsey what his theological basis is for arguing for his differing covenantal views.

Müller sees Calvin's and Beza's Covenantal work as paving the way to the Westminster Confession, so he dismisses the essential research Cornelis Grafland's has done in writing his three volume *Van Calvijn tot Comrie: oorsprong en ontwikkeling van de leer van het verbond in het Gereformeerd Protestantisme* (1992–1994) all too lightly. The worthy Dutch scholar sees problems in Calvin's thoughts and criticises Beza and allegedly, so Müller, pits Calvin against the so-called 'Calvinists'. If Müller means the Calvinists such as Thomas Cartwright, whom Woolsey praises, I would agree that Calvin and such as Cartwright are very much different cups of tea. Müller then refers to Peter Golding's *Covenant Theology: the Key of Theology and Reformed Thought and Tradition* of 2004, finding it unscholarly and weak. I found it a delight and encouragement to read as it was designed for 'ordinary people' and, as such, served its purpose well. If I were Woolsey, I would have hoped for a more scholarly, subject orientated Introduction to my book!

---

[178] Introduction p. 2.

Woolsey leaves gaps rather than fills them

Though Müller claims Woolsey fills a gap in examining the primary sources,[179] I find that Woolsey creates many gaps as he has failed to research in detail alternative views to his own. Müller portrays Woolsey as arguing backwards from the *Westminster Standards* and using what he finds there as his criterium for judging the historical continuity in the covenant debate. So Woolsey goes from what he feels is the 'more concise, nuggetory statements of the *Confession*'[180] back through the growth of Presbyterianism to his central source in Calvin in a most zig-zagged manner. In his exhaustive overview of Woolsey's conclusions, Müller leaves Henry Bullinger and his followers and those past stalwarts who influenced him out.

Woolsey's 'followers of Calvin' are ill-chosen

Woolsey complains that Continental writers leave out the British testimony which is far from being true. Woolsey, in his historical overview of the English contribution to covenant thought, picks out Thomas Cartwright (1535-1603) as a major link between the Continental Calvinistic Reformation and the Westminster understanding of the Covenant. Here he has chosen the wrong man. When the Heidelberg Protestants protested against Luther, Bullinger and Calvin as being too soft and lax in theology, Cartwright joined them and took over their extreme legalistic views. He protested at the 'low Calvinism of Calvin'.

Edwin Sandys, exiled by Mary, had had enough of religious persecution himself and was to suffer further under the criminal energies of the so-called English disciplinarians who held extreme legalistic ideas of church management. He wrote to Rudolf Gwalther, Bullinger's adoptive son and successor and Zwingli's son-in-law at Zürich on August, 1574 expressing great concern regarding the extraordinary new love of severe discipline on the Continent which was uniting Hyper-Lutheran legalism and Hyper-Genevan legalism where doctrine and Christian fellowship had seemingly failed. This was being exported to England through such as Cartwright who had picked up the new foreign discipline from Heidelberg rather than build on the work

---

[179] Introduction p. x.
[180] *Sources and Covenantal Doctrine of the Westminster Standard*, p. 73.

of the less-extreme English Dissenters. Thus Cartwright can hardly be praised for setting up an 'English Theology' as his ideas and those of his ordinee Walter Travers were developed in an anti-Calvinistic foreign background. Rather too confident that the new church-splitting foreign bubble of the new discipline would soon burst, Sandy's says:

> Our innovators, who have been striving to strike out for us a new form of a church, are not doing us much harm; nor is the new fabric of theirs making much progress as they expected. Our nobility are at last sensible of the object to which this novel fabrication is tending. The author of these novelties, and after Beza[181] the first inventor, is a young Englishman, by name Thomas Cartwright, who, they say, is now sojourning at Heidelberg. He has lately written from thence a treatise in Latin, in defence of this new discipline which he wishes to obtrude upon us. I have not seen the book, but I hear that it is printed, and has been brought over to us. As soon as it shall come into my hands, I will take care it shall be sent to you.[182]

On 16 March, 1574, Gwalther told Cox that these More-Calvinist-than-Calvin rebels wished to 'revive' a Presbyterian system as the answer to the church's needs, but he adds, 'I wish they would think about reviving that simplicity of faith and purity of morals, which formerly flourished.' And continues:

> I greatly fear there is lying concealed under the presbytery an affection of oligarchy, which may at length degenerate into monarchy, or even open tyranny. Nor do I fear this without reason. For I know (to give one instance out of many) a city of some importance, in which, after this form of discipline had been introduced, within the space of three years were exhibited such instances of tyranny, as would put the Romanists to shame.[183]

---

[181] Beza erred often in striving to become 'all things to all men' in an exaggerated manner. He quickly altered his opinion regarding Cartwright and Co. admitting he had been deceived by them.
[182] *Zürich Letters*, First Series, pp. 312, 313.
[183] *Zürich Letters*, Second Series, p. 251.

Here Gwalther is thinking, in context, of Heidelberg which had 'progressed' from a Reformed doctrine of church discipline to the new doctrine which caused a veritable reign of terror to proceed through the churches. Cartwright was instructed in radicalism in Heidelberg and sought to Heidelbergise England. This was a circumlocution of Calvinism.

Woolsey criticises Whitgift's strictures on Cartwright but does not mention that these were fundamentally doctrinal, historical and scriptural. Has Woolsey really studied Cartwright's low doctrine of Justification and high doctrine of monarchical elders? Cartwright's ecclesiology is far different from Bullinger's and Calvin's. Woolsey's emphasis that Cartwright was 'the nexus between English Puritanism and the Continental Reformation' in church government and theology demonstrates that Woolsey has not done his homework and is leaning on the wrong historical traditions. Having to admit the strong Calvinism of Whitgift and the Lambeth Articles, Woolsey backs out of the argument by agreeing with C. D. Stevens that 'Whitgift was not a Calvinist as Cartwright was'. Nor was Calvin a Calvinist as Cartwright was. Here we must ask what influence had Cartwright on the Covenant in general and on Woolsey's views in particular and how did Cartwright differ from Calvin's Calvinism? Woolsey does not attempt to answer such questions. Nor does Woolsey explain why Cartwright altered his theology and views of Church Government so often and sought by deceit to obtain high posts,[184] though he is so often depicted as 'a man of the people'.

Then Woolsey branches off to a discussion on Predestination without embedding it in scriptural Covenant Theology and introduces many other matters way off his theme showing a great lack of research. This is also exemplified in his description of the Reformed Church of Exiles in Frankfurt and his presentation of Andrew Melville. So what we are finding in Woolsey's book is that for the most part, Woolsey leaves the unity and continuity of covenant thought out and replaces it with a most lop-sided history of Presbyterianism which he sees ramified and ratified in the *Westminster Confession*. He seems to be oblivious to

---

[184] *Historical Background to the Westminster Assembly* pp. 17 and 20, also Chapter Sixteen: The Puritan Stream: Thomas Cartwright and Dudley Fenner.

the fact that Calvin was far from being a Presbyterian and had criticised their rebellious activities strongly.

Woolsey seeks backing by James Ussher

On dealing with James Ussher Woolsey admits that though Ussher wrote in 1645 that he had not authored the work of *A Body of Divinity* which had allegedly been published in his name from 'rude draughts … presented in a very faulty manner', mainly based on student notes he had made on Cartwright, and repeated this denial on several occasions, Woolsey, nevertheless in his frequent usage of this work refers to it as 'Ussher's'. Here Woolsey is arguing on uncertain ground. He did not state that Ussher confirmed his denial in the 1648 publication which makes Woolsey's use of an alleged Ussher even more dubious. Nor does he note that the only witnesses to a connection between Ussher and the work in a 'Letter to the Reader' prefaced to several editions is that those who criticise the work claimed that Ussher came to approve of it in his old age as it had been useful. Harrison Perkins writing in the *Evangelical Quarterly* states that, 'Andrew Woolsey likely accepted the *Body* too uncritically, although he usually incorporated evidence from Ussher's other catechisms as well'[185]. This is putting it very diplomatically and mildly. It is true the many editions of 'The Body' are wrapped up in authentic works of Ussher but the core bearing the name 'Body' does not appear to be his. Even the very detailed biography of Ussher appended to the 1677 edition and others does not mention any work of Ussher's on a 'Body of Divinity' but states he had studied many such 'Bodies' in his youth. Even the alleged Prefaces of John Downam give different information on dating the work. This author has read through some six editions of the supposed 'Body' which display highly different reasonings concerning authorship. Woolsey seems to have only considered one 'version'. I shall refer back to this subject in an Appendix showing how Ussher was involved in working with John Durie and a good number of London ministers from 1628 on concerning a *Body of Practical Divinity* from which Ussher had to

---

[185] 'Manuscript and Material Evidence for James Ussher's Authorship of *A Body of Divinitie* (1645),' EQ 29.2 (2018) 133-161, quote from p. 138.

withdraw in 1553 because of the unsettled state of the Cromwellian era.[186]

A spark of light comes with John Ball

Arriving at John Ball,[187] whose theology differed from Bullinger's to some extent and Calvin's to a greater extent, Woolsey shows clear original reading, though he is obviously using the Westminster Confession as a yardstick to understand Ball who died in 1540 before the Westminster Assembly had commenced. At last, through Ball, we have a glimpse of scriptural findings concerning the Covenant of Grace. Woolsey even states that Ball 'devoted the opening chapter of his Covenant of Grace to 'The Signification of the Word Covenant' which Woolsey sees as a reference to Bullinger's *De Testimento* which will be taken up later in this chapter. Ball was certainly closer to the Bullinger tradition, illustrated by his view of election and predestination taking final place 'after being brought into grace by Christ'. Thus Ball did not follow the deterministic Zwinglian doctrine which Woolsey appears to accept. So, too, Ball sees Moses as acting under Christ's directions in writing out the law and pointing out its tenors.[188] However, Ball was a contemporary of the troubles which gave rise to the Commonwealth and not a pioneer writer on the Covenant. One wonders why Woolsey omits dealing with John Bale's (not to be confused with John Ball) pioneer work on the Covenant which was contemporary to Bullinger's. Woolsey complains that foreign writers do not quote English-speaking writers but he himself leaves out the very best.

Woolsey goes on in the next few chapters to give an overview of post Westminster Assembly research centred more or less on the Covenant. On the whole he leaves out discussions on Bullinger's Covenant views even when discussing such theologians as Gerhard Vos who emphasized Bullinger's teaching on the Covenant, which Woolsey does not take up in his brief review of Bullinger in Chapter Seven.

---

[186] It is obvious that those who consider Ussher to be the author of *The Body of Divinity* have, in part, confused his cooperation with John and George Downam with a planned work sponsored by Durie for a *Body of Practical Divinity* which never came to be because of George Downam's death and Ussher's precarious situation under Commonwealth powers.

[187] See Chapter Two, Sources and Covenantal Doctrine of the Westminster Standards and *passim.*

[188] *A Treatise of the Covenant of Grace*, pp. 292ff. See also entry under Election in the Appended Table (no pagination).

Woolsey's dismissal of Baker's works

Only when dealing with Wayne Baker's work *Heinrich Bullinger and the Covenant* does Woolsey take up Bullinger in any detail only to question the 'historical truth' of Baker's findings on him. Woolsey obviously disagrees with Baker's (and Bullinger's) rejection of a deterministic double-predestination outside of the Covenant and is not prepared to study Baker's historical evidence. Indeed, Woolsey's main weakness is that he does not consider past and contemporary works on Bullinger, in spite of his wide reading but claims:

> Baker's insistence that Bullinger's sermon on Providence and predestination must be interpreted by the fact that he earlier affirmed universal calling of God, and that God was not the author of sin, is suspect since neither of these points can be considered contrary to Calvin's predestinarian position.

Again, Woolsey boils everything down to predestination which was not Bullinger's position and arguably not Calvin's either, and in so doing ignores the central teaching of Bullinger who did indeed tell Calvin not to write as if he thought God were the author of sin.

In his chapter 'The Covenant in the Early Reformers' Woolsey devotes a few pages to Bullinger, but the entire next seven chapters are devoted to Wooley's understanding of Genevan theology which is most superficial but which he feels overtook Bullinger and formed the basis of the *Westminster Confession*. I am familiar with several extant written minutes of the Westminster Assembly records, including those of John Lightfoot and Adoniram Byfield and have read an immense amount of correspondence between the Assembly and foreign churches, touring Europe to find it. I never found Woolsey's extreme position broadcast in such correspondence. Woolsey's views are certainly not in accordance with those of John Durie, the compiler of the records and main correspondent, or with those of Byfield, the main minutes-taker at the Assembly. Here certainly, Woolsey has lost the historical Calvin as he has also lost the historical Westminster Assembly.

Bullinger side-stepped in Woolsey's Covenant links

Woolsey's position seems to be that there was a break in Covenant theology in Bullinger's day and Calvin took over directly from Zwingli because of Zwingli's ideas of a double predestination and reprobation which Bullinger did not share. This is all part of a lead-up to establish, not the unity and continuation of the biblical Covenant of Grace but to justify the *Westminster Confession* division of the Covenant *as he sees it*.[189] In order to emphasise his alleged 'Calvinistic' thrust, Woolsey accuses Wayne Baker of centring on Bullinger to the exclusion of Calvin and his supporters in his various works. Here, he is echoing Müller's criticism of Schrenk in his Introduction. However, Woolsey fails to present a solid case for both a detailed study of the Covenant as found in scripture and history and evidence to show that the *Westminster Standards*, which he takes as the norm for Covenant teaching, are an improvement on Bullinger's and the bulk of the Swiss and British Reformers' teaching. One might also turn Woolsey's criticism of Baker back on him as he moves Bullinger after a brief recognition to the side in his devotion to what he believes is the 'Calvinistic' position, not taking into account scores of Bullinger's works based on his Covenant teaching. Indeed, because Calvin so often took over Bullinger's views, as also Bucer's we can argue that Bullinger was more 'Calvinistic' than Woolsey, as Calvin was so often a Bullingerite or Bucerite. Indeed Gustav Anrich claims it was Bucer who was the father of Calvinism and not Calvin.[190] Nor has Woolsey taken into consideration the flood of works on Bullinger's covenantal ideas between 1988 and the time of the book's publication in 2012. After reading both Woolsey and Baker, I realised all too well what Baker meant by speaking of criticism against his evidence being 'Hyper-Calvinistic Scholasticism'.

Bullinger was before Zwingli in his work on the Covenant

Contrary to the historical facts, Woolsey insists that Bullinger depended on Zwingli for his Covenant views. Obviously, as the records show, this was a topic of much discussion between the older and the younger man but here Woolsey does not take note of the dates of Bullinger's

---

[189] My italics.
[190] *Martin Bucer*, Strassburg, 1914, pp. 143, 144.

publications and the fact that Zwingli asked Bullinger to delay going to press with his reforms. Zwingli never came up with anything on the Covenant which was of the quality of Bullinger's work and his riper views came long after Bullinger had first published his own findings but these were highly philosophical and deterministic. Nevertheless, Woolsey sidesteps Bullinger and links Zwingli directly with Calvin because of his 'double predestination' which Woolsey emphasises more than Calvin ever did. Of course, such views are foreign to Bullinger's understanding of a Covenant which embraces all the elect in Christ who have been granted repentance and faith. There is no predestination whatsoever outside of this Covenant.

The *Confession* queried

Chapter VII of the *Confession* on 'Of God's Covenant with Man' is open to grave misunderstanding. The Reformed doctrine of the Covenant of Grace was between the Father and the Son on behalf of man. Our Reformers denied that a saving Covenant could be made between two unequals, God and man. Nor is the *Confession* at all clear on the use of the term the 'Covenant of Works'. Is this meant as a separate covenant doctrine? Does the *Confession* teach different Covenants? Nor is the *Confession* clear in its mention of different dispensations. Are we facing a kind of Dispensationalism here? We read also of different administrations in the *Confession*, none of which are clearly defined. The *Confession*, on the whole, presents a different story to the unity and continuation of the Reformed doctrine of the Covenant of Grace.

What is certain is there is no mention of predestination whether single of double in the *Confession's* definition of the Covenant which is Christocentric. But this is also a divergence from Reformed theology which speaks of being predestined in Christ. Chapter VII, which appears orthodox on the surface, however, is spoilt in its meaning by Chapter III 'On God's Eternal Decrees' which is far from Christo-centric and allows for different reprobations and different salvations. In Chapter III, we find the elect saved with no reference to Christ and the reprobate damned also with no reference to Christ. Then we are told that Christ comes in as a kind of second thought or Plan B and saves the already saved and the already damned are damned again for their unbelief. This quite destroys the arguments of our Reformers such as John Bale; 17th Century Puritans such as John Durie and 18th Century stalwarts such as John Gill who place predestination within a Christo-centric Covenant. The *Confession* postulates quite a different philosophical scenario of God's actions from eternity. Surely God's election from eternity is an election in Christ from eternity in time for eternity? Our God is always immanent in His actions from eternity in the purpose and progress of salvation. Our Reformers and Gill clearly taught that salvation was aevi-eternal, that is, it begins in time for eternity. The *Confession* confuses time with eternity as if election came in a fictive past eternity and salvation came in time as the second of two separate 'predestinations'. This breaks the back of God's Covenant of Grace in Christ and is worse than the thoroughly un-reformed philosophy of Zwingli.

Zwingli and Bullinger again

Woolsey points out that Bullinger wrote his work on the Covenant whilst debating with the Catabaptists as if this meant that he could not deal with the topic in a relaxed and thorough manner. However, this would go for Calvin, too, as many of his writings were written even in anger as his controversy with Jérôme-Hermès Bolsec, Westphal and others show. Most of Zwingli's works between 1524 and 1528 on the Lord's Supper, for instance, were written in his controversy with Luther and which were limited to technical but scholarly points as to the meaning of 'is' in Christ's words 'This is my body'. Up to 1526, they could hardly be called 'Reformed' and not Reformed at all in Zwingli's final year or so.

The fact that a number of Christian writers look upon Zwingli as having handed over his doctrine of the covenant to Bullinger, seems to be based on the belief that Zwingli was older than Bullinger who thus must have served as a kind of apprentice to him. However, whilst Zwingli was busy debating on the Lord's Supper with the Lutherans, he was at the same time urging caution in carrying out reforms in his own church. Such a further reformation was highly necessary as Zwingli surprised the Bern and Basle Reformers as late as 1528 at the Disputation of Bern by dropping to his knees and crossing himself every time the morning Mary bells were rung.

Zwingli had lived a wastrel life before becoming a Roman Catholic priest and sadly also afterwards. His father constantly told him he was only good enough to play bawdy tavern songs. Unlike Heinrich Bullinger's father who had kept faithful to his dear common-law wife from the start of their courtship and married her as soon as he had accepted Reformation truths, Zwingli, of whom it is claimed was Reformed in 1519 waited until 1525 before he married his mistress of several years, Anna Reinhard, but, as V. H. H. Green states in his *Renaissance and Reformation*, 'it was not so much an affair of the heart as an attempt to regularise a dubious relationship'.[191] We note that as late as 1524, the pope still counted Zwingli as a loyal Roman Catholic. Adrian VI spoke highly of Zwingli and his successor Clement VII negotiated amiably with him for a time.

The early date of 1519 so often given for Zwingli's spiritual conversion and departure from Rome does not meet the facts. When Francois Lambert of Avignon arrived in Zürich on 12 July, 1522 on a pan-European preaching tour, he visited Zwingli who had already served three years as a Roman Catholic priest and was still in Roman Catholic orders which Lambert had already thrown off. Zwingli had, however, become influenced by those in Basle who were now challenging Rome such as his mentor Thomas Wyttenbach and also Johannes Oeclampadius and Conrad Kürschner, better known as 'Pellican.'

Zwingli had indeed begun several minor reforms within the Roman Catholic Church which alarmed some and encourage others. This moved the sympathetic city council to propose a series of four debates between Zwingli and his Church concerning his new views. Lambert arrived shortly before these debates and both men conversed closely concerning the whole spectrum of Christian doctrine which would have helped Zwingli order his thoughts aright in preparation for the debates which proved highly successful. It was not until 1522 that both Zwingli and Lambert realised they must break with Rome. Lambert did so abruptly but Zwingli now took his time, sounding both Rome and the Zürich Council out so he could keep his office and church in Zürich. During this time teenager Bullinger had totally cast off all his Roman

---

[191] P. 161.

Catholic fetters and in 1523 started teaching Reformed theology in a former abbey college near Zürich where he caught the older man's new interest in Reformed theology.

After mentioning the fact that it was Bullinger who encouraged the printing of Zwingli's works after his death on the battle-field in 1531, Jon Balserak and Jim West in their book *From Zwingli to Amyraut: Exploring the Growth of European Reformed Traditions* wrote:

> However, the position advanced here is that it was actually Zwingli who gleaned much from Bullinger with respect to the Eucharist as well as the theme of the covenant. Bullinger's understanding of the Eucharist was intimately linked with his understanding of God's covenant which he viewed as foundational for God's plan of salvation from the Garden of Eden in Genesis 3 to the garden of Revelation 22. For Bullinger, the Eucharist is a covenant sign and seal of God's grace (Staedtke 1975, 227-228; Williams: 1975, 131).

My research shows that this verdict is accurate as Bullinger opened Zwingli's eyes to a number of Reformed doctrines not only concerning the Covenant and the Lord's Supper. Indeed, Zwingli wobbled between three distinct theories of the sacraments from 1523 to 1531, these being, the Real Presence in flesh and blood, the Spiritual Presence and a mere memorial ceremony. Personally, I am convinced for reasons I have emphasized in other publications, particularly in *New Focus Magazine* that Zwingli opted for the Reformed position of Christ's Spiritual Presence, whereas both Calvin and Beza never came down on one side of the argument concerning a Real Presence and a Spiritual one.[192]Even the *Consensus Tigurinus* of 1549 proved to be a *Dissensus Tigurinus* because neither Calvin not Beza kept to it but preferred a more Lutheran interpretation where the term 'substance' was highlighted. This term Bullinger managed to keep out of the *Consensus Tigurinus* and led to Calvin's complaint that Bullinger never moved an inch whereas he was forced to compromise time and time again.

---

[192] Of course, Calvin and Beza were long divided on this issue. See my detailed analysis of the matter between Bullinger, Calvin and Beza in my *Henry Bullinger: Shepherd of the Churches*, especially by examination of the Consensus Tigurinus.

In an important entry in his *Diarium* dated 12th September, 1524 Bullinger stated that 'Zwingli disclosed his mind to me concerning what he understood about the sacrament of the body and blood of the Lord' in response to Bullinger sharing 'in good faith' his own view of the Eucharist to Zwingli. Bullinger explained that his conclusions concerning the Eucharist from his own study of scripture and his grasp of the theme of the covenant were reflected in the writings of both Augustine and of the Waldensians (Burnett 2011:77-90, 103, 104). Bullinger also noted in his *Diarium* that 'Zwingli forbade me to explain this mystery to anyone' as he deemed it not the appropriate time to do so because Zwingli 'desired to mention it himself at the proper time (pp. 59, 60).' It does appear here that Zwingli was rather worried that Bullinger would run ahead of the older man in his Reforms.

It might well be the case that Calvin links up somewhat with Zwingli rather than Bullinger here as Calvin's first edition of the *Institutes* came at a time when the reformers were discussing Zwingli's 1531 exposition of the Christian faith[193] which was distributed in manuscript form until Bullinger published it shortly prior to Calvin's publication of the first edition of the *Institutes*. Calvin's small publication of 1536[194] echoes much of Zwingli's work, besides Bucer's, including Zwingli's dedication of his work to the French King. However, Zwingli had already shown his flattering interest in Francis I in his 1525 work *On True and False Religion* in which Zwingli, however, does not take up the matter of the Covenant. He refers to the Covenant once in his previous work addressed to Emperor Charles V *Rechenschaft des Glaubens* where he uses the term in conjunction with what baptism signifies but he does not go into any further detail. Years later, after Bullinger's thrust into publicising his work on the Covenant, Zwingli came up with his 1530 work *De Providentia Dei (1530)*. This work is highly philosophical and Humanistic and there is little scriptural work in it. Indeed, Zwingli argues here that God's predestination and reprobation are outside the realms of faith and even outside the work of Christ which he hardly mentions in the essay. There is no sign in the work of Bullinger's doctrine of being elected in Christ within the

---

[193] *Christiana fidei brevis et clara exposition.*
[194] See Ford Lewis Battles' translation and annotations to this early edition of Calvin's *Institutes.*

Covenant of Grace. Furthermore, Zwingli argues deterministically that God predestined man to sin and does not fight shy of calling God the author of sin. This was going too far for Calvin in its bluntness so during the predestination debate with Bolsec, Calvin wrote to Bullinger in January, 1552, saying:

Zwingli's book (*de Providentia*), between you and me, is so full of hard paradoxes, that it is far from the restraint that I practise.

This might be taken for a disagreement with Zwingli's arguments or not, but at least we know that Calvin protested at the harsh way Zwingli described Providence.

If Calvin is Zwingli's successor, Bullinger hardly fits the picture
Naturally Bullinger is bound to be left out here in the process of Woolsey's 'unity and continuity' because he would not accept the fatalism and arbitrary nature of both Zwingli's and Calvin's theologies which destroyed the doctrine of the Covenant of Grace. Bullinger felt free to advise his friends on this subject without any falling out on any side. However, we must note that Jacques Courvoisier opens his book *Zwingli: A Reformed Theologian* by claiming that Zwingli was quite ahead of Calvin in a number of central theological doctrines, especially ecclesiology, and went beyond him in his intellectual capacities. Indeed, towards the end of his book when dealing with Zwingli's doctrine of the sacraments, a term Zwingli detested, Courvoisier still complains that Calvin was 'totally unaware' of the ecclesial dimensions of Zwingli's thought.[195] This goes for his understanding of Bullinger's ecclesiology also. Such 'dimensions' are entirely absent from *De Providentia* but very much present in all Bullinger's works. Courvoisier does not refer to any teaching of the Covenant in Zwingli's writings whatsoever, but nevertheless claims that Calvin owed more to Zwingli than he thought. This can be said also of Calvin's indebtedness to the French, Swiss, Flemish, German and English Reformers which is made very apparent when comparing the various editions of the *Institutes*, although acknowledgements to other writers are scarce in Calvin's

---

[195] See Chapter IV and especially the long footnote 45.

works. The Basle and Bern Reformers were quick to point out this weakness on Calvin's side when he presented Bullinger's views as if he had authored them. After reading most of what Calvin wrote and nearly all of what Bullinger wrote and very much of what Zwingli wrote, this writer has come to the conclusion that Calvin, though remaining less of a philosopher than Zwingli and less of a theologian than Bullinger, went his own way along the Covenant path cataloguing but not synthesising other men's ideas as he went along.

Woolsey, however, roots his idea of 'Calvinism' in Zwingli's doctrine of what we may call 'reprobation-in-a-vacuum' which Bullinger for good Christ-centred reasons did not share and which, however, did become a permanent feature of Calvin's systematic, case-study thinking. Bullinger had a most balanced doctrine of predestination and reprobation which he also placed firmly in his gospel view of the *Gnadenbund* or Covenant of Grace. Calvin tended to view Predestination and Election as if they were factors outside of the Father's arrangement with the Son to choose out a People for Himself, thus showing that he had, indeed, side-stepped Bullinger and put the clock back to Zwingli without developing a Christo-centric ecclesiology of the Covenant of Grace. Thus J. Wayne Baker writes in Chapter Two of his *Henry Bullinger and the Covenant* in the section entitled 'Predestination and Covenant in Bullinger's Thought':

> Predestination, insomuch as it was incipient in sola gratia, was a generally accepted doctrine from the very beginning of the Reformation, although it was not a source of contention in the early years. The importance of the teaching grew, however, until after mid-century, absolute double predestination increasingly became the test of orthodoxy in Reformed circles. But this did not happen without a struggle. Calvin himself was the author of the controversy, particularly in his argument with Bolsec in the early 1550s.

This discussion greatly harmed the Reformed insistence that the Covenant of Grace was the hub of ecclesiology and not a deterministic predestination outside of the Covenant. After Calvin, Reformed theology took two different paths. Of course, this is one of the major weaknesses of the *Westminster Confession*, too which sought to out-Calvinise Calvin and quite departed from Bullinger.

God is not the author of sin

Calvin did place a more general emphasis on his 'double-predestination than most other Reformers of his day. It is in this connection that Woolsey places Bullinger's advice to Calvin not to give the impression that he believed God was the author of sin[196] in the double-predestination debate. Woolsey mentions on two occasions, that this advice was exaggerated, and argues that Calvin was as much against accusing God of being the author of sin as Bullinger. This is ignoring both Calvin's and Bullinger's clearly stated views. Woolsey here is confusing the issue and moves the controversy out of its historical context. Bullinger always presented God as the loving Father who created a people to be loved, rather than the abstract, impersonal God who created man solely for His own honour. Bullinger emphasises that God created man in the form His Son took upon Himself as a means of fellowshipping with man in Christ. This is the core of the Covenant for Bullinger. His Covenant was based on Pre-Fall creation as a work of Christ in his inter-Trinitarian fellowship with the Father and the Spirit for man's sake. It was not built on a highly fictive pre-fall theory of reprobation which leaves God's Covenant and Christ's work and purpose in creation aside. Bullinger further believed, because of Christ's unity with His elect, that when the Father said of the Son that He was well-pleased with Him, he was also including those who were placed in Christ. Bullinger argued also that in His love for Adam, God created him as a free agent, able to withstand sin. This Calvin denied and told the Genevan Council, who happily rarely agreed with Calvin, on 6 October, 1552,

> However, I am free to confess, that I have stated that God not only has foreseen, but also foreordained, the fall of Adam, which I maintain to be true, not without good grounds and evidences from holy writ.

---

[196] See Chapter Seven footnote 226.

Here Calvin is defending his 1551 edition of the *Institutes* which Jean Trolliet had criticised correctly for its alleged teaching that God ordained sin. In the 1551 version of the *Institutes*, Calvin strives both to eat his cake and keep it, arguing that Adam was created with the intention that he should fall to the glory of God's Name but that he was also damned because of His own (God given?) perversity. Calvin is also suggesting that God condemned Adam for what he foresaw he would do, though he otherwise argues that election was because of foreordination and not fore-knowledge. This is all light-years from Bullinger's biblical stance. Indeed, Calvin had written in his *Institutes*:

> Although that by the eternal Providence of God *man has been created for that state of misery in which he is*, yet notwithstanding he has deserved the cause of that misery for himself, and not from God. For he perishes only because of his having through perversity, degenerated from the pure nature which God had given him.[197]

One might ask how can Calvin speak of man's 'pure nature' when God decreed it to be defiled? The very idea is horrible, to say the least. However, not only Bolsec and Trolliet but also Bullinger have been criticised by modern 'Calvinists' for misunderstanding Calvin here, though one would think it impossible to misunderstand the fact that Calvin is teaching that God created man to sin.

Calvin now accused Bullinger of letting him down in not supporting him on the matter of an alleged decree of God that Adam should sin and his ideas of a double-predestination outside of Christ's Covenant. Bullinger's reaction to his protégé's move came on February 20, 1552 when he told Calvin that he gave the impression of teaching that God had not only foreseen Adam's fall but predestinated and activated it so that He is made the author of sin. Such a teaching would only scare people away from listening to the gospel, Bullinger added. This was exactly the point Bolsec, too, had made against Calvin. Calvin,

---

[197] See Calvin's address before the Council and the editor's quotes from the 1551 *Institutes* in the Ages Ultimate Library, Letter 301, p. 371ff.. The italics are mine.

however, took Bullinger's mild words as an insult.[198] Reformed Bern's reaction was far from mild as they still considered themselves responsible for Geneva's Reformation. Thus Geneva's deliverers from the Roman Catholic yoke reacted with great anger to Calvin's un-Reformed attitude and forbade the people of the Vaud to take Communion in Geneva. Again, Calvin turned to Bullinger and begged him to mediate. Bullinger saw that the Bernese Council were now going to extremes themselves and told them their reaction was too strong. As a result of Bullinger's mediation, Bern lifted the Lord's Supper embargo on Geneva. This was one of the many times Bullinger rescued his friend from his own temper and helped him stabilise his theological balance. Without Bullinger's mediation, Calvin would never have returned to Geneva after his exile.

It seems, however, that hard core predestinarians who place an alleged decree to predestinate and reprobate outside of the work of Christ within the Covenant of Grace are still with us. In his article Heinrich Bullinger: Covenant Theologian, published in the *Standard Bearer* in 1993 (Vol. 69 #19), Herman Hanko departs from his otherwise positive assessment of Bullinger and says:

> In one controversy, however, he showed a weakness. When Calvin in Geneva was struggling with the heresies of Bolsec, the Consistory of Geneva sought the advice of the other Swiss theologians. Although in general these theologians agreed with Calvin in his doctrine of predestination (Bolsec denied sovereign predestination), with the exception of Farel, they cautioned Geneva to proceed with care and questioned Calvin's strong statements on God's predestination of sin and sovereign, unconditional reprobation. Bullinger was among them.

If 'sovereign predestination' means God is the Author of sin, this author who believes we are predestined in Christ and not outside of Christ and the Fall was man's sole fault not God's, would say Hanko has placed himself outside of the Covenant of Grace, I trust from ignorance, which is forgivable, and not intention. Furthermore, the

---

[198] See Chapter Five: 'Ridding Geneva of Heresy' on these Geneva problems in my book *Henry Bullinger: Shepherd of the Churches.*

major Swiss theologians certainly did not agree with Calvin and censured him harshly, leading to his appeal to Bullinger to help him out of his difficulties. This demonstrates how accuracy in theology is determined by historical facts.

Woolsey ignores world-wide acceptance of Bullinger's doctrines
Woolsey, in his quick dismissal of Bullinger's importance, quite ignores the widespread positive reception of Bullinger's theology after Calvin's death, especially in Switzerland, Great Britain, Germany and the Eastern European countries. Indeed, after Calvin's home call, Beza was advised by the Council to follow Bullinger first and foremost and they had always forbidden Calvin to publish his *Institutes* in Geneva without their publishing Bullinger's works to help balance them off. A good number of articles concerning Bullinger's special contribution to the Church of England whose Reformers called Bullinger, 'The One Pillar of the English Church' have been published including several from my pen. The final triumph of the Reformation under Bullinger's leadership in Hungary came on 24 February, 1567, three years after Calvin's death, when the Hungarians called the Council of Debrecen and ruled that Bullinger's doctrinal works should become the confessions of their faith and doctrines. These works also became the basis for Hungary's state-Church relationships for several hundred years to come. Bullinger's ministry to Hungary, however, was to spread still further when the Trinitarian Controversy broke out and Bullinger was relied on by the Hungarians to defend Orthodoxy in their country as did also the Poles. Correspondence between these countries became so brisk that Bullinger had to appoint Ludwig Lavater (1527-1586), Josias Simler, Conrad Gessner and Johannes Wolf (1521-1571) to help him with his witness to Hungary and Poland. It was Bullinger's theology that the early Pilgrims in the New World took with them as Calvin's influence was still a long way off.

Up to 1536, Calvin was quite unknown in wider Continental Reformed circles and did not reach the international eye until a full decade later. Even then and as late as 1550, Calvin had published little, especially on sermons and preaching, whereas people were reading literally hundreds of Bullinger's sermons and doctrinal works in several languages. Furthermore, few scholars have taken the trouble to compare

Calvin's *Institutes* with Bullinger's works. Walter Hollweg in his *Heinrich Bullingers Hausbuch* devotes an entire chapter to Bullinger's enormous influence on Calvin's *Institutes*, in particular the 1550 version, and the Heidelberger Catechism.[199] He states that Calvin is not guilty of plagiarism but leaves the impression that Calvin avoids the charge merely by rewording Bullinger in the numerous passages taken from him and he include not only Bullinger's themes and scriptural proofs but even the examples Bullinger gives to illustrate them. Gillian Lewis has obviously little to say about Bullinger's influence as Calvin is his subject. As soon as Calvin died, however, Lewis turns his gaze on Bullinger and, not surprisingly, but rather critically, says that Bullinger sat like a spider in the centre of the web of the Reformation.[200]

We remember, too, that when Beza, Calvin's successor in Geneva, was asked by the Scottish Assembly to send them a statement of the Genevan Reformed doctrines, Beza said he and Calvin had had nothing to do with the founding of their church and that they had no Confession of Faith of their own so he was enclosing Bullinger's *Second Helvetic Confession*. This great international scope of Bullinger's theology is more or less ignored by Woolsey.

Bullinger's Decades

It is interesting to note that Woolsey cites Bullinger's *Decades* to show he wrote little on the Covenant of Grace, though others, such as myself, would find it pervading the entire work. Gerhard Vos, for instance, tells us that the *Decades* are 'structured entirely by the covenant idea'.[201] Woolsey omits to mention this fact when dealing with Vos. Peter Opitz shows in his 458 paged work on the *Decades* how Bullinger's Covenant teaching is there from the first Decade on and that this was Christo-centric. Obviously one who has not the same 'covenant idea' or ideas of a Covenant based on deterministic logic and not on the love of Christ for His People will not find it there. I have a dear friend who cannot

---

[199] See Chapter 3, Der Einfluss des Buches auf die *Institutio* Calvins und den Heidelberger Katechismus.

[200] *International Calvinism*, p. 67.

[201] *Redemptive History and Biblical Thought*, Phillipsburg, 1980, p. 236. I am indebted to Angus Stewart for this source and would heartily recommend a thorough study of Stewart's British Reformed Journal article 'Heinrich Bullinger', the First Covenant Theologian, also published in a slightly abridged form on the *Covenant Protestant Reformed Church* website.

come to faith because of his fear that he is a castaway and God has determined that He is reprobate, though he loves the word of God and adores Christ. Sadly, he has been influenced by those who prefer to preach on God's alleged double-predestination in some 'past eternity' and final judgment on sinners irrespective of Christ's Covenant Work and not on the great plan of God to save mankind from such a situation. I have often discussed 1 Corinthians 9:27 with this man who lives in permanent horror of being a castaway and showed him that Paul is not preaching on being cast away but on the way he has found in Christ to avoid it. I have also expounded Hebrews 10:39 explaining that:

> We are not of them that draw back unto perdition; but of them
> that believe to the saving of the soul.

This is the difference between Zwingli's, and often Calvin's, expression of the Covenant and Bullinger's.

Woolsey's main complaint is that Bullinger has not presented a specially worked out thesis on the Covenant in his *Decades*. But why pick especially on the *Decades* and not on the other 126 works we have extant from Bullinger's pen, many of which refer to the Covenant? Woolsey obviously demands a special thesis in the *Decades* on the subject for want of looking elsewhere. But the *Decades* are a collection of sermons given originally in Swiss-German to his humble hearers, many of whom were land and forest workers and ex-soldiers so as to win them for Christ. They were meant as a House Book or 'Andachtsbuch' for home-devotions and edification. The sermons therein are highly evangelical and gospel-bound throughout, and outrivalled all other works of this kind by its enormous reception in many countries. This is why Archbishop Whitgift made them essential reading for those who wished for a preaching licence. In the Advertisement to the Parker Society's edition of the First and Second Decades we read:

> In the convocation of the province of Canterbury, held in
> 1586, among the orders for the better increase of learning in the
> inferior ministers, introduced by Whitgift, Archbishop of
> Canterbury, the following direction stands foremost: every

minister having cure, and being under the degrees of master of arts, and bachelor of law, and not licensed to be a public preacher, shall before the second day of February next provide a Bible, and Bullinger's Decads in Latin or English and a paper book, and shall every day read over one chapter of the Holy Scriptures, and note the principal contents thereof briefly in his paper book, and shall every weeke read over one sermon in the said Decads, and note likewise the chief matters therein contained in the said paper; and shall once in every quarter (viz. within a fortnight before or after the end of the quarter) show his said notes to some preacher nere adjoyninge to be assigned for that purpose.

Bullinger's pioneer work on the Covenant cannot be evaded
But from 1523 on, Bullinger expounded the Covenant for theologians and ministers under a number of titles some of which Woolsey notes with short comments. A brief look at the many volumes of *Heinrich Bullinger Werke*, with many still to be published, made available by the Theologischer Verlag Zürich, will reveal that Bullinger authored far more material on the Covenant than did Calvin. If Woolsey had applied the same criticism to Calvin as he does to Bullinger, he would have had little to work on. Throughout his 'Calvinistic' arguments, Woolsey seems to be highly unfamiliar with the exact contents of Bullinger's special work on the Covenant *On the One and Eternal Testament or Covenant* though it is available as a freebie through various sources online. My copy came free of charge directly from the Zentralbibliothek, Zürich. Woolsey could also try Bullinger's later work *Der Alt Gloub*. Should Woolsey wish for a modern English translation, of *De Testamento seu foedere Dei* which appeared in both German and Latin, this is provided by McCoy and Baker in their book *Fountainhead of Federalism: Heinrich Bullinger and the Covenantal Tradition*. Where, we may ask is such a thorough-going exposition of the Covenant, as the gospel of world-wide evangelism from Bullinger's pen, given in Calvin's works? Of this work of Bullinger's though he agrees that it is 'a First', Woolsey says in Chapter Seven:

> While Bullinger was the first clearly to organise the ideas of the continent in a polemic work, *De Testamento* (1534), it is

possible to focus too much on this and make more of the covenant theme in Bullinger than he himself made of it.

This is typical of Woolsey where he gives praise to Bullinger with one hand and takes it back with the other. Woolsey just will not allow his readers to make their own conclusion, especially from the evidence which Woolsey keeps to himself or is not aware of it. A further example of this strange manoeuvre follows immediately after the first. Woolsey adds, '*De Testamento*, nevertheless, represented a milestone in the history of covenantal thought.' This sounds most positive yet Woolsey takes back much of what he has just written by saying: 'Bullinger gathered together and expanded in a more concise and systematic way all the points made by Zwingli.' Then he adds, 'and it (Zwingli's points?) can be justly called the first extended exposition of the Covenant of Grace.' This most unfounded view of Woolsey's leads him to claim, 'It is now generally accepted that Zwingli was the father of Reformed Covenant theology'. He says this because he erroneously thinks that Zwingli led the Reformation in Switzerland a generation before Bullinger.

Nevertheless, Woolsey's quotes from Bullinger's publications, as far as he has them at hand, present a synergised, biblical view of the Covenant which Woolsey's later chapters on Calvin fail to provide and which Zwingli and the *Confession* fail to promote.

Although Woolsey is apparently appealing to a general public in his brief survey of Bullinger, the footnotes he provides will be more than off-putting for those wishing to hear what Bullinger has to say. Though contemporary translations of Bullinger's works appeared in English shortly after being written Woolsey gives quotes from Bullinger's *Decades* in Latin. Miles Coverdale, correspondent and friend of Bullinger's, was at the forefront of these translations followed by John Stockwood. Significant enough is the fact that the Parker Society translation of the *Decades* was available to Woolsey via his own publisher's reprint of 2004[202] with introductions and comments both from Joel Beeke's pen and mine. Also Joel Beeke published my long

---

[202] See Band 1 and Band 2 (Erste Abteilung) *Bibliographie*, Theologischer Verlag Zürich 1972.

essay on Henry Bullinger 1504-1575 in the early summer of 2004 which puts Bullinger in quite a brighter light.

Oddly enough, when Woolsey quotes the *Institutes*, which is not too often, he uses the English language and not Calvin's original Latin and French. It may be said that I quote Latin freely in my doctoral thesis on the life and works of that great apostle of the Covenant John Durie, but this was according to the university's specifications and translations and quotes had to be given untranslated in the original language. The work was not published as a handbook for every man. However, very many important works of Durie's have still to be translated into English.

All doctrines of grace are centred in the Covenant
Bullinger, above all our Reformers, pointed out how the same essential message of salvation is seen throughout the entire Bible from Genesis to Revelation. The Covenant provides a focal point for all the doctrines of grace. All Christian doctrine and rites such as predestination, election, reprobation, law, gospel, forgiveness of sins, justification, sanctification, baptism, the Lord's Supper and the perseverance of the saints are all to be understood in the covenant context of God choosing a People for Himself in Christ from eternity and binding them to Him for eternity. Thus we need the entire scriptures from Genesis to Revelation to understand these matters. This Covenant centres alone in the work and eternal offices of the Lord Jesus Christ through whom all believers have access to every covenant blessing from the foundation of the world. Bullinger's insight into scripture is thus far more plausible than the horrid idea that an arbitrary deity in a presumed 'past-eternity' played the game of 'Eeny, meeny, miny moe' to count a person out in a game of 'tig' or 'tag'. I notice a number of British schools have banned this game from their playgrounds. Bullinger banned it from theology.

As a nineteen year-old, when looking back on his coming to faith in Christ through reading the scriptures, Bullinger wrote in his *De Scripturae negotio*, published in November 30, 1523:

> In brief, I discover that the New Testament is nothing other than the interpretation of the Old, in that the latter promises, the former teaches what has been made real; the latter more

concealed, the former more open; the latter in veils and figures, the former with clear evidence and the things itself.[203]

This is the basis of Bullinger's Covenant teaching. In a footnote, he thus adds 'The New Testament is a commentary'.[204] In this passage, Bullinger also shows that Christ based His calling on the Old Testament scriptures and proclaimed that the Old Testament bore witness to Him (John 5:39-47). Likewise, Acts 15:14-21 shows that the Apostles saw their work as carrying out the message of the Old Testament. So, too, Paul, when he told Timothy that all scripture was written on inspiration of God, he was chiefly referring to the Old Testament (2 Timothy 3:16, 17).[205] It is of note that in Zwingli's *Taufbüchlein* (Baptism Booklet) written two years later than Bullinger's own work, we find the older man who was slower to grasp the full Reformation than Bullinger, still emphasising the distinctions and contrast rather than the unity of the two Testaments. Woolsey has obviously missed this important fact. Later works of Zwingli showed he had come very near to Bullinger except for his insistence on a reprobation act of God inconsistent with Bullinger's view of the Christian gospel. If Woolsey's main argument is correct and Calvin obtained his idea of a so-called double-predestination from Zwingli, then Calvin relieved Zwingli's doctrine from its gospel and ecclesiastical context which was shown in his earlier works before the warrior-politician became too involved in violent controversies with the surrounding cantons which cost him his life. So, too, by such a step Calvin would have separated himself from Bullinger's more gospel tones.

Rather than view the Covenant with Abraham as one of Law only or merely concerning land possessions, as a number of modern political, Christian radicals, in tune with the old Catabaptists, do, Bullinger sees that one of Abraham's major covenantal tasks in preparation for deeper and wider revelations was to institute circumcision as a covenant sign pointing to the grace God offers. In his work *Studiorum ratio*, published in 1527 but based on a former letter to his friend Werner Steiner of

---

[203] Unveröffentlichte Werke aus der Kappeler Zeit, *De Scripturae negotio*, p. 25.

[204] *Novum testa(mentum) est commentarius.*

[205] *De Scripturtae negotio*, p. 25.

uncertain date, which was filled out up to the time of publication, Bullinger points out that all the books of the whole Bible point to the one eternal covenant which is thus the central theme of God's Word. Bullinger's major work on the Covenant *De testamento seu foedere dei unico et aeterno expositio* or *On the One and Eternal Testament or Covenant of God* was published in 1534, the probable year of Calvin's conversion, and quickly went into 15 editions. Here, Bullinger outlines that all God's covenant promises in both the Old and New Testaments are centred in the eternal Son of God and are thus 'one and eternal' in themselves. The subtitle of this work is Bullinger's most used text, 'This is my beloved Son in whom I am well pleased; hear ye him' (Matthew 17:5), a text with which Bullinger prefixes many of his works. We are justified in, through, by, for the sake of, and because of Christ's Work from eternity proclaimed in Old Testament times and throughout all further time. This is why we meet Christ in all the scriptures, historically, chronologically and spiritually.

In his *De testamento*, Bullinger uses Eusebius to show how his Covenant view was not only scriptural but also historical and the accepted doctrine of the Early Church and it had always been world-wide in its application. Quoting this ancient church historian, Bullinger writes:

> The religion of Christians is neither a new, nor foreign one, nor has it arisen recently. Rather, since we are permitted freely to indicate what is the truth, it was the first religion of all, originating with the beginning of the world, from the beginning receiving shape and form by the same Christ as God, creator and teacher.[206]

Here, Bullinger is in agreement with early Irish Reformer John Bale whose Covenant writings have also been a constant comfort to me for very many years. He also looked on the entire scriptures as a testimony to the true, Christian Covenant religion throughout all time as we shall see in my final chapter.

---

[206] I am using the McCoy/Baker translation here.

Bullinger's works should be read by all those who see no continuity from the Old to the New Testament

Most of Bullinger's works on the eternal Covenant were written against contemporary 'Modernists', such as the Catabaptists who taught a new gospel concerning a radical distinction between and even a radical break between the two Testaments, seeing in them two covenants with two concepts of salvation. Only their New Testament version was accepted as valid and worthy of all acceptation. Many of these various protest movements rejected the entire covenant idea as being merely Jewish and part of an Old Testament which had no relevance to Christians who were believers of New Testament truths only.

Bullinger claimed that in rejecting the Old Testament, Catabaptists rejected not only the true Covenant and the signs pointing to the work of grace in Christ but to a right use of the ordinances and the central themes of law and gospel. In his *On the One and Eternal Covenant* Bullinger sees the term 'covenant' as being often synonymous with 'testament'. This testament is bi-lateral because it outlines not only the eternal inheritance of God's people through an act of grace, but also the duties of believers in living according to the covenant. The German word for covenant used by Bullinger to translate the biblical words is *Bund* which is similar in meaning to the English word 'bond' or 'binding'. It includes not only the idea of the Covenant itself as used in English but also the idea of '*keeping* the Covenant' and being bound to it by God's Grace. Of course, it is Christ who thus 'bounds us' to Him as the apple of His eye. Christ is our Covenant-Keeper. It is difficult to compare German terms for 'Testament' and 'Covenant' with English equivalents because there is no 'one to one' translation of the different synonyms in both languages. Indeed, most of the diversities found in international theological debate are merely over two narrow indigenous renderings of the Greek and Hebrew where other language speakers have no problem there though perhaps in other theological areas. Throughout all my writings, I have thus always had at least five dictionaries at hand besides my Hebrew, Greek and Latin lexica, so as to work out closer meanings. This has helped me to avoid the efforts of many modern scholars who are far too narrow in the use of words, especially when translating.

Keeping to the idea of 'binding', Bullinger shows secondly that through the Covenant of Grace, God first unbinds the sinner from his bondage to sin and then binds him to Himself, placing him under a mutual obligation to serve his God. Thus the Swiss pastor and theologian emphasises not only Psalm 103:8ff. and Romans 11:36 when stressing that the covenant is all of grace, but he equally emphasises Genesis 17:1 which states that the believer must walk before God and be perfect. The Zürich Bible in High German which Bullinger and his team of translators brought out some years before Luther's work translates Genesis 17:1 as 'I am the almighty God, walk before me then you will be unpunishable.'

For Bullinger, the perfect man is the man whose condemnation has been removed from him and who has been justified and sanctified in Christ. The Covenant People are those whom God has no cause to punish eternally because our Covenant Head, the Lord Jesus Christ, has sealed the Covenant in His own obedience to the Law and His vicarious death under its penalties. As Isaiah preached, 'With His stripes we are healed'.[207] Bullinger further outlines the relationship between the Old and New Testaments, body and spirit, law and gospel and also the relationship of baptism to the covenant gospel. In his *Von dem Touff (Concerning Baptism)*, he sees the covenant sign of circumcision as pointing ahead to the blood sacrifice of Christ. After that sacrifice was made once and for all eternity, the covenant sign became the unbloody sign of water baptism demonstrating the cleansing powers of Christ's work on the cross and the outpouring of the Spirit of God on His people. Baptism is not an individual testimony to one's own belief but a universal testimony of Christ's sin-cleansing work on the cross. It is a visual reminder and promise of what Christ has done and does for his People.

Bullinger closes his major work on the Covenant with the words:

Now I ask, therefore, who is ashamed of or regrets the most difficult labours undertaken on behalf of the covenant of God, since it is now evident that from the beginning of the world all the saints have worship God in this covenant and have even laid down their lives on behalf of it? Who has not been greatly

---

[207] Isaiah 53:5.

fortified, even though sweating in the midst of great labours, by the fact that the eternal God has bound himself to us by an eternal bond and has most faithfully kept that eternal covenant with all his saints from the beginning? For often the saints have been thrown into dangers, often religion itself has been threatened with destruction, and more often it seemed to be defeated and buried, and even God was quite frequently thought to have deserted his own people. But rising up at the right moment, God has always protected the true religion, having defeated and crushed the destroyer's ones. This same God is immutable and eternal. This same God, therefore, even today will not fail those of his own who are bound to him in the eternal covenant, no matter how the world might be seized with madness. To him be the glory!

As a brief postscript, Bullinger adds Psalm 25:10:

All the parts of the Lord are grace and faith to those who keep his Testament and his covenant!

Summing up

Henry Bullinger was the first Reformer to emphasise the centrality of the Covenant for all Christian doctrine from Genesis to Revelation and one of the first writers to attract my attention to this biblical fundamental teaching. Bullinger felt he must publish on the Covenant which had been the basis of the Christian faith so long because the Catabaptists were now denying it and robbing the New Testament of its Old Testament basis. Sadly, some evangelical, Reformed people are now misusing the name of Calvin to put forward the theory that both Calvin and Zwingli were the essential creators of Covenant of Grace theology. Hereby they are guilty of what has been called High-Calvinistic Scholasticism and a rejection of the fundamental Christocentric teaching of Bullinger which they replace with deterministic double-predestination theories which side-step the biblical teaching recognized by Bullinger. Thus such modern writers on the Covenant forget that it is a Covenant of Grace in all its biblical, salvational, ecclesiastical and Church historical aspects and rather dwell on philosophical theories of double-predestination and double-reprobation which such as Andrew Woolsey claim Calvin took over from Zwingli. Woolsey seems to base his unwarranted theories on the *Westminster Confession* (which he greatly misinterprets) rather than God's Word.

Symptomatic of Woolsey's approach is that those writers who give good, sound documentary evidence for Bullinger's pioneer views are dismissed for leaving 'Calvin and his followers' out of the picture. His attempts to show that Zwingli influenced Bullinger on the Covenant question are groundless as Bullinger developed his theology quite independently of Zwingli and published before him. Documents from Zwingli's pen show a radically different understanding of the Covenant to Bullinger's. From the written evidence and dates of publications from both Zwingli's and Bullinger's pens it is obvious that Bullinger influenced Zwingli to some extent but the older man, who was converted from Rome at about the same time as the younger, was unable to follow Bullinger.

Woolsey's arguments are typical of those who cannot reconcile *Westminster Confession* teaching with Bullinger's solid biblical exegesis and show a most limited knowledge or at least understanding of Bullinger's many works. It is strange that, writing for Reformation Heritage Publishing, Woolsey has come up with a totally different view of Bullinger's works which appeared in the Introductions and commentaries on Bullinger's *Decades* printed by the same publisher' just a few years previously.

Bullinger pointed out that the same Christo-centric Covenantal message is to be found throughout all the scriptures and the New Testament was a commentary on the Old and carried on its Messianic thrust. All Christian doctrine is united in this pan-biblical Covenant so the New Testament writers carried on the message of the Old. Both Testaments point to the same Saviour so both Testaments are Christian in their teaching.

In cutting out the Covenant outlined in the Old Testament and with it the Law that our Reformers claimed 'biddeth good, and forbiddeth evil', Bullinger argued that such people cut out Christ in the Old Testament in all His salvational tasks and rob the scriptures of their teaching concerning God's righteousness and thus throw out the central teaching of both Law and Gospel. Furthermore they erase the sinner's responsibility before God forgetting the binding nature of the eternal Covenant of Grace. Anyone who discards all the Old Testament signs pointing to Jesus, cannot complain if he remains voluntarily in unbelief. This attitude of scoffers against the Old Testament Bullinger calls 'madness' which will not stop God from carrying His purpose out.

Bullinger is also very useful in showing that the Old Testament revelation concerning the Covenant was not one of Law only but Law and Grace went hand in hand in the Old as they do in the New. This is because Christ is in all the scriptures reconciling the World to Himself, and He keeps the Covenant in both its properties of Law and Grace for us.

Chapter 10

John Durie On God's Covenant People

My indebtedness to John Durie (c.1599-c.1680)

From 1640 onwards, there was a great protest amongst Reformed theologians against spreading errors propagated by supposed Reformed people who looked on the Covenant as some sort of religio-political contract between God and their faulty view of their own particular institution thought to be the true 'Church'. The leader of the movement of some fifty stalwarts in England, many on the Continent and a faithful handful in the New World to restore the Reformed faith and unite the now highly fragmented Church was John Durie (c.1596-c.1680). Of his still-well-known followers were Samuel Hartlib, James Ussher, John Davenant, William Biddel, Joseph Hall, Adoniram Byfield, William Gouge, John Stoughton, John Downam, Henry Burton, George Walker, Nicolas Morton, Sidrach Simpson, Richard Culverwell, Obadiah Sedgwick, George Hughes, Joseph Symonds, John Cotton, the Nye brothers and Richard Sibbes – all great names in true Reformed theology. There were also great men who supported the Reformers where they could such as John Owen, Thomas Goodwin and Joseph Mede. I mention these to show that Durie was a leader of a great company, though few acknowledge him today as his theology is abandoned by those who profess to be 'Reformed'.

This Puritan Reformer and man of seemingly endless capacities was also the writer who took me further into Covenant mercies and blessings. Durie, Cromwell's ambassador to Europe and compiler of the Westminster Standards and Minutes, who worked closely with Adoniram Byfield, the official minute-taker was the only Church of England minister left at the Assembly after 1643 and the only minister appointed directly to the Assembly by Charles I. He was just too proficient and useful to be thrown out like Daniel Featley. Ussher never attended the Assembly in spite of many reports to the contrary. Durie was also the only Scotsman to receive full voting rights and to be given the freedom of petitioning Parliament as Member for Westminster and as a private man. When Durie was abroad, working as Cromwell's right-hand man in Europe, John Owen and a number of other Independents, represented Durie's interest before Parliament. Durie is still widely known on the Continent under the Latinised name of Johannes Duraeus for his Practical Divinity reforms in theological training and free education for all children, including free access to libraries. He planned the setting up of think tanks in several continents with free access given to all.

Basing all knowledge on God-Only-Wise

The novel thing with Durie was that he based both his curricula for theological training and all his educational reforms, which he called Universal Learning, on tracing the ways of God-Only-Wise[208] in the Covenant teaching of the scriptures. He was the first true knowledge-engineer. Nowadays he is almost unknown in Britain, though he led the Reformed Puritan Party in Britain between the reigns of Charles I and II and influenced Germany, Holland, Sweden, Finland, Denmark, Switzerland, the Baltic States, Poland, Hungary, and other East European countries in realms of theology, pastoral training, education and international diplomacy. Indeed his outreach was far greater, though not as lasting as Bullinger's international influence.

Durie was highly successful as a diplomat in paving the way for the end of the Thirty Years' War, being advisor to the Swedish Royal family and the German Protestant princes over several generations. It is a great myth that Britain never took part in the Thirty Years' War as

---

[208] Romans 16:27 and passim.

Britain provided many thousands of troops under James and his son Charles to support the Protestant Cause on the Continent. Sadly, growing criticism of heredity Royalty in Parliament, curbed Britain's help and King Charles was executed confessing his deep faith in Christ.

However, most of the Continental Protestant Princes and Dukes were related somehow to the Stuarts and it was a German Stuart, George I, who eventually took over Great Britain through the descendants of Elizabeth, Charles I's sister. Durie travelled so widely internationally for the gospel's sake, often moving with the troops as a number of high-ranking Scottish officers were related to him, that church historian Shaw in his two-volume work on the Church throughout the Commonwealth period called him 'ubiquitous'.

The Covenant of Grace was not between God and fallen man
Through his studies in the Old and New Testament Covenant, Durie, a Hebraist and Greek scholar of note,[209] found that God had initiated a pact with His Son to give mankind a direct contact with the creator of all knowledge and its use for the common good through God's own revelation in His Word and His creation. This covenant was not between man and God as two unequals, the one being the receiver and the other the Giver. It was between two equals, God the Father and God the Son on behalf of fallen sinners. The Old Testament was the Bible of the Early Church and all her doctrines were thus grounded in this source of knowledge pointing to Christ the Maker of all things. He believed that to know Christ was to discover all knowledge because all knowledge and wisdom came from Christ and pointed back to Him. Durie believed, following the English and Swiss Reformers, that there was one continued Covenant and one continued Testament in the scriptures, the words *chadash* and *kainos* referring not to new in the sense that the old was no more but in the sense of ever-new, renewing, re-establishing and refreshing.[210] Durie's key verses here were Isaiah

---

[209] Durie also wrote and published in five different modern languages and was taken as a native in several European countries. He always dressed and cut his hair and beard in the fashion of the countries he visited and nobody noticed he was a foreigner.

[210] It is said that James VI could never throw away his old slippers as they had become his best friends because of their comfort. He bought new slippers for other practical uses as new friends. Thus we must think of 'old' in the sense of 'well-proven and an old friend' rather than something

11:9ff., Jeremiah 10:23, Jeremiah 31:31-34 and Proverbs 16:1. He was obviously influenced in his position by Johannes Wollebius the Swiss Puritan at Basel whose works he recommended to ministerial students and teachers. For Durie, the history of Salvation was the history of constant Reform in which the truths of the Covenant of Grace were repeatedly made clear to a generation who needed enlightenment in God's ways. Sadly, today in our dumbing down of language, we have given the terms 'old' and 'new' restricted meanings not supported by their old usage and the meanings of the Hebrew and Greek words they are thought to represent. Most theological problems today are because of linguistic misinterpretations. It is interesting to note, for instance, that the various Hebrew words for 'sin' are mostly associated with 'confusion'. The Early Church Fathers pointed out that Mankind has made its sin worse by our consenting to confusion and not by following God who is entirely free of confusion as Paul tells us.[211] Babel is sadly still with us!

Durie, like my other mentor William Cowper, believed in the restitution of all things before the Second Coming of Christ and that what sin had marred, God would mend. Thus when well-meaning John MacArthur tells us that 'all Israel shall be saved', I can live quite well with that providing MacArthur tells us who 'all Israel' are and how they are being and will be saved. John 19:12 is often used to back up MacArthur's Dispensational theory, 'They shall look on him whom they pierced'. We must, however turn to the Old Testament in order to understand this phrase. If we believe the Covenant is continuous, this is no problem. In Zechariah 12:10 we read:

> I will pour upon the house of David, and upon the inhabitants of Jerusalem, the spirit of grace and of supplication: and they shall look upon me whom they have pierced.

First of all, Zechariah is dealing with God's Covenant with the House of David and refers to a spirit of grace and supplication falling on it. I believe we can take 'me' to refer to our Saviour as in the light

---

to be discarded. Sadly, because of the dumbing down of English, the meanings of 'old' and 'new' have been grievously curbed, a fact that happily has not occurred in other modern languages.
[211] 1 Corinthians 14:33

of John 19 this cannot be avoided. So the salvation here intended must be through belief in Jesus and John tells us this was his intention in referring to this Old Testament text (v. 35). There is no salvation by '*sight*' in the scriptures but only through *insight* into the wonders of Christ provided by the Holy Spirit. Until Christ brings us Home to Glory, we live by His Faith.[212] The wall of partition between Greeks and Jews is demolished by Christ who makes one flock of His sheep and places them in one fold.

That all the People of God can only find salvation in and through the Great Shepherd is made clear in John 10:1-9:

> Verily, verily, I say unto you, He that entereth not by the door into the sheepfold, but climbeth up some other way, the same is a thief and a robber. But he that entereth in by the door is the shepherd of the sheep. To him the porter openeth; and the sheep hear his voice: and he calleth his own sheep by name, and leadeth them out. And when he putteth forth his own sheep, he goeth before them, and the sheep follow him: for they know his voice. And a stranger will they not follow, but will flee from him: for they know not the voice of strangers. This parable spake Jesus unto them: but they understood not what things they were which he spake unto them. Then said Jesus unto them again, Verily, verily, I say unto you, I am the door of the sheep. All that ever came before me are thieves and robbers: but the sheep did not hear them. I am the door: by me if any man enter in, he shall be saved, and shall go in and out, and find pasture.

Durie's vision of the universality of the Gospel found in Isaiah 11.9
The central pivot of all Durie's teaching of God's sure and certain Covenant with Christ on behalf of man was the conviction that one day the knowledge of the Lord would cover the earth as the waters cover the sea and would one day be the lot of every man, woman and child on the earth, according to age and capabilities but not restricted to social standing or nationality. This future which every minister and teacher

---

[212] Galatians 2:20.

should aim at was Durie's sole millennial thought and he based his educational reforms on scriptures such as Psalm 76 and Isaiah 11:8, 9 where we read of war being abolished and that every human being would learn to praise God for the knowledge received from Him helping them in their personal growth, occupations, usefulness to mankind and preparation for their heavenly inheritance. Durie outlines his doctrine concerning the spreading of the knowledge of the Lord in his *A further discovery of the Office of Address* and *Some Proposals towards the Advancement of Learning*. Durie's two main works on the Covenant *Earnest Breathings* and *A Summarie Platform of the Heads of a Body of Divinity* transformed my thinking as did his *Reformed Librarian*, a book still used in training Librarians. Durie saw his work as Librarian, especially when he took over the neglected King Charles I's library after the Cromwellians had left it to rot and be plundered, as providing free international centres of knowledge so every person would have access to God's Covenant wisdom.

The spiritual and intellectual movement of 1630-1680 in which Durie played a major role, was, however, also an inner reaction to the warring political and religious revolutions which were severely disrupting English and European society and national traditions.[213] As a result, an international hope arose amongst Protestants that a revival of religion and world-wide peaceful cooperation in religion, politics, science and education would arise out of the ashes of a ruined Europe and the knowledge of the Lord would spread all over the world. Writing to Hartlib on 30 November, 1638 John Durie says:

> The scripture hath promised unto us that this shall bee at last brought to passe in the Church of God & foretelleth us also of the meanes by which it shall bee accomplished: Esa. 11. 8, 9. wee there are told that the greatest enimitie & exasperation that is in nature shall bee taken away from amongst the creatures; & that there shall bee no hurting nor destroying any more in all the holy mountaine of God; because the earth shall bee full of the

---

[213] It is often thought that the Thirty Years' War was solely a Continental disaster where Protestants and Roman Catholics were in battle. In England, there was a very similar battle going on which, for many years, was equally bloody. In England, it was between the Church of the Reformation and the Monarchy on the one side and the usurping Presbyterian and Republican ideologies on the other. The world of England and the Continent became changed for ever.

knowledge of the Lord as the waters couering the bottome of the sea. here the exasperat spirits of men are reconciled; & the meanes wherby God will bring this to passe is said to bee the abundance of his knowledge & the euidence of his will reuealed unto all those that shall bee in his Church.' [214]

The Restitution of All Things

It is a surprise to many modern Reformed believers to find that Durie's views were common amongst the Puritans of his age who spoke of making Britain a New Jerusalem which would prepare the world for that eschatological restoration of Eden called by many church historians The Puritan Hope.[215] This conviction has now waned in Reformed thinking. After checking with Jonathan Edwards concerning his teaching on the restitution of all things at the end of time, I asked two most active writers on Edwards why this did not appear in their Edwards biographies. Both told me that Edwards did not touch on the subject. They had overlooked it as being of no interest. When we read the works of these seventeenth and eighteenth century Reformers, we realise they were not burdened by our contemporary pseudo-theological speculations about whether all Jews will be saved or not. They looked forwards to the knowledge of Christ being a universal revelation and also the clear way to Him taught in the Covenant of Grace. Then Gentiles will not be worse off than Jews and the latter will certainly not be worse off than the Gentiles.

Systematic Theologies destroy synergy of the Covenant of Grace

Up to the Reformation, the analytical logic and understanding applied to the scriptures exercised by most Roman Catholic theologians was based mostly on misunderstood theories allegedly propagated by Aristoteles. This led to the study of parts rather than wholes and gradually these parts became wholes in themselves to those who studied them. It was like classifying the wings, legs, beak, feathers etc. of a dead bird and pawning each part off as real, living, integrated creatures.

---

[214] Ref: 2/6/12A-15B and passim, HP.
[215] See Iain Murray's excellent Banner of Truth book under the same title.

In theology this philosophy paved the way for what has been called Systematic Theologies.

During the Reformation this idea of reducing a whole to its supposed parts was abandoned by many for a more biblical, holistic, integrated and synergized knowledge pioneered by Bullinger and Francis Bacon (1561-1626) and extended by John Durie and later John Gill. This writer is heavily indebted to all four of these men for his own theology. Scripture was seen by these men as an inseparable unity with one certain message – God's Plan of Salvation. Sadly, many of our Puritans influenced by Continental second generation reformers returned to Aristotelian, Systematic Theology striving to outdo Calvin's *Institutes* which was never intended to be a 'rule of life and faith' for Christians but an anthology of learning picked from here and there for the education of the French. Throughout my studies and long years of writing, I have carefully scrutinised Calvin's *Institutes*, edition by edition, and also traced many of Calvin's extensive sources where they were not acknowledged. I have gained much help from this 'potted' mixture of doctrine with which Calvin took the cream of English, German and Swiss-German doctrines and make them available to a French-speaking public. Wisely, the Geneva council gave Calvin permission to print his *Institutes* only if the Swiss printers published Bullinger's more synergistic and original works at the same time to balance off the picture. However, I would challenge anyone to read Calvin's *Institutes* and thus equip himself with a comprehensive and all-embracing Covenant teaching on the way of salvation. His work is a catalogued hotchpotch of sayings of various spiritual values in anthological form but it is not a comprehensive, thorough-going gospel that will answer all that mankind needs for a step into faith and a continuation of it. When one has found the way, then the *Institutes* is often useful for referring to as a kind of theological Wikipedia.

I would rather have no Systematic Theologies but of those we have, I prefer Bullinger's *Decades* any time as it grew out of sermons preached from the heart, all with an evangelical thrust to 'consider Him'. If one requires an overview of sound theological doctrine, though it is couched in a language a little unusual for those speaking the dumbed-down language of today, there is perhaps nothing better than John Gill's *Body of Divinity* which was also formerly evangelistic sermons given in a number of churches and public halls. Gill's knowledge of history, ancient literature, theology and the biblical languages was, like Bullinger's, vastly superior to Calvin's. So, too, though Calvin made much of his knowledge of the Church Fathers, this was minimal in comparison with his fellow Reformers and opponents as shown by his controversies with Pighius. Sadly, Practical Divinity has been greatly neglected in theology in place of analytical studies which destroy the unity of the Gospel. John Durie has a good deal to teach us on this matter.

Summing up
John Durie, theologian, linguist, educator, diplomat and Westminster Assembly member was extremely effective in teaching Covenant mercies throughout Europe and taking the lead in many inter-Protestant conferences which also affected European politics. He defended the Covenant of Grace teaching of the Bible against new ideas of a dual covenant which mixed theology with political contracts between man and God.

Durie saw God in Christ as the source of all knowledge, as all knowledge pointed to God-Only-Wise outside of whom there is no knowledge. Those who knew Christ were enveloped in His wisdom and knew what the aims and goals of knowledge were. He emphasized how the Covenant was not between man and God as the Covenant had to be between two equals who were able to keep to the Covenant programme. Thus Christ, the Perfect Man, took on the nature of man to perform the conditions of the Covenant perfectly thus keeping a Covenant between two equals; God and the Man Christ Jesus. This was no 'social contract theory'.

This one-and-only Covenant provided continuous revelation and was thus one of constant reform, reestablishment and progression according to the needs of the ages it bridged. It was also constantly widened in application to embrace all mankind. Thus for Durie, the New Jerusalem was not merely for believing Jews but for all God's People everywhere who awaited the Second Coming of Christ in Glory.

Durie, in keeping with a number of Reformers, Puritans and men of the Great Awakening after him believed in the restitution of all things before the coming of the Lord when all people everywhere would be enabled to hear the Gospel. He thus dwelt often and long on Psalm 76,

Isaiah 11:8, 9. This conviction solves problems concerning the future of the Jews such as aired by John MacArthur as Durie looked forward to an ever increasing world-wide evangelism embracing all Jews and Gentiles and with it a world-wide revival, nevertheless, Christ remained the one door of entry into the New Jerusalem. All theological or 'secular' training which did not follow this biblical maxim was without meaning. This he outlined in the works mentioned above dealing with education within the Covenant.

I close this chapter with a brief analysis of Systematic Theology, rejected by Durie in preparation for the next chapter on Durie's Covenant Teaching in his 'Practical Divinity'. My remarks on the *Institutes* must be understood against the claims of the More-Calvinist-than-Calvin people who look to the *Institutes* as their mine of information and the *Westminster Confession* wrongly as Calvin's prophet.

Any theology is only a theology worthy of all acceptation when it is capable of presenting the Covenant of Grace as a united whole in seeking the salvation of mankind. The Everlasting Gospel is not to be divided and if it is, it can never be united again but remains a sum of parts for the analysts.

Chapter 11

Practical Divinity According
To The Covenant Of Grace

The difference between Practical Divinity and Case Divinity
Practical Divinity entails applying scripture immediately to the conscience, situation and behaviour of the seeker. It emphasizes that theology is something to be done. Systematic theology offers a conglomeration of different case studies which have no direct application to the overall needs of either the lost sinner or the saved. Preaching or teaching based on uncoordinated, incomplete arguments is worse than unhelpful. Durie called this 'Case Divinity' as opposed to 'Practical Divinity'. Durie taught me that continually dividing knowledge of any kind never leads to a synthesis of that knowledge as each separate study merely develops its own framework leaving out all other essential parts. In theology if one divides the scriptures, one loses the scriptural message. In other words, the Covenant of Grace must be studied and taught *in toto* or it will never be discovered at all.

So Durie and his followers decided to compile a Practical Divinity as opposed to the Aristotelian Systematic Divinities of their politically Puritan and philosophical[216] contemporaries. It was to be a great

---

[216] 'Philosophical' in those days meant 'scientific'.

undertaking, planned from the late twenties but especially at the wish of the Continental Protestant churches in the early thirties. It was to be based on the practical outworking of God's covenant with his Son on behalf of man. From 1628 on they had hoped Archbishop Ussher would have shouldered the main burden but his difficulties with the new regime and the fact that those who were to assist him were gradually dying off or suffering under the turbulent years of revolution and warfare both in Britain and on the Continent made this task difficult. At last, after many years of anxious waiting, in 1653, Ussher asked John Durie and the co-workers still active around him to take up the task themselves.[217] Durie soon found he was left quite alone with this burden on his shoulders and produced several works on the subject which have been almost completely ignored. In Durie's days, his plans for a Practical Divinity based on the Covenant of Grace continued to be highly influential on the Continent into the following century. I trust that my Marburg doctoral thesis *The Practical Divinity of Universal Learning: John Durie's Educational Pansophism* might create a little more interest in the endeavours of this first rank Puritan of timeless worth to develop a meaningful Reformed theology of world-wide application.

Durie's starting point

Durie had been working on various essays concerning Practical Divinity between 1628 and 1651 as illustrated by his *Reformed School* and *Supplement to the Reformed School* where Durie appeals to the church-goer, pupil, student, minister, employer and teacher to follow the path of experimental Divinity. As the Continental Protestant Churches had asked Durie to send them his conclusions concerning a practical divinity which was still absent from their curricula for theological studies, Durie sent them his *A summarie Platform of the heads of a Body of Practical Divinity* in 1654 with an introductory letter by Ussher to his 'beloved friend' Durie. This was followed by his work *The Earnest Breathings of the Forreign Protestants, Divines and*

---

[217] I was thus surprised to read a few years ago that a *Practical Divinity* had been published from Ussher's pen. Any such work at the time could have been only a product of the Durie workshop but Ussher stressed he was not in a position to continue the work or even to edit and publish the workshop's findings but gave Durie his blessing and advice as to how to continue. See Appendix I.

Others: to the Ministers and other able Christians of these three Nations, for a Compleat Body of Practicall Divinity. In this work, Durie claims the beginning of all learning must start with a thorough understanding of the Covenant of Grace to which all the scriptures testify. On considering 'What is meant by a Body of Practicall Divinity', under the sub-heading 'Concerning the Principles' Durie claims:

Now all the truths which beget divine faith and love, proceeds from one root, which is the tenor of the Covenant, which God hath appointed to be offered from the scriptures, by the preaching of the gospel in his name, to be believed and entertained by all: for all the God doth aim at in his dealing with mankind, next unto the manifestation of the glory of his goodness over all his creatures, is chiefly this, to show himself a Saviour, in uniting man by a Covenant of Grace unto himself, that he being guided by his counsel, and having kept the faith therein, may afterward be received into glory.

The Covenant of Grace then is, the great and fundamental principle of all the principals of the life of godliness: for as there is none other way appointed to unite man unto God, and restore us again from our fall to integrity, but this way of a Covenant: so there is nothing which we can do acceptably towards God, or profitably for our own salvation; but that which is done in order to the tenor thereof. Whence followeth also, that all our knowledge is not otherwise useful, nor to be sought after upon any other ground, but as it leadeth to the observation of the Covenant; nor to be entertained for any other aim but as it is subordinate unto the tenor thereof: for as no man ever was, is, or can be saved, but he that is faithful in the Covenant of Grace with God; so no matter of knowledge can be saving to any man, but that which enableth him to keep the tenor thereof. Hereunto then all truths, both theoretical and practical, are finally to be referred; and therefore in the doctrine of the life of godliness, the Covenant must be made the ground of all the principals of faith, from which the duties of obedience must flow: and I am fully persuaded, both upon the grounds of sound reason, which a natural moral man is capable of; and upon the grounds of Divine testimony and spiritual experience, that all doubtful matters in divinity, whether they concern the points of knowledge, or of practice, may not only be resolved by the right understanding of God's aim towards us, and of our duty towards Him in the Covenant; but that the resolutions thereof, of what kind soever, must be examined by, and applied to the analogy of faith concerning the Covenant, before ever they can bring true peace to the conscience of any man; and therefore my advice shall be unto those who will undertake any part of this work, that they keep always the Covenant in their eyes, as mariners to the north point of the compass, to steer their course by it in all their meditation; for it is mainly for want of this directory, that both in our notions and actions concerning religion, we run such wild courses: nor is it possible, as I conceive, ever to unite the professors of Christianity to each other, to heal their breaches and divisions in doctrine and practice, and to make them live together as brethren in one spirit ought to do, without the same sense of the Covenant, by which they may be made to perceive the terms upon which God doth unite all those that are his children unto himself, and upon which everyone that is in Covenant with God, is bound in conscience through love unto God, to maintain the unity of the Spirit in the bond of peace with those who are his children, who all alike, and by the same very way, are in Covenant with him.[218]

Though Durie's several works on Practical Divinity and the Covenant of Grace were the clearest and most detailed descriptions hitherto, Durie still considered his works as a mere 'Platform', trusting that his 'steering committee' would carry on. However, times became more turbulent and Durie found himself in his second exile at the Restitution, this time until his death which no one recorded, nor do we know where he was buried.

A Covenant contracted with Christ on behalf of man
After establishing the history and characteristics of the canon, Durie goes on to discuss what he calls its 'precognitions' or 'principles' (or

---

[218] Page 11. I have up-dated the spelling somewhat.

'premises' as we would say today). These are, for Durie, generally accepted truths which lead to true godliness via a Covenant teaching which shows how the Covenant is revealed, made and confirmed and how man is motivated in his conscience to keep it. Durie perhaps took too much for granted concerning what the common man could absorb in theological debate and thus Ussher told Durie to make his 'precognitions' as low as possible before building on them. Concerning the tenor of the Covenant man must be taught who the Persons are who take part in the covenant, namely God, mankind and Jesus Christ and that God is the Author of the Covenant as revealed in scripture which outlines man's dependence on Him in His Covenant. Jesus Christ is the sole Mediator between God and man within this Covenant by virtue of His nature as God and Man in one person and thus a true Medium and centre of all God's and man's properties. Christ is placed in His covenant function as Prophet, Priest and King of all the saints in Heaven and earth for which His two-fold state of life qualifies Him, that is, His humiliation on earth and His exaltation in Heaven and His work of mediation in both these capacities.

The Covenant is directly contracted solely with Christ and with man only in, by and through Him. Thus we distinguish between the things promised and the terms by which they are promised in relation to Christ directly and to believers and professors indirectly.

The Covenant performed and accomplished
The performance and accomplishment of what is to be done by both sides is thus two-fold. Christ, by His vicarious and substitutionary sufferings vouchsafed all the conditions of fulfilment for such as believe and profess His name and He thus secured the blessings of the Covenant directly and properly for them. On the Father's part by means of His power and glory, He made good unto Christ all His promises by raising Christ from the dead and setting him at His right hand and by giving Him all power in Heaven and in earth to administer his own Testament by sending forth the Holy Spirit and the preaching of the gospel. In this administration of the Testament of Christ by the Spirit in the Gospel a general call is given and an offer of grace made by Christ on God's part unto all that hear and believe the Gospel. This grace secures the terms of the Covenant to all believers, by their effectual

calling and conversion unto God, and by their constant perseverance in grace unto the end. The motives which oblige men's consciences to entertain the offer are the happiness which is the lot of those in Covenant with God (Psalm 25:10), and the obligation which lies upon the conscience of men to obey God's commandments and calls and prepare them for the Day of Judgment

The confirming of the Covenant

After teaching what the Covenant *is*, Durie shows how the Covenant is *confirmed* via the manner of its institution through its doctrines appointed by God to place a seal on the reality of His working in the inner man. Following these doctrines equips believers for a life confirmed in grace and godliness and provides us with all the benefits which God purposes for mankind in them. In this way the believer experiences the power and practice of all the truth whereby God is enjoyed in the Covenant relating to the inward and outward man of God. The inward man is the New Creature who must learn what regeneration of the soul is and how it is wrought by God's Spirit in fellowship with God. He must also learn how this differs from the unregenerate soul. To stabilise him on this path, he must know what the deceits of natural imagination and the wiles of Satan are and how to resist unclean things.

Durie follows Paul

Durie thus starts where Paul starts, seeing the full revelation of the Bible as God's written Covenant with His Son regarding man's salvation. He thus outlines God's plan of salvation for Christ's Bride in all the scriptures, in the two clauses of the one Testament explaining the one Covenant. Durie continues his Covenant exegesis by demonstrating the reliability and sufficiency of the entire scriptures before dealing with the Being of God, Father, Son and Holy Spirit to whom they testify and the sorry state of man for whom they are testified. Then, before outlining the form of the 'Contract' for which we usually use the word 'Covenant', Durie describes Christ in his office of Mediator in both Testaments.

A commonly accepted theology Reformation

This was not a one-off notion of a group of religious cranks. This writer has studied official documents from between 1631 and 1680 from all the main European churches and universities and archives, including Oxford, Cambridge, Leipzig, Hamburg, Duisburg, Marburg, Heilbron, Uppsala, Rinteln, Sedan etc. ... One major find were documents signed by John Owen which were being used as a door-stopper in an old paper parcel keeping an ancient archive door from closing. I found documents from over a hundred true British Puritans, including Owen, Nye and Goodwin, and large numbers of Continental Europeans, including Calixtus, Bergius and Crocius all affirming that they stood four-square behind John Durie's initiative and saw in him the person most fitted out by God to restore the Reformation in Europe with his teaching on Practical Divinity. Geneva gave Durie and his Covenant Gospel a good hearing and the Swiss gave Durie their strong financial backing and support.

Durie's thrust is almost unknown today
This thrust of Durie's is ignored by modern Counter-Reformation so-called 'Reformed' works. Woolsey does not even mention Durie's massive contributions to Covenant of Grace theology though Durie played a central role in the Westminster debates. However, when I was sent to trace the Westminster Assembly's correspondence with Sweden by Cambridge's Department of History, (a Post-Doctoral initiative), I found that the bulk of this work was done by Durie and grateful Sweden was celebrating his memory in special church services. I found this high recognition of Durie's labours was the same in the German, Dutch, Polish, Swiss and Czech seventeenth century churches. Indeed, I found documents and publications written by Durie or about him in over fifty Continental archives and also in Britain's university libraries especially those of Sheffield and Oxford. I went 'begging' at the doors of owners and of families who had sheltered Durie during and after the Thirty Years' War and still had letters and writings in their possession. Here I think especially of Wolfgang Ernst Fürst zu Ysenburg und Büdingen and his archivist Dr Decker who opened their private library to me and the kind help of Sweden's then Archbishop Anders Wejrud, an old friend of this author's from their student days together at Uppsala University.

Durie's day is still to come

Graham Windsor in his refreshing work 'The Reunion Views of Archbishop Ussher and His Circle' says of Durie and his supporters Davenant, Ward, Hall and Bedell who backed him from 1630 on:

> Though they could get little hearing at home, they were celebrated and respected abroad, and this lent added weight to their comments on the inter-church situation. They were men of international reputation, honoured by Lutherans, Arminians, and Reformed.[219]

Though a prophet is seldom honoured in his own country, this author believes that John Durie's day is still to come in theological appreciation in the Anglo-Saxon world as it has been valued in knowledge-engineering in the so-called secular world for some time as illustrated by my dissertation. He will soon stand with the world's greatest Covenant theologians if his present day followers are able to educate present day friends of the Covenant by God's Grace. Sadly, little of him is still in print and much untranslated, but for those who have the interest, time and energy there are literally hundreds of his works to be had in odd corners of the internet, some with over 500 pages, and at least two university research groups are working on the *Hartlib Papers* which provide a gold-mine of material on Durie which is gradually being published. Some of his works, used by this author such as his *Supplement* to his work on the *Reformed School* built on his Covenant teaching are now extremely rare and are said to be limited to one copy only for each. So, too, many of Durie's preserved manuscripts and even printed works lack pagination so the reader must invest much time and energy tracing Durie's thoughts.

Samuel Hartlib was Durie's advisor, editor, publisher and agent from 1628 to his death in 1662, and laid the foundation for Durie studies by collecting and preserving well-over two thousand documents appertaining to the Durie circle. Also, even during Durie's life-time, a number of university dissertations were written on the subject of Durie's aims and ideals as theologians from quite different camps

---

[219] Churchman 77/3 1963.

discussed his policies.[220] For those who read Latin, my lengthy list of Durie's works given and used in my dissertation will prove a mine of blessings. Neglecting all these precious documents has caused modern Reformed witness on the Covenant in particular and Practical Divinity in general to be but a pair of worn socks just longing to be darned or re-knitted.

Seventeenth century opposition to Durie
Durie's ways were, however, not always strewn with roses. He was attacked bitterly by William Prynne the Presbyterian lawyer who stole his letters and published them interspersed with evil comments. He had found them in the papers he had stolen from Archbishop Laud's private chest after putting him under arrest. He also stole Laud's diaries part of which Prynne 're-wrote' in order to denounce Laud and Durie who had worked together in striving for a union of Protestant, Reformed churches in Britain and on the Continent. The isolationist Presbyterians rejected Laud's overtures to the Presbyterians, Lutherans and the Continental Puritans, saying he was secretly wooing these people back to Rome. Durie was also treated with contempt by Charles II who banned him from Britain though he had helped Charles I to defend his case. Durie had been too near Cromwell for Charles II's liking. France went further and put a price on Durie's head, though it appears Durie found his last spiritual home in the French Reformed Church which was, at the time, strongly influenced by Pierre Du Moulin (1568-1658).

Durie opposed the Roman Catholic Aristotelian system
Durie firmly opposed Aristotelian Systematic Theologies which cut up essential doctrines into what they called 'cases', and claimed that theology and other subjects must be taught by separated case studies in order to get a general overview. Such bits and pieces cannot be parts of any comprehensive whole. Durie longed for a volume of Practical Divinity for general and international use because:

---

[220] Please consult my book *The Practical Divinity of Universal Learning* for an overview of Durie scholarship up to date.

... the study of Practical Divinity, is of farre greater concernment unto all, and far more to be heeded, esteemed, and entertained in the Schools of the Prophets, than the study of contemplative Mysteries and notions of Divinity; whereupon Controversial matters are ordinarily attendants. And feeling there are so many bodies and Systemes of Theoretical and Controversial matters, that it would be no easie task to any man to reckon them all up; and yet there is not so much as one compleat body or System of Practical Divinity found in all the Churches; whereunto we see nevertheless, that all Theoretical Truths ought to be referred, and directed as to their end; it is evident that therein there is a manefest defect, and that much is wanting hereby, to the increase of publique Edification, to the supply of Spiritual Consolation, and to the settlement of a sound Reformation in all the churches, which may be remedied by a Body of this nature.[221]

Systematic Theology for Durie never points to the ultimate ends of man and a right knowledge of God. The whole body of scripture must be studied in its practical and utilitarian entirety and not through piece-meal, artificial analysis. No dissection of feathers, sinews, muscle, skin and skeleton can describe a living Bird of Paradise. Put the bird in the mincing machine and it is gone. Nearly all controversies in modern theology are caused by separating what belongs together by Aristotelian Systematics, inherited from Rome. Durie felt they did not lead to 'Gospel Communion'.

Durie returns to this theme repeatedly from 1628 on in the various editions of the *Reformed School*, and the *Supplement to the Reformed School* but probably nowhere so firmly as in his 1654-8 works *A Summarie Platform of the Heads of a Body of Divinity* and *The Earnest Breathings of Forreign Protestants, Divines and Others: etc. For a Compleat Body of Practicall Divinity*.[222] In *Earnest Breathings*, Durie enclosed a translation of the foreign ministers' pleas and a letter sent from a Professor of Theology at Leyden University supporting the international ministers. He also enclosed a letter from James Ussher explaining why he could not take on the task himself though some

---

[221] *Earnest Breathings*, pp. 3, 4.
[222] Appendix I will deal with problems attached to the writing of this *Practical Body of Divinity*.

twelve members of the Durie circle had begged him to do so in 1633. In his response Durie declares that a Systematic Divinity beginning with 'cases' in order to work out a Body of Divinity is a 'preposterous course every way'[223] as by isolating parts, one can never conclude their whole and it is not known by what criteria these 'cases' are to be ruled or merged. Durie, as always, was looking for a *filum Ariadnae* which he found in the Covenant of Grace.[224]

One of the reasons why Durie was so long in responding to the Continental call for a Practical Divinity was that Hartlib, Durie's right-hand man, for the first time in many years disagreed with Durie. He was for merely gathering articles from various theologians on various subjects; talks given at meetings such as the Invisible Society's; and correspondence both received and sent with which he could make an encyclopaedic compendium of Christian knowledge before working out a pansophical overview on this basis. This was the method which Alsted and Comenius practised. This would account for the Hartlib Papers being preserved which deal with almost every subject under the sun but have no order, cross referencing, summing up or framework of any kind. This would scarcely suffice as an encyclopaedia of knowledge as even encyclopaedias have always some kind of framework and order, even if only alphabetical. Hartlib's approach is thus the very opposite of Durie's. The latter wanted stable terms of reference with which all case studies could be compared, amalgamated, synergised and thus find their rightful and useful place. Durie thus told his friend Hartlib in a letter appended to *Earnest Breathings*:

> Practical Divinity containeth properly the determination of the ends of all our actions, to show how they are subordinate to godliness and the rules whereby the actions are to be directed to their own proper ends.[225]

After showing what confusion Case Theology brings, Durie says:

---

[223] *Earnest Breathings* p. 51.
[224] Working out *a filum Ariadnae*, or how to find the way through a labyrinth was a main point of debate in the co-working of Durie, Hartlib and Comenius.
[225] *Ibid* p. 50.

… from whence you see that I am not of your mind when you say that Case Divinity must first be ruled before Practical Divinity: for Case-Divinity cannot be ruled unless you have first a rule to rule it by. Now the rule is that which I say is the matter of Practical Divinity; *viz.* all such express determinations as the scripture doth deliver concerning all the parts and actions, either of the general and substantial, or of the particular and accidental state of Christianity.

Happily, Durie goes on to explain what he means but I leave that enlightenment to those who care to read the entire work for themselves. The long and short of Durie's thesis is that he re-introduced the teaching of his Reformed Fathers that all knowledge was one reflecting the mind of Christ who is *Pansophia* (Romans 16:27), All-Wisdom, and God's revelation is all one in Christ and cannot be cut up and dissected. He saw Christ being revealed in all the scriptures and that all the scriptures were the product of God's Covenant of salvation with His Son. All theology is thus Covenant theology and all theology must be taught as a unity. We do not teach theological 'subjects' or 'case studies'; we teach the wisdom of God as revealed historically in scripture in its synergetic synthesis and wholeness.

Durie's Reformed Covenant Theology
Two things must be understood. Durie teaches in *Earnest Breathings*, if one wishes to grasp Covenant truths: we must know for whom the contract is made properly and directly, and for whose sakes. Then we must consider what the terms of agreement made with each party are.

First: The parties in the Covenant agreement
The contract is directly a Divine contract as hinted at previously but as this point is so neglected today, it must be repeated and hammered home. The Covenant is properly and directly an *agreement* made between the Father and the Son. Indirectly, however, it is made for those who believe in Christ and profess His Name. Why is this? Because Christ, according to scripture is the Covenant of God in Person. He is the living *contract* bringing perfect Divinity and Perfect Manhood together. No one else can do this. Here Durie quotes Isaiah 42:6 a verse

very familiar to the ears of his time, but to those of us who are today unfamiliar with Old Testament preaching, verses 1-7 will make Durie's point clearer:

> Behold my servant, whom I uphold; mine elect, in whom my soul delighteth; I have put my spirit upon him: he shall bring forth judgment to the Gentiles. He shall not cry, nor lift up, nor cause his voice to be heard in the street. A bruised reed shall he not break, and the smoking flax shall he not quench: he shall bring forth judgment unto truth. He shall not fail nor be discouraged, till he have set judgment in the earth: and the isles shall wait for his law. Thus saith God the LORD, he that created the heavens, and stretched them out; he that spread forth the earth, and that which cometh out of it; he that giveth breath unto the people upon it, and spirit to them that walk therein: I the LORD have called thee in righteousness, and will hold thine hand, and will keep thee, and give thee for a covenant of the people, for a light of the Gentiles; To open the blind eyes, to bring out the prisoners from the prison, and them that sit in darkness out of the prison house.

Christ is the Fulfiller of the Divine Covenant

Here we see how the Divine Godhead sets up Christ as the fulfiller of the Divine Covenant. So, too, we see that Isaiah, a Jew of the Jews and both a priest and prophet, refers twice to Christ's work amongst the Gentiles in these few verses, and the fact that He is the righteous judge of all the earth. So, too, God goes back to His Covenant purpose in Christ for His Elect which is the entire reason behind the creation of the world. Christ was thus Covenant Keeper from the beginning to the end of creation and into eternity. So Christ, according to the words God gave Isaiah, shows that He has already instigated the world-wide round-up of His flock.

Durie also quotes Isaiah 49:8:

> Thus saith the Lord, in an acceptable time have I heard thee, and in a day of salvation have I helped the, and give thee for a

covenant of the people, to establish the earth, to cause to inherit the desolate heritages.

Again, we have a world application of the Covenant whereby sinners are received into the Covenant for Christ's sake only and not for anything in themselves. Those who are in Christ are in the Covenant. Those who have Christ, have the Covenant. Christ and He alone IS the Covenant. This is the teaching of the whole Covenant Bible.

Second: The terms of the Covenant Agreement

The Covenant is thus a contract and an agreement, which is outlined in the two-clause Testament which, as a whole, refers to the inheritance of all the People of God, past, present and future. These Covenant terms show how the Covenant came about and how it is to be enjoyed. These terms are made with Christ not fallen man. Thus whosoever is redeemed by Christ, whether Jew or Gentile, is one having no righteousness of his own but receives the righteousness of God through faith and becomes a child of God and heir of eternal glory. To this both the Old and New Testaments testify as in Isaiah 59:21 and Romans 3:24. Thus the People of God are those justified freely by His grace through the redemption that is in Jesus Christ and found in him as Titus 3:7 and Romans 8:29 testify. They are predestinate to be conformed to the image of His Son that He might be the first born among many brethren. He gave them the power to become the sons of God (Romans 5; John 1:12); and Christ should lose nothing of all which He has been given, but raise it up again at the last day (John 6:39).

The terms by which the Covenant is made in Christ for believers specify that God will be merciful to their unrighteousness, and remember their iniquities no more. He will write His laws on their hearts, and give them understanding that He will be to them a God, and they shall be to him a People, that they shall all be taught of God from the least unto the greatest, Hebrews 8:10-12.

Concerning the terms in the hands of mere professors to belief in Christ, Durie distinguished strongly between true believers and mere professors. He teaches that the Church knows no theoretical members. Thus all who name the Name of Christ must depart from iniquity (2 Timothy 2:19). Such as separate themselves unto the Lord, and touch not the unclean thing shall be received by Him; that He will dwell amongst them, and walk in them and be their God and they shall be His people: that He shall be a Father unto them, and they shall be His sons and daughters (2 Corinthians 6:16-18), and that every one who doth suffer with Christ shall also reign with him (2 Timothy 2:12; Romans 8:17). Durie calls this the tenor, or settled course and direction of the Covenant and goes on to write of its confirmation under the title: 'The conditions of the Covenant which Christ took upon Himself'.

The Conditions of the Covenant
So that the contract could be ratified and unalterably confirmed and believers receive their due inheritance, Christ had to die and rise again from the dead and is now in Heaven where He administers the Testament for those to whom He bequeathed it. To this effect the gospel of Christ's covenanted Testament is to be preached and published throughout the world. This is done through the gifts of the Holy Spirit which is part of the Covenant which the Father has made with those who are in Christ for His benefit, ensuring that Christ's promises will not depart out of His mouth, nor out of the mouth of His Seed, nor out of the mouth of His Seed's Seed, from henceforth and for ever' (Isaiah 59:20, 21). Again Durie takes his 'New Covenant' ideas from the Old Testament. In this Administration of the Testament for the establishment of the Covenant, two things are to be acknowledged: What the general offer of Grace is on God's part, calling all men to Christ to partake of the Covenant and how the particular terms of the contract are made good regarding believers and mere professors.

How does the sinner receive Grace?
Since the late eighties, I have come under heavy fire from three Banner of Truth editors and some five other leading 'Banner' men on the subject of the sinner's reception of the gospel, leading to a BOT article claiming I did not believe in bringing the gospel to the unconverted. Indeed, one of the people who started feeding the BOT ears with such nonsense wrote several books with the BOT's support arguing against my beliefs which he did not seem to grasp. This main denunciator of my theology has now turned on the BOT and denounced them. After going through at least five extreme theological systems, he has now become an adherent of the NCT, driving it to a new radicalism. It is

strange that this BOT criticism came parallel to their contention that I believed God justified the ungodly, so mixed up was their theology. At the same time these people took a U-turn from men of God they had honoured in the past such as John Gill, William Huntington and William Romaine, men I still honour but the BOT associate me with their teaching and that alone is worthy of their denigration.

The point of controversy was whether an evangelist can warrant sinners with what they call a 'well-meant' offer based on their duty to respond in faith to the gospel. They felt they could point to every sinner and say 'Christ has died for you'. This is, at least, how I understood them via their criticism of my beliefs in the general call to sinners to repent and believe. I felt, and still believe, that my duty was to present Christ in the gospel to sinners and the rest was the work of the Holy Spirit. The preacher does not impart saving grace, but the Holy Spirit does. To this end, I denied that the sinner had any ability to co-work in receiving faith apart from being a recipient. I called their 'well-meant', 'duty-faith' warrant of salvation to man's unfallen abilities a gospel of deceit and argued that the general call to believe was certainly an offer of grace to those who repent and believe but it was to people dead in trespasses and sin who had not the ability to exercise any faith duties at all unless given a saving faith by Christ. I thus took it that my former brethren associated with the BOT had left the true gospel path. I later picked up a book by Durie on the same theme and realized that I thoroughly agreed with him and that my call to sinners was scriptural to the core.

Concerning the general offer of grace

Durie tells us concerning how Christ calls woos and commands us in the gospel that God has appointed the Gospel to be preached to men dead in sins and trespasses who have no ability of themselves at all to will anything which is spiritually good, far less to convert themselves or to prepare themselves for such a new birth. Durie does not talk of an awareness of duty-faith in sinners nor even a duty of sinners to prepare themselves for conversion as in the modern 'well-meant' evangelism mentioned above. Durie then asks what those in Christ are called to experience and says that they are called to receive pardon of their sins, rest and ease to their souls and the light of life, quoting 'Come unto me all that labour and are heavy laden, and I will give thee rest' (Matthew

11:28); 'And it be known unto you, that through this man is preached unto you forgiveness of sins, and by him all that believe are justified from all things, from which ye could not be justified by the law of Moses (Acts 13:38, 39).

Covenant preaching is calling and commanding, as only God can, sin-slain men to awake from the dead and approach Christ who draws them into His forgiving arms.

What way must sinners take to come to Christ?

The question now is, however, what way must these lost sinners take in approaching Christ? Durie explains the way by urging sinners to repent from dead works and exercising faith towards God. 'The kingdom of God is at hand: Repent ye and believe the gospel' (Mark 1:15): 'Testifying to the Jews, and also to the Greeks, repentance towards God, and faith towards our Lord Jesus Christ' (Acts 20:21). Durie explains how the particular terms of the Covenant of Grace are made good to believers and tells us that those who hear the Word of God, answer the call, and embrace the promises of the Covenant, are those moved to do so by the free and special grace of God conferred on them in God's good pleasure through the gift of faith; both to will conversion and perform the same. Then, unto all who are given faith, they are also given justification and adoption and sanctified by the Spirit of regeneration, sealed until the final day of redemption and enabled to walk in obedience of faith and in the enjoyment of grace unto the end. Note that all these points are separated in today's pseudo-Reformed teaching. Our gracious Saviour gives us everything at once in a gorgeous whole of saving Grace.

Making sinners sensible

Then Durie touches on the point that made my above mentioned critics grind their teeth. He tells us how sinners are 'made sensible of their happy condition in Grace to apprehend their right to Glory.' Whenever I used the word 'sensible' in the sense that sinners are awakened to their fate as such and to God's Covenant mercies in Christ and also to their well-being in God, I was challenged in book and blog-form for using Hyper-Calvinistic and Antinomian terms. The word 'sensible' was, however, used by Bunyan, Gill, most of the 18th century evangelists,

267

and even Andrew Fuller whom these people cited against me. Indeed, it was common evangelical parlance until the duty-faith, well-meant offer people came on the scene with their strange anti-Covenant of Grace gospel. However, I have never understood what these people have against this term. People who are insensible to their sins are not the People of God.[226]

Triumphantly and passionately in his fervour as a soul-winner, Durie says:

> We believe that all true believers may have a comfortable assurance of the blessed estate in grace, by the testimony of the Spirit of Adoption unto their conscience, given them in the sincerity of their walking with God in the Covenant, according to that which the Apostle saith (Romans 8:15, 16); The Spirit of Adoption whereby we cry Abba Father, the Spirit itself beareth witness with our spirit that we are the children of God.

Our gospel is certainly to waken the dead and make them sensible to their plight and to their salvation.

Believers must not neglect worshipping together

Durie's next point is that believers must not neglect their coming together in a body so that the world shall see how the People of God behave. Even I am rather pessimistic here as our modern churches are often hot debating societies or narrow-minded channels of hate for their brethren rather than groups of 'just men made perfect'. Nevertheless, Durie says:

> 1. Such as profess the Lord Jesus Christ are bound to join themselves together in one body as members one of another in Christ. To effect this, the Lord has given various gifts to His Church. At first Apostles, Prophets and Evangelists to lay the foundation. Now Pastors and Teachers to build on it.
> 2. The gathered members are to be perfected and built up by the work of the ministry, towards the effecting of the Covenant.

---

[226] I have dealt with these, we hope, well-meant criticisms in various articles, mostly by courtesy of *New Focus Magazine* and also on my website *Bibliographia Evangelica*.

Durie continues by saying:

> We believe also that the gathering together of Protestants into one body, is lawfully performed, when they professedly give up themselves unto God through the ministry of the Testament which Christ has instituted, and by their professed subjecting of themselves to all the Ordinances of God's House, which make the believers as one in the Covenant with each other before the World in the profession thereof to God's glory. These spiritual exercises which build up the faithful to the full measure of the stature of Christ in the Covenant are two-fold, relating to both the inward man and outward man.

Those gifts relating to the inward man, Durie explains are: the duties of public worship, attending to the word of prophesy, prayer and praise. Those relating to the outward man are:

> The exercise of love in the communion of saints, watching over one another, caring for one another and supplying all needs. Particularly Elders are called to supervise and direct these exercises and the deacons to make sure that bodily and health needs are met, distributing the monies which the members have contributed for this cause.

Ridding ourselves of the veil of confusion

Reformer William Whitaker in his *Disputation on Holy Scripture Against the Papists*, taught that God's Covenant is completely revealed in both Testaments which is the full will of God. He teaches, that whoever adds or rejects any of it or seeks elsewhere for God's will has still the veil of sin over his eyes. We complain about Islamic women wearing their veils. Are not those Christians who cut up God's one and only way of salvation until there is little left, as in so much modern Covenant teaching, more guilty than those Moslem women who do not know Christ? Reformer Roger Hutchinson, author of the famous *Image of God* insisted that both Testaments are one legacy and the Old is valid in the New as the New is in the Old. Condemnation through the Law and acquittal in Christ belong to the Covenant rule of the whole scriptures. This is why Peter in Acts 15, referring to the Old Testament saints, says, 'We believe that through the grace of the Lord Jesus Christ we shall be saved, even as they,' because we are under the same Covenant. Stop, you might say, 'Old' in 'Old Testament' means done away with and 'New' means it did not exist before. Oh no, this is certainly not the case, 'Chadash' in the Old Testament means 'refreshed', 'renovated', 'rejuvenated,' or even 're-applied' and has many by-meanings such as 'sweet' and 'refreshing'. We must get back to the roots and the original intended meaning. In the New Testament 'Palaios' (old) means 'In existence for a long time.' 'Neo' means 'ever fresh' and kaisos used in Hebrews for the Covenant has just the same meaning as chadash used in Jeremiah 31 for the same Covenant. Our old-time, eternal Gospel is ever new and fresh and brings renewal with it like the morning dew. It only makes sense, however, to renewed and restored sinners. It must be remembered that in the scriptures 'old covenant' is not the same as New Covenant as, the old covenant, as Jeremiah explains in his 31st chapter, was broken before Israel received the revelation from Sinai. The Old Testament, on the other hand has as its main theme the New Covenant.

When Cromwell was dying, he spoke much of the Covenant, affirming in his last breath that from eternity there is but one Covenant. In his dying prayer, he said, 'Lord, though I am but a miserable and wretched creature, I am in Covenant with Thee through grace.' His friends told him to eat and drink and gain strength to live. He refused and answered, 'My design is to make what haste I can to be gone.' He trusted in the Covenant-Keeper. Such are the People of God whether former Jews, former Gentiles, or whatever. These nationalities and titles are nothing as when they are all one in Christ, there are no dividing issues.

Dear Brethren, the one Covenant is the only Covenant to die happily in. I have not told you half of what the scriptures and God's faithful witnesses have taught. There is much good news still to be learnt. Perhaps we have learnt enough to accept God's gracious Covenant in its entirety and not become bogged down in artificial parts which will give us but a piece-meal faith to quarrel over. However, who will ever learn and know of all God's covenant mercies this side of enjoying our

Heavenly inheritance? May God help us to learn more and more as we grow in grace and the knowledge of our Saviour and find that, in the original sense of the word 'new' we can say that 'His love for us is new every morning'.

Summing Up

Durie felt that systematic or 'case-divinity' as he called it, was of little use in describing the Covenant of Grace as this central all-comprehensive doctrine cannot be studied by separating what belongs together. Having worked on the idea since 1628, he was asked in 1633 to author a Practical Divinity by many Continental theologians, chiefly with a view to ministerial training and pastoral work. Durie hoped Archbishop Ussher would take up the task but nothing came of this so Durie had to carry on the task himself.

In his subsequent work, Durie argued that all learning must start with the Covenant of Grace worked out by the Father and the Son for the salvation of mankind. Outside of this Covenant no true knowledge was possible and inside of this Covenant all knowledge was to be gained in fellowship with God-Only-Wise. The way to this end was centred in true Covenantal preaching which provides confirmation of the Covenant through the new life attained in it for the believer in Christ, giving him due revelation as to the benefits of being in the Covenant and a clear understanding of what the wiles of natural, fallen, human understanding are. In order to grasp the full tenor of this gospel, a thorough study of God's Word is necessary in both clauses of Christ's one Testament.

This view of the Covenant was widespread in Durie's day but was already coming under heavy fire from rationalistic preaching of a pseudo-Reformed nature. Many on the Continent, especially in Germany, the Netherlands and Geneva, saw Durie's thrust as a continuation of the Reformation in Europe and Durie is still recognized more on the Continent than in English-speaking countries. Indeed, I found most of Durie's printed works and hand-written manuscripts in Continental archives, private and public. However, Sheffield and the Oxford college libraries have also thousands of separate MSS from Durie's pen or correspondence to and from Durie. University

271

dissertations on Durie have continued from Durie's day to the present time.

Even in his day, however, there was intense opposition to Durie's teaching and influence from denomination-bound critics who realised Durie was aiming for a united Protestantism world-wide based on unity in the Covenant teaching of the Bible instead of the inessentials of denominational differences. Though the French Protestants welcomed Durie, the Roman Catholic government wanted him hunted down and 'punished'. Sadly, King Charles II persecuted Durie.

An avowed opponent of any form of Systematic Theology, Durie believed it was a mere wasteful contemplation of mysteries, notions and case-studies and designed for controversial debating but not for teaching the whole Body of Divinity. It did not present the gospel as a whole, showing the divine goal in the teaching of scripture, nor the golden thread which pervades the gospel.

Durie, in preparing his Practical Divinity had trouble persuading his agent, editor and closest friend Samuel Hartlib who felt, like Comenius, that one must work from parts to wholes, forming general rules from the parts. Durie felt that one must have a rule to go by in working out a Practical Divinity and this was the Covenant of Grace. However, one must first learn from scripture who the Covenant parties are and what part they play. It was an agreement between the Father and the Son who was to be its sole Mediator between God and man with Christ keeping the conditions as God-Man for both God and man. This truth is outlined in both Testaments. All the terms of the Covenant are thus kept by Christ with the outcome that the righteousness of faith can be enjoyed by the believer for eternity and new hearts are given to appreciate and follow God's law as it was intended. Here, Durie distinguishes, as always, between doers and professors of the Covenant. There are no theoretical members of the Covenant so that all who stand behind the Name of Christ must be doers of His Word.

This Covenant was secured by Christ's vicarious death and resurrection which enable Him to ratify and administrate His Testament for His Bride and fit its inheritors out with the Holy Spirit and promises which are fulfilled for ever. This is all received by the believer through Grace and before belief there is no ability, duty or capability in man to do anything to assist God. All the necessary deeds of atonement have been performed by Christ. God justifies the ungodly whilst they are ungodly and the ungodly can do nothing to enhance their salvation of themselves.

General offers of grace are for totally depraved sinners only, otherwise salvation would not be 'of grace'. Salvation is built as far as man is concerned on repentance and faith but these are not natural properties of man but the sinner must be made sensible to his plight outside of Christ and given an awareness of the joys of being in Christ. This is through the medium of Covenant preaching in the Spirit which can awaken the dead.

To grow in Grace one needs a home and a place of refuge which God has designed by having us take care to fellowship together in public testimony and worship within the Body of Christ. Here, the believer is equipped for the perfecting of the Covenant within him learning to teach and be taught through the unity of faith. Nor should the fellowship's social responsibilities be forgotten as this is also part of God's Covenant wish.

The Covenant of Grace was never an old, covenant of the man-made type but the same one-and-only, ratified, renewing and reforming Covenant of God wherever it was preached and entered into throughout all the times in the Bible accounts. Even Cromwell, with all his evil doings was in this Covenant as was Abraham and David who were far from perfect, but saved by Grace. Thus the worst of sinners, as Paul called himself, can die happily in Christ. We know Our Redeemer is eternally alive and we in Him.

Chapter 12

John Gill: The Exegete Of The Covenant Of Grace

The everlasting council of the Covenant of Grace
Most people who read my books will know how I am indebted to that
great Baptist scholar John Gill (1697-1771) in his guiding Christians
through the scriptures from Genesis to Revelation showing how Christ
is the same yesterday, today and forever. Under the heading 'The
Everlasting Council and the Covenant of Grace', Gill shows how the
gospel of God's love to the people of His choice is made apparent to
mankind through God's revealed Covenant in the scriptures. This
Covenant arises from God's grace alone and is thus entirely unilateral.
It is thoroughly binding in its specifications and does not allow for any
retraction from it either on God's part or man's. For Gill, the Covenant
of Grace is the outcome of the eternal council of God concerning the
salvation of the elect. Gill's actual definition is:

> The Covenant of Grace is a compact or agreement made from
> all eternity among the divine Persons, more especially between
> the Father and the Son, concerning the salvation of the elect …
> Which lay the foundation of all the grace, comfort and happiness,
> of the saints in time and to eternity.[227]

---

[227] *A Complete Body of Divinity*, Book 2, p. 813, 1796 edition.

Gill deepens this truth by declaring that not only was the Covenant of Grace contrived and planned from eternity, but it was always fixed and settled there as an essential factor in God's eternal nature, choosing out a covenant people. Our God is a Covenant God and a God of Grace in His very nature. He created the world to fulfil His desire.

Entering into the Covenant in time for eternity
A further point to note here is the phrase 'in time and to eternity'. Most of Gill's critics argue that he teaches eternal justification in the sense that the saints were always justified by some fiat of God in a 'time' beyond the beginning of time and not as a result of predestination in Christ's atoning work. This they call 'eternal Justification'. Gill, however, teaches that grace comes to the elect 'in time' and this is election 'to eternity'. In other words, the elect are chosen *in* time *for* eternity. Gill goes deeper into this question elsewhere where he distinguishes, as did the old Reformers and Puritans between 'eternity' and 'aevi-eternity'. The former meaning eternal *per se*, which can only be used of God, and the latter that which is created in time for eternity.[228]

Covenant in the Old Testament
Gill argues that the main word for 'covenant' in the Old Testament *berith* which comes from the root *bara* referring to creation. This created covenant was not in time but from eternity, though it was applied to both the time-needs and eternity-needs of man as soon as he fell. For Gill, however, the term can also mean to order or dispose of things in the sense of a testament which rules how things are to be managed. Furthermore, the word can also mean to cut and divide referring to the practice of cutting up an animal and the covenanters walking between the parts themselves to show their newly won unity.[229] Though all these meanings are very relevant to the Covenant process, the Baptist pastor, lecturer, preacher, teacher and author concludes that the basic meaning of 'Covenant' must be 'selecting or choosing'. A

---

[228] Consult Chapter Six of Gill's '*Body*', 'Of the Infinity of God, His Omnipresence and Eternity' for a comprehensive survey of this teaching.
[229] Jeremiah in Chapters 31 and following shows how Israel erred in understanding such covenant meanings but gave them the true meanings.

covenant thus relates to God choosing freely to associate with whom He will. In this case, God in Christ chose to associate first with His Old Testament people from the pre-Jewish era through to the wider opening of the gospel world-wide in the first century A.D.. Thus, for Gill the outworking of the atonement through the fulness of time is in its embracing all time in preparation for eternity.

Covenant in the New Testament
Turning to the New Testament, Gill shows the equivalent word here to *berith* is *diatheekee*, a word handed down from the O.T. Septuagint to describe the Covenant. Here the root meaning of the word is make a payment to secure something on behalf of another. Thus in Luke 22:29 we find that Christ appoints His disciples to a kingdom as the Father has appointed the kingdom to Christ. The word is also used for a testament or will as in Hebrews 9:17. Gill believes one should refer to both meanings with their wider implications when considering the Covenant of Grace and proves his case by numerous examples from the scriptures. However, Gill equates God's covenant with God's ordinances, precepts and commands as when God commanded the sons of Aaron to make heave-offerings (Numbers 18:19) or the command to release servants after six years' service (Jeremiah 34:13, 14). Likewise, the so-called covenant of works[230] with Adam and the Ten Commandments (Deuteronomy 4:13) are in this category as God commands what is to be done and not done. Gill sees the Covenant as a promise from God as in Isaiah 59:21 where the prophet refers to the covenant in terms of the giving of the Spirit and Ephesians 2:12 tells us that the unsaved are strangers from the covenants of promise and thus without hope. That promise is salvation in Christ which brings with it eternal life (1 John 2:25). Such usage shows that whatever conditions are required in the covenant, Christ is the only fulfiller of them. Furthermore, Gill argues covenants can be made between the Father and the Son or between men and men but cannot be made between men

---

[230] I use the term 'so-called' here because it is becoming more and more popular amongst once Reformed circles to entirely separate Law from Grace in the Covenant whereas all God's dealings with mankind are within one Covenant which includes Law as much as Grace. Indeed, as my old Principle, Ernest Kevan outlines in his book, *The Grace of Law*, redemption, mercy and grace are part of the one Covenant with the Law embedded in it.

and God. We note that whenever Gill speaks of the Covenant, he backs up his exegesis from both Testaments because they both refer to the one and same Covenant.

The Bible of Christ's times, the Septuagint is helpful here

The LXX translators used *diatheekee* especially to emphasise that One Person was providing all the commitments and they did not use the nigh-synonym *suntheekee* because the meaning of this word tends to refer to two or more equal parties in a transaction. There are such covenants between men in which both sides draw up stipulations and rules for their mutual observance, but this is different to the Covenant of Grace. Thus Abraham enters into a covenant with Aner, Eschol and Mamre, Abimelech with Isaac, and David with Jonathan. Such covenants cannot be entered into between men and God. Man can have no claims on God which do not stem from God's Covenant will and promise and he has no powers but what God gives him. Furthermore, God has a right claim on man's absolute fidelity without making him any promises or concessions whatsoever. All this makes Gill stress that the Covenant of Grace is made between God and the Son with the elect being in Christ as their Head and Representative. All stipulations and re-stipulations, all claims and agreements are mutual (Isaiah 49:1-6; 53:10, 11; Psalm 40:6-8 and John 17:4, 5).

The relationship of God's wrath and God's grace

Some modern writers have a bone to pick with Gill because he believes under the Covenant all men are in Adam until death releases them. But the sinner can, nevertheless, according to Gill, be saved by Christ's Covenant mercies. Thus Gill is accused of believing Christians are under two separate covenants with two separate covenant Heads, Adam and Christ. This led, for instance, the author of a book entitled *Picking up a Pin for the Lord*, to claim that Gill's doctrine can only lead to confusion. He feels that Gill's statement in *Sermons and Tracts*,[231] cannot stand where Gill says:

God's elect may be considered under two different *Heads,* and as related to two different covenants at one and the same

---

[231] Vol. 2, p. 500.

time. As they are the descendants of *Adam,* they are related to him, as a covenant-head, and as such, sinned in him; and, through his offence judgment came upon them all to condemnation; and so they are all, by nature, children of wrath, even as others. But then, as considered in Christ, they were loved with an everlasting love: God chose them in Him before the foundation of the world; and always viewed and accounted them righteous in Christ, in whom they were eternally secured from eternal wrath and damnation. So that it is no contradiction to say, that the elect of God, as they are in *Adam,* and according to the covenant of works, are under the sentence of condemnation; and that as they are in Christ, and according to the Covenant of Grace, and the secret transactions thereof, they are justified and freed from all condemnation. This is no more a contradiction, than that they are loved with an everlasting love, and yet are children of wrath at one and the same time, as they certainly are. And again, this is no more a contradiction, than that Jesus Christ was the Object of His Father's love and wrath at one and the same time; sustaining two different capacities, and standing in two different relations when He suffered in the room and stead of His people.

Gill's exegesis challenged as being contrary to Ephesians 2:3

Gill's view of the elect, his critics maintain stubbornly, is in contradiction to Ephesians 2:3 where we read that 'we are by nature the children of wrath'. With this, however, Gill is in thorough agreement! However, the critic in question, as several others, argues that the meaning of Ephesians 2:3 is that it is impossible to be under wrath and under grace at the same time. One must leave one covenant to be put into another. Gill, they maintain is talking about the dual position of the unsaved elect sinner before conversion. This, however, is not what Gill is talking about in the context at all but he is listing objections to his doctrine of justification from eternity and meeting them. He is viewing the elect as they stand in time in Adam and yet in eternity in Christ. The fact that a sinner is condemned in time for being in Adam does not negate the fact that in God's eternal Covenant of Grace ruled from eternity the elect are put in Christ. Furthermore in picking out these words from Gill's sermon on Justification, such critics do not allude to Gill's previously given backing for his statement which, I believe, is irrefutable.[232] Gill can safely argue that just as a loving father scolds his child who is naughty, God is angry whenever His people sin, but this does not mean that he does not love them in Christ. Isaiah 54:7-10 sums up nicely God's attitude to His elect in their period of darkness:

> For a small moment have I forsaken thee; but with great mercies will I gather thee. In a little wrath I hid my face from thee for a moment; but with everlasting kindness will I have mercy on thee, saith the Lord thy Redeemer. For this is as the waters of Noah unto me: for as I have sworn that the waters of Noah should no more go over the earth; so have I sworn that I would not be wraith with thee, nor rebuke thee. For the mountains shall depart, and the hills be removed; but my kindness shall not depart from thee, neither shall the covenant of my peace be removed, saith the Lord that hath mercy on thee.[233]

The testimony of the Covenant of Grace throughout the Bible is that God shows love and mercy to those under condemnation so one wonders what scriptures such as Naylor have as their basis. Isaiah shows how God reminds His people of all the blessings of the Covenant throughout the ages and uses Noah here to illustrate His Covenant grace. God loves His people from eternity and He has placed them in covenant with His Son. But before conversion there is a time when He hides His face from His elect because of their sin until the time when his great mercies in Christ pour into their lives in the fulfilling of His covenant plan of salvation. The doctrine of God's loving the elect in union with Christ as their Father but still condemning them in Adam as their offended Judge, pervades all the doctrines of salvation, whatever they are and is in no way merely existent in justification but in all aspects of the atonement and with Christ's purpose in dying for His elect.

---

[232] Sermon VI and VII on *The Stability of the Covenant of Grace*.
[233] *Of the Object and Acts of Justification*, pp. 40, 41.

Smeaton on God's wrath allied with His grace

Referring to that great chapter on reconciliation, Romans 5, George Smeaton, pointing out that reconciliation was worked out in the atonement and not on the basis of a moral change in man, deals with the very same problem i.e. that critics argue that God cannot love the elect and be wrathful at the same time. Of course He can, says Smeaton:

> To this, however, it is urged as an objection, that such a mode of viewing reconciliation makes us at once enemies and friends: and it is said, Can we regard God as both hating and loving us: as evincing displeasure, and concerting the means of taking us into favour? This difficulty vanishes when we come to see that love and wrath well enough consist together, because men are presented to His view both as the creatures of His hand, and as sinners, yet the objects of His grace. He had wrath and enmity against their sin, according to His holy nature and the inalienable claims of justice; but He had love to His creatures, and a disposition to do them good. And the atonement, as an arrangement interposed between divine wrath on the one hand, and the sinful human race on the other, was the removal of all the impediments that stood in the way of the divine love. The text shows that free love provided the atonement, but that men were actually taken into favour only on the ground of satisfaction.[234]

Gill's critics have problems with the Atonement

It is no surprise, therefore, to find that the author of *Picking up a Pin for the Lord* has problems with the atonement itself. He finds it hard to imagine God being well pleased with Christ yet at the same time chastising Him for our sins. Gill should never have used this example, he argues, to draw a parallel with the state of the elect. Gill chose this parallel correctly as it is the very parallel that the gospel draws. It was Christ's voluntarily and vicariously taking upon Himself the wrath of God that found acceptance in the Godhead and secured our salvation. The author's reference to Andrew Fuller here indicates that his mentor

---

[234] *Atonement According to Christ and His Apostles*, Smeaton, p. 73, Second Part.

is being a stumbling block to him as Fuller taught clearly in his doctrine of justification that God only turned to man after man had turned with what he calls 'a holy disposition' to Him.[235] Since when did unsaved sinners have a 'holy disposition' to turn to God unless God turns them? It is clear such people object to Gill's doctrine that the Holy Spirit makes men sensible of their sins as they believe this 'sensibility' comes from man's own holy disposition. In *Picking up a Pin* the author complains that such a verse as Romans 4:5, "But to him that worketh not, but believeth on him that justifieth the *ungodly*, his faith is counted for righteousness" is a unique passage in scripture so we must compare it with clearer passages on the subject in order to discover its true meaning. This is a strange thought for a Christian as the Bible tells us throughout that the ungodly are justified by God. Paul, for instance, says:

> But God commendeth his love towards us, that while we were yet sinners, Christ died for us. Much more then, being now justified in his blood, we shall be saved from wrath through him. For if, when we were enemies, we were reconciled to God by the death of his Son, much more, being reconciled, we shall be saved by his life.[236]

It is thus clear that Romans 4:5 is not a 'one-off' statement after all. We have a clear exposition of the fact that God justifies the ungodly in Christ's own words. He tells us through Matthew 9:12ff. that 'They that be whole need not a physician' and 'I am not come to call the righteous, but sinners to repentance.' This is repeated in Mark 2:17 and Luke 5:31 so it is far from being a 'one-off' piece of gospel truth. The Fullerites might argue that here Jesus is not speaking of justification. This would certainly be an error of judgment on their part as Jesus is rejecting false views of righteousness and showing how He grants true righteousness. 'To justify' means, of course, 'to make righteous'.

Those who criticise Gill on this basic Christian doctrine are blindly following Andrew Fuller here who argued that the words cannot mean that God justifies anterior to belief, i.e. while we were yet in our

---

[235] *Remarks on God's Justifying the Ungodly*, Vol. 3, pp. 714-719.
[236] Romans 5:8, 9.

unforgiven sins, so it must refer to something else. As the Bible only speaks of *believers* being justified elsewhere, he claims quite wrongly, this cannot mean that *unbelievers* are justified in Romans 4:5. Thus, the word 'ungodly' here does not refer to our state prior to belief at all but to the simple fact that believers remain ungodly until death. The saints are always ungodly! Fuller thus actually interprets Romans 4:5 to mean that Christ justifies *believers* who are *ungodly* and that 'ungodly' does not refer to a pre-faith state but the permanent state of sinners and saints alike. Thus Christ's words given above in Matthew, Mark and Luke, we presume, are re-translated by Fullerites as 'I am not come to call sinners, but the righteous to repentance.' Be that as it may, this is the 'gospel' that Fuller claims is 'worthy of all acceptation'. Here he joins hand in hand with the Pharisees.

I once asked as a tiny tot my Sunday School teacher Mr Lee what a 'Pharisee' was. He answered 'those who are far I see' and explained how far the Pharisees were from the truth. I asked what 'Sadducee' was and he told me that they were 'sad you see' because they had no resurrection hope. This totally uneducated great theologian was looked down on by the other 'educated' Sunday School teachers and was finally asked to leave the staff as he was an embarrassment to them. The other teachers were Pharisees and Sadducees, you see.

God's love goes out to those at enmity with Him
This writer holds to the same Covenant truths as Gill, namely that God's love for the people of His choice is from everlasting, is unchangeable and not dependent on man's love for God. Indeed, God's love goes out to those who are clearly at enmity with Him. Atonement means healing sinners to make them into saints. God sees no sin in His elect people who have their sins atoned for and remitted. This is because God sees His own as clothed in Christ's righteousness by virtue of Christ being their federal Head and His removing all guilt and condemnation from them. Gill teaches however, as few men in his time or afterwards, that the wages of sin is death but he is quick to add that the gift of God is eternal life. Gill taught that though man's sanctification in Christ is complete, as he has put on Christ, he is still in the body and in this dual state must grow in grace and faith and a deeper knowledge of his Saviour until he is released at death from his bodily remnants of Adam.

This is all in God's covenant plan with His people which was contrived, fixed and settled in eternity.

This Covenant of Grace is exercised as a command and promise to man but it is not between man and God but solely between the Father and the Son as our Head and Representative. The Covenant is to bring life, peace, grace and redemption to the people of God. It is not *four* different covenants, as Dispensationalists and some uncertain NCT people now tell us, each made under different conditions. It is one single Covenant made perfect by the redemption freely given us in Christ and it is through grace alone.

Adam knew both what law was and what was grace

Some scholars have difficulty with Gill's view that one is in Adam and under God's natural covenant with Adam and co-responsible with Adam for breaking it but at the same time in the spiritual covenant under Christ's Headship which releases one from the penalties accrued through breaking the natural, Adamic covenant. Gill sees this two-fold covenantal state as the good news of the gospel. He denies that Adam was merely under the Law as Adam was experiencing God's Grace at the time in being placed where he was at the birth of history. This continued when Adam fell as though in Adam all die, so those in Christ, the Second Adam, shall all be made alive. This is the Covenant of Grace which was made from everlasting and which places us in and under Christ as our federal Head and Representative. This covenant was not made with Christ alone but with Him as the federal Head and Mediator of His spiritual offspring. Thus Gill can say:

> Christ represented His people in this covenant, and they had a representative union to Him in it; all that He promised and engaged to do, He promised and engaged in their name and on their account; and when performed, it was the same with God, as if it had been done by them; and what He received, promises and blessings of grace, He received in their name, and they received them in him, being one with Him as their common head and representative.[237]

---

[237] *Body of Divinity*, Vol. 1, Of the Eternal Union of the Elect Unto God, p. 287.

Gill's scriptural backing to this section is found in Psalm 89: 2, 3, 33, 34; Isaiah 54:10; Proverbs 8:23; Micah 5:2; Titus 1:2; 2 Timothy 1:9; Romans 5:14 and he draws a parallel between Romans 5 and 1 Corinthians 15. We note Gill bases all he says on a pan-biblical gospel. This was as relevant to the saints called in through grace after Adam's fall as it is for us today so long after Christ's resurrection.

Macleod's sinful New Man
Since the nineteen-seventies, however, there has been a strong rejection of the two natures doctrine taught by Gill and most preachers and teachers since biblical times. The traditional view envisages Christ's Bride in her life-time on earth being still in the First Adam physically with all her fallen weaknesses but in the Second Adam spiritually as forgiven sinners. The Elect can thus be condemned in the flesh for their sins yet be regarded in Christ as spirits freed from all condemnation. I was always an enthusiastic reader of the Banner of Truth Magazine from the late fifties on and their writers appeared then to believe that we are only truly released from sinning at death when all vestiges of fallen Adam will be gone. I had already been attacked for my views as a young convert around 1956 by holders of the Keswick sanctification views which, to cut their lengthy arguments short, taught that Romans Seven was Paul's story of his life as an unsaved sinner and Roman's Eight was the story of Paul's later triumphant Christian life. I could not believe this as Paul, all along, had been testifying to his state as being a wretched sinner struggling under the continuing sins of his flesh but rejoicing in the experience of not being condemned for this as he stands in Christ. Is not this the normal experience of every Christian? It is also clear from the two chapters that becoming free from the sinful body inherited from Adam will only occur when we reach our heavenly inheritance. Until then, even as redeemed men we sadly do that which we hate. In other words, there is still indwelling sin in the Elect Adam race but this sin has no dominion over them as they are safe in the arms of Jesus who has given them total forgiveness.

Then, in the early summer of 1971,[238] Donald Macleod, led the
B.O.T into the open arms of the Wesleyans and the false 'holiness'
enthusiasts. This was an act which pioneered many B.O.T trips into
Wesleyan pastures in the following years. However, Macleod avoided
almost fully the evidence given in Romans Seven and Eight in his desire
to prove there are no remnants of the Old Man in the converted
Christian. So Macleod, who still reckoned with sin in man, seemed to
be teaching we now sin in our new creation as Children of our Holy
God in Christ. Macleod tells us the doctrine he is denying was 'for long
dominant in Reformed circles' until, it appears, Macleod came along to
disprove it. However his new perspective on mankind was that of
ancient Arminius which gradually developed into that Arminianism
which has sought to stifle the doctrines of Grace for so long. It would
appear now as if Macleod had stopped striving to clean out sin from
Adam's stables but was now at work cleaning out Christ's stables
accusing the New Man in Christ of being the same sinner in Christ as
he was in Adam. In order to convince his readers of what he is saying,
Macleod argues two-fold, basing his views on his re-interpretation of
Colossians 3:9; Romans 6:6 and Ephesians 4:20ff. He thus starts to re-
translate these texts in opposition to the A.V., taking infinitives and
aorists which are not tense or timing agents and using them to put
scripture under the timing of his own Arminian clock to make it appear
that Old Adam is with us no more. We notice that this 'correcting' of
the Authorised Version of the Bible has been the method of a number
of B.O.T writers including John Murray, since Macleod's doctrinal
dam-buster in 1971. Secondly, on the basis of this most dubious
linguistic reasoning, Macleod argues that 'the Old Man', our Adamic
nature, cannot be confused with indwelling sin as the former has gone
but the latter remains in the New Man. What then, we must ask, is
'New' about the 'New Man' if he is still in his sins? Macleod is arguing,
what we might call 'ideally', by saying the Christian's present life is
determined by three great past events: He died, He put off the old man
and He rose with Christ.' Macleod's use of the capital in 'He' is rather
confusing here but he is most obviously saying of man that he did die,
he did put off the old man and did rise with Christ. However, this is to

[238] 'Paul's Use of the Term 'The Old Man', Banner of Truth Magazine, Number 92, May 1971, pp. 13-19.

be fully accomplished for man when he actually is resurrected with Christ when sin shall be no more and God shall wipe away every tear. Indeed, Paul explains his reference to the dying of the 'Old Man' by saying, 'henceforth we should not serve sin'.[239] He does not say 'Henceforth, sin is no longer there to be served'. Until his resurrection, man is still living in the vale of tears and burdened by his sin, which Macleod oddly enough admits, takes for granted but gives no valid reasons for it.

Here, we must take into consideration the First Adam-Second Adam comparisons of the Bible with its applications to the Elects' death and resurrection and Christ's death and resurrection. Paul teaches in 1 Corinthians 15:22-25:

> ... for as in Adam all die, so also in Christ shall all be made alive. But every man in his own order: Christ the first fruits; and afterwards they that are Christ's at his coming. Then cometh the end, when he shall have delivered up the kingdom to God, even the Father; when he shall have put down all rule and all authority and power. For he must reign, till he hath put all enemies under his feet. The last enemy that shall be destroyed is death.

Herman Ridderbos thus relates the 'Old Man' to our Adamic nature and says:

> Because the old man was condemned and put to death in Christ's death on the cross, the body of sin, the flesh, the old mode of existence of sin, has lost its dominion and control over those who are in him. In Christ's death and resurrection they have been transferred to the new order of life – the life order of the new creation, the new man.[240]

Thus Macleod's distinction between the 'Old Man' and 'the Body of Sin' is merely one of terms but not of meaning. Where does this sin

---

[239] Romans 6:6.
[240] 'In Christ, With Christ. The Old Man and the New Man', taken from 'Paul: An Outline of His Theology', Chapter 2 found online under above title.

come from? Obviously from man's fallen Adamic nature which will only be removed at death. This fallen nature can never be called the 'New Man' in Christ. I have read Macleod's most speculative, hazardous argument's many times and studied his hypothetical Greek as also his most dogmatic conclusions which leaves the confused reader still asking the same questions as he did before looking at Macleod's own confusion. Furthermore, I find Macleod's arguments for indwelling sin in the New Man far less convincing than arguments for indwelling sin based on the fact our sinful flesh is Adamic which we know from scripture.

God's moving cause in choosing out a people according to Gill

The death, atonement and resurrection of Christ are all now past time features in God's eternal will. However, they are not past features in mankind as God in Christ accompanies His Elect, member after member, from birth to death throughout all ages until all the Elect are gathered in which will be completed at their final glorification and, according to Gill, though this thought is often denied him, their final justification. The moving cause of God's redeeming a People for Himself, according to Gill is the everlasting love of God, the source and spring of every blessing found in Christ, God's greatest gift to His people throughout all times, past, present and future. 'In this was manifested the love of God toward us, because that God sent his only begotten Son into the world, that we might live through him. Herein is love, not that we loved God, but that he loved us, and sent his Son to be the propitiation of our sins' (1 John 4:9, 10). This love is free, unmerited by sinful man and where applied, it is thus by grace alone. As all of God's evidences of love, Gill sees them administrated through His immutable Covenant of Grace for His people, of which he says:

All these workings in the heart and will of God, issued in a covenant between Him and His Son; in which He proposed to His Son, that He should be the Raiser up, Restorer, and Redeemer of His people, both among Jews and Gentiles; and to which He agreed, and said, 'Lo, I come to do thy will!' which was no other, than to work out the redemption of His people, Isaiah 49:5, 6 Psalm 40:7, 8. Hence this covenant is by some called, the covenant of redemption, in which this great affair was settled and

288

secured. Now upon all this, the love, grace, and mercy of God, the good will and purpose of His heart, His council and covenant, the plot of man's redemption is formed; this is the source and spring of it.[241]

Gill demonstrate that this Old Testament truth is emphasised in Hebrews 9:15-17:

And for this cause he is the mediator of the new testament, that by means of death, for the redemption of the transgressions that were under the first testament, they which are called might receive the promise of eternal inheritance. For where a testament is, there must also of necessity be the death of the testator. For a testament is of force after men are dead: otherwise it is of no strength at all while the testator liveth.

This truth is based on the fact that all power is given unto Christ who is God blessed forever and all things own their being to Him who is the Creator of all. Christ has His divine right to dispose of His inheritance as He sees fit. All the promises in the covenant refer to the vicarious work of Christ who made His soul an offering for sin and poured out His blood in death, Isaiah 53:10-12, as the Spirit breathed Word tells us. As Christ is the Lamb slain before the foundation of the world, His Testatorship works both backwards and forwards in time, securing all God's elect from condemnation and reconciling them to God.

Nothing can be given man in the Covenant of Grace without Christ's counsel and consent and all that Christ has to give man could only be obtained through Christ making His soul an offering for sin and pouring out His soul unto death (Isaiah 53:10-12). All this was planned from eternity with the drawing up of the covenant so the Bible can truly speak of Christ as the lamb slain from the foundation of the world. All that is the Father's was given the Son from eternity and all that was the Son's was given the elect by a testament. Thus Christ, when facing death,

---

[241] Ibid, Vol. 6, Book 6, Chapter 2.

could say to His followers, 'And I appoint unto you a kingdom, as my Father hath appointed unto me'.[242]

Summing Up

Gill is a great writer on the unilateral everlastingness of God's wise council and His Covenant of Grace made between the Father and the Son for the eternal happiness of man. This is all without man's help because man can give no help. Contradicting extreme views of God's election of man in some past time in eternity, a nonsensical concept, Gill shows us that time was created for the work of Christ in choosing out and redeeming His Bride in the fulness of time which, by its very name fills out the whole of time. The just are hereby chosen, made just in time and prepared for eternity. This is what God's 'Covenant' means.

In the New Testament use of the term 'Covenant' we find also the meaning of appointment, command, redemption, promise and fulfilment. The likeness of meanings of Covenant in both Testaments leads Gill to the conclusion both Testaments are necessary in order to recognise fully God's Covenant. This view is endorsed by the Greek Old Testament which was Christ's Bible.

Gill is criticized for allegedly insisting man is under God's wrath as a sinner but love as a saint at the same time. Gill sees all God's work of Law as all God's work of Grace within the same Covenant. A good parent always scolds the child he loves when the child does wrong.

Ephesians 2:3 can never mean Christians are not by nature the children of wrath and the idea one must be taken out of one covenant 'of wrath' and be put into another Covenant 'of Grace' is quite un-biblical. There is only one Covenant. The elect die in Adam and are made alive in Christ within the one Covenant of Grace. The very meaning of Christ's redemption is that He adopts into His family those whom the Law has led to Him. This is also the argument of Smeaton who influenced Gill positively by arguing that reconciliation was worked out in the atonement and not on the basis of a moral change in man. The saving factor is not rewards and punishments but the overriding love of God. Sinners are included in the Covenant on grounds of the satisfaction of God, not on their fallen status.

---

[242] See Gill's commentary on Hebrews 9:15.

Here Smeaton puts his finger on the weakness of Gill's critics who have, on the whole, a faulty view of the Atonement. They find Gill's teaching that God showed his wrath against sin in Christ's atoning death which secured our salvation wrong, thus denying the very purpose of the Atonement that Christ should become 'sin' for us. Such critics speak of Christ saving those who have a 'holy disposition' based on their own capabilities. They object to the teaching of scripture that God justifies the ungodly. Justification is for sinners. God justifies anterior to belief. His gospel goes out to His enemies to whom He grants eternal peace.

Adam was never under a separate Law Covenant to earn his place within the Covenant of Grace but he was under the full Covenant state of Law and Gospel. His sin did not annul the Law and certainly not God's Covenant of Grace which includes the Law. Nor did God's Grace leave Adam at his sinning as God told him of the downfall of Satan.

Man is not left alone to decide whether he should follow God or not as he has been given Christ as the Mediator of a Better Covenant than one merely of works which the Old Testament clearly teaches is a broken man-made Covenant. The tenor of 'works' is that they do not work and the tenor of God's Covenant of Grace is that it always works in God's administration of it through our Mediator.

The Banner of Truth doctrine that there is no Adam in believers, though the scriptures teach that all men must taste death for their being in Adam is a great breach in Gospel teaching as it postulates a new sinful man as a new creation in Christ. This is blasphemy pure. It would mean man would be in need of a further offering for sin to cleanse the sin in Christ's Body, the Church, which is Christ and all the saints with Him. The point is that the sin inherited from the Old Man has no claim on the New Man in Christ Jesus. Until our resurrection day we remain unprofitable, sinful souls helpless without God's Covenant of Grace in which we stand. As in Adam all die, so in Christ shall all be made alive.

The moving cause of salvation remains the love of God shown to His redeemed People through Christ's vicarious death as outlined in the Covenant of Grace which thus can be called the Covenant of Redemption as redemption is its goal. This gospel was preached in the Old Testament as it was in the New. We can speak of Christ being the Lamb of God slain from the foundation of the world. For this purpose God set up the Covenant of Grace in time for all time and eternity.

291

Chapter 13

The Mediatory Office Of Christ Within The Covenant

The Humanity of Christ in Salvation

Theologians are seldom all-rounders in their studies and tend to follow each other in their research as it saves much spade work and one remains 'on the ball', that is, one deals with aspects of Biblical Studies which have become popular. Few, like John Gill are called to tackle the whole doctrine of God. The theological fashion in the recent past has been to isolate the work of the Holy Spirit, the doctrine of justification, the alleged wills of God, the agency of man in salvation, the extent of the atonement and the efficiency of the atonement and duty-faith from full gospel teaching. Call this 'Systematic Theology' if you like but it is not biblical or Practical Theology. These doctrines, with the exception of the last, which is post eighteenth century, have all been taken out and aired in a regular sequence throughout Church History.

As one who has been watching this progress of theological fashion for over sixty years through close connections with some seven British and European universities there appears to be two basic trends of interest to Protestant, evangelical, Reformed believers. First, evangelicals are playing a far greater role in theological research and second and far more disastrous, Theology, or Divinity as it is also called, is becoming more man-centred and less Christ-centred. Indeed, man's alleged duty-faith which arose out of the Enlightenment theory of the infallibility of the will is again a major theme in scholarly debate.

In spite of the recent Jubilee celebrations of Luther's 'Bondage of the Will', it is sad to see so many Reformed evangelicals ignoring such works and celebrating the freedom of the will as in pre-Reformation times.

This development can, of course, be explained by the truth that it is to man we are called, and to his needs, so why my caution? Man must be dealt with anthropomorphically. The big disadvantage here is that within fallen man there is no salvation. However, all men's needs are met salvation-wise by Christ and without a thorough study of the question raised in Anselm's ancient words, *Cur Deus homo*, 'Why did God become Man?', we cannot even start to build up a soteriology (study of salvation) of man. Anselm's question needs to be asked and answered before we can start to tackle this re-emergence of the 'Modern Question'[243] of whether man is an agent in his own salvation or not.

Nowadays, those who answer this 'Modern Question' in the affirmative such as Sam Waldron, Curt Daniel, Tom Ascol and Tom Nettles, who all have been granted the title of 'Dr' whether of Theology or Philosophy, claim they are in the majority amongst Christians and at the peak of biblical research. David Mark Rathel, whose views I have examined in various academic media including the *Baptist Quarterly*, is now striving to follow in their wake and argue against those whom he accuses of belittling man's agency in salvation.[244] All these modern theorists oppose John Gill's teaching concerning man as fallen man and also Man as the Incarnate Christ. What is clear is that Gill based his view of man's lost state on scripture backed up by decades of study regarding Christ as the Man *par excellence* who obeyed all the conditions placed before man in order for him to be saved so that the Second Adam could right the wrong performed by the First Adam. Thus Man died for man. This would be truly maximizing Christ-the-Man's agency in salvation but it would be the whole truth and nothing but the truth. Rathel, following such as Daniel, somehow sees this as 'minimising' the agency of lost man in the salvation process. It might

---

[243] Developed by the Congregationalists in the 18th century and taken over erroneously by Baptist Andrew Fuller as a pillar of his faith, thus splitting the Baptist, Congregationalist and Presbyterian movements.
[244] 'Was John Gill a Hyper-Calvinist? Determining Gill's Theological Identity', *Baptist Quarterly*, Vol. 48, 2017., Issue 1. Pp. 47-59.

well be asked who is the more accurate scholar here Gill or his modern opponents?

It can be truly said that most of those theologians who criticize John Gill's studies concerning man are weak on coming up with a true doctrine of man as God sees him and as he is described in the Bible. Though they say Gill minimizes man's duties, they minimize man's responsibilities and maximize his abilities. They follow the high view of man proposed by Andrew Fuller who minimizes the outcome of the Fall radically. They also neglect to portray the role of the Man Christ Jesus in salvation. I had hoped that up-and-coming young Rathel would correct this error of judgment but he has made the same error himself by not basing his view of man's salvation on the Incarnation and Atonement but on faulty logic based on the idea of a free offer pointing to the duties of fallen man as if Christ had never died as the God-Man for him.

Maximal man minimized by the Fall

Since the early nineteen fifties, many theological students, pastors and gospel witnesses have profited from Otto Weber's large two-volume work on basic dogmatics *Grundlagen der Dogmatik*. In his exact study of the Incarnation, he shows how Christ takes over from Adam as *the* maximal Man when Adam minimalized himself in the Fall and broke God's Covenant with him. Weber points out that Adam is often referred to in the Greek Septuaginta (LXX)[245] by name as 'anthropos', that is 'man' as a type for or figure of all men. However, we read in Romans 5:12ff. that the first man Adam was also a figure or type of the real Man Christ who rights all Adam's wrongs. We see here, too, that as all who remain in Adam are lost, all who are chosen in Christ are saved. This is emphasised in 1 Corinthians 15:21, 22; 45-49 where we read that the first Adam was merely earthly with a living soul but the last Adam is a quickening (life-giving) Spirit without which no soul can live.[246]

The whole doctrine of God is revealed in the Son of Man's triumph over sin and death. This can never be maximized enough. This triumph was all part of the Divine Covenant plan of setting up Christ as the

---

[245] The Bible used by Christ and the Apostles.
[246] Weber, pp. 589ff.

Messiah and Mediator of the Covenant of Grace in choosing out a People of God, alias Christ's Bride, alias the Elect, alias the Church. This chapter therefore deals with Christ's mediation of the vastly 'better Covenant' than fallen man allowed himself. As so often, I am dependent on Gill for many of these thoughts.

Christ's Qualifications as Mediator

The whole New Testament but especially the Epistle to the Hebrews, describes Christ as Mediator and this title and office is allied to Christ's further title and office Covenant Head and as such He is described as the Mediator of the new and better covenant.[247] Christ alone bears this office as 'there is one Mediator between God and men, the man Christ Jesus'.[248] Many say that Moses, too, was a Mediator. His office, however, was that of God's spokesman. Christ does not merely hold the office of a spokesman-messenger, revealing the Father's mind, but He is a true Mediator in that He reconciles sinners to God on behalf of both God and man. He is the Ideal Mediator of reconciliation between two parties because He is of the two parties.

The Mediator of Reconciliation

Christ, therefore, stands *between* and yet *for* both parties, that of God who initiates the mediation and man who needs it. Christ's office entails being a Mediator by His proposing to His Father that He make satisfaction for the offence committed and appease injured justice. Christ proposed this in Eternity as a Covenant of Mercy, which was acceptable to the Godhead. Christ is thus the Mediator of the Covenant of Grace.[249]

Man was created in friendship with God but fell to temptation and was alienated from God by his own sin. Christ's task is to mend what was broken.[250] As Colossians 1:21 says, 'And you, that were sometime alienated and enemies in your mind by wicked works, yet now hath he reconciled'. Now Christ's loved-ones share a greater friendship with God than Adam experienced before the Fall. Furthermore, Christ is a

---

[247] Hebrews 8:6; 9:15; 12:24.

[248] 1 Timothy 2:5.

[249] 'Mercy' and 'Grace' are synonyms in the Testaments.

[250] When Jeremiah refers to the New Covenant in Chapter 31:22ff into chapter 32, he is protesting against the broken covenant of the Jews who did not understand the everlasting Covenant of Grace.

Mediator who is continually needed. Unfallen Adam needed no Mediator as he lived in natural harmony with God but fallen man can now only live in harmony with God by the mediatory merits of Christ. Man lost his integrity with the Fall. His present integrity as a child of God is found solely in His union with Christ who has mediated a better covenant for him. The atonement was a once and for all action on the cross announcing the fulfilling of time. The propitiation which ensued from it is forever maintained for us by our eternal Redeemer who will never leave us, nor forsake us. We share Christ's unity with the Father through our unity with the Son.

This necessary reconciliation does not contradict the everlasting love of God for His elect. Reconciliation is from everlasting. As David loved his rebellious son Absalom, so God loves His elect, though they rebelled, but God provided a way for His elect to return to Him. God does not change from a hating Deity to a loving Deity in His attitude to His elect but always loves His own, though He is angry at their sin. However, Christ ever covenants in the Spirit with the Father to save His elect Bride.

The Mediator of Intercession and Advocacy
Christ thus continually keeps His flock from falling, preserving them before the face of the Father by interceding for them and representing them as their Advocate. 'If any man sin, we have an advocate with the Father Jesus Christ the righteous; and he is the propitiation of our sins.'[251] Just as sinners are reconciled through Christ's atoning death, they are preserved through His interceding life. Christ is the medium of access to God and none can draw nigh to God but through Christ's advocacy. He is the new and living New Covenant way of which He is Mediator. We are accepted in God because we are accepted in the Beloved. Christ is not only the medium of the saints' happiness and communion on earth but also in Heaven, for all eternity.

The Fitness of Christ for His Work and Office
Christ is the perfect Mediator because He is perfect Man and perfect God. Thus He is perfectly suited to be both the human and Divine

---

[251] 1 John 2:1, 2.

agents in salvation. The modern deadening emphasis on God's provisions being activated by each man using his own duty-bound agency, shows ignorance of Christ's mediatory work.

The Mediator must be Truly Man

The Son of God is thus the only human agency in salvation, mediating for us to save us from the mess our fallen nature has caused. Gill says this human Mediator must be:

a. Our Goel who has a just right to redeem us according to the law, in our room and stead.[252]

b. Our Goel kinsman must be of the same nature as the ones to be redeemed.

c. A divine person would not be subject to the law but a human person must show He is able to obey the law his fellow-men have broken. So Christ was born under the law, not above it. Those who teach that Christ stands above His own law, rather than uses the law to reflect His own nature, err. Not wanting a Saviour who humbled Himself so much, putting Himself under the law for our sakes, they preach Christ was above the law and gained our freedom by virtue of this high position. They deny Christ was punished on our behalf and that He paid the penalty of sin vicariously. In this, they follow Fuller who taught:

> The sufferings of Christ in our stead, therefore, are not a punishment inflicted in the ordinary course of distributive justice, but an extraordinary interposition of infinite wisdom and love; not contrary to, but rather above the law, deviating from the letter, but more than preserving the spirit of it. Such brethren, as well as I am able to explain them, are my views of the substitution of Christ.[253]

When the Bible teaches that the letter kills but the spirit gives life, it does not teach that the just man should deviate from the letter but that he should follow it in the way advised by the Word of God. According to Gill, following the Bible, if Christ did not stand where we stood and fulfilled the law in its entirety and to the letter on our behalf, exactly

---

[252] Leviticus 25:48, 49.
[253] *Works*, Vol. 2, p. 689.

where we failed, then He could not be our Mediator. He would not have fulfilled the claims of the law on human beings which was the purpose of His vicarious life. How can Fuller say Christ deviated from the letter when he fulfilled every jot and tittle of it and also all its spiritual requirements? Could Christ have taken on the penalty of the broken law which was the purpose of His vicarious death if He had dispensed with the Law He came to fulfil? Of course not.

The fact Christ was made of a woman and made *under* the law,[254](we note not '*above* the Law'), fitted Him out to be our Mediator. It was by His obedience that many are made righteous.[255] Thus, Christ showed Himself to be fit for the office of Mediator in taking upon Himself the sufferings of death which were necessary to obtain atoning reconciliation. A sacrifice for sin was necessary and Christ gave Himself to His Bride as that perfect sacrifice. The Captain of our salvation was demonstrated as perfect through His sufferings which were acceptable by imputation to reconcile the elect to their God because 'In that he himself hath suffered being tempted, he is able to succour them that are tempted.'[256] Hereby, Christ demonstrated His fellow-feeling for man and His sympathy with them in all their temptations and afflictions. He also showed His will to relieve them from their troubles by offering Himself as the only sacrifice possible and acceptable to present them, with Himself, spotless before God.

The Mediator must be truly God

a. The Mediator must be on equal terms with God to plan salvation with Him and enter into covenant with Him.

b. If the Mediator were mere man, His virtue, obedience and righteousness would not have sufficed to justify men nor would His sufferings and death be a proper sacrifice and atonement for sin. Modern Fullerite Probationists see enough natural and moral capacities in man to restore him through obedience to his former Adamic stature. Even if this were possible, however, it would be senseless. Christ does not mediate with His Father to reform Eden but to give mankind a

---

[254] Galatians 4:4.
[255] Romans 5:19.
[256] Hebrews 2:18.

higher justification making him an inheritor of Heaven. In Christ, we receive a greater righteousness than that of Adam. Those in Christ can never fall. Christ's righteousness is the righteousness of God, not Adam, and it is this divine righteousness with which He imputes His elect-ones. Believers are thus made to partake of the divine nature. Adam's nature was never sufficient to open Heaven's gates to mankind but only the gates of Eden. Only God can justify by imputing Christ's righteousness and only God can atone.

c. Fallen man has thus no agency in salvation. God will not give His glory to another. Thus for a Mediator to be a proper object of trust, worship and honour, He must be God Himself.

The Mediator must be God and man in one Person

Human nature must be taken up, united to and subsist in the Person of the Son. It must be a union of two natures in one Person. The Mediator must be divinely human and humanly divine. He cannot mediate as sometimes God and sometimes man. He must be both in unity or He is neither in separation.

How Christ comes to be Mediator

Christ's mediatorship is on the initiative of the Godhead. This is the party offended by man but also the party who then sues for peace. 'All things are of God, who hath reconciled us to himself by Jesus Christ, and hath given us the ministry of reconciliation; to wit, that God was in Christ, reconciling the world unto himself, not imputing their trespasses unto them; and hath committed unto us the work of reconciliation.'[257] For this office, Christ is set up from everlasting[258] to be a demonstration of God's forbearance and a propitiation for sin.[259]

What Christ's mediatorship entails

a. He is the only Mediator. Not the angels, not saints, not Mary and definitely not fallen man. The Bible tells us, 'There is one mediator between God and man, the man Christ Jesus.'[260]

---

[257] 2 Corinthians 5:18, 19.
[258] Proverbs 8:23.
[259] Romans 3:25.
[260] 1 Timothy 2:5.

b. Christ is the Mediator of all God's chosen vessels of mercy[261] for whom He died and whom He calls to salvation. He is the Mediator of the New Testament.[262] He is thus a Mediator for mankind only. The good angels need no Mediator and the fallen angels have no Mediator.

c. He is the Mediator of the Old Testament saints as well as the New Testament saints. The People of God are to be found in all times since the Fall. There is only one Name under Heaven in which salvation is to be found, the Name of the Lord Jesus Christ. Dispensationalists who deny members of Christ's Bride existed in Old Testament times, claiming Christ is Lord of the Church in New Testament times only, are Marcionite deceivers. Christ's Bridegroomship is not a mere matter of post-resurrection religion.[263] Isaiah shows clearly that Christ has His Bride amongst the Old Testament saints and the Shepherdship and Lordship of Christ is everywhere testified within the Old Testament's pages. One cannot separate the Lordship of Christ over His Bride, the Church, from His office of Mediator. Where Christ is Mediator, He is also Lord, Saviour, Reconciler, Redeemer, Bridegroom and Covenant Head of His Church.

Christ came not in time but in the fulness of time.[264] His atonement was from eternity and impinged on time at a special, chosen point of time-fulfilment. From thence, His atoning and reconciling mediatory mercies permeate and fill all time, fulfilling time's purpose as a handmaid of eternity. Thus at any point of time since the Fall or in any eternal outworking of God's purpose, Christ is Reconciler and Mediator. Where the Bridegroom is, there is the Bride. This is the glorious testimony of Ephesians 1 which describes Christ's electing work from the fulness of time, before the foundations of the world, to that Day when He will present His body, the Church as 'the fulness of him that filleth all in all'.[265]

We see, then that:

---

[261] Romans 9:23, 24.
[262] Hebrews 9:15.
[263] See Reisinger's *Christ the Lord of the Church*, pp. 1, 2 and *Christ, Lord and Lawgiver Over the Church*, p. 7.
[264] Galatians 4:4.
[265] Ephesians 1:23.

a. Christ is an effective Mediator. His mediatory work always succeeds. He is entirely successful as Reconciler, Intercessor and Advocate. The modern teaching that Christ died in vain for the masses of mankind, as if Christ failed in His attempt to mediate for them, is the 'God is Dead' blasphemy of modern rational Liberals. Christ's blood speaks peace and pardon for whom it was shed. Christ never intercedes for us in vain.

b. Christ is an everlasting Mediator. His pardoning blood is eternally effective and Christ ever lives to make intercession for us. So, too, His priesthood is unchangeable after the order of Melchizedek, without beginning and end.

c. Christ's office of Mediator includes his Kingly and Prophetic offices.[266] For Gill, all other names and titles of Christ are reducible to them. Gill stresses these titles were from everlasting and have been exercised both mediately and immediately throughout the Old Testament period and are not new functions which Christ earned through His ministry and sufferings on earth as per John Reisinger.[267] They were then demonstrated with power in the fulness of Christ's saving work but Christ was ever Prophet, Priest and King as He was also Mediator and Lord. The Lord who is King and Judge for ever and ever (Psalm 10), is the same Lord, King and Judge today as on the day the Psalmist made this statement of faith.

Christ's Engagements as Mediator demonstrated in Suretyship

Christ is our Surety because He transfers our obligations and debts to Himself, leaving us free from them. Those who preach that Christ was not imputed with our sin and did not pay a ransom for sinners' debts, leave the sinner with his obligations, guilt and debts. He is forgiven, but still guilty, as if Christ had never unburdened him. Nowadays, we hear that Christ brings us pardon but not freedom from guilt, so we must constantly mortify ourselves through the moral law, to put into practice

---

[266] See Book IV of Gill's *Body of Divinity*.

[267] See Reisinger's *Christ Lord and Lawgiver Over the Church* where he claims Christ had to earn His right to be Saviour and Judge, p. 2. Perhaps Reisinger is thinking of his remark in *Abraham's Four Seeds* where Adam, he claims, was put under the obligation to 'earn' the blessings of the covenant of works regarding Life. Naturally, Reisinger is wanting to show that where Adam failed, Christ succeeded but both statements are false. Christ took on the tasks of Saviour and Judge in His own right as such as established by the Godhead, not by His success which was never in question. Adam was not given anything to 'earn' but was given free grace which he rejected.

what Christ has gained for us in theory. The entire Mosaic law could neither save nor sanctify a sinner, so how can a cut-down version of it work such miracles? Christ's Mediatorial Office is to present us guiltless before the Father. Christ does not perform a mere half-work in us, leaving us to do the rest. He whom Christ saves is saved to the uttermost and stands spotless before God. Where nothing is owed, there is no debt and no guilt.

Sadly, the NCT believes the Roman Catholic *limbus patrum* myth whereby Old Testament believers were detained until Christ set them free after His Resurrection. NCT works are full of the idea that the Old Testament saints had to wait until Christ's resurrection before they could be counted as real Christians. The myth that all O.T. glorified saints were still under their fallen obligations until Christ paid the price of their sins in time, is to misunderstand what 'the fulness of time' means. Christ had obligated Himself to redeem all saints in Eternity, not after they were born, or before they were born for that matter. John Reisinger claims that Old Testament believers had their 'hope realised' only after Christ came in time. There was a suspended salvation for O.T. saints which turned into real, empirical salvation at Pentecost. However, the nature of the Church has always been *faith* in Christ and not *rational trust* in Christ *by sight*. There is no saving difference between Abraham's faith and Paul's. Indeed, the scriptures call Abraham the father of the faithful. 'Hope realised' will be the lot of the entire Body of Christ on the Resurrection Morning. Hebrews commends the faith of the fathers in times past and, before listing their names, tells us that, 'Faith is the substance of things hoped for, the evidence of things not seen' (11:1). They had that faith, the Christian's present duty is to see that modern man follows in their train.

The Old Testament saints were thus conscious of the suretyship they had in Christ and prayed and pleaded for the application of such benefits to them and thus received and enjoyed these benefits.[268]

Gill comments:

> From this suretyship of Christ arose both the imputation of sin to Christ, and the imputation of His righteousness to His people;

---

[268] Job 19:25; Psalm 119:122; Isaiah. 38:14.

this is the ground and foundation of both, and on which the priestly office of Christ stands, and in virtue of which it is exercised.[269]

What Christ engaged to do as a surety

Using the example of Paul and Onesimus, Gill says Christ 'engaged to pay the debts of His people, and satisfy for the wrong and injury done by them'. Concerning Onesimus, Paul said to Philemon, 'If he hath wronged thee, or oweth thee ought, put that on my account; I Paul hath written it with my own hand, I will repay it'.[270] The debt Christ paid for His Bride, the Church, is two-fold:

1. Christ paid the debt of obedience to the law of God

Christ summed up His task by saying, 'Lo, I come ... to do thy will O God',[271] teaching that the old shadowy sacrifices are done away that the law might be fulfilled and established in Himself. Thus Christ was incarnated under the law to yield obedience to the law so those for whom He took upon Himself this dreadful burden could receive His righteousness.

2. Christ paid the debt of punishment for sin

Christ paid the debt of punishment incurred through the failure of man's obedience which is the curse of the law, the penalty of death. Gill concludes, 'by paying both these debts, the whole righteousness of the law is fulfilled in His people, considered in Him their head and Surety'. Sin, Gill stresses, 'deserves and requires punishment in body and soul, being transgressions of the righteous law of God'. The legal and spiritual deadness of a sinner reveals the deceit of the common-grace, free-offer, duty-faith gospellers. They accuse us of not believing in human responsibility or accountability. If man were totally dead in trespasses and sins, they say, God cannot hold him responsible. Dead men cannot shoulder responsibilities. Man must be sufficiently alive to recognise his own defects. They believe in the probation, second

---

[269] 2 Corinthians 5:21; Hebrews 7:20-22.
[270] Philemon 18, 19.
[271] Hebrews 10:7-9.

chance, theory of Joseph Bellamy, copied slavishly by Andrew Fuller. For them, the true and final fall is when man rejects Christ. He is a probationer and potential Christian until then.

Man's damnation does not arise from any present rejection of Christ but from his fall in Adam which was so utterly foreign to God's character and will that God pronounced the only penalty possible on man – death. All men, because of their fallen nature are hell-bound when left to their own agency. Because man was responsible for his God-denying actions, God struck him down. It is totally impossible for natural man to accept Christ. Gill's doctrine of man's responsibility goes far deeper than the watered-down doctrine of responsibility preached by many pseudo-evangelicals based on their low view of the fall, the gospel and the Trinity and their high view of man. To argue that man is merely fallen in his morals but not in his basic natural capacities is to argue man is not fallen at all. He has, to use their word for sin, merely a 'moral defect' which only needs an effort of the will to set it right. The Fullerite slogan that man 'can if he only wills' is a mockery of the fall, man's condemnation and redemption.

Though the wages of sin is death, the gift of God is eternal life. God's gift of grace would not be a gift of grace if there were any agency in man that could assist God in His giving. Sadly, modern critics of the faith of our fathers do not base their gospel on saving grace but on what they call 'common grace' or 'natural theology' and 'Natural Law'. Can such erroneous teaching be called 'Christian'?

Christ, our Surety brings all the elect safe to glory

Judah pledged his suretyship for Benjamin by saying to Israel, 'I will be surety for him, of my hand shalt thou require him; if I bring him not unto thee, and set him before thee, then let me bear the blame for ever'.[272] So Jesus presents His Church to the Father, saying 'Lo, I, and the children which God hath given me'.[273] The work Christ covenanted to do was to bring back Jacob and to restore the preserved of Israel,[274] and to recover and ransom lost sheep. The entire initiative of the

---

[272] Genesis 43:9.
[273] Hebrews 2:13.
[274] Isaiah 49:5, 6.

sinner's surety is a covenant action within the Godhead in eternity. Salvation is not a time-phenomenon, aided by the initiative or agency of man. It is not a general offer to be accepted or rejected at will. God has a fixed and definite number of adopted children, all of them His beloved Benjamins. Christ has pledged Himself to keep them safe for ever. None can remove them from the Father's love as they are eternally safe in the surety of Christ Jesus Himself. Thus, those evangelists who speak of salvation as being a provision of God, rendered efficacious by man's agency, are preaching a false gospel.

Christ's Mediatorship is also in the form of a Testatorship

1. The Covenant of Grace is in the form of a testament, founded on the absolute and sovereign will of God. Drawn up because of God's loving desire to call a people as joint heirs with Christ who was chosen as their Testator.

2. The testament contains several legacies. Those given by the Father to His Son, Christ, as His portion and inheritance, and those legacies of grace and glory given to those chosen as joint-heirs with Christ.

3. God disposes in His testament only that which is His own to dispose. He alone has the sovereign right to do with His blessings as He will.

4. This testament is very ancient. It is called 'new', not because it was newly made but because it was newly revealed, published and declared from time to time as a 'better covenant' than that with Adam and that which the Jews failed to keep in the Wilderness. Actually, this testament was made in eternity[275] and is thus not time-bound, though it is time-applied.

5. This testament is unalterable. It is a yea and amen testament.

6. The testament is sealed, though not by circumcision, baptism and the Lord's Supper which some teach are the seals of the Covenant of Grace. The seals are the Holy Spirit of God who witnesses to the covenant, and the blood of Christ which ratifies and confirms it.[276]

---

[275] 2 Timothy 1:9.
[276] Zechariah 9:11; Matthew 26:28; Hebrews 13:20.

7. A testament needs witnesses. God swore by Himself because there was none greater. There were no fit human witnesses,[277] but John nevertheless teaches there are three who bear witness to it in eternity, the Father, the Word and the Holy Spirit.

8. The Covenant of Grace or new testament is registered in scripture, the public notaries being the prophets and apostles.

Re-stipulation impossible from man's side

Inheritors named in a human will cannot alter it. Likewise, no man can alter what God has decreed. The new covenant is a covenant of promise of what surely shall come to pass. Thus, the legacies are solely owing to the good will of the testator. Salvation is not of law or human claims on it, but of promise. Here our modern duty-faith movement makes a mockery of the Covenant of Grace as they claim that God expects every sinner to do his duty and believe savingly in God. Salvation is not of duty but of promise, that is, of grace.[278]

Christ is the Mediating Testator of the Covenant of Grace

Hebrews 9:15-17 teaches:

> And for this cause he is the mediator of the new testament, that by means of death, for the redemption of the transgressions that were under the first testament, they which are called might receive the promise of eternal inheritance. For where a testament is, there must also of necessity be the death of the testator. For a testament is of force after men are dead: otherwise it is of no strength at all while the testator liveth.

All power is given unto Christ who is God blessed for ever and all things own their being to Him who is the Creator of all. Christ thus disposes of His inheritance as He sees fit by His divine right. The Covenant's promises point to the vicarious work of Christ who made His soul an offering for sin and poured out His blood in death.[279] As

---

[277] 1 John 5:7.
[278] Romans 4:14; Galatians 3:18.
[279] Isaiah 53:10-12.

307

Christ is the Lamb slain before the foundation of the world, His Testatorship works both backwards and forwards in time, securing all God's elect from condemnation and reconciling them to God.

Man receives nothing in the Covenant of Grace without Christ's counsel and consent. This was planned from eternity when the Covenant was concluded, so the Bible can truly speak of Christ as the lamb slain from the foundation of the world. All that is the Father's was given the Son in eternity and all that was the Son's was given the elect by a testament. Thus Christ, when facing death, could tell His followers, 'I appoint unto you a kingdom, as my Father hath appointed unto me'.[280]

Christ's death is necessary to put His will in force
The ruling regarding the enforcement of wills is clear. The testator himself must die before it is effective. Unlike human wills, however, which are only of benefit to contemporaries or people to come, Gill says concerning Christ's Testament:

> ... such is the virtue and *efficacy* of it, that it reaches backward to the beginning of the world, as before observed: wherefore the Old Testament saints not only received the promise of eternal inheritance, but enjoyed it before the death of Christ, though in virtue of it, for they are said to inherit the promises, that is the things promised,[281] but the death of Christ was necessary to confirm the covenant or testament, that the legatees might appear to have a legal right to what was bequeathed to them, law and justice being satisfied thereby; so that no caveat could be put in against them, and no obstruction be made to their claim of legacies, and their enjoyment of them; and no danger of this will being ever set aside.[282]

Summing up
Christ was appointed from eternity as the Mediator of the New Covenant between God and man. His office was not merely to reveal

---

[280] Luke 22:29.
[281] Hebrews 9:15 and 6:12.
[282] Of Christ, As The Testator Of The Covenant, *A Body of Practical and Doctrinal Divinity*.

the Father's mind as Moses did but to reconcile sinners to God. Here Christ by virtue of His two perfect natures represents both sides perfectly. We gain unity with the Father through our unity with the Son. This unity is kept upright by the intercession and advocacy of Christ. Nothing man can do can alter or enhance this work of Christ's so those who speak of man's agency in salvation speak of a nonentity. Christ's mediation as the Son of God entailed His redeeming us from the curse of the law by putting Himself under the law and fulfilling it to the last jot and tittle. Theories of mediation whereby Christ is seen as carrying out a token obedience to the law where quality is shown rather than quantity, always being above the law and not placing Himself under it, is not the gospel of Christ's Mediatorship. Christ could only redeem us by suffering the full curse of the law. He could only redeem us by fulfilling all the law in His Person. As Mediator, Christ mediates only for the elect of all ages for whom He died. He is the Mediator of the Old Testament saints as He is of the New. There was never a time when Christ was not Mediator. Christ's Mediatorship is fully successful and is for eternity. He never mediates in vain.

This is because Christ has given Himself as the elect's surety, guaranteeing freedom from punishment, guilt and condemnation for all eternity. In this suretyship, Christ guarantees to pay the debts of His people to the law and to the punishment for sin and to preserve them safe for ever in glory. Again, the initiative to be our surety is entirely Christ's and man's agency plays no part.

Christ's Mediatorship also includes His Testatorship. All the blessings in Christ appertaining to the Covenant of Grace are the eternal legacy of the saints. This bequest can only come into being through the death of the Testator. Christ offered up His life so that redemption, justification and glorification, which He alone can give, could be inherited by His Bride, the Church. May we all be given grace to say 'Amen' to that!

Chapter 14

Establishing The Relevance Of The Covenant Of Grace For God's People

The Covenant of Condition

We cannot understand who God's People are if we ignore the Covenant of Grace. In searching the scriptures in order to find out who the true People of God are we find that believers in the Messiah-Christ in both Testaments are God's Covenant People. They believe in the one Covenant given to the world at different times according to the necessities of the times throughout history via God's own revelation as recorded in the scriptures. This manifestation of God's grace is a Messianic Covenant between God the Father and the Messiah. The purpose of this Covenant is to choose out a People of God through salvation in Christ the Lord and Messiah. He alone is worthy to pledge Himself to be its Author, Fulfiller and Keeper because He alone is able to keep what He has ordained. Thus this is a conditional Covenant which demonstrates God's eternal nature and eternal grace and demands the same standards from its recipients. Though it is meant as a bilateral understanding between God and man, all fallen men are shown by the Law revealed in the Covenant as not being able to keep it. Who could, except God Himself? This is why Christ bound and limited Himself to appearing in the flesh to fulfil the conditions in His own Manhood which the rest of mankind fail to keep and cannot keep.

True religion is found in man's keeping the Covenant through faith in the Messiah who keeps the Covenant for him and gives him the faith to be ruled by His Messianic choice.

This true religion in the form of what the Jewish heart seeks and in which the Christian heart rejoices has never been attained by either Jew or Christian as fallen human beings and never will. It is wrought out solely through means the Messiah Man has brought about in placing Himself under the Covenant and keeping it on behalf of His people. 'As in Adam all die, even so in Christ shall all be made alive.'[283] This is the promise which both the Old and New Testaments reveal. This is God's Everlasting Covenant with man, stretching from Adam to eternity in Christ. There are no two administrations of this as the Presbyterians tell us and no two different covenants here as the NCT followers tell us but it is one Covenant of Grace embracing man's fall and the triumph of our Messiah. Law and Grace bring new life to dead men. The First Adam fell to sin but the Second or Last Adam, as Christ is also called, rose from the dead and conquered sin. Thus the scriptures tell us, 'The first man Adam was made a living soul; the last Adam was made a quickening spirit ... The first man is of the earth, earthy, the second man is the Lord from heaven'.[284] The Covenant is thus bilaterally a Divine Covenant but at the same time a Human one, kept by the Messiah Man Himself who fulfils all its conditions on fallen man's behalf. He alone has proved Himself to be the sole condition-keeper between God and man. This is why we call this Eternal Covenant the Covenant of Grace. It was given by the Father out of love for His wayward children and accomplished by His beloved Son.[285] Greater love for his brethren can no man have.

The Covenant of Grace as a Biblical Fact

Recently teaching concerning the Covenant of Grace which stretches from the beginning of time into eternity has been challenged as being un-biblical. Some say it started with the Sermon on the Mount where allegedly Christ disestablished the Old Law and established a New Law. Others say their 'new covenant' started with the atoning death of Christ,

---

[283] 1 Corinthians 15:22.
[284] 1 Corinthians 15:45-47.
[285] John 3:16.

others with the resurrection. Some are looking for an eschatological establishing of their new covenant. This writer has seen modern professing Reformed Christians go from a 'One Covenant' teaching through most of these positions in the development of their ideas. This confusion of covenants and their dispensations has led them even to deny that the Covenant of Grace is a biblical term and they substitute it by the most questionable term 'New Law'.

The quest for a 'New Law' leads away from the teaching on Divine Law in both Testaments

As God's Covenant with His Son clearly says in both Testaments that Law does not save sinners but drives them to seek grace, it might seem strange that our NCT friends seek for a New Law and thus depart from Covenant of Grace thinking. It is even odder that NCT followers go so far as to define Christ's Lordship as *'New Lawgiver'*. Ernest Trenchard in his article on 'Grace, Covenant and Law' written in the late fifties, before New Covenant Theology had re-challenged biblical thinking, saw this 'new Law' teaching as a second century falling away from the biblical gospel. He argues that such writings as the 'Shepherd of Hermas', the 'Epistle of Barnabas' and the 'Teaching of the Twelve' show 'how quickly they (Christians) had lost contact with the fundamental teaching of the Apostle to the Gentiles and lost their vision of the absoluteness of Grace and thus began to present the gospel as 'the new law of our Lord Jesus Christ'.[286]

Through dismissing the Old Testament as a reliable source on everlasting Covenant teaching, including Law and Grace, such revisionists also dismiss Christ's Messianic and Mediatorial status as Covenant-Keeper in the Old Testament. The Mosaic Law was a schoolmaster to bring students to Christ[287] and was the Law God ordained for that purpose. In fulfilling the Law Christ kept it. He did not abolish it as many now maintain. Indeed if keeping the Law meant doing away with it, what purpose has the Law in our salvation and why

---

[286] P. 132.
[287] Galatians 3:24, 25.

did Christ die to keep us from its curse?[288] If the law has no curse for sinners, all sinners are free. The NCT followers tell us there is now a New Law but for the saved only. But the saved are under grace, not Law. It is unrepentant sinners who are still under the Law.

NCT abolishes the Law for both believers and unbelievers

Does this mean that, according to New Covenant Theology teaching, sinners condemned by the Law given to Moses and what orthodox people take to be an ever-new eternal Law, are now free from this Covenant Law given to God's People in the Old Testament and maintained in the New? If so, the NCT should call itself BCT – Broken Covenant Theology! It is so very, very difficult to obtain a biblical answer to this question from NCT people and it is obviously one of their very weak spots. They must, however, think it strange that Jesus allowed Himself to be condemned and punished under the old Law but, they nevertheless teach that Christ annulled this Law for a New Law which the NCT hold as a secret revelation and will not spell it out. Romans 3:19 claims that in New Testament times both Jews and Gentiles are under the same Law and the purpose of this Law as part of God's Covenantal care is explained carefully and repeatedly in both Testaments. Indeed, Paul emphasizes there is one Law for both Jews and Gentiles which shows all sinners from whatever country, class or creed they might come, that they are fallen creatures in need of redemption. 2 Timothy 1:5-11 is of great significance here as Paul warns against those who talk about the Law but do not know at all what they are talking about. Paul also outlines the work of the Law in the Gospel with which He has been entrusted. When Paul here teaches that the Law is good when put to good use, he is speaking about the Law in his day and not the Law as a mere Old Testament institution, now rendered invalid for saints and sinners alike. Similarly, in Romans 7:12-14, Paul argues that the Law is holy, just, good and spiritual, that is when put to its right use in addressing sinners in the Gospel.

---

[288] When I use the term 'Law', I do not see that law as being the opposite of 'grace' but see law in grace and grace in law. They belong together and were never intended by God to be found contradictory.

Has the NCT abolished sin with its abolishment of the Law?

Once in my boyhood Bradford, a church put up a notice along the road to Saltaire which said, 'This Church is for sinners only'. People tell me I am joking when I tell this story but I passed this church every day on my way to work in Cottingley Woods and I knew the minister. He complained hardly any strangers had visited his church since he put up the notice. Certainly Paul, when referring to the Law which condemns sinners, is speaking of the one and only Law here under which all are placed. He is not speaking of a New Law and a New Lawgiver. He is saying that though the Law once delivered, condemns them, Grace can save them. Christ did not create a New Law, thus contradicting an Old Law, but Christ died under that Law He gave in the Old Testament to be applied also to Himself in the New. Christ did not die under the fictive Law he is supposed in NCT mythology to have established shortly before His death. This is the view aired in John Reisinger's booklet. *But I say unto You* ... with the New Law beginning through the Sermon on the Mount. However, in his work *Abraham's Four Seeds*, the same author maintains that his New Covenant with His new Lawgiver started at Pentecost when the Church was founded. It is rather frustrating that such people can never spell out in unison what the New Law is and when their New Covenant (which appears to be the same thing) started and what relation to it have those who died as believers though under the times of a supposed Old Law. However, the NCT-followers are no different from many other denominations such as the Anglicans, Presbyterians and Baptists who rally around their institutions when challenged but believe quite different things amongst themselves. In their similar behaviour, the NCT have certainly become a Denomination rather than a Church.

One can hardly believe that a number of NCT writers[289] maintain that not only the Old Testament knew no New Covenant although this was ardently preached by the O.T. prophets, but also the witness of Matthew, Mark, Luke and John to the Old Testament has no relevance to a People of God or a Church in their gospels. However, the bulk of Christians will surely notice that Paul in Romans 3 and 4 teaches that the gospel combination of both Law and Grace, as in the Old Testament,

---

[289] See Bibliography for their works.

does not mean that God's revealed Law is abolished but it is established through faith. Here, we must study Romans chapter 4 carefully and in its entirety. In order to explain how the Covenant works, Paul starts with Abraham, who lived at least 480 years before the foundation of the Jewish nation, who was saved, not by works, but by faith within the Covenant as all the People of God must be past, present and future. Paul also explains that salvation by works merely reveals man's debt which means his natural duty to make recompense, which he cannot do, so the only alternative is God's grace. Next, he moves to David whom he deals with as a saved man who has received righteousness without his own working. Obviously, from what Paul says, both non-Jews as Abraham and Gentiles are all condemned under sin but, 'Blessed are they whose iniquities are forgiven, and whose sins are covered. Blessed is the man to whom the Lord will not impute sin'.[290] This is a reference both to the circumcised and the uncircumcised, irrespective of the curse of the Law. Nevertheless, Paul sees both the work of the Law and that of grace as a necessity in the Covenant life of the believer, saying in versed 16:

> Therefore it is of faith, that it might be by grace; to the end the promise might be sure to all the seed; not to that only which is of the Law, but to that which is of the faith of Abraham who is the father of us all.

Paul hammers this truth home my emphasizing that Abraham is thus the father of many nations and this Old Testament truth was not merely for Abraham but for us all.

The New Testament never teaches that the Law revealed in the Old Testament as part of the eternal Covenant of Grace, has been abolished and a New Law substituted. Neither Testament teaches a go-it-alone of Law and Grace but that God's righteous character displays both.

The NCT lacks research into their judgment of scripture

Most NCT arguments appear not to come directly from the scriptures but from their own testimony and have developed through debates with certain Dispensationalists, Catabaptists and Presbyterians who were not representative of either Reformed or biblical covenantal faith. Indeed,

---

[290] Romans 4:7, 8.

my criticism of so-called New Covenant Theology which I have aired both in my books and very extensive correspondence with them, is that they stand too near the Dispensationalists in their multiple ideas on biblical covenants which often run parallel to what others call 'Dispensations'. So, too, the NCT people as a body are far nearer the Presbyterians with their two-covenant teaching than to the One Covenant teaching of the Bible and our Reformed fathers. Many NCT people, like Reisinger, also make the mistake of accepting the Westminster Confession as the general standard of the Reformed faith, obviously not knowing how the Confession came to be and how it was published in its unfinished form. There are at least fifty other great Reformed documents which they ought to have studied but, as I have seen through my correspondence with a number of leading NCT men, they leave such research to others. Having said this, I must honestly confess that there is a great deal of confusion amongst other supposedly 'Reformed' people who look on their covenant teaching as a form of a socio-politico-religio-contract between God and 'the Powers that Be'.

Trenchard has again a wise word to say concerning the idea of God's Covenant laying conditions on fallen man. He quotes the Westminster Dictionary of the Bible which declares that God's 'covenant with man is a free promise on His part, generally based upon the fulfilment of certain conditions by man'. Here the dictionary obviously speaks of conditions to be fulfilled by fallen man, not by the Man Christ Jesus. As Trenchard points out:

> ... a free promise on the part of God cannot be made dependent on certain conditions to be fulfilled by man, neither generally nor in certain stated cases, though a right attitude on man's part is necessary if the free promise is to be appropriated.[291]

The Bible followed by our Reformers, sees this appropriation being the work of the Holy Spirit in man showing that the Covenant is all of God.

---

[291] Grace, Covenant and Law, p. 133.

God indeed put Abraham under a Covenant of Grace

The NCT people deny, oddly enough, that God put Adam, Abraham etc. under a Covenant of Grace, arguing that we cannot relate the gospel to such a Covenant. This must come as a surprising challenge to those who believe the Covenant of Grace is our gospel in its entirety, leaving nothing out appertaining to the doctrine of salvation, obviously including that basic gospel truth that the wages of sin is death but the gift of God is eternal life. To back up his negative idea the author of *Abraham's Four Seeds* quotes Galatians 3:8 as summing up what he assumes is the gospel to Abraham and which he thinks by definition excludes a Covenant of Grace with Abraham:

> And the scripture, foreseeing that God would justify the heathen through faith, preached before the gospel unto Abraham, saying, In thee shall all nations be blessed.[292]

Though these words, in context, are a clear reference to a Covenant of Grace, the author concludes it is wrong to use such a term referring to the gospel and says:

> Nowhere in all the Word of God does the Holy Spirit call the gospel the Covenant of Grace nor does any verse remotely imply that when God graciously makes known the gospel promise to an individual, or to a whole nation, that he is thereby putting the individual under a Covenant of Grace. If Covenant Theology[293] is correct, then Paul should have said, 'God made a Covenant of Grace with Abraham.[294]

---

[292] *Abraham's Four Seeds*, p. 38.

[293] Reisinger defines Covenant Theology for his argument's sake as a belief in two covenantal administrations which separates a covenant of works from one of grace. This reveals the source of his ideas which are found in Presbyterian thinking. Neither the Presbyterian idea nor what the NCT have made of it is a biblical, Reformed position but was established in the Cromwellian regime under Presbyterian pressure in order to place a political, totalitarian clamp on Britain. At the back of this, urged by Samuel Rutherford, was the thinking of Plato and Aristotle on which Rutherford based his view of the relationship between King (or Government) and people in his *Rex Lex*. This became the text book of the Westminster Presbyterians from approximately 1643 to 1648 which ushered in that period of darkness commonly called 'The Enlightenment'. Covenant Theology proper is that the Covenant of Grace binds the Old and New Testaments together and the 'new' is a continuation of the 'old'.

[294] *Abraham's Four Seeds*, p. 38, 39

Happily, others think otherwise. Ernest Trenchard concludes his essay on 'Grace, Covenant and the Law' by saying, 'The Abrahamic covenant was a manifestation in time of the Eternal Covenant, and as such was purely of grace, unconditional, and guaranteed by God alone.' Trenchard adds, 'When our Lord instituted the Last Supper He declared that the Eternal Covenant of Grace was established 'in His blood'. He sees this as a confirmation and completion of the Covenant with Abraham in the promised 'Seed'.[295]

Reisinger thinks the Covenant with Abraham was merely material
At first, readers might be puzzled by Reisinger's words denying God made a Covenant of Grace with Abraham. However, on reading down the page we find the author takes God's promise of grace to Abraham merely as an earthly promise that his physical seed would inherit 'the land'.[296] The idea of Abraham being the Father of the faithful in all nations is thus lost to our NCT friends here. Surely all God's transactions with Abraham were so He could choose out a People of God for Himself. This, as we shall see more in depth later, was the Covenant of Grace.

It is strange that the author of *Abraham's Four Seeds* rejects terms here which he feels, albeit wrongly, are not to be found in scripture though many of his own terms, whether orthodox or not, are not found in scripture at all. Indeed, NCT writers sometimes provide glossaries at the end of their works to explain their special and particular NCT jargon. We note that the author does use the very acceptable term 'the doctrines of grace' but this term has less to back it up as verbatim scripture than 'the Covenant of Grace'.

This anti-Covenant of Grace author constantly claims that his NCT novelties are true Baptist teaching but he is not in a position to convince anyone that he represents Baptist theology. A greater representative was surely John Gill who was a Baptist of the Baptists and denounced what later was falsely termed 'New Covenant Theology' in its mistaken

---

[295] Pp. 147, 148.
[296] *Ibid* p. 38.

understanding of Law and Grace. Gill uses the term 'Covenant of Grace as do all our Reformers and tells us the term Covenant of Grace is:

> ... properly enough, since it entirely flows from and has its foundation in the grace of God: it is owing to the everlasting love and free favour of God the Father, that he proposed a covenant of this kind to his Son; and it is owing to the grace of the son that he so freely and voluntarily entered into engagements with the Father; the matter, sum and substance of it is grace; it consists of grants and blessings of grace to the elect in Christ; and the ultimate end and design of it is the glory of the grace of God.[297]

This is the gospel and Gill knew it! In his work on the everlasting Covenant of Grace cited above, Gill refers to the confusion of those who split up the essential nature of the Covenant, arguing, with illustrations from biblical passages that the Covenant of Grace is also a Covenant of Life (Malachi 2:5; 2 Timothy 1:1; Titus 1:2), a covenant of peace (also Malachi 2:5; Isaiah 54:10). Gill also sees the Covenant of Grace as one of Redemption, though the author under scrutiny here, John Reisinger, accepts the latter title but not the former. This helps us to examine Reisinger's claims that he represents Baptist theology as he criticizes those who confuse the Covenant of Redemption with the Covenant of Grace but in His work on the *Everlasting Covenant* John Gill treats the terms as synonymous. The 'confusion' appears to be with Reisinger.[298]

The Old Testament knows no legal 'stand-alone' dictated by God
In his book *Abraham's Four Seeds* where the single biblical 'seed' in the Covenant prophesies is split into an alleged four different lines, Reisinger argues that Covenant Theologians, a term he defines far too narrowly and inaccurately, are 'forced into inventing' such terms as 'Covenant of Grace', 'simply because they fail to see the uniqueness of God's dealings with a special nation "put under law" as no other nation ever was before and ever will be again'. As far as it goes, given a very

---

[297] *A Body of Practical and Doctrinal Divinity*, Book II, Of the Covenant of Grace', p.144, 1810 edition.
[298] See *Abraham's Four Seeds*, p. 37 and passim.

wide range of interpretations, this statement might stand as a basis for discussion between those who are for or against the NCT position. However, this chance of debate is smothered by Reisinger concluding that the Jews were merely put under a legal covenant which he calls the 'covenant of works'. Where Old Testament Law is, to Reisinger, there can be no Grace.[299] Reading this, one cannot help but think Reisinger puts all post-O.T. Gentiles under the New Law, however, NCT deny this and claim that only Christians are put under the New Law and the Mosaic Law is abolished. But how then shall we bring sinners to conviction if the supposed 'Old Law' is abolished? If Law is only for already saints, what hope have the fallen for salvation?

The term 'Covenant of Grace' is fully Biblical
The term 'Covenant of Grace' has always been used in the history of the Church to depict God's mode of choosing a People for Himself. It is found in the early church as '*pactum gratia*' but it was given renewed vigour and understanding in Reformed circles since Henry Bullinger first expounded the doctrine in a Reformed manner. Good doctrine is as old as Genesis and Bullinger was influenced by Oecolampadius, the chain of influence going way back in history. Bullinger influenced Ursinus and Olevanus who gave us the Heidelberg Catechism. Both Ursinus and Olevanus stressed that the basis of the Covenant was that Christ died for sinners by fulfilling and keeping the Law for them as His eternal prerogative which stretched throughout all history. This school through Wollebius influenced John Durie who passed the truth on to Ussher, Davenant, Howe, Sibbs, the Nyes and some forty other leading British Puritans besides an equal number of Continental ministers of the gospel. This thinking reformed their theology. Sadly, the Presbyterians in power at the time of the Westminster Assembly opposed Durie and his staunch Reformed friends, mostly Church of England and Independents, maligning them with rude names and split the one biblical Covenant taught by such as Tyndale into two separate Covenants paving the way for modern Dispensationalism and the so-called New Covenant Theology. My own tutors in this matter were Bullinger, Bale, Durie, Gill and Ball and the Independents and

---

[299] *Ibid*, p. 134.

Anglicans who did not bow the knee to the totalitarian religio-political covenant thinking of the Presbyterians expressed in their *Solemn League and Covenant*. When referring to the Father's Covenant with His Son on behalf of mankind, Bullinger used the exact German equivalent of the 'Covenant of Grace in German which is '*Gnadenbund*'. This is still the standard term (when translated) used in most languages where Reformed thinking is discussed. The French have 'alliance de la grâce'; the Dutch have 'genadeverbond'; the Swedes have 'förbund av nåd'; the Danes have 'nådens pagt'' the Welsh have Cyfamod gras' and modern Greeks have 'diathiki tis charitas' (transcribed). Most English-speaking NCT people do not bother to read expositions of the Covenant in other languages. Indeed, after living most of my life speaking other languages I am of the opinion that most theological quarrels amongst English-speaking evangelicals are caused by the dumbing-down of the English language which Durie and the budding Royal Academy warned about in the mid-17th century.

'Grace' has its synonyms

However, even English, like, Greek and Hebrew, has several exact synonyms for 'grace' which are mostly found in equivalent terms for 'mercy'. 'Grace' and 'mercy' are thus translations of the same term in Hebrew and Greek and are used synonymously throughout the 1611 English Bible. Without spoiling the meaning, indeed, the biblical expression 'Covenant of Grace' can be rendered 'Covenant of Mercy' and 'Covenant of Peace' as it is also called, using non-synonyms, an Everlasting Covenant and a Holy Covenant[300]

To be in the Holy Covenant is synonymous with being in Grace and under God's mercy as witnessed from Genesis to Revelation. This fact may be a little confusing for some because of the sheer wealth of synonyms used to translate Hebrew and Greek words for 'grace' which English-speaking theologians of the traditional rival schools are afraid of using as they spoil their denominational programme. I remember a dear friend of mine, an editor, criticizing an author for using different translations of the same Greek word in different contexts. He argued that one Greek word must have one English word as its translation. I could not convince him that English has often very many synonyms for

---

[300] See Luke 1:72; Ezekiel 37:26.

the same Greek word and one Greek word carries often meanings that one English word cannot express. We have only to think of the Greek word for 'baptism' which has over forty meanings and is still proving a headache for translators. The Old Testament words 'chesed' and 'chen', for instance, can be translated as mercy, kindness, lovingkindness, goodness, goodliness, good deeds, bounty, preciousness, well-favoured and favour besides 'grace' in the English Bible. The Covenant of Grace contains all these aspects. When NCT people deny there was ever a Covenant of Grace, they deny that God's Covenant contains all these attributes also. All these synonyms can be grouped together under the heading 'grace'. Furthermore, different words of mercy and grace are used in parallel pairs in the Old Testament to stress God's merciful grace and His gracious mercy in respect of His Covenant, commandments and testimonies. Thus we see Daniel referring to a Covenant of Mercy/Grace in Daniel 9:4 'keeping the covenant and mercy to them that love him'. But it was also so back in Mosaic times as there we read in Deuteronomy 7:9 of the very same truth. This is also repeated and emphasised in 1 Kings 8:23; Nehemiah 1:5; Nehemiah 9:17; Nehemiah 9:32; Joel 2:13. and especially Luke 1:72 where High Priest Zacharias sees the Covenant of Grace continued in New Testament times and calls the Covenant one of 'mercy'. He teaches that God's covenantal mercies stretch from the Old Testament into the New. The Greek word 'charis' often used in the New Testament for 'grace' covers all the meanings of its Old Testament counterpart and many more. Yet I have books from four NCT authors, each denying there is such a biblical teaching as 'The Covenant of Grace'.

So, too, the word 'eleos' used in Luke 1:72 of God's Covenant mercies is used by Paul in Romans to express 'grace' throughout chapters nine and eleven. In 1 Timothy 1:13-16 it is used to denote the obtaining of pardon and forgiveness. The Bible often relates grace, mercy and peace together as in Titus 1:4 and we find God's Covenant called by Ezekiel the Prophet 'a covenant of peace' (Ezekiel 34:25 and Ezekiel 37:26) which is to be for everlasting. Of course, 'grace', 'mercy' and 'peace' in the Bible all have overlapping meanings, especially in the realms of favour and being set right with God. One can only conclude that the idea of a Covenant of Grace, mercy and peace is central to the scriptures and thus to the gospel. It is spoken of by the minor prophets at the end of the Old Testament and taken up again at the beginning of the New. The fact English-speaking people have settled on one term 'the Covenant of Grace' as a *terminus technicus* is merely a matter of utility and does not rule out synonymous terms as 'un-biblical'. A good pastor should teach his flock what these synonyms mean instead of jumping on one meaning and then altering it.

Cutting out the ongoing features of the Old Testament into the New
When Wells and Zaspel conclude their book on NCT dogmas with the words, 'The conclusion seems clear: when N.T. writers use the word covenant, they normally want to assert discontinuity',[301] they only show they are poor linguists and exegetes and do not understand the way Hebrew, Greek and English express themselves. One can only deny 'the Covenant of Grace' is not to be found in scripture by denying its true meaning as NCT followers do. Nothing is more continuous than God's Covenant of Grace and Mercy which is everlasting. On the other hand, NCT teaching, like Dispensationalism, is one of absolute discontinuity and their interpretation of the 285 references to berit[302] in the Old Testament Hebrew, is speculation galore. Yet this word is only one of many synonyms in the Bible for 'Covenant'. Their teaching concerning the Covenant in the New Testament is based on a total break between the history of salvation in the Old Testament and the history of salvation in the New. They see two Peoples of God, two separate covenants and two kinds of hope in salvation. For them, there is no one history of salvation revealed and experienced in both Testaments. They not only argue for discontinuity in the Bible, they are very near being left with two different Bibles! Though they deny it, they attribute merely a partial faith and not a full saving faith to those men whom the letter to the Hebrews call our examples in real faith, arguing this is because they did not see their Messiah with their own eyes and had to rely on hope only. But what does the Book of Hebrews tell us? 'Faith is the substance of things hoped for, the evidence of things not seen'.[303] Surely the underlining truth of the gospel Covenant as already hinted at, is that by

---

[301] *New Covenant Theology*, New Covenant Media, 2002.
[302] Beriit, b'ryt, B.R.H., the transcriptions are numerous. We must also add the most numerous uses of Greek equivalents in the LXX and Novum.
[303] Hebrews 11:1.

faith we are saved and not by 'sight'. Hebrews 10:38; Romans 1:17 and Galatians 3:11 teach us this truth.

'The just shall live by faith' is an Old Testament truth

Is true saving faith a New Testament revelation only? No, the old prophets preached this as exemplified by the very clear statement of Habakkuk 2:4, 'Behold, his soul which is lifted up is not upright in him: but the just shall live by his faith.' This is a truth which France's Jacques Lefèvre outlined in his Romans commentary in 1512. After Lefèvre, the truth of justification by faith, was taken up by Lambert, then Luther and many others and became the motto of the Reformation. This is a truth, however, outlined in the abundant gospel teaching of the Old Testament.

Part of this Reformed faith is the knowledge 'the earth shall be filled with the knowledge of the glory of the Lord as the waters cover the sea' (Habakkuk 2:14) but this does not mean only those who see that in action in New Testament times are saved. I have often heard this prophetic utterance belittled by people who say that knowledge of the Lord does not mean belief in Him. But this is how the scriptures use the words we translate as 'knowledge'. John 17:3 explicitly emphasizes that eternal life is for those who know God.[304]

We all wait for that glorious time in faith which is our redemption. We note that Habakkuk closes his preaching with the joyful words, 'I will rejoice in the Lord, I will joy in the God of my salvation.' This is the New Testament faith the author to the Hebrews recommends with biblical authority. Thus, this author accepts fully the statement of Bullinger in his *Studiorum ratio* (1527/28) for his students that:

All the books of the Holy Scriptures have a common goal ...
The God of Heaven, the Almighty God has laid down for eternity
a testament, a contract, a covenant with mankind.

Bullinger was far from being alone in such thinking which was common understanding in his day and is today amongst modern scholarship worldwide. The common Covenant goal of the Testaments

---

[304] See how often John uses the word 'know' in a saving way in this chapter.

embraces both Law and Grace. Brill Publications in Holland has featured many interesting accounts of Luke's and Paul's handling of Law and Grace in the one Covenant. I have before me a paper from Brill's *Novum Testamentum*, with its subtitle 'an international quarterly for New Testament and Related Studies'. In edition 56, 2014, pages 335-358 Sigurd Grindheim gives an abstract from his thesis *Luke, Paul, and the Law*, saying:

> The emphasis on continuity between the early church and Israel's traditions is very characteristic of Luke. He portrays Jesus and his followers as faithful keepers of the Mosaic law. In this respect, Luke's Gospel contrasts with several statements in the Pauline corpus, where the law and the gospel are seen to be in tension (e.g., 2 Corinthians 3:4-18).

He goes on to distinguish between Paul's and Luke's emphasis by saying,

> The purpose of this article is to reopen the question of Luke and the law. In particular, I intend to argue that Luke's understanding of the law is compatible with that of Paul. Whereas previous studies have tended to focus on direct statements about the law, I will cast the net wider and examine the function of the law in Luke's narrative. Luke uses explicit and implicit references to the law as he develops his characters. Attention to this narrative strategy reveals a tension between law and faith in Luke. Unlike Paul, however, this tension is not between faith and the law as such. Instead, Luke consistently draws a contrast between characters that are defined by obedience to the law and characters that are defined by faith. People are not accepted by God through obedience of the law, but through faith.

Perhaps our NCT friends are in danger of forgetting that the Old Testament was Christ's Bible and that of the Early Church and it was preaching from it that saved those early Christians.

Summing up

It is impossible to understand who God's Chosen Ones are without reference to the Covenant of Grace revealed in both Testaments. It declares the whole story of salvation in time for all time and eternity. Had not the Christ-Messiah, the Lord from Heaven, created and as True Man kept the Covenant there would be no People of God. This gospel news pervades both Testaments. The broken-covenant theology of the NCT is thus a No Covenant Theology as the roots of New Testament understanding of the Divine combination of Law and Grace, each with its own function in the one goal of saving sinners are in the Old Testament. You cannot have one without the other. Christ did not need to create a new Law as the NCT maintain as the old one served and still serves its purpose perfectly. Christ bore His People's sins under the condemning power of the Law which still comes as a savour of death to those outside of Christ. The truth of recognizing Christ and His righteousness was known by Abraham and David as it was known by Paul and all believers.

Most of the NCT's arguments are not scriptural but denominational, picking out those denominations who are also weak on the Covenant question and when they have proven such theories wrong to their own satisfaction, they tell us that their own breech of the Covenant is the only alternative left to those searching for the truth. Since when did one wrong make another wrong right?

Ernest Trenchard has clearly pointed out that 'New Law' teaching reflects the falling away from the biblical account as erroneously taught by second century pseudo-epigraphic gospel imitations. Those who dismiss the gospel of Covenantal teaching concerning Law and Grace also dismiss with it the Messianic and Mediatorial role of Christ as our Covenant-Keeper. The 'New Law' of the NCT for saved sinners only, releases them from the Christian commitment of preaching 'repent and believe' thus rejecting Christ's Covenant provisions. The nature and purpose of the Law in condemning sin and leading sinners to Christ is absent from the witness of these professing Christians though Christ's Church is for sinners only. However, typical of their Marcion background, the NCT reject very much of the New Testament which deals with applying the Law both in the hands of sinners and saints as

327

a Jewish anachronism, foreign to their 'New Age' religion. Yet Christ's righteousness embraces both Law and Grace.

NCT theology is merely a theoretical application of ideas developed through debating with other 'Christian' movements and their lobbyists who also show weakness in their Covenant thinking. Thus both the NCT and their partners in debate are to be blamed for their blind leading the blind. As Trenchard also pointed out in his criticism of the Westminster Dictionary, a gospel dependent on man-made conditions is no gospel at all.

The denial of the NCT that Abraham's world-wide status as Father of the faithful has anything to do with the gospel and that it was only a matter of 'land-rights' is a grave misinterpretation. Reisinger scolds his critics for not using what he feels are correct gospel terms within his NewSpeak but his own renderings rid the scriptures of its gospel. Despite such NCT denials, our Reformers exemplified by Bullinger, Bale and later John Gill held to an everlasting doctrine of Grace promised to Abraham on very strong biblical, exegetical and linguistic grounds. Any discontinuation the NCT finds in the Covenant teaching of the Bible is purely because they have decided at their peril to discontinue the Covenant.

Reisinger's boast that his NCT is the true expression of the Baptists' faith is contradicted in full force by the Baptist Confessions and such as John Gill's corner-stone Baptist Theology. Gill demonstrated that the term Covenant of Grace is fully biblical as anyone with a smattering of understanding for biblical terms in both Testaments would see. The history of the Church and theology show that not only Baptists but our Reformers and all Christians with few exceptions believe that Christ fulfilled the Law by placing Himself under it and not by abolishing it, though its condemnation has been lifted for saints but not for sinners. Admittedly here, the Presbyterians, Fullerites and NCT-ites have hypothetically a different head-reasoning but Christ, deals with their hearts and most Christians are such in spite of themselves. All the great theologians of history world-wide speak of the Covenant of Grace as the cradle of the Gospel story. This is clear from the many renderings of the phrase not only in English synonyms but those of most foreign languages. This is true of Hebrew and Greek usage where one idea can be expressed in many different words expressing the same thing. Indeed, the Old Testament loves to say one thing one way and then give a parallel rendering in different words. Our Old and New Testament are rich in examples and the message of the Covenant of Grace pervades in this manner the entire biblical, united and ever continued gospel.

Actually, because of their cut, down and out version of the Covenant which they deny is of Grace, NCT followers live in opposition to the message of Hebrews which raises the Old Testament saints up as being our fathers in the faith and examples of true faith. Both the Old Testament as the New Testament saints looked forward, as all Christians do, to a realization of their faith in the New Jerusalem and this made and still makes them rejoice in the Lord. Thus the fact that the just shall live by faith, that is, the same faith, is the teaching of the entire Bible with its one, continued, united doctrine of the Covenant of Grace.

Chapter 15

The Everlastingness Of The Covenant Of Grace

The Covenant Given in Old Testament Times is not redundant
Grindheim's statement given in the previous chapter concerning the continuity of the Old to New Testament points a finger at the weakness of NCT exegesis. They see only a redundant Law in the Old Testament and deal with it as if grace and faith did not exist in union with it. To them, the Covenant in the Old Testament applies solely to the naked-letter *laws* on Mount Sinai, leaving aside the rest of the Torah, the Prophets, Wisdom Literature and other O.T. writings which teach the *Grace* of God. Indeed, in their minimalised view of the Covenant in the Old Testament both in its gracious and legal capacities and in spite of the fact they call it the Sinai Covenant and the only covenant under which the Jews were put, they, nevertheless, leave out very much of the Sinai story itself, not explaining how it came to be written and how Moses wished it to be firmly based on the Covenant with Abraham to choose out a People of God. Similarly, they lift the land rights promised to the Jews out of their contextual and historical place in the scriptures regarding the Covenant of Grace. Though they often speak of 'types', when it suits them, the 'types' of Canaan, the Promised Land and the New Jerusalem leave them cold. The NCT is ever dissecting the inseparable. One cannot cut out either Law, Grace or Faith from God's Old Testament revelation, especially when dealing with the main

exponents of the Covenant such as Abraham, Moses and David. So one cannot limit what the Bible calls 'the Everlasting Covenant' to land promises to an ethnic Israel which they depict as slaves to a short-term Law.

Conscious of this difficulty but wishing to avoid it, Reisinger devotes nine pages to analysing terms such as 'everlasting' and 'for ever' in his section, 'How long is "Everlasting"?'[305] to demonstrate that 'everlasting' with regards to the biblical Covenant cannot possibly mean 'never end'. His purpose is simple and obvious. He wishes to show that because the Covenant with Israel was merely a Law covenant which was abolished in New Testament times, 'everlasting' cannot mean 'everlasting' and we cannot thus find the 'everlasting Covenant' in the Old Testament. None of Reisinger's examples are valid as they are not analysed within the Covenant of Grace and are argued as if there was no covenantal continuity between the Old Testament and the New. He thus starts with his dissected bits and pieces of his own system instead of the biblical whole.

Reisinger's first example concerns 'the covenant of an everlasting priesthood' (Numbers 25:13), also described as a 'covenant of peace' (v. 12). This covenant, says Reisinger was 'done away in Christ' when Christ was offered as a sacrifice and died and 'the forming of the Body of Christ at Pentecost.' Is Reisinger saying that God has not placed the Priesthood at the heart of the everlasting Covenant and that the Covenant of Peace ended with Malachi, the last book in the Old Testament? This cannot be the case as Malachi deplores the fact that Israel, like the NCT, has misunderstood and corrupted the priesthood which was a covenant of life and peace.[306] He informs Israel that a 'messenger of the covenant' shall come, sent by the Lord who never changes in His plans.[307] This appears to be very much a prophesy concerning John the Baptist whose name is mentioned in the very next book.[308] Furthermore, the New Testament starts with a confirmation that the Everlasting Covenant is still working as a Covenant of Grace and Peace.[309]

---

[305] *Abraham's Four Seeds*, pp. 87-95.
[306] Malachi 1:1-8.
[307] Malachi 3:1-6.
[308] Matthew Chapter 3.
[309] See especially the opening chapters of Luke which will be discussed in more detail below.

Remission of sins through the shedding of blood

When Jesus instigated the Lord's Supper in remembrance of His saving work, He told His disciples, 'This is my blood of the new testament, which is shed for many for the remission of sins.'[310] For the background of Christ's words we must turn to Exodus 24:8 which tells us, 'Moses took the blood, and sprinkled it on the people, and said, Behold the blood of the covenant which the Lord hath made with you concerning all these words'. From then on a right keeping of the Covenant was referred to as keeping the spiritual 'New' Covenant as opposed to the Covenant merely kept to the lettering of it which the refugees from Egypt did not keep, either.[311] Of course, this 'New Covenant' is taken up by the New Testament and enlarged in its application. It is thus difficult to fathom why the NCT make much of Hebrews 13:20, 21 to back up their dogma of discontinuity between the Testaments. Contrary to NCT teaching the author says:

> Now the God of peace that brought again from the dead our Lord Jesus, that great shepherd of the sheep, through the blood of the *everlasting covenant*, Make you perfect in every good work to do his will, working in you that which is well pleasing in his sight, through Jesus Christ; to whom be glory for ever and ever. Amen.

Old Testament priestly terms taken up in the New

This takes us again immediately back to the Old Testament and is clearly what Ezekiel envisaged in chapter 37:26 and passim in the Old Testament. Indeed, the rest of Ezekiel 37 emphasises the Eternal Covenant of Peace when all Israel shall be gathered in and an everlasting sanctuary and tabernacle set up. He is here using priestly terms. The author to the Hebrews explains as seen above, that this is the task of our Great High Priest who fulfils eternally all the duties of the Priesthood.

---

[310] Matthew 26:28.
[311] Jeremiah 31:31.

So, too, the author to the Hebrews tells us in Chapter 10:29:

> Of how much sorer punishment, suppose ye, shall he be thought worthy, who hath trodden underfoot the Son of God, and hath counted the blood of the covenant, wherewith he was sanctified, an unholy thing, and hath done despite unto the Spirit of grace?

Again, this is couched in the priestly terms of the Covenant teaching in the Old Testament. The author to the Hebrews did not say, 'my terms are foreign to our new religion but you might understand what I mean'. The facts of Pentecost, according to Peter were foreseen by Old Testament patriarchs and prophets and believed. That Christ allegedly did away with the 'eternal priesthood' promised to Aaron, as Reisinger will have it, is quite a new thought. Did not Christ establish and fulfilled the Priesthood in Himself and make all His People priests? Is Christ not our High Priest for ever?

The Old Testament priesthood points to the everlasting High Priest
This writer sees the description of the Aaronic priesthood in the Old Testament as an eternal pointer to Christ. Reisinger supports his argument by saying the Aaronic priesthood was no longer needed after Christ's vicarious sacrifice and was thus not 'everlasting'. Has not the blood of the Covenant everlasting effects? And is not Christ still our High Priest according to Hebrews 2:17; 3:1; 4:14, 15; 5:1; 5:5; etc., etc. which is an everlasting order? Indeed the author of this faithful book on the everlasting Covenant of Grace insists that though Christ is now in the Heavens, He is still our High Priest. Indeed, the priesthood of all believers is based on the sure and certain office of Christ as our High Priest. Yet why does Reisinger claim that Aaron's priesthood lapsed at Christ's death when its witness still points to Christ and the Christian faith is explained through it? Most Sunday School children learn, or used to learn, that Old Testament prophetic features pointed to greater things to come. Shadows pointed to greater light. Continuation, extension and fulfilment do not indicate abolishment just as the Law fulfilled in Christ does not mean we are now under a New Law. Continuation in revelation is one of the key-notes of the Bible. We

understand the function of the priesthood through the way Christ used it as part of the Everlasting Covenant open to all believers. Here we are not bothered about proving that Christ was a physical descendent of Aaron, though He *was* obviously related to the High Priestly line. The Bible maintains that He was of the tribe of Judah and a priest of the order of Melchizedek.[312] This priesthood, founded before Aaron ever was, is forever, without beginning and end. One cannot get more 'everlasting' than that! This eternal truth was preached in the Old Testament at the same time as Aaronic theology was displayed as part of the Covenant.[313] It was believed then as it is believed by Christians today. We note that Malachi depicts Levi as Christ's upholder of the Covenant of Life and Peace showing that Christ, the Lord of Hosts, the same yesterday and forever, was present in the Old Testament reconciling the world to Himself.[314] This truth is worth repeating: the author of Hebrews emphasizes that Christ's priesthood is from eternity and was there in the past as it is in the present and in the future, so it is clear from these repeatedly emphasized statements that the Author and Keeper of both Law and Grace in the Covenant, our Saviour Jesus Christ, was ever at work in Old Testament times, choosing out a people for Himself as her High Priest, Messiah, Mediator, Prophet and King. We must not forget all the blessed offices of Christ.

Concerning the Levitical Priesthood, Ernest Trenchard has some very pithy things to say about its relation to the law within the Covenant in his *Evangelical Quarterly* article entitled 'Grace, Covenant and the Law'. He is seeking an answer to the question:

Can the inter-relation of Grace, Covenant and Law be expressed in a way which does justice to the unity of divine principles throughout scripture, and yet does not do violence to the contrasts and emphases of scripture?[315]

---

[312] Hebrews 5:6, 10; 6:20; 7:1, 10, 11, 15, 17, 21.
[313] See Psalm 10:4.
[314] Malachi 2:4-8.
[315] P. 132.

Trenchard emphasizes that the Law did not play the most prominent role within the Covenant but yet it was an intrinsic, essential part of it. Concerning the work of the Levitical priesthood which the NCT place merely on the law-bound 'shadow-side' of scripture the author shows that those theologians:

> ... were wholly right who regarded the Levitical ritual as a symbolic' 'covering', speaking of the eternal work of the Cross, which made it possible for God to declare of Himself through Balaam: 'He hath not beheld iniquity in Jacob, neither hath he seen perverseness in Israel'. The terrible lesson of the paidagogos was accompanied by a series of object-lessons, which, according to Hebrews, spoke of 'good things to come', and without which the rod of the paidagogos would have at once become an exterminating sword. The order of presentation in Exodus is significant: first the Decalogue, and some basic ordinances were given. As soon as they were given, Moses ordered the offering of sacrifices and sprinkled the blood upon the people, which was a rough and ready anticipation of the complicated ritual soon to be given, and spoke of the 'blood of the covenant' (Exodus 24:4-8, with the significant commentary of the writer to the Hebrews on this scene in Hebrews 9:19-22). Then the plan of the Tabernacle was given to Moses in the mount. By this time the people had committed the sin of the golden calf by which they had broken their 'covenant' and placed themselves under the wrath of God, and therefore Moses broke the first tables of the law in pieces at the foot of the mount. Partial judgment follows, with Moses' intercession on the basis of the Abrahamic covenant. Then the Tabernacle was set up and the Levitical system instituted in detail, with the new tables of the law hidden in the Ark of the Covenant. The lesson is that even a partial application of the covenant of works was inconceivable apart from a ritual which spoke continually of the value of the expiatory work of Christ, basis of the Eternal Covenant, which was to be manifested in 'the consummation of the ages' (Hebrews 9:26). The whole of Hebrews is a commentary on this principle, but the key verse is found in Hebrews 7:11: 'For on the basis of it (the Levitical priesthood) hath the people received the law'. That is to say, the

Levitical system was not a strange appendage to the Decalogue, judgments and ordinances, but the very basis which made possible their promulgation. Our conclusion is, therefore, that the 'gracious' elements of God's dealings with Israel from Sinai to the Cross stem entirely from the Abrahamic covenant, which in itself was to be fulfilled in Christ, while the Levitical sacrifices kept constantly in view the righteous basis on which God could bless His people. On the other hand, any attempt to find a direct manifestation of the grace of God in the thunders of Sinai tends to undermine some of the fundamental postulates of Pauline theology. [316]

The Old Testament pointed not to shadows but to the real Christ
This might serve as a hint to NCT people who tell us that the Old Testament only dealt with shadows and the thundering of Sinai. Trenchard is arguing this is not true at all. And, by the way, Trenchard puts his fingers on the greatest mistake those would-be theologians make who talk so much of a New Covenant as a post-Old Testament phenomena and not as the central teaching of the Old Testament. The Tyndale Fellowship member speaks of the setting up of the Golden Calf as a breaking of the Covenant and Moses interceded on the basis of the Abrahamic Covenant with a fresh and sweet (Old Testament synonyms for 'new') revelation of the true Covenant. He is arguing that partial and broken covenants do not count and these needed to be rectified in the understanding and faith of those who seek God. This can be read up in Jeremiah 31 and the chapters adjoining it. It is clear that with Jeremiah's reference to the New Covenant, he is talking about events which everyone knew about and many understood after the Children of Israel had run off after their own partial and broken understanding and interpretation a law which they had not grasped and which, indeed, was still in the process of being revealed. These self-thinkers and free-willers were what my Oklahoma friends call 'Sooners' who had jumped the gun. Yet our NCT friends tell us that Jeremiah spoke about matters

---

[316] *Op. sit.*, pp. 141, 142.

which were to be revealed many hundreds of years later through their post-biblical exegesis as an eschatological event and could not have been understood by Moses and Jeremiah's contemporaries. The New, ever freshened and refreshing Covenant was there even long before Moses. Any denial of this is breaking the covenant and rendering the broken parts void, useless and a jeopardising of eternal salvation within God's true Covenant. May those who have still ears to hear amongst the NCT take note that their covenant is a broken one.

The Old Testament had an active Messiah

What has Aaron to do with Melchizedek and the Everlasting Covenant? A great deal, indeed. This is explained by the author of Hebrews throughout his book. In the context of the author's references to Melchizedek, Aaron is mentioned most positively as one called by God for a particular purpose. This purpose was part of Christ's priestly plan for both Law and Grace in both Testaments. Again, the fault here is that followers of New-Covenant-Theology isolate Aaron, Moses and the other upholders of the everlasting Covenant from the Messianic realm and Christ's Mediatorial work by saying they represented a pre-Christian and pre-Church era that Christ not only corrected but annulled. They misunderstand the function of priesthood just as the priests in Malachi's days did and the Old Testament Prophet had to put them right in the same way the NCT need correction. They follow the way of the Jews who departed from the faith which the prophets preached. They remove Christ from His Old Testament Messianic participation. Aaron and other O.T. stalwarts mentioned and not mentioned here were signposts who pointed to a fuller definition of Priest and Lawgiver in the Messiah. But Christ was working His purpose out both in Aaron and Moses. They did not point to a different Covenant and different Law in the future but were Christ's servants working that Covenant out in their lifetimes. Christ was reconciling the World to Himself in the Old Testament as He was in the New and is still so doing.[317] To argue this was not Christ's function as Covenant Maker and Keeper in the Old Testament is to make the New Testament meaningless and to believe merely in a half-truth. I have spoken with several leading NCT men who admit this but instead of accepting

---

[317] 2 Corinthians 5:2.

biblical revelation with its sufficient explanation they look forward to a Third Great Revelation which will explain the New Testament.[318] Then they will probably say the New Testament is now too old to be relevant. The Muslims feel they have such a Testament in the Koran, yet even they appeal to Moses and Abraham as witnesses as did Moses!

The Law was never Graceless and Grace never Lawless
Within the Covenant of Grace, the Law was never intended to be effective of itself but serves to show man's ineffectiveness in dealing with his own sin. This was an act of Grace on God's part. In the same eternal plan the Covenant shows God's effectiveness in dealing with man and his transgressions. God first revealed Himself to Moses as the God of his father and Abraham.[319] This is repeated throughout all the books dealing with the Pentateuch which understand the Law within the terms given to Abraham. Moses personally anchored his correct understanding of the Law in the promises made to Abraham in his pleas with God for blessings on Israel.[320] Paul confirms all this in Galatians Chapter 3. Indeed, God never promised anything conditionally at Sinai which he had not promised unconditionally to Abraham. The Covenant with the part law plays in it was always effective in balancing out the interaction between law and grace so law was never graceless and grace never lawless. The demands of the Law were never effective in their accomplishment by man but were there to show the absolute inability of man to stand alone without God's grace. One cannot have one without the other and be a just man made perfect by God.

God's Word reveals the Christ of both Testaments
This writer believes that the New Testament exists as God's Word because it is built on the eternal Testimony of Christ in His status as

---

[318] In his book *In the Last Days*, Randy Seiver gives hints as to expected post-realised-eschatological revelations and adds 'We do not understand the fulfilment of the new covenant in such a way that there cannot be a fuller realisation of the same promises in the future.' P. 231. Seiver sees the Old Testament Covenant as appertaining merely to Israel's land-rights. This is the type, he says, of 'the spiritual inheritance that God has granted to His new covenant people' (p. 230fn.).
[319] See Exodus 3:6 and passim.
[320] Exodus 32:13.

Covenant-Keeper. Here we should look at Hebrews Chapter Three where Christ's work in the Old Testament is outlined. Our Saviour is introduced as the Apostle and High Priest who is identified as God who built the house of faith in which He placed Moses as Christ's servant and who testified as His Master commanded. Christ is thus the original, eternal and only Law-Giver and Grace-Giver who appointed Moses to teach both Law and Grace. Obviously, as Hebrews tells us, the builder of the House is more worthy than he who is merely appointed to run it and do as he is told. But it is Moses' faithfulness which is emphasized here. There are many who strive to ruin God's House not run it. Malachi emphasizes that the original Covenantal priesthood performed its tasks correctly but, like Israel on the whole, became corrupted. I am not putting this forward as a theory, all the Prophets witness to this. One can only take such passages as meaning that Christ appointed Moses to point the way to Him and that Christ is thus the Author of the Mosaic Law which is thus a Divine, Messianic and Mediatorial Law. Aaron's priesthood pointed to Christ who is the Author and Upholder of all that priesthood entails. To call Christ, 'The New Law-Giver' as if the Pentateuch was none of His making is to deny Christ's Messiahship and to play down His role in both Testaments. Mark's gospel opens by telling us that the people were astonished because Christ spoke with authority and not as one of the scribes.[321] Yes, He spoke as the Master of Law and Grace and not like a servant; as the Author and Finisher of our faith and not merely as a go-between. As James 4:12 tells us, 'There is only one "Lawgiver"'. Christ, however, is both Law-Giver and Law-Keeper in One. Indeed, all the 'proof-texts' Reisinger lists in pages 87-89 to show 'everlasting' means 'temporary' have an eternal application which is 'typical' of Christ's everlasting Covenant. It is the same with the NCT insistence on discontinuity between the Old and New Testaments. Their 'proof-texts' for discontinuity are taken and badly re-interpreted from a context which displays continuity. They are committing the errors of those pre-Sinai renegade Children of Israel who broke the Covenant and perished for their sins.

---

[321] Mark 1:21, 22.

The Covenant is old as man and lasts as long as Messiah reigns
We see the Covenant of Grace being applied from the very beginning in the fall of man, making it quite clear to him he could not honour God in his own strength. Many give Eve the blame for breaking the creation Covenant but Eve was not yet created when God drew up His Covenant with Adam, telling him, 'And the Lord God commanded the man, saying, Of every tree of the garden thou mayest freely eat (Grace): but of the tree of the knowledge of good and evil, though shalt not eat of it: for in the day that thou eatest thereof, thou shalt surely die (Law)'.[322] From creation on, man was dependent on God's Grace which could not be separated from God's own standards displayed within that Grace. In God's Covenant, Law and Grace continue forever. As a sign of this, a new human seed was prophesied which would restore what sin had marred showing that Law is always cradled in Grace but also that Grace is always cradled in Law. The wages of sin always brings death but the gift of God, nevertheless always brings Eternal Life to the believer. Though sin marred all, the Jewish prophets in the Old Testament and the authors of the New were enabled by God to predict the Restitution of All Things leading to a Paradise Regained. 'As in Adam all die, so in Christ shall all be made alive.' These earlier prophesies in the Old Testament concerning Adam were clarified more and more by Jewish and Gentile prophets after the constant failure of Adam's descendants to keep them. This was to be expected as the basis of the Covenant was never national, limited to one nation but designed for the People of God who were given grace to be Covenant Keepers throughout the entire world. This is called by some 'progressive revelation' but I think this does injustice to God's Covenant. The entire scriptures from Genesis to Revelation are one continuous commentary on what the Covenant signifies. It is an ever renewing covenant and one that is always freshly affirmed in the history of man. It is an ever-continuous Covenant of Grace.

The Covenant was always to all people everywhere
Thus the first Covenant promises were given to new-created man and non-Jews with special attention to Adam, Noah and Abraham. This fact

---

[322] Genesis 2:16 but also read the more extensive wording in Genesis 1:28-30.

has strangely enough caused many to claim that the Covenant was to the Jews only because it was given solely to the ancestors of the Jews who were Adam, Noah and Abraham. To argue that only Jews were Adam's, Noah's and Abraham's offspring would be folly indeed. We see clearly in the history of Noah a foretaste of world-wide destruction was given but also of world-wide blessings. The centre of this new world population was Mount Ararat[323] in present day Turkey from where Noah and his family were to 'replenish the earth' so it was said concerning Shem, Ham and Japheth that they were sent out over all the earth. Genesis 9:17 also clearly says:

> And God said unto Noah, This is the token of the covenant, which I have established between me and all flesh that is upon the face of the earth.

So we see Turkey, a Gentile country as the centre of worldwide evangelism and not Israel! Thereafter all renewing expositions of the Covenant were related to the entire world. Two great examples here may suffice. One of the bravest, godliest and wisest of the main Old Testament pointers to the Messiah was Job of Uz. No scholar has yet placed Uz in present day Israel or even Davidic Israel or ever associated him with 'The Children of Israel'. He was long before their time in the earlier years of the Edomite and Persian power which later gave Israel so much trouble. So, too, the Non-Jew Balaam gave one of the most detailed prophesies of the Messiah ever but is listed as an enemy of Israel. Many of the Patriarchs descendants were declared enemies of the Jews as a political people and gave rise to many kingdoms and nations speaking many different languages as we see from the earliest connections the 'Children of Israel' had with them. Seen historically and chronologically, the Covenant was promised long before these 'Children' came into being and continued on after Israel split into two kingships and countries (Israel and Judah), shrunk greatly under the Herodian Monarchy and then perished as a national enterprise altogether. In the same book from the beginning of time that tells us a Man will be raised up to tread down the Serpent Satan,[324] we also read

---

[323] See Genesis Chapters 8 and 9.
[324] Genesis 3:15.

that in Abraham, all the nations (families of the earth) will be blessed. The Covenant of Grace was never to the Jews only. This is one of the many great errors of modern Christian Zionism. Christ is more than *Lux Judaei* He is *Lux Mundi.*

Summing up
The eternal Covenant of Grace was not emptied of the righteousness of the Law at the end of the Old Testament. This would have meant also the end of God's Grace and the end of Faith. There was no Sinai Covenant which functioned apart from and contrary to God's Covenant with Abraham. Moses was quite aware of this and so were all the Old Testament prophets and writers. None envisaged the ending of either Law or Grace or Faith before the coming of the Messiah but all were convinced that only then would they reach their full functionality. The NCT idea that Law, Grace and Faith in the Covenant were merely limited to land promises is merely reading the Old Testament with blurred, falsely prescribed glasses so the NCT cannot believe what they ought to see.

Nor can the everlastingness of the Gospel or the everlasting Covenant be done away with through the radical logic of a Reisinger who first cuts out the main essentials from the Bible then forms his judgment on the bits and pieces he is prepared to accept from God's Word. Reisinger in doing away with the types is really doing away with what they anticipate. The Old Testament types are signs for New Testament sinners, pointing out the way they must go and why they must 'consider Him'. Thus there is no discontinuity between the Testaments but a smooth and immediate move from one chapter Malachi to the next chapter Matthew. The Covenant blood that Christ shed was for the sins of all ages and woe be to those who tread this truth under their feet!

To say once Christ has been found types are unnecessary is a selfish notion the NCT has of its own supposed status in Christ. They feel no responsibility for those still under the Law which they have abolished with all the pointers to Christ. They maintain that the gospel is for saints only. They forget how sinners are made saints according to the everlasting Covenant. The Bible teaches the gospel is for sinners to make them into saints and the gospel includes the work of the Law in

343

leading sinners to Christ. The Law is not the overruling part of the Covenant but is essential as a gospel aid in its fulfilment. The paidagogos is a 'bearer of good things to come'.

Trenchard reminds us the breaking of the old covenant was before the giving and ratification of the Mosaic Law so the NCT cannot argue the Mosaic Law has nothing to do with the New Covenant made with Abraham. The broken Covenant had, however, certainly nothing to do with Abraham. This scriptural and historical truth, according to the NCT, has only reference to New Testament times and was not grasped until Christ came in Person. Thus they rob the eternal Gospel of the Covenant of Grace from the Old Testament and rob it of its God inspired purpose, making it meaningless. Yet Christ was in the world, reconciling the World to Himself then as now.

The Law was never intended to be savingly effective of itself and was never designed to effect salvation. Nothing was promised unconditionally in the Law but the Law depended on the conditional promises made to Abraham which pointed to faith in the Messiah, the Covenant Fulfiller of whom Abraham, as Job of old, was well aware. Moses' God was the God of Abraham and all the faithful People of God as is confirmed in Galatians chapter three. God built the House of Faith in which he placed Moses as Christ's servant and all Christ's other servants as a witness to both Law and Grace within the Covenant. Both are necessary in establishing a just man made perfect. To call Christ 'the New Lawgiver' is to reduce Him to His servant Moses and to deny the outworking of the Covenant between the Father, Son and Holy Ghost in establishing the Law in the Old Testament for all time. The New Testament is not a Plan B.

God's one and only Covenant plan was put into practice when needed at the Fall and showed man was no covenant-keeper of himself and was lost without Grace. The wages of sin were always death and the gift of God was always eternal life. This is how the Covenant has always worked as testified from Genesis to Revelation. It was also always a gospel to all men everywhere in all times. Indeed the renewing of the Covenant with Noah was outside of Palestine, in modern Turkey, enhancing its message to the Gentiles. Abraham supposedly lived in present day Turkey or Iraq that is in the lands of the Gentiles, and his faith was expressly designed by God to be established throughout all nations. The identification of Israel with the Covenant was short-termed, God-willed and intense but the Jewish prophets always claimed this relationship of type was secondary to the relationship of true believers to the true Jerusalem which was a place preserved in Heaven for all Covenant members. Indeed, though Israel for a time was a united nation under the Covenant of Grace, it soon became dispersed amongst the nations because of its transgressions but God used this to His Glory as true, believing Jews pioneered the evangelization of the world so that *Lux Judaei* was seen to be *Lux Mundi*.

Chapter 16

The Covenant Gospel Of The
Old Testament Highlighted In The New

The New starts by confirming the Old

The New Testament starts by declaring that the everlasting Covenant given to the People of God in former (Old Testament) times is continued through the birth and life of John the Baptist and, above all, the birth of Jesus. John's task, according to this fulfilment, was to point the way to Jesus, the promised Messiah as the Old Testament foretold. Rather than claiming the Old Testament Law and its alliance with Grace within the Covenant is abolished, the constant truth concerning both is re-enforced, re-established and repeated in the New especially in the Gospels and Pauline Epistles. Like love and marriage, as the song goes 'you can't have one without the other'. It was not possible to divorce Grace from Law in the Old Testament and is not possible in the New because the One Messiah is the One Covenant Keeper throughout all time and eternity and through His grace the Law is fulfilled. I often disagreed with my old Principle, Ernest Kevan at the London Bible College but his essays on lawful grace and graceful law were a real blessing to me and I treasure his doctoral thesis on that subject.

David our Forerunner in the Faith

I have always been influenced by David who could say as a believer in the Covenant of Grace, 'I love the Lord because he hath heard my supplications. Because he hath inclined his ear unto me, therefore will I call upon him as long as I live'.[325] Because of a balanced covenantal faith, David can also say 'Oh how love I thy law! It is my meditation all the day'. This is because he knew from experience the Law pointed to the Lord and not to one's own capacities and achievements. This demonstrates that the righteousness of the Law is clear to those who love God as it displays His righteousness forever. This is surely what Paul means when he writes that the requirements of the Law are fulfilled in those who walk according to the Spirit and not the flesh.[326] Indeed, when Moses gave the Children of Israel the Law after praying he might continue in Abraham's footsteps, he began by saying, 'Thou shalt love the Lord thy God with all thine heart, and with all thy soul, and with all thy might.'[327]

Anyone who maintains that such gospel sayings are evidence of a mere legal code needs to be taught what is spiritual and what is legal. Thus, when the Pharisees strove to trap Jesus into saying something they could find fault with, they asked Jesus which was the greatest commandment, possibly thinking they were all equal. Christ's reply, quoting Deuteronomy 6:5, was an answer they could not gainsay. However, on the Sermon on the Mount where Christ underlined the spirituality of the Law, He put the Scribes and Pharisees again to shame by showing them even hidden sins such as covetousness were condemned equally with all sins by God as all committed sins, open and hidden, show the fallen nature of mankind. Thus one can say that all the Ten Commandments are spiritual rather than legal as breaking them means not displaying love for God. So, God condemns sin where no legal system could act. This true examining of the Law as Christ applies it cannot be put away as it describes to all for all eternity, God's Holy Nature. The Law was meant to be applied in this way, side by side with the overtures of Grace provided through God's Promises to Abraham.

---

[325] Psalm 116:1ff. The entire chapter is well worth reading as it shows a believer trusting in his Lord through life and death.
[326] Romans 8:3.
[327] Deuteronomy 6:5.

It in no way annulled the Covenant of Grace with Abraham but proclaimed death to sin. It had no power in itself to deal with this sin but when used spiritually, that is lawfully, it was and still is used by the Spirit in His Word to lead men to find Grace and forgiveness in Christ. Where Law is recognized for what it is, only then can Grace be seen for what it is. Mankind never sinned merely 'legally' but always sinned as a breach in the Covenant of Love with God.

John Ball teaches us in his *Treatise on the Covenant*:

> The Covenant that God made with Abraham was the Covenant of Grace, as it is acknowledged: but the Covenant made with Abraham is for substance the same with the Covenant made with Israel upon Mount Sinai: the promise is the same, and the things required the same.[328]

The relation of the Covenant to the Testaments

The Old and New Testaments are a natural outcome of the Covenant but not the Covenant itself which brought them into being. The Old Testament was the story of the grain of mustard seed finding growth-nutrition amongst the Christ-filled witness of the elect Patriarchs, the elect Prophets and the elect Jews. It was the leaven hidden by God, working secretly, unknown to the bulk of the Gentile world. The New Testament is the story of the growth of a great tree in whose branches all God's elect birds find shelter and nourishment. It is the once hidden leaven, now leavening the whole lump for the whole world to see. The Old Testament was the inheritance of a few believers in a few Near Eastern states only. The New Testament is the inheritance of all saints everywhere, going into all the world, and preaching the gospel. The Old Testament is the First Clause in the only will left to us after the vicarious human death of our Saviour-Testator who was slain before the foundation of the world,[329] manifested to us at the Fulfilment of Time. The New Testament is the Second Clause in that gracious will, proclaiming that not only the Good Shepherd's first sheep come under

---

[328] Ball, p. 102. Peter and Rachel Reynolds edition.
[329] I understand the word 'before' as prepositional not as an adverb of time.

Christ's inheritance but also God's Gentile adopted offspring. God's will and testament for the Church past, present, future and eternal is thus to be found in all the scriptures, in Christ's entire Testament. If we throw one sentence, paragraph or clause of it out, destroy or dismiss any part, however, small, we destroy not only God's revealed will for the salvation of the Church but also the knowledge of our inheritance as if Christ died intestate. There is one fold and one shepherd where neither Jews nor Gentiles in Christ have any separate identity. Neither race, gender, learning, nor social standing can stand in the way of those who are chosen to inherit their Heavenly inheritance as the People of God.

Christ our Testator and Executor
However, due to the unique Nature of the Lord Jesus Christ who after His vicarious punishment and substitutionary death was restored to Life from that death by His glorious resurrection, Christ is now not only the Testator but also the Executor of His own will. Notice, however, in the New Testament, Gentiles are told they may enter into the privileges of God's Old Testament people, not the other way round. It is not that God has done with the Jews, as modern New Covenant Dispensationalists tell us but the Gentiles are given the same privileges as the Old Testament saints from Genesis to Malachi and beyond. This is the only evolution you will ever get in God's creation and it is the only one necessary for real life. It is divine soteriological evolution, which brings with it the development of Christ's Kingdom on earth, preparing it for Heaven. Similarly, the Lord's Covenant People build their faith on the revelations of both Testaments unrestricted by colour, class, or, we must also say, 'creeds'.

Why did God wait, from the perspective of time, so long before the seed grew and the yeast fermented? If we look at the matter from the perspective of eternity, we need not speculate about the whys and wherefores of time. The Fulness of time was to marry time with eternity, the course of time is to bring in the elect. If we look at the matter from the perspective of time, we are in God's world, run by God's laws in which seeds in different soils do not develop simultaneously, nor does yeast ferment equally in all environments. There can be no better Gardener and Provider than God who has His own schedule in the establishment of His Kingdom.

The Covenant was always at work throughout the world's history
There is much talk nowadays about different covenants at different times. The Bible has one Covenant of Grace between God and Man. However, some modern movements who call themselves biblical speculate from between two to an ever increasing number appertaining to salvation. They build their movements, laws, rules and church order around the new forms and shapes they give to God's plan of salvation turning themselves thus into para-churches. Some Covenant Theologies speak mostly of everlasting covenants throughout the Old and New Testaments, others appear to reject all mention of an everlasting Covenant. Indeed, Wells' and Zaspel's book on NCT ends with the words, 'The conclusion seems clear: when N.T. writers use the word covenant, they normally want to assert discontinuity'.

The good news of the New Testament is not discontinuation but is continuous at a greater pace and to a greater extent. Christ's task now is to promote the gospel to the Gentiles but still caring for His Jewish sheep. John tells us Christ said:

> Other sheep I have which are not of this fold: them also must I bring, and they shall hear my voice: and there shall be one fold, and one shepherd.[330]

That all the Jews were not in the first fold is made clear by Christ's rejection of unbelieving Jews as seen in verses 24-29. I also take Christ's words to mean that His Shepherd-hood is for both believing Jews and Gentiles who become Christ's one flock.

Rationalism versus Revelation
However, some modern professing Christians who even call themselves 'Reformed' deny the soteriological nature of the Covenant in the Old Testament and others deny its presence in the gospels. They argue God's Covenant first begins in Acts and is Gentile-orientated only. Many who carry that blessed word 'Covenant' in their denominational names do not even rely on Acts to Revelation but tell us of a new covenantal dispensation to come. Why is this? It is because they have

---

[330] John 10:16.

little idea what a biblical Covenant is and have substituted their own rationalism for Divine Revelation. It is as if Christ's words about His flock seem too easy for them and they boast of finding some deeply hidden meaning which they alone have discovered in these 'last days'. The NCT leaders refer to this as 'Realised Eschatology'.

The Covenant dissected
Sadly, the sixteenth century Reformation in England soon cooled down on the larger scale and became fragmented and the leaven often turned sour or found no nutrition. The main reason I give for this was the dissecting of the Covenant into Aristotelian bits and pieces. Besides, legalism once more took over from grace. The chopping and hacking at the One Covenant of the Bible and the Reformation became popular during the early part of Cromwell's government until the penny dropped and Cromwell expelled the Presbyterians. By propagating a Covenant split down the middle one will never understand God's covenantal purpose in establishing a People for Himself. The first Counter-Reformation mistake the Presbyterians made, trained in Hyper-Lutheran and Hyper-Calvinistic schools on the Continent (see Cartwright and Travers etc.) was to define the term Covenant in non-biblical terms as a religio-political contract of law between a less than ideal God and a supposed ideal Case-Law-ruled State. See here the teachings of Knox who apparently built his Christianity on case-law so his chief editors and biographers had to complain he never discovered the New Testament but remained on a par with the earlier prophets.[331]

Building up Britain on Jewish misconceptions
These people had misunderstood God's dealings with the state of Israel for the very short time of forty years it existed and wanted to force their false idea of a non-functional God's State in the Old Testament eternally onto the green and pleasant land of England. The Notorious 'Solemn League and Covenant' of the Cromwellian totalitarian state with its harsh, inhuman administration is a typical example of this. However many, still rejoicing in the Reformation now called England *The New Eden* because of the progress of the Reformation there which

---

[331] See, for instance, Andrew Lang's chapter 'Knox's Lost Opportunity' in his Knox biography. Better to read the entire biography!

had gone further than in all other countries. I have copies of letters from seventeen great German theologians led by Germany's Synod of Dort delegates such as Dr Paul Tossanus, writing to the Church in England, outlawed in 1643, saying, 'Tell us your secret. What are your doctrines of Practical Divinity which are so superior to ours?' The Continentals still regarded Britain as the centre of Reformed theology as formerly taught by Wycliffe, Jewel, Lever, Latimer, Tyndale, Grindal, Coverdale, Bale and many more. The last of these stalwarts were now dying out with Davenant, Hall, Mede, Ward, Ussher and the older members of Durie's 'steering committee'. Tossanus was mistaken concerning the then supposed British love for Practical Divinity. Durie had made the doctrine so popular on the Continent and as he was sent abroad with the King's backing and that of the Archbishops from England, Ireland and Scotland and later with Cromwell's blessings, the Continentals felt that all British ministers were well-trained in Practical Divinity. However, Durie complained from the thirties to the late fifties that there was not a single work on Practical Divinity in all the British Universities.

Rebuilding Britain on a broken Covenant
Durie's pan-European hope of an international and united Reformed Church built on Covenant of Grace teaching was rejected by the ruling churches in Britain intent on continuing to misinterpret the ideas of Law and Gospel which went hand in hand in the Old Testament. To gain power in Parliament, the Presbyterians spoke of the Covenant of Works and the Covenant of Grace and used their artificial Covenant of Works, rather than grace, as their basis on which to build their New Britain. They looked, however, to the secular military arm of British troops to enforce it. They were at a loss in understanding what a rule by grace entailed. Indeed, they boycotted Cromwell's attempts to set up a Ministry for Tolerance in Parliament and the recognition of all the major Protestant Churches and paid William Prynne to denounce those seeking pan-Reformed unity in the courts. Their idea of Old Testament inheritance was of a human Government taking over God's wrath against sin, dictating the 'shalts' and 'shalt nots' of case law to a people whom they enslaved to their law, putting saved and unsaved alike under the yoke of Sinai. If an over eighteen year-old refused to sell away his

Christian inheritance for a mess of pottage by signing the Scottish Solemn League and Covenant, he at worse lost his life and at best his property and was banned from Church fellowship and civil rights. As all Episcopalians, who were outlawed in 1643 came under this umbrella and most Independents, who were ranked with the Anglicans as 'Malignants', a reign of persecuting terror ensued. Why? One party of fallen men thought they could set up a Demi-Paradise by terrorising the common people who are usually the worse off when tyranny reigns. This was not the New Covenant but old rationalism and pagan tyranny. Sadly, the greatest sins ever committed since the Fall are sins of the would-be churches. What do we learn by this? When man enters into covenant with man under conditions imposed by one side, one can forget the notion of 'Covenant' altogether.

Striving to merge day and night

However, most modern covenant-based believers, of whatever kind, do not so much speak of a Covenant of Man to man but speak of a Covenant of God with man, as if man and God could be placed in equal partnership. I notice in this new theology of the Covenant which I have been looking into from time to time during the last fifteen years, their gurus explain what they think the term 'Covenant' means by giving examples of man's covenants with man before applying them to God's covenant with man as if the one confused view made the other more enlightening. One might as well try to merge night with day and produce an eternal twilight as talk of partnerships between our righteous God and sinful man. Or combine summer and winter and have the sun beaming down icicles at us and the ground producing freshly-packed frozen foods. Such things do happen in the make-believe Neverland of science fiction. This is the Ersatz-Religion of many modern would-be Covenanters. What a high view of man and low view of God such people must have!

I must be more provocative. Be suspicious when you hear of God entering into separate covenants with sinful Adam, with sinful Noah, and sinful Abraham, or even sinful Jews and sinful Gentiles. None of us can stand before God as one worthy of partnership in a Covenant with God. It has been complained to me that this is nihilistic thinking and the discarding of all theologies connected with the Covenant overboard'. It is not so. All false theologies based on fallen man as an equal partner in any covenant whatsoever must be discarded because neither a fallen, nor even a redeemed man can stand as his own Covenant-Keeper.

Our Covenant Keeper is the Man Christ Jesus Man
What about the idea of a God making a covenant with a God which is surprisingly taught in a number of churches in the States some of which profess therefore to be 'Calvinistic'. Calvin gets blamed for the strangest things! They maintain correctly that God cannot enter into a partnership of equals with man but claim there can be a partnership of equals between Gods. Thus God the Father can enter into a partnership with God the Son. This seems tempting. But wait! Why then the need for the Incarnation? Why did God have to become man? Old Anselm's question *Cur Deus homo*, (Why did God become man?) was the best question ever asked. These would-be-Calvinists answer the question wrongly by saying that Christ never identified Himself with sinful man for our sakes but was ever a divine being in human ethereal form, like the bodies of the resurrected saints. He did not need to become man. The Incarnation was thus a sham, they tell us, as one could not imagine the holy God-Man feeding on the blood of sinful woman and passing through her sinful womb. They conclude thus that it was Christ as a divine Partner with whom the Father made a covenant and not with a Man among men. I was once in an American pastors' chat-group and this was their daily theme. I was soon told by these holier-than-thou ministers of the gospel that I was 'the son of a whore' and even filthier insults so I left them to their idle speculations.

Christ tempted in all ways as we are – but yet without sinning
These disbelievers in Christ-Manhood tell us that had Christ become a mere man amongst fallen men, He would have gone the way of all flesh. They even say Christ withstood the Devil's temptations only because of His Godhood as He would have failed if He had taken on our manhood. Imagine how useless such a divine contract would be, apart from the fact the idea is pantheistic. A righteous God barters with another righteous God and comes to an agreement. But God remains God in His righteousness and man remains man in his unrighteousness. Of course, if Christ did not carry our sins away from us as a Man among

men, there could be no reconciliation between God and man. God so designed our salvation that it took a perfect, unfallen Man to become sin for us in exchange for His righteousness. I had to leave another chat group because they would not accept the biblical doctrine of imputation either way and told me I had 'a polluted Saviour'. I thank God that though it was me who was polluted, sinless Christ brought death to my pollutions through His triumphant vicarious bearing of our sins and by His stripes we were healed.

Novel views of the Covenant seem legion today
So much fanciful thinking about the Covenant since the Reformation has turned our churches into institutions and denominations more to be classified with Secret Societies, Debating Societies, Rabbit Clubs, Lodges, Business enterprises, Football Associations and the like. We can talk about the Covenant of Grace, the Covenant of Works, the Covenant of Redemption, New Covenant and Old Covenant or the Solemn League and Covenant but they are all false theologies if they are based on an imagined mixture of God's provisions and man's duties. God only knows His duty to His own Righteousness. Man only knows his duty to his own sinfulness. This is what makes all the talk about salvation being by God's provisions and man's agency, or dutiful exercise of faith, all my eye and Peggy Martin.

A perfect covenant must be a transaction between trustworthy, competent, indeed, perfect partners. If there is to be a perfect covenant of any kind between God and man it must be between a perfect God and a perfect Man. In the entire universe, there are only two who meet the correct criterion for both Partners. The God and Father of our Lord Jesus Christ and Christ our Righteousness. A covenant between men cannot be eternally effective; a covenant between God and man can only fail because of man. Covenants between gods only happen in mythology and fairy-tales and leave mankind quite out of the picture. There is only one pure righteous Man in this whole universe who has shown Himself worthy to be our advocate before God and that is the Lord Jesus Christ who, when God asked in the Heavenly Tribune, with whom can I establish a Covenant so that I can establish a People for Myself and a Bride for my Son, Christ volunteered Himself to take on those tasks.

Theories based on a discontinuity of the Covenant of Grace invalid

All theories of covenants based on Dispensational grounds are wrong headed because they teach a discontinuous and not an eternal covenant in Christ. Again, the Covenant is not discontinuous, it is not divided, and it is not Dispensational. The Covenant of Grace in both Testaments is a seamless, uncut, robe. As Christ is the Author and Finisher and Keeper of the Covenant and is the same yesterday, today and forever, His Covenant is permanent and everlasting. It stretches through all eternity, and thus cannot be limited in time. Christ never changes His redemptive mind. Likewise, any idea of splitting up Law and Grace into two separate Covenants is quite false. Unity divided is disunity. The one Covenant declares 'the wages of sin is death but the gift of God is eternal life'. 'All in Adam die but all in Christ are reborn'. Condemnation of sin and justification through Christ's righteousness go hand in hand in the one biblical Covenant. Players in the amalgamated league Dispensationalism and NCT-ism combine the errors of false Old-Covenant theology with false New-Covenant theology and are thus doubly wrong.

Modern ignorance concerning the Reformation

We should be familiar with the biblical truth reintroduced by our Reformers, but the Reformers are the most neglected writers in Christendom. Instead, modern pseudo-Puritan teaching refers to the brief Presbyterian era as a Second Reformation, as if it replaced the first. This is a mistranslation of the more Bible-based Dutch *Nadere Reformatie* and *Nadere uitwerking* which they claim to promote. The Dutch term refers to the continuation of the 16th Century Reformation, not to a new 17th Century one. Remember, Witsius came over to sort the Westminster Assembly's errors out, telling them their Antinomian covenantal mistakes were caused through their not believing in God's actions from eternity. It was professing Reformed Christians who launched the notorious Antinomian Controversy of the Cromwellian era.

The Covenant of the Father's dealings with His Son Jesus Christ through the outworking of the Holy Spirit is revealed from Genesis to Revelation. This is the full revelation of God and does not allow for the neglect of one jot or title. This truth is almost lost because we have been drilled since the 1950s to believe that the minority Counter-Reformed party who dominated Britain from 1643 to 1648 has pronounced the first and last word on the subject in their so-called Second Reformation. What they did was empty God's Covenant of its historical, scriptural, doctrinal and theological content and introduced the spiritual anarchy which has spawned all our denominations. Christians have become denominational builders and not Church builders. Any Covenant Theology that deals with isolated particulars, periods or people in the Bible and leaves out other scriptures, periods and people, is an un-biblical fake. Our Reformers taught us God's Covenant is revealed in all the Bible's pages with no picking and choosing.

Return to true Biblical, Reformed exegesis is necessary
William Tyndale, when writing his Prologue to Exodus around 1530, taught that God's Covenant was with Christ on behalf of man from the beginning, witnessed by both Testaments. The Old Testament Law and the Prophets spoke of Christ just like the New Testament and, though less detailed, was still sufficient to bring in the elect. Of the New Testament, he said, 'the New Testament was ever, even from the beginning of the world. For there was always promises of Christ to come by faith in which promises the elect were then justified inwardly to God, as outwardly before the world'.

So the Testaments complement each other backwards and forwards. Henry Bullinger, called the 'one great pillar of the English Church', spoke of the one revelation of God's Covenant with man in both clauses of the Testament. One of his proof texts was the one the NCT so terribly misuses, Hebrews 11:13:

> These all died in faith, not having received the promises, but having seen them afar off, and were persuaded of them, and embraced them, and confessed that they were strangers and pilgrims on the earth.

The NCT says, 'Abraham never received the promises so His generation did not experience the New Covenant.' Bullinger explains that the Old Testament saints, like New Testament saints, died in the same faith, under the same Covenant. Both they and we believe the same promises but none of us will experience them until the

Resurrection Morning when we enter into our Heavenly inheritance together. As 2 Corinthians 4:18 says:

> While we look not at the things which are seen, but at the things not seen: for the things which are seen are temporal, but the things which are not seen are eternal.

This is why we can groan with Abraham, 'earnestly desiring to be clothed upon with our house which is from heaven' until we arrive in our Heavenly Mansion promised us by Christ. His Bride, the Church, whether B.C. or A.D., walks by faith not by sight. We, like our O.T. mentors in the faith are pilgrims and strangers in this world. Bullinger tells his congregation:

> I have, I trust, sufficiently proved that the faithful fathers of the old testament, and we believers of the new covenant, are one church and one people, which are all saved under one congregation, under one only testament, and by one and the same manner of means, to wit, by faith in Christ Jesus.[332]

This is Reformed Covenant Theology and our sole platform in our witness to those in error either on the Reformed side or on the NCT side. When we study those who rejected Reformed theology in the 17th Century through speaking of two covenants, and not one, we find that though they presented themselves as mainstream Reformers, they were a short-term mistaken minority.

Summing Up
The New Testament starts as a 'next chapter' and continuation of the Old Testament with the birth of John the Baptist and the announcement of Gabriel, and Luke's testimony as a Gentile that the Old Testament Covenant of Grace is continuing as it will until the elect are gathered in. In the New Testament testimony Law and Grace continue their marriage together. Believers of all times, like David of old, experienced the Law in Grace and Grace in the Law fulfilled in walking in the Holy

---

[332] Third Decade, p. 293, Parker Society.

Spirit and not in the flesh. Moses, too, knew how to love the Lord with all his soul and with all his might because the true object of the Law was faith in Christ the Lord. Christ thus taught the Scribes and Pharisees that the Law was to work in the inner man as much as the outer profession. It could not cleanse from sin but it was purposed to lead the defiled sinner to the Cleanser from all sin. Ball says truly that the Abrahamic Covenant is in substance the same as the Covenant made with Israel via Moses as Jesus made clear on the Mount.

This is the continued story of both Testaments, which reflect the two clauses of Christ's one Testament. If one paragraph from this Testament is erased, the whole is jeopardised. Christ did not die intestate and is now in His resurrected state both Testator and Executor of His own Will, enabling Gentiles to enter into the same inheritance already enjoyed by believing Jews in God's good time in preparation for eternity. All this shows how erroneous those are who boast of their fallen wisdom in rejecting the Law which is of faith. Neither Law nor Grace work without faith and the Christian's task is to bring this faith to Christ's other sheep who are still to be gathered into the fold. The Modernist argument that world-wide evangelization began with the Book of Acts and is Gentile-orientated only are certainly breakers of God's eternal Covenant with man in all ages.

Sadly in our Churches since the decline of Reformation preaching, there is much dissecting of the Word of God and much building of new theologies illustrated by 'New Divinity', 'New Covenant Theology', 'New Perspectives', 'New Age Theology' and now even simply 'New Theology' all of which are no theologies whatsoever but crumbs from under the table now turned mouldy, tiresome and far from the truth and no use to anyone.

All this is the direct result of the breaking up of the Covenant in the Commonwealth period and the humanizing of the Gospel which came with 'Enlightenment' radicalism. This merging of politics with the Christian faith, and rule by case-law and an acceptance of the pseudo-Jewish legal set up foreign to the Covenant of Grace as a pattern for Christian faithful behaviour, turned indeed Sinai into a legal covenant which it never was.

The cooling down of the Reformation in the 17th Century was clearly the result of the splitting up of the Covenant of Grace and the re-systematising of theology back to its Roman Catholic days of 'case studies'. Fancy basing a new denomination on the Hyper-legalism of Cartwright and Travers who strove to force through their rational religious views and church directories by rule of Parliament! The idea of building a British ideal Christian state on the ruins of the old Jewish system as practiced by former unbelieving Jews was folly indeed.

During the 17th century, the Continental churches looked to England for leadership, thinking of the great times of the British Reformation. Sadly, these great Fathers in Israel were no longer there or quickly dying out and there was great opposition to former Reformed theology which was deemed too conservative 'Church of England' by the contemporary fiery spirits who now built their politics on a covenant of works. Tolerance was now laughed at. Man was acclaimed as being able to covenant with God but the real Covenant is undivided and stems from the eternal unity of the Trinity to bring to man what he cannot produce himself. This is the only Covenant to be trusted.

Christians today must rescue the Eternal Gospel from its century long degrading and dumbing down and pray and act for a new Reformation in Faith and Order as the old is hidden or lost. This can only be built on the theology of a united Godhead that has been redeeming His Church throughout all ages through the one eternal Gospel of the one eternal Covenant of Grace centred in Christ's atoning Work for those whose true Home is in the New Jerusalem of Heaven.

Chapter 17

The New Jerusalem: The Gathering in of God's Covenant People

The folly of breaking God's Word off in the middle

If ever there was proof of the folly of breaking scripture off at Malachi and starting off afresh with Matthew as if the Covenant scriptures up to then had not been revealed, that proof is found in the Book of Revelation. Revelation crowns the whole Bible from start to finish, summing up all God's ways throughout the entire Covenant of Grace in both Testaments. Obviously, there is fuller revelation in the New Testament as in the Old as we would expect when reading the Old Testament where revelation is seen to be renewed and strengthened continually until its completion in the New Testament. In every good book the best comes at the end when we read 'and they all lived happily ever after'.

Revelation testifies to the fact Christ was electing His Bride from the dawn of creation until the end of time when the great Feast of the Marriage of the Lamb occurs and every Christian has a place at the Lord's reception table. The book describes the gathering in of God's Covenant People throughout the one continuous period on earth during which Christ has adorned them as His True Love for Eternity. Revelation may mean nothing to Covenant-breakers as it brings nothing new to those who have not taken note of the Spirit's work in all the scripture which perpetually points to the Holy One of True Israel from start to finish. I say 'may mean nothing' because the culmination of Divine things on this earth which the Book of Revelation describes provides all the then living with a final opportunity to repent and believe before Christ gathers in His New Jerusalem to be with Him forever. After that glorious appearance those then living who are not in that body of believers will not have another chance. They will have refused to be married to the Bridegroom. So Revelation sums up not only the teaching of the New Testament but also, and perhaps more especially, the Old. I say this because almost all Revelation's teaching on our future hope as the People of God is taken from the Old Testament in the one Word of God and built further on it.

Learning from our Reformers

Some main pointers to put me on the right path in understanding Covenant mercies, were the works of John Bale, the former Bishop of Ossory in Ireland who was born in 1495 and was called Home in 1563. Bishop Bale on becoming a child of God was severely persecuted and imprisoned by the Roman Catholic clergy and faced with the death penalty. He was compelled to flee to the Continent several times before taking advantage of the Emperor's offer of citizenship and employment in Frankfurt for all the Protestant Refugees and the so-called Strangers' Churches persecuted by Queen Mary. The Emperor and city patricians even provided financial assistance to those willing to settle down in Frankfurt, open businesses and become citizens. A number of prominent Reformers took advantage of this generous offer and the Frankfurt church grew to some 350 members with much coming and going depending on the political and religious system in England. The Frankfurt Fair (Messe) founded a century before was dying but was revived by the industrious members of the British church, now turned merchants and the Fair is still going strong. Bale spent some eight years in Germany and some time in Switzerland leading exile churches and writing on Reformation history. John Foxe and Miles Coverdale also fled to Frankfurt, and Foxe used Bale's writings, as also Coverdale's, as important sources for his *Book of Martyrs*. Indeed, Tom Freeman in his *Journal of Reformation* article 'John Bale's Book of Martyrs', argues that Bale especially mentored Foxe's work.[333] I have referred repeatedly to Bale in my book *Troublemakers at Frankfurt* where Bale, not knowing what manner of man Knox was, invited him to be co-pastor at Frankfurt with Thomas Lever but was the first to call for his dismissal when Knox strove to bend all to his iron will and put the Reformation clock back, even denying lay men to partake in the service and the public reading of scripture.

Bale was a many-sided man making a name for himself in literature and theology producing a good number of 'firsts' in both areas and pioneering the use of English in his writings rather than Latin, though he was also a master of the latter. Bale wrote several historical pageants, morality and mystery plays in a strong Protestant spirit as all the contemporary semi-religious entertainment was Roman Catholic. His aim was to illustrate the fall of Rome when faced with the true gospel. Shakespeare is said to have used Bale as a source for his *King John*. Bale's Protestant plays, like Foxe's were to be performed '*profanus*', that is, 'before the Temple' for the benefit of the unlettered and as an admonition to the unrepentant clergy encased in their 'temples' by their popish system.

A man of the Covenant
John Bale was a man of the Covenant and was the first to write a full English paraphrase and commentary on the Book of Revelation with the odd sounding title of *The Image of Both Churches*[334] which views Revelation as a summary of God's Covenantal teaching throughout the entire scriptures. Bale had suffered greatly through those whom he argued were in a false church, so after his conversion, he campaigned loudly and with all his energies for the true Church as opposed to the false one. The truth or falsity of a Church, he found in its acceptance or rejection of God's Covenant teaching. He had strong, critical things to say about the Roman Catholic Church and Islam which he viewed as the two sides of the same coin. When I published William Huntington's similar view of a merging of Rome with Mecca, Huntington was

---

[333] *Journal of Reformation*, Vol. 3, Issue 1.
[334] There are an abundance of free sources for this exceptional book but I am using the more modernised Parker Society edition for my quotes.

ridiculed for such a 'far-fetched' idea and this author, too, for airing it. Be this as it may, mosques are now being erected in Germany with Roman Catholic donations and Roman Catholic community grants and I hear it is the same elsewhere. So, too, reports on the bishop of the Vatican's meeting with Islamic leaders in the Arabian Peninsula are reported as covering all points of religious cooperation apart from the Gospel.

Bale thus called his paraphrase and commentary on Revelation *The Image of Both Churches*, because he believed the book of Revelation revealed the true Church which he terms New Jerusalem as opposed to the church of man which he likens to fallen Babylon. It is also the philosophy of Babylon as we have seen which is hindering modern Jews from trusting in the Covenant of Grace. I was long pestered in my youth by Dispensationalists and those who prophesy that either the pope or the President of the United State of America will turn into an Anti-Christ. He was then 'predicted' to lead a war of the people with the mark of the beast, alias those with National Health insurance card numbers, against those who wish to rebuild the Temple destroyed for good reasons by God. After hearing such rubbish, reading Bale came as a healthy breeze and warm sunshine revealing how much better is the everlasting Gospel than the fantasies of man. Bale preached on our eternal home a hundred years before all these useless eschatological 'horror-scopes' came into being. He sees the Anti-Christ as being all the machinations of the devil in fallen man and sees Christ coming gently and peacefully again to take His Bride home with Him.

Bale wrote this work in exile from a Britain who had become an Anti-Christ and rejected the Gospel. He identified himself closely with Saint John who wrote Revelation whilst exiled on the island of Patmos. The full title in the 1550 edition which I have used myself is: *The ymage of both Churches after the most wonderful and heauenly Reuelacion of Saincte John the Euangelyst, contaynyng a very frutefull exposition or paraphrase vpon the same, wherin it is co(n)ferred with the other scriptures, & most auctorysed histories. Co(m)pyled by John Bale an exile also in this lyfe, for the faithfull testimony of Iesus.* Bale's works are in the Old Middle English dialect similar to that which is found in the York, Wakefield and Towneley mystery plays outlining God's deeds from creation to the last judgment. These were performed regularly in the schools and outside in my school days and are still regularly performed in Yorkshire. Knowing these plays which I took to be normal English helped me pass my Middle English exams at university. However, for those not having this background I quote from the Parker Society's one-volume *Select Works of John Bale D.D.* which includes the Martyrdoms of Lord Cobham, William Thorpe and Anne Askewe. All my quotes and sources given are from this volume.

In his Preface, Bale sees the Book of Revelation as a summing up of the history of the Church on earth and says:

> Not one necessary point of belief is in all the other scriptures, that is not here also in one place or another. The very complete sum and whole knitting up in this heavenly book of the universal verities of the Bible. All that Moses taught in the Law, David in the Psalms, and the prophets in their writings concerning Christ's spiritual kingdom both here and above, meet[335] for this present knowledge, are herein briefly comprehended. So is his eternal victory for us over sin, death, hell and the devil, with his perpetual clearness, authority, and empire world without end.

After showing that a belief in or rejection of this truth is the dividing line between being in or out of Christ, Bale concludes:

> After the true opinion of St Augustine, either we are citizens in the new Jerusalem with Jesus Christ, or else in the old superstitious Babylon with antichrist the vicar of Satan.

We note that Bale writes of the spirituality of the Old Testament Law and argues his case for such an interpretation carefully and exactly. Wherever Bale looks into the Book of Revelation, he finds mention of the everlasting gospel witnessing to the everlasting Covenant and affirms the gospel *is* the everlasting Covenant. Our antagonists, whether they break the Covenant after reading Malachi, at the birth of Christ, at the Sermon on the Mount or wherever, will certainly say that Bale exaggerates his case and the doctrines he sees in Revelation are not really there. Here one must note that when one denies a continuous

---

[335] Suitable.

Covenant gospel from Genesis to Revelation, one will hardly take the trouble to find it there. Once convinced by the Word that the gospel is as everlasting as the Covenant, one will see this bright and shining truth in all the scriptures especially and including Revelation!

For Bale, quoting David and Paul, the everlasting gospel is:

> ... not the gospel for reading of the letter, but for the belief that men have in the word of God; that it is the gospel that we believe, and not the letter that we read; for because the letter, that is touched with man's hand, is not the gospel but the sentence,[336] that is very[337] believed in man's heart.[338]

So Bale refers to 'the living spirit of the gospel'[339] and calls it 'everlasting' because it declares that:

> His eternal testament and covenant of peace hath the Lord given to them (His People), to preach deliverance to the captive, health to the wounded, life to the dead, and remission to the sinful; yea, to utter that word that is stronger than is heaven and earth, and that shall never fail him that truly believeth.[340]

On commentating on Revelation 6:6 on the measure of wheat and the three measures of barley, Bale says:

> So precious are the scriptures of the old law for the Christian's erudition, as of the new: for both they are verity, spirit and promise of God. So perfect also is the one as the other (each grain in his kind considered), as the law to condemn, and the gospel to save. So necessary is it to the sinner to know his fall as to see his rise. In that the barley is three measures, and the wheat but one, is signified that the Old Testament contains the old law, the psalms and prophesies, and the New the only doctrine of Christ,

---

[336] M.E. 'sense', 'gist'.
[337] M.E. 'truly'.
[338] *The Works of John Bale*, Parker Society, p.114.
[339] P. 58.
[340] P. 457.

and confessing altogether three distinct persons in one Godhead.[341]

On dealing closer with the Covenant of Grace, Bale refers repeatedly to Christ as its first Angel, Messenger and sole Keeper, thus giving it its perpetual, everlasting, eternal nature. He thus majors on the theme of the:

> ... perpetual covenant of peace and love to all them that hath faith, which are so dear unto him as is the apple of his own eye.[342]

It is in the Book of Revelation, Chapter One and following that we gain an overview of the Church in the Asia of those days, a region which now laps over far into Europe. Seven churches are mentioned listing all the strengths and weaknesses of all local church bodies since that time. Ephesus, Pergamos, Thyatira, Smyrna, Sardis, Philadelphia and Laodicea. Obviously, these churches, though possibly founded by the Jewish Christian Diaspora in their obedience to Christ's command in Matthew 28, taking for granted John's old age and the spread of the gospel over the previous thirty years, were now churches of both Jewish and Gentile Christians who had left their former religions behind them. The seven churches represented are thus Christian churches, although their 'Christianity' at times comes very short of Christ's Covenant norm. The prophets refer repeatedly to the Gentile nations looking to the Jews for their messianic faith which thus covers Patmos and post-Patmos times. The Covenant of Grace is now equally revealed to both Jews and Gentiles.

The message to all these churches is the same, they are being prepared for that final day which will end all time when God's New Jerusalem, a Christian Jerusalem, shall descend from Heaven and usher in true Eden, true Sion and true Canaan. Some ten times Bale displays Revelation's accounts of the story of the New Jerusalem where all the Covenant saints world-wide and throughout history are chosen to join one another in the true Promised Land of the Bible.

---

[341] P. 318.
[342] P. 298.

In mentioning the advent of the New, Heavenly and Ideal Jerusalem on the earth, we must remind ourselves of what has happened to the earthly Jerusalem which was specially chosen for a centre of international peace and harmony but broke God's Covenant miserably. One of the lesser known declarations of Isaiah concerning the future of Jerusalem gives us some insight into why earthly Jerusalem failed as a type of the true New Jerusalem. Isaiah says regretfully, the city on a hill has turned everything upside down.[343] It had all to do with God's Covenant which Jerusalem had not only broken but turned, according to the Prophet, into a Covenant of Death. Isaiah thus preaches:

> Wherefore hear the word of the LORD, ye scornful men, that rule this people which is in Jerusalem. Because ye have said, We have made a covenant with death, and with hell are we at agreement; when the overflowing scourge shall pass through, it shall not come unto us: for we have made lies our refuge, and under falsehood have we hid ourselves. Therefore thus saith the Lord GOD, Behold, I lay in Zion for a foundation a stone, a tried stone, a precious corner stone, a sure foundation: he that believeth shall not make haste. Judgment also will I lay to the line, and righteousness to the plummet: and the hail shall sweep away the refuge of lies, and the waters shall overflow the hiding place. And your covenant with death shall be disannulled, and your agreement with hell shall not stand; when the overflowing scourge shall pass through, then ye shall be trodden down by it. From the time that it goeth forth it shall take you: for morning by morning shall it pass over, by day and by night: and it shall be a vexation only to understand the report. For the bed is shorter than that a man can stretch himself on it: and the covering narrower than that he can wrap himself in it. For the LORD shall rise up as in mount Perazim, he shall be wroth as in the valley of Gibeon, that he may do his work, his strange work; and bring to pass his act, his strange act. Now therefore be ye not mockers, lest your bands be made strong: for I have heard from the Lord GOD of

---

[343] Isaiah 29:16.

hosts a consumption, even determined upon the whole earth. Give ye ear, and hear my voice; hearken, and hear my speech.[344]

The descriptions that Isaiah gives of the once Holy City can be likened to the state of debauchery in Sodom and Gomorrah but here, Isaiah is not talking about pagan heathens who have never heard the Gospel but about the Jewish priests and prophets which Bale classifies as 'the wrong Church' and thus Antichrist. Where spiritual life should reign the now Unholy City is in covenant with death and hell which has spread an evil disease throughout the whole earth. No wonder that, as a final sign of Jewish spiritual death, the Temple was destroyed. As the saying goes, a dead fish first begins to stink from its head.

However, God declares that in the ruins and rubble of Jerusalem, there is a tried and precious corner stone which is a sure foundation for believers in the true Covenant. 'There you are', say the NCT. 'That corner stone is Christ. We see that the Old Testament had no law of salvation and Christ first established His New Law in the New Testament.' One has heard such cries enough in the last few decades but those who cry in this way have not taken heed to Isaiah's words, nor to those of the bulk of the Old Testament Prophets. The theme of the destruction of the Temple in Jerusalem and the stone which has caused stumbling was preached throughout the Old Testament by the true Old Testament saints with a strong world-wide emphasis and clear spiritual meaning concerning the times they were in and the times which were to come. Their prophesying was not soothsaying but a proclamation of the spiritual state of the times and that which could cure it there, then and always. David tells us in Psalm 118:22: 'The stone which the builders refused is become the headstone of the corner.' Isaiah echoes this in the words:

> Therefore thus says the Lord GOD: Behold I lay in Zion for a foundation a stone, a tried stone, a precious corner stone, a sure foundation: he that believeth shall not make haste.[345]

---

[344] Isaiah 28:14-23.
[345] Isaiah 28:16.

The Old Testament knew more about this corner stone and the everlasting gospel than some modern re-interpreters of their preaching are prepared to admit. Even in New Testament times Christ had to ask his disciples if they had ever read about this fact which the scriptures make plain (Matthew 21:24). Even today, professing Christians of the NCT kind do not seem to have grasped this truth. What is clear is that Christ explained His own everlasting task and His own Person by referring to the Old Testament testimony to Him and there were no others at the time. Christ here told His disciples their knowledge of the Old Testament would explain everything! Christ, is indeed the Corner Stone of the Covenant of Grace and Old Testament believers, as Jesus pointed out, knew this. By Zechariah's time, right at the end of the Old Testament story, we find mention of the rejected stone and that Jerusalem would again be built up and believers would dwell in it from all the nations of the world. Then the true prophet links these second inhabitants of a restored Jerusalem with the New Testament truth of Christ's journey into Jerusalem and the salvation which it entails.

'Rejoice greatly, O daughter of Zion; shout O daughter of Jerusalem: behold thy King cometh unto thee: he is just, and having salvation; lowly and riding upon an ass, and upon a colt, the foal of an ass.'[346]

Micah also at the end of the Old Testament period preaches the downfall of the earthly Zion of Blood and the Jerusalem of Iniquity before the setting up of a New Jerusalem for all the world's believers.[347] Old Jerusalem shall be levelled to the ground but the 'daughters of Jerusalem' whether this refers to the true remnant of believers just mentioned in Chapter 4:7, or Christ Himself with His Bride the believing daughter of God, it is obvious that the New Jerusalem shall be for believers throughout the Earth (4:2). Then Micah develops the gospel theme further in Chapter 5, explaining the Covenant which unfaithful people had broken. However, the Covenant in Christ's keeping had been there all the time especially for His Bride because Christ's 'goings forth have been from of old, from everlasting (5:2).

This writer is aware of the fact that Jerusalem and the Temple were destroyed and again rebuilt in Old Testament times but all the Prophets linked this new building with declarations concerning what the spiritual

---

[346] Zechariah 9:9.
[347] Micah 3:10 and Chapter 4.

New Jerusalem would be like and what the true People of God would be like. To them, the earthly Jerusalem and Temple which they rebuilt, and which again fell, was a mere pointer to the Jerusalem and Temple made 'without hands' which would last forever. Thus modern so-called Christian Zionists who are collecting funds to rebuild the fallen and desecrated Temple built by hands argue against both the Old Testament Prophets and the witness of the New Testament. They are neither true Jewish nor true Christian in their pseudo-works of righteousness.

It is significant that the two books of Jewish Chronicles in the Bible end their accounts in 2 Chronicles, chapter 36, by recording how the ruling people in their stronghold of Jerusalem 'did evil in the sight of the Lord' and so God 'burnt the house of God and brake down the walls of Jerusalem, and burnt all the palaces thereof with fire, and destroyed all the goodly vessels thereof'.

Still there is a hope given the desolate Jews by King Cyrus, the far-sighted one,[348] who claimed to rule 'all the kingdoms of the earth which the Lord God of heaven' had given him and appealed to those Jews who were willing to follow the Lord their God in building up Jerusalem. There is no mention of a re-building here and Cyrus was obviously appealing to a believing remnant.

In Micah, we are immediately led from the Old Testament gospel of faith to the New Testament gospel of fulfilment which still needs the same God-given faith in the Messiah today in order to understand it. It is no wonder that Zechariah speaks of one believing Jew per ten Gentiles who sought the same faith as the Jew in the future world-wide acceptance of Covenant faith. True faith, as Old Testament believing Jews showed, accepts the event before it happens as God has revealed it in His Word and it is thus the greater faith. We also note that the New Testament expressly refers to the Old Testament's prior belief in this event in John 12:14-16. Even the disciples took some time to see the association. In condemning the Jewish clergy and false prophets for leading Jews astray, the great Prophets of the Bible denounced unbelievers and Covenant-breakers and unbelieving Jews and their

---

[348] The linguistic controversy over the meaning of the name of 'Cyrus' as being 'Lord', 'Sun', 'young man' and even the 'Lord's anointed one' is for me an entrance into Babel. We know, however, that God used King Cyrus and that is enough.

word is still Gospel today. Here, we are not talking about a New-Testament-only truth but of a lasting biblical truth passed on from the Old to the New and shared in its true pan-biblical manner. It is also of note that believing onlookers associated the prophesied action of Christ entering into dead Jerusalem as a sign of the resurrection from the dead (v. 17). John continues these truths during his Patmos exile with the culminating arrival of the Heavenly New Jerusalem, ushering in Christ's perpetual reign with His Bride. There is now no more talk of a re-built earthly Jerusalem and a Temple for sacrifices as the New Jerusalem is God's Temple and Christ has paid the needy sacrifice once and for ever more.

John Bale speaks very much of the New Jerusalem and the simple and straightforward eschatology attached to it. Bale's version might seem too 'simple' for many. We must take into account that Bale lived before the 17th Century with its superstitious eschatological systems introduced by the Jesuits and Continental Jewish seekers for the real Promised Land. Millennialism then became a religion in itself with as many 'denominations' as found previously in the 17th Century split up of the churches. Indeed, these growing fables of the future, as believed by Cromwell himself, were little better than horoscopes as our Dispensationism, Lindseyism, Pre-, Post-, and A-millennialism are today and which have split the seamless Robe of Christ into tatters. Many a preacher's gospel has been destroyed because his sermons were mere speculative assumptions concerning future occurrences ignoring Christ's plea not to entertain such folly.

I once attended a gigantic meeting of some 2,000 believers in Uppsala who had invited a Norwegian preacher of fame to preach. I knew him well as we shared family ancestors and we had been each other's guests a number of times. However, during his preaching, the preacher sadly departed into using the Bible as a 'horror-scope' of soothsaying and told us about the extension of worldly Israel and her armies and the coming of the Antichrist with the world turned into a second Sodom and Gomorrah where Christ played second fiddle in urging the Armageddon battle to end all battles on. Later, I heard that this wonderful brother of great capacities and intelligence and love for his fellow men was busy tracking UFOs and a possible alien occupation of the Earth from outer space. Bale would have told him he was in the wrong church.

What does Bale then say of the New Jerusalem in his Revelation commentary? He refers to Chapter Three, verse 12, which is verse 18 for him as he starts the versification at our verse seven which opens God's words to Philadelphia. This reads:

> Him that overcometh will I make a pillar in the temple of my God, and he shall go no more out: and I will write upon him the name of my God, and the name of the city of my God, which is new Jerusalem, which cometh down out of heaven from my God: and I will write upon him my new name.[349]

Bale comments on the man with a new name:

> Evermore shall he be called a servant of the Lord, an apostle or witness of God, a lamb of Christ's fold, a sheep of his pasture, a branch of his vine, a member of his church, an imp[350] of his kingdom, a citizen of heaven, and an inheritor of everlasting life.[351]

It is quite clear here that Bale understands the scriptures as liking the New Jerusalem to the Christian fold with no talk about Jews and Gentiles. It is also clear for Bale, and I presume for any other Christian, that this New Jerusalem is to be understood spiritually and world-wide and not as a vision of bricks and mortar. The coming down of the New Jerusalem will come as a time of world-wide revival when the false Church of Babylon will be defeated and a time of rest has come for true Christians who can freely rejoice in the Lord. When the elect are gathered in throughout this time of peace, this New Jerusalem of Christian saints will rise and meet their Saviour to be forever with Him. Bale tells us, commentating on Revelation 21:

> Jerusalem is she called both here and there, our peaceable city of the Lord, in that all her citizens are of one faith, and there shall

---

[349] P. 289.
[350] Offspring.
[351] P. 292.

375

be one glorious unity and concord. Here are her dwellers citizens with the saints, and the household servants of God; there shall they be both His children and heirs together with Christ. From God she came down, and out of heaven first of all. Neither out of flesh nor blood hath sprung her Christian belief, but from the gracious opening of the Father, which is in heaven. 'That Jerusalem (saith Paul) which is free and our mother, is from above'. She is that city, whose builder and maker is God. With none other laws is she governed, but with his eternal testament and gospel of peace. With the constitutions of men hath she nothing to do, be they never so holy and precious: for alone she dependeth on God and His Spirit. Of Him she is prepared through the gift of faith. She is cleansed with the fountain of water in the word of life, to seem a glorious congregation without blemish or wrinkle. From her sins is she purely washed in His blood; And so garnished as a beautiful bride to her husband with love, joy, peace, patience, meekness, long-suffering, and other glorious fruits of the Spirit. 'Upon thy right hand, Lord (saith David) standeth a queen in a garment of most fine gold, compassed with diversity.' But every man shall not see this her apparel; for it will be rather a raiment of the heart than of the outward body. Figured was this decking of her at large in the wonderful adorning of the temple and tabernacle of God in the days of Moses and Solomon, whose mystical meeting also he describeth in his canticles. How marvellous this new Jerusalem will be in the regeneration, when she meeteth her spouse in the air, and how glorious her continuance with Him, it lieth not in us to declare in all points, considering that neither eye hath seen, nor ear heard, neither can the heart conjecture, what God hath there prepared for them that love him.[352]

So the Bible ends as it begins with an appeal to follow the Lord always. We, the People of His Choice will be no longer in Adam but fully taken up in Christ in our resurrected bodies and spirits as we patiently await His call to our heavenly mansions. It comes quickly for some and seemingly far too slowly for others, yet it will come at last

---

[352] Pp. 583, 584. Revelation Chapter 21.

for us all. Our Saviour tells us speculation as to the timing of this and that in the future will not help us at all, indeed, it has hindered many. Our duty is to be watchful and when that great clarion call comes, we shall be lifted out of this world of tears and our eternal joy is to see Jesus' loving face and be forever with Him.

The pan-biblical message of the eternal New Jerusalem
Let us look then at some of these pan-biblical gospel treasures to be found in Revelation which are drawn from the Old Testament to prepare us for Eternity.

Isaiah the great Prophet of the New Jerusalem concerning his day and all time, tells us of the time growing ever nearer, when time itself will be wound up and the old creation will end. Then he tells us the blessed, comforting news that God has reserved a New Jerusalem for a believing remnant of this earth which will last forever. In Chapter 65:17-19 Isaiah relates not what God has merely planned for the future but what God is doing in Isaiah's very day and will do so until Christ comes to take home His own.

> For behold, I create new heavens and a new earth: and the former shall not be remembered, nor come into mind. But be ye glad and rejoice for ever in that which I create: for behold I create Jerusalem, a rejoicing, and her people a joy. And I will rejoice in my people: and the voice of weeping shall be no more heard in her, nor the voice of crying.[353]

Isaiah relates this truth to the Covenant God has made for His People in chapter 54:10, saying:

> For the mountains shall depart, and the hills be removed; but my kindness shall not depart from thee, neither shall the covenant of my peace be removed, saith the Lord saith the Lord that hath mercy upon us.

---

[353] See also Psalm 102:25-28.

I take the departing of the mountains and the removing of the hills in context to mean the fall of worldly Jerusalem, the renegade city on a hill, because of inner corruptions leading to corruptions throughout all the earth. Usually when Isaiah speaks of mountain or mountains he is speaking like Micah and the other Prophets of Jerusalem and the Temple[354] which will be reduced to heaps and Zion plowed like a field. There is hope, however for both Jews and Gentiles. In this chapter, Isaiah also emphasizes repeatedly the Covenant is also for Gentiles and refers to them (v. 3) and their Maker, Lord Redeemer and Bridegroom who is the Holy One of Israel and will be recognized as the God of all the earth (v. 5). Here Isaiah is surely referring to the New Covenant or the Covenant of Grace echoed a hundred years later in Jeremiah. This was the new song the Lord gave to believing Israel based on the new things told Israel by God concerning the Covenant of Grace and the evangelization of the world. Indeed we find this 'new thing' and 'this new' song referring to a 'new spirit' and a 'new heart' mentioned not only here in Isaiah and Jeremiah 31:22 and Ezekiel 11:19, 36:26 but throughout the Psalms and other books such as Lamentations where we read in the Lamentations of Jeremiah 3:23 that God's mercies are new (renewed) every morning. Clearly, when Jeremiah speaks of 'new' he is referring to God's ever-renewing of His Covenant when unbeliever's go out of their way to forget it. The meaning of 'new' here is that which is renewed or ever new, and we know from Ecclesiastes 1:9, there is nothing absolutely new to God under the sun but everything goes according to His one plan.[355] Given the obstinacy of fallen man it is no wonder God tells the Covenant-breakers in Isaiah 48:6 and context:

> Thou hast heard, see all this; and will not ye declare it? I have shewed thee new things from this time, even hidden things, and thou didst not know them.

This shows that Isaiah, long before Jeremiah, knew what the New Covenant was all about which was followed by believers in his own day and was not in cold storage until Old Testament times were over. Here, also, God in His revelation as the Messianic First and the Last, goes on

---

[354] Isaiah 2:2ff; Micah 3:12; Jeremiah 26:18.
[355] Isaiah 42:9, 10; Psalm 33:3 and passim, Ecclesiastes 1:9.

to tell wayward Israel why He has brought creation into being which has come and will go when God's purpose in Christ is fulfilled.

This work of God related in Old Testament times for the benefit of the people of that time, was re-echoed throughout the Old Testament and into the New so we find Peter saying hundreds of years after Isaiah:

Nevertheless we, according to his promise, look for new heavens and a new earth, wherein dwelleth righteousness.[356]

Then, in the last book of the Bible the Apostle John now exiled to Patmos, true to his everlasting faith and the eternal truth of God's Word, says:

And I saw a new heaven and a new earth: for the first heaven and the first earth were passed away, and there was no more sea. And I John saw the holy city new Jerusalem coming down from God out of heaven, adorned as a bride for her husband ... And God shall wipe away all tears from their eyes; and there shall be no more death, neither sorrow nor crying, neither shall there be any more pain: for the former things are passed away.[357]

Here we see that God's New Jerusalem was not solely a New Testament conception but had been taken over from the preaching of the prophets many hundreds of years before.

The Lamb's Book of Life known throughout all history
Most Christians know about the Lamb's Book of Life which contains a list of the Elect's names as a key to open the doors of Glory for them. Surely this is part of New Testament eschatological doctrine, we might say. Yes, it is but this was a truth known throughout the ages by the Lord's people. Just as Gabriel gave the New Testament Good News of Christ's birth, so he gave the Old Testament the news of Christ's Bride, the Church. The Prophet Daniel, one who was on speaking terms with the Angels, was told:

---

[356] 2 Peter 3:13.
[357] Revelation 21:1, 2, 4. See also Matthew 24:35.

At that time shall arise Michael, the great prince who has charge of your people. And there shall be a time of trouble, such as never has been since there was a nation till that time. But at that time your people shall be delivered, everyone whose name shall be found written in the book. And many of those who sleep in the dust of the earth shall awake, some to everlasting life, and some to shame and everlasting contempt. And those who are wise shall shine like the brightness of the sky above; and those who turn many to righteousness, like the stars forever and ever. But you, Daniel, shut up the words and seal the book, until the time of the end. Many shall run to and fro, and knowledge shall increase.[358]

Then John takes up this blessed theme on Patmos and says:

Then I saw a great white throne and him who was seated on it. From his presence earth and sky fled away, and no place was found for them. And I saw the dead, great and small, standing before the throne, and books were opened. Then another book was opened, which is the book of life. And the dead were judged by what was written in the books, according to what they had done. And the sea gave up the dead who were in it, Death and Hades gave up the dead who were in them, and they were judged, each one of them, according to what they had done. Then Death and Hades were thrown into the lake of fire. This is the second death, the lake of fire. And if anyone's name was not found written in the book of life, he was thrown into the lake of fire.[359]

This is the glorious gospel believed by the People of God in all ages
Paul had certainly more than an inkling of this where he gives his Christian readers comforting words concerning their wonderful home call:

---

[358] Daniel 12:1.
[359] Revelation 20:11-15.

Behold, I shew you a mystery; We shall not all sleep, but we shall all be changed, In a moment, in the twinkling of an eye, at the last trump: for the trumpet shall sound, and the dead shall be raised incorruptible, and we shall be changed. For this corruptible must put on incorruption, and this mortal must put on immortality. So when this corruptible shall have put on incorruption, and this mortal shall have put on immortality, then shall be brought to pass the saying that is written, Death is swallowed up in victory. O death, where is thy sting? O grave, where is thy victory?[360]

Paul is echoing the words of his Old Testament mentors in the faith Was this a home truth revealed to Paul on the spur of the moment as a first ray of hope? Not at all! This comforting truth had been a support for believers through many centuries. Paul was following the teaching of his father in the faith Isaiah and Isaiah's fellow Old Testament believers. The Lord had thus placed these never to be forgotten words in his mind and heart:

And he will destroy in this mountain the face of the covering cast over all people, and the vail that is spread over all nations. *He will swallow up death in victory*; and the Lord GOD will wipe away tears from off all faces; and the rebuke of his people shall he take away from off all the earth: for the LORD hath spoken it. And it shall be said in that day, Lo, this is our God; we have waited for him, and he will save us: this is the LORD; we have waited for him, we will be glad and rejoice in his salvation.[361]

We notice how Isaiah mentions the blindness in Jerusalem in one breath with 'all people' and the vail that is spread over 'all nations'. He had the whole world in view. Isaiah, like the other Prophets, is a universal preacher with a Gospel that covers all time.

---

[360] 1 Corinthians 15:51ff..
[361] Isaiah 25:7-9.

After the falling asleep the awakening in Glory
Thus Paul can, under the work of the Holy Spirit in all time, comfort believers world-wide with the words:

> But I would not have you to be ignorant, brethren, concerning them which are asleep, that ye sorrow not, even as others which have no hope. For if we believe that Jesus died and rose again, even so them also which sleep in Jesus will God bring with him. For this we say unto you by the word of the Lord, that we which are alive and remain unto the coming of the Lord shall not prevent them which are asleep. For the Lord himself shall descend from heaven with a shout, with the voice of the archangel, and with the trump of God: and the dead in Christ shall rise first: Then we which are alive and remain shall be caught up together with them in the clouds, to meet the Lord in the air: and so shall we ever be with the Lord.[362]

Here is a wonderful blending of Old Testament and New Testament teaching so that one can hardly say which is which. Why should we try, it is all the pure Word of God revealed to us so that we might enter into God's Covenant by faith.

Good news from past times
William Plumer wrote a fine commentary on the words in Romans 5:2 'We rejoice in hope of the glory of God'[363] and goes on to quote blessed words from the New Testament concerning our Heavenly home. Yet when we look at these verses of hope, we find them embedded in God's revelation from the very beginning of time when Adam sinned and the Covenant of Grace began. In Ephesians 4:4 where Paul is speaking of being in 'one body, and one hope, even as ye are called in one hope of your calling, though he is addressing Gentiles, he teaches the righteousness preached in the Old Testament to them through using the Law lawfully. In Colossians 1:5, Paul speaks of the 'hope which is laid up for you in heaven' gained through believing the gospel which Paul

---

[362] 1 Thessalonians 4:13-17.
[363] This wee commentary is offered free of charge by the Inheritance Publishers P.O. Box 1334, Grand Rapids, Michigan 49501, USA and multiple free copies can be ordered for free distribution.

establishes in the Old Testament creation story showing that 'all things were created by him and for him'. In Titus 1:2 we read of 'the hope of eternal life, which God, that cannot lie, promised before the world began'. They are told, however, not to give 'heed to Jewish fables and commandments of men, that turn from the truth'. Obviously covenant-breaking Jews are meant here and not those who were given to understand the true tenor of the Law in the Covenant of Grace who are 'Looking for that blessed hope, and the glorious appearance of the great God and our Saviour Jesus Christ Who gave himself for us, that he might redeem us from all iniquity, and purify unto himself a peculiar people, zealous of good works'.[364]

A heavenly mansion for each and every Christian
One passage of scripture, straight from the mouth of our Lord has been a comfort to me since my earliest Sunday School days and is my greatest comfort now, aged eighty, in my preparations to meet my Saviour face to face. It is found in John fourteen verses one and two and is, I believe, unique in scripture. It reads:

Let not your heart be troubled; ye believe in God, believe also in me. In my Father's house are many mansions: if it were not so, I would have told you. I go to prepare a place for you. And if I go and prepare a place for you, I will come again and receive you unto myself; that where I am, there ye may be also.

Perhaps no other passage of scripture is so intimate, loving, soothing, comforting and assuring. It is also so matter-of-fact, direct and straightforward in its message. The Lord hath spoken. Blessed be the Name of the Lord! How wonderful is this gospel of certainty!

---

[364] Titus 2:13.

Appendix I

Review Article Concerning David H. Wenkel: Only and Alone the Naked Soul: The Anti-Preparation Doctrine of the London Baptist Confession of 1644/1646.

In this book *The Covenant of Grace and the People of God* I have striven to demonstrate the purpose of both Law and Grace within the Covenant of Grace. This work left me with the rather soothing conviction that the NCT with its broken-covenant teaching was a lost cause and would make no headway into orthodox theology and especially mainstream Baptist thinking. However, I recently received the January, 2019 issue of the *Baptist Quarterly* of which I am a life-time subscriber. The above article immediately caught my attention as I have always been a severe critic of 'Preparationism' which I always understood as persuading sinners to follow a programme of spiritual exercises such as praying, Bible-reading, hymn-singing etc. so they might through hard trying come to faith. This questionable method was made clear to me recently by a visiting Baptist pastor and his wife whom my wife and I had invited for a meal. He told us how he encouraged unbelievers to join his church choir. I asked him how he expected still lost sinners to praise God for the blessings of the Christian life when they did not believe in them nor had every received them. I also asked him what evangelistic purpose he had in mind with his action. Our friend's answer came as a surprise. He believed that in the preparational singing of God's salvation, his choir members would begin to believe what they were singing.

It was with this background I turned to David Wenkel's analysis of Article XXV of the First London Confession which Wenkel claims is 'Anti-Preparational'. The Article states:

> That the tenders of the Gospel to the conversion of sinners, is absolutely free, no way requiring, as absolutely necessary, any qualifications, preparations, terrors of the Law or preceding ministry of the Law, but only and alone the naked soul, as a sinner and ungodly to receive Christ, as Christ, as crucified, dead and buried, and risen again, being made a Prince and a Saviour for such sinners.

> (John 3:14, 15; 1:12; Isaiah 55:1; John 7:37; 1 Timothy 1:15; Romans 4:5; 5:8; Acts 5:30, 31; 2:36; 1 Corinthians 1:22-24)

I must confess that I have always considered the First London Confession as superior to the Second London Confession and I have always held that merely preaching Law without its place within the Covenant of Grace is wrong as Law was never meant to be a stand-alone way of salvation or punishment in either the Old Testament or the New. This, however, is the way Wenkel appears to understand 'the terrors of the Law' and 'preceding ministry of the Law' though the passage in context is clearly refuting what Wenkel makes of it. Those old-time Baptists knew their Covenant Theology and are contrasting true Covenant-Gospel teaching with mere pulpit thumping efforts to frighten sinners to the cross. However, Wenkel clearly refers to this wrong use of the Law outlined in the Article as being 'almost certainly' that of Moses. Here Wenkel is mistaken. The Mosaic Law carried 'tenors' with it which were in keeping with the Covenant of Grace given to Abraham in God's work of preparing a People for Himself through the mediation of Christ. One cannot place the Law outside of the Covenant of Grace as it has then no meaning or purpose.

Wenkel argues for the NCT position that the Mosaic Law is not an essential part of an eternal Covenant of Grace which was drawn up by the Holy Trinity from eternity leading to the foundation of the world for the calling in of Christ's Bride, the Church. The Law given to Moses, it

386

appears for Wenkel, was God's Plan A which failed. His second covenant, or Plan B, then came as a completely New Covenant which is truly forever. This appears to be a contradiction of Article X of the *First London Confession* which declares:

> Touching His office, Jesus Christ only is made the Mediator of the New Covenant, even the everlasting Covenant of Grace between God and man, to be perfectly and fully the Prophet, Priest and King of the Church of God for evermore.

Here, there is no talk of two covenants but one everlasting Covenant of Grace with Christ as its Mediator, Prophet, Priest and King. Christ's Mediatorship was from the foundation of the world as Article IX makes clear. Nevertheless, Wenkel, who has isolated Article XXV from its context, speaks of a historical, failed Covenant and an 'ahistorical' Covenant (whatever that means) which is eternally successful. The Bible, however, presents the one Covenant of Grace as being historical and eternal in the aevi-eternal sense of being revealed in time for eternity. There is nothing 'ahistorical' about the Father's Covenant with His Son to provide a way of salvation in Christ. We see, therefore, that Wenkel is unashamedly a New Covenant Theologian who, in the terms of Isaiah, that great One Covenant Theologian, turns God's one-and-only plan of salvation in the one-and-only Covenant of Grace preached in the one-and-only everlasting Gospel upside down.[365]

If the first step is not on firm ground, the second usually also falters. Wenkel now argues himself into believing that there is thus a discontinuation between a supposed Mosaic Covenant and a New Covenant. However, the Mosaic Covenant as Moses himself emphasized, followed by Paul was added to the Abrahamic Covenant which was eternal and of world-wide application. Furthermore, preaching concerning the New Covenant in the Old Testament was continually being renewed and reformed as Moses himself testified and nearly all the other Old Testament writers. Jeremiah clearly places the preaching of the New Covenant before the Mosaic addition because of pre-Mosaic covenant-breakers. Yet NCT-friend Wenkel claims that:

---

[365] Isaiah 29:16.

This willingness to see strong discontinuities between the Mosaic era and the New Covenant era reflects the Baptists' distinctive doctrine of credo-baptism.

Such a willingness, thrust onto the *First Confession*, is solely a product of Wenkel's independent thinking. The Old Testament ends with God's plea to remember the Law of Moses His servant and the story of John the Baptist[366] who baptized Christ as part of the Covenant of Grace which Zacharias[367] and no less a personage than Gabriel announced was continuing in the New Testament where the people were admonished to 'remember the Covenant' of mercy. The latter word used here is synonymous with grace. Wenkel's theology of cutting up the Covenant can hardly be used as an interpretation of or as an alternative to traditional Baptist doctrine.

Next, Wenkel repeatedly wonders, though his readers do not, why the 1644/1646 editions 'do not cite passages of scripture that one would expect?' He quotes Galatians 3:23-25 here, obviously quite out of context, which he believes the early Baptists should have used. We must add, 'Providing that they agreed with Wenkel's interpretation of what they had written'. To a less biased writer it would appear that Galatians 3:23-25 was not mentioned in the XXV Article because it had no application there and did not illustrate the point they were making. In typical NCT manner, Wenkel explains that as our Messiah has come and we have come to faith, we do not need a Schoolmaster, Guardian or Pedagogue. He concludes therefore the Law has been abolished. But what about those who are still under the Law and have not yet found their Messiah and are still under condemnation by the Law until Grace enters their lives? What about those who are no longer under the Law but see in the Law portraits of God's eternal righteousness? One does not take all the sign-posts down along the way to a town because the town has been reached. There are other travellers on the way.

Wenkel believes no Gentile is under the Law of Moses, quoting Paul's words in Romans 2:14 as 'proof'. Again, Wenkel is cutting out Paul's words from the context which is that all sinners are covenant-

---

[366] Malachi 4:4ff..
[367] This is the message of Luke 1 and 2, especially 1:72.

breakers,[368] though historically, most Gentiles did not know the written Law, or Grace, for that matter, they are now put under the same gospel obligations towards both Law and Grace as unbelieving Jews. They are put under the same gospel as the Jews. Christ thus fulfilled the one Law by Grace for both Jews and Gentiles. He did not fulfil two separate Laws requiring two separate acts of Grace. The Law and the Prophets also teach Gentiles that the just shall live by faith in Christ (v. 21), thus experiencing the tenor of the Law. In Chapter 4, Paul argues that this gospel story was the same in Abraham's days, remembering he was the Father in the faith to all nations, a message Paul continues. He then speaks of the action of the Law on all men without having to refer to distinctions between Jews and Gentiles which play no part in God's salvation. This gospel is repeated in Galatians 1-3 and beyond. When Paul speaks of those under the curse of the Law in Galatians 3:16, he is not distinguishing between Jews and Gentiles.

As to be expected, Wenkel is also amazed that Article XXV does not refer to Romans 2:14, and again it must be said that as the early Baptists obviously understood their Article differently to Wenkel, his 'proof-texts' are non-applicable.

Now, Wenkel becomes theologically very vague in arguing the Gentiles have a 'moral law' written on their hearts. What does he mean by this 'moral' idea and from where has he obtained his evidence? We might also add, why should he think that the Article XXV author's divided up the Law into Wenkel's three parts, the moral, the ceremonial and the judicial? There is no mention of a 'moral law' in the Article, just as there is no mention of Galatians 3:23-25 and no mention of Romans 2:14. However, Wenkel takes all the non-applicable 'evidence' he has collected to argue that Gentiles because of their supposed 'moral law' written on their hearts 'are already prepared to receive Christ'. So now we are back to the problem of 'duty faith' which apparently Wenkel sees as a Gentile help to salvation. He is not so insistent that the Jews also have this 'preparation'. This argument comes as rather a surprise because Wenkel started off by denying a preparational use of the Law. What he really means is that he does not agree with the

---

[368] Romans 1:31.

preparationism which he argues, but does not prove, the authors of Article XXV rejected.

Now Wenkel comes up with the idea of a 'tension theology' which is often used to explain the inexplicable. He believes the Baptist articles reject the Mosaic Law though they yet claim that those who receive Christ must do so as 'sinners' and 'ungodly'. Wenkel maintains this was the 'quandary' of the First London Confession, though the Confession gives no evidence of such a quandary. It appears this is a quandary of Wenkel's own 'tension theology'. So Wenkel states in the confusion he has put himself, 'It simply is not clear how sinners come to know themselves as sinners and ungodly'.[369] Wenkel suggests this is because we use the wrong *ordo salutis* in determining the relationship between regeneration, repentance, faith and belief. Wenkel began to get too complicated for me here but seems to conclude 'repentance follows faith', which is, again, not an issue in the First London Confession so why raise it? Also, why then do the scriptures tell us to 'repent and believe'?

Now Wenkel, by way of summing up his thoughts, uses Article XXV as a spring board from which to jump into his most speculative airing of NCT theology and states:

> The only way logically to explain the language of Article Twenty-Five in the LBC of 1644/1646 is to conclude that it teaches a soft or chastened preparationism through the instrumental causes of preaching while rejecting preparation as a material cause of conversion. It is possible that this instrumental preparation happens through the presence of God's moral law and the resulting conflict in the conscience of all people – but this is not explicit.

I found this a most unclear, foggy statement. This is a highly unsatisfactory way of saying that the Article could be this, that or the other, whereas the First London Confession in no way beats about the bush but states confidentially what was believed and accepted amongst the London Baptists. Wenkel's most personal interpretations are backed up by his 'four salient conclusions' which are:

---

[369] P. 27.

1. The authors of Article XXV intentionally distanced themselves from their Reformed contemporaries who sought to use the Law of Moses to prepare sinners for conversion.

Here Wenkel separates the London Baptists from the Reformed teaching of their contemporaries whether Baptists, Church of England, Independents or Presbyterians without giving any evidence whatsoever from their works to prove his case. Wenkel mentions Calvin who was no contemporary of the 1644 men and also William Ames who can hardly be called a contemporary having died in 1633. The mention of these two Reformers is in conjunction with their *ordo salutis* and not on their view of the Law. Wenkel's novel criticism appears to be that the 1644 authors' Reformed contemporaries were not NCT followers but the First London Baptists of the Confession were. He has not given the least backing for such a theory.

2. The Article XXV authors had a mind to practical divinity in pastoral praxis on a sound doctrinal basis which is found outlined in Article XXIV.
Article XXIV reads:

> That faith is ordinarily begot by the preaching of the Gospel, or word of Christ, without respect to any power or capacity in the creature, but it is wholly passive, being dead in sins and trespasses, does believe, and is converted by no less power, than that which raised Christ from the dead.

I cannot think of a Reformer or Reformed 17th Century believer who could not subscribe to this article. However, we must truly ask how these people were pronounced 'dead in trespasses and sins' without the gracious work of the Law, written down in God's Word by the Spirit to lead sinful souls to Christ. This would not be 'preparationism' but hearing, receiving and believing the gospel through the Grace of the Lord Jesus Christ. When Paul addresses the Gentiles who were dead in trespasses and sins in Ephesians 2:1ff, he tells them that their salvation is due to Christ:

... having abolished in his flesh the enmity, even the law of commandments contained in ordinances; for to make in himself of twain one new man, so making peace.[370]

Paul then lays out the tenor (not terror) of the Law in the following chapters to those ignorant of the Law that they might serve the Law in Christ.

This writer, who does not share Wenkel's novel theology, nevertheless would argue that Article XXIV is soundly Reformed because it is biblical and in no way contradicts the historical Reformed faith though Wenkel would seek to separate the Baptists from those exegetical, practical, methodical and spiritual doctrines.

3. The doctrine of anti-preparationalism 'relies on an unstated but critical distinction between instrumental and material causation. The preaching of the gospel and the scriptures are the instruments of conversion yet the act of conversion has no material cause outside of God's sovereign act of grace that changes that which was dead to life.'

Wenkel would have done well to define what he means by 'instrumental' and 'material' in a way more appropriate to the theology expressed in the London Baptist Confession Articles. Though Wenkel admits his views are 'unstated' in the Articles, he believes they, nevertheless, exercise the same 'critical distinction' he does. Wenkel, however, has not commented on the Articles themselves but on what he feels they ought to have said but did not say. There is nothing to be said about such a flimsy argument.

4. The conclusions of this paper also suggest a need to re-visit the early Baptist doctrines of ordo salutis because these two early confessions point to the primacy of faith before repentance.

Wenkel is surely wrong again on this issue as the *ordo salutis* which he prefers is not made an issue in either the First or Second London Baptist Confession. The First does not mention repentance and the Second in Chapter 15 on the subject speaks of 'repentance unto life and salvation' some thirteen times. Here surely is a belief in repentance coming before faith. In Chapter 20 there are another two references, one

---

[370] Ephesians 2:15.

to faith and repentance as being begotten of God and one to 'faith or repentance' and the Chapter seems to deal with faith and repentance as synonyms. If Wenkel wishes to draw an *ordo salutis* from this, which the Confession found no reason to do, the evidence would indicate the early Baptists saw repentance preceding faith, though I would doubt whether a time period between the two has any saving significance as it is all of Grace and God grants both as free gifts. However, Wenkel's last theory in his defence of NCT-ism disappears as the Articles obviously contradict him.

The Covenant Of Grace And The People Of God

Appendix II

The Story Behind Durie's *Body of Practical Divinity*

The need for a Practical Divinity on the Continent
Durie's own publications such as his *Capitum de Pace religiosa* appeared in various forms and languages and was published almost simultaneously in London, Amsterdam, Stockholm, Berlin, Cassel, Frankfurt-on-the-Oder, Bremen and several cities in Eastern Europe. This was because Durie wrote his works out in some five different languages and had publishing contacts throughout Europe. His linguistic gifts were not shared by the bulk of his co-workers who were aware of the need to spread sound British theological literature throughout Europe and the New World. Thus Durie, supported by German and Dutch thinkers, canvassed throughout Britain for translators who would put English and Scottish works into the languages of the Continent. Amongst those forty or so who committed themselves were William Twisse, himself of German extraction, Samuel Hartlib who was half Polish, the German Henry Oldenburg (Durie's Secretary and son-in-law who became the Secretary of the Royal Society), John Cotton, Henry Burton, Samuel Ward, Richard Sibbes, Henry and Philip Nye, Jeremy Burroughs and Daniel Featley. The help of James Ussher was especially requested as a leading writer in this project. A number of Durie's 'Committee of Foreign Language Speakers' such as Philip Nye had gained their knowledge of foreign languages like Durie whilst in exile or pastoring foreign churches.

These men began to collect material for a *Body of Practical Divinity*, in answer to a request from members of the Diet of Leipzig (1631) and Diet of Hanau (1634), which could be translated into the Continental languages. Durie set up his final 'steering committee', as it has been dubbed by writers, for the project in 1633. The members, mostly London ministers, were William Gouge, John Stoughton, John Downam,[371] Henry Burton, George Walker, Nicolas Morton, Sidrach Simpson, Adoniram Byfield, Richard Culverwell, Obadiah Sedgwick, George Hughes and Joseph Symonds who all promised to cooperate in producing suitable English writings on Practical Divinity based on the Covenant of Grace to be translated into foreign tongues. James Ussher was approached then by the ministers in Durie's committee, mostly from the London area, with a request that he should lead them in compiling a *Body of Practical Divinity*.[372] This fact is of interest as supporters of the idea that Ussher eventually wrote a '*Body of Divinity*', confuse the London minister's request for '*Practical Divinity*' with a *Body of Divinity* they attribute to Ussher, though he denied repeatedly that he was the author. Ussher was unable to contribute to the '*Practical Divinity*' for reasons he gave over twenty years later, enclosed below. Continental theologians such as Johann Crocius joined in begging Ussher to take on the work but Ussher remained silent. These Continentals then lobbied Archbishop George Abbott who died in August 1633 and also William Laud who succeeded him. Ussher, Abbott and Laud all supported Durie in word and deed in his work as did also Davenant, Ward, Hall, Biddel and Roe with other leading Reformed men and Charles I made Durie one of his Chaplains.

In the anonymous Life of Ussher appended to several editions of Ussher's alleged *Body of Divinity*, the writer mentions the findings of the German Herborn Synod of 1633, organised mostly by Durie. This, however, was a plea for the compiling of a *Body of Practical Divinity*, which never got underway in the form originally intended, and not to the compiling of a case-study of doctrines as in the anonymous '*Body*'. In several editions Ussher is mentioned as working on the '*Body*' with

---

[371] Variously spelt Downame, Downham.
[372] See *The Copy of a Letter which was written by several Godly Ministers, Undertakers in this Work of compiling a Body of Practical Divinity, to Doctor Usher the Primat of Armach in Ireland* (undated) appended to Durie's *Earnest Breathings*.

Bishop George Downam, though Ussher tells us this early cooperation, which came to nought, was concerning a planned *Body of Practical Divinity* and Downam's death in 1634 put an end to this cooperation so Ussher dropped it. So, too, the 1677 edition of the alleged 'Body of Divinity', featured a Preface brought up to date by the long dead John Downam, who had urged Ussher in vain to write a 'Practical Divinity'. Other 'Prefaces' to the increasing number of different 'Bodies of Divinity', though probably from Ussher's pen, have little if anything to do with the 'Body' itself. Though the 'Life' and Postscript in the 1677 edition are *said to be* the work of John Durie this would provide new problems in working out when Durie could have written this work. In this 'Life' there is no mention of the *Body of Divinity* which it is supposed to introduce. The only reference is to Ussher's reading various 'Bodies of Divinity as a young student. So, too, Durie had been living in Exile, chiefly in Germany since 1660 and, in his minutely kept record of his writings by Samuel Hartlib, also a friend of Ussher's, up to 1680, Durie's agent and editor had given no hint that he was aware of such a work from Ussher's pen. Indeed, in his 1653 work *Some Proposals towards the Advancement of Learning*, Durie who was in correspondence with Ussher at the time, wrote concerning his educational plans for children's and adults' education:

> First, that some course may be thought upon to compile out of all the best authors a Complete Body of Moral or Practical Divinity, whereby we shall not only benefit ourselves, by gathering the marrow of all our authors as it were in one dish, to set it before the godly to feed upon, and by reaping the fall harvest of all the labours of our predecessors in one storehouse, to be dispensed upon all occasions to such as shall stand in need of such provisions: but we shall all so exceedingly gratify the desires of the evangelical divines in foreign churches, who have made it long ago their joint and earnest suit unto us (as by their letters to that effect may be evidenced that we would perfect this part of learning, for the use of the prophetical schools of the churches; and because they perceive that God hath furnished this nation with more means to do it, then all the churches besides,

therefore they have a earnestly pressed us not to do this precious talent in the ground.[373]

If Ussher, had been compiling such a collection of authors himself with a similar aim, it is quite astonishing that he would keep this from his very good friend.

Durie's team found the task too difficult
Coming back to Durie's initial appeals of 1628 to 1633 to move Ussher to take the leadership in collecting works for a 'Practical Divinity' which would also be suitable for translation into the Continental languages, nothing happened as Durie's team protested that the English theological language was so rich in vocabulary and eloquence that it just could not be translated easily. They also argued that English theologians had developed such a specialised theological language that there were no counterparts in other tongues. Also, there was no response whatsoever from Archbishop Ussher on the issue.

Durie, working hard on the Continent for a joint-recognition of one another by the Protestant churches was terribly disappointed because he heard nothing positive from either Ussher or his own 'steering committee' and began to show signs of frustration. By 1636 though he was busy canvasing for support in Sweden and assisting Johannes Mattiae in the education of Queen Christina and supporting the Finns, Czechs and Poles in their theological and educational reforms, the matter of Practical Divinity weighed heavily on his conscience. He wrote to Ambassador Thomas Roe, his faithful friend and financial supporter from Stockholm on 3 December, 1636 saying:

> The excuse of such as remain at home for doing nothing in the Worke of Practical Divinity or Pacification show their irresolutenes and needles fears. But what shall I say? God hath all things in his owne hand, so also Mens hearts.[374]

---

[373] *Hartlib Papers*, 47/2/1A-12 B, No. 53.
[374] Turnbull's collection, p. 227. The entire correspondence of Durie with his British colleagues including Ussher shows no mention of a 'Body of Divinity' having been or being compiled by Ussher. Otherwise Durie would have immediately considered what part of it could be taken over in a Practical Divinity, so keen was he to collect material.

Durie gains new hope
In 1641, Durie who believed he had the Monarch and his archbishops behind him, petitioned both the King and Parliament repeatedly for backing for his work in his *A Memorial concerning Peace Ecclesiasticall: To the king of England and the pastors and elders of the Kirk of Scotland meeting at St. Andrews* and *Petition to the Honourable House of the Commons in England now assembled in Parliament*; *A Discourse concerning Peace Ecclesiasticall*; *Petition to the House of Commons, for the Preservation of True Religion* and *Petition to the House of Commons; whereunto are added, certain Considerations, showing the necessity of a Correspondence in Spiritual Matters, between Protestant Churches*. It was in this latter petition that Durie included a description he had sent to Alexander Henderson, his fellow Royal Chaplain, and the Scottish Assembly concerning his views for a common Practical Divinity based on the Covenant of Grace to be used throughout the British and European Protestant churches. The Scottish Assembly responded at first positively but objected later to non-Presbyterians being involved.

Durie was always an over-optimist and now thinking success was near, he published *A Motion Tending to the Publick Good* in 1642 composed of introductory thoughts and views aired in two letters to Sir Cheney Culpeper. The work was to demonstrate 'how by the best means of reformation in learning and religion it may be advanced'. Its further aim was given in the extended title, as encouraging text book authors 'to set forward pious and learned Works'. Amongst a list of generalities, Durie plead for:

The setting up of agencies; spiritual counsellors and agents appointed to work out a foundation of evangelical religion for educational purposes, avoiding the scandals and differences of denominationalism and showing the benefits of ecclesiastical pacification. Unblameable and peaceful conversation with all men should be taught, even when opinions differ. A lively correspondence should take place between the Protestant churches concerning pan-educational matters and this should be printed for general distribution.

Chairs should be appointed in Practical Divinity and in colleges and universities and one each at Sion and Gresham Colleges in London, teaching the practical application of public good. Works on *Practical*

Divinity should be compiled from the practical writers of the age. Durie defined 'practical writers' as those who use their knowledge of whatever kind for the public good.

Taking a great risk as the Church of England was outlawed in 1543 and Durie himself had been ordained by Bishop Hall whom Cromwell had robbed of his living, Durie could not give up the idea of having Ussher in his team and sent him further material to entice him into the project. Ussher finally answered in 1653, the year Durie wrote his *Proposals for the Advancement of Learning*, in a letter which must have disappointed Durie further:

For his loving friend M. John Dury,[375] These

Mr. Dury, I am glad that you are still willing to take some pains about the procuring of a Body of Practical Divinity: a work which I have long wished for; and which formerly my heart was in, and my hand would have been in, if God had been pleased to continue our peace: for when you brought over the letters from the foreign churches, wherein they make it their request unto us to gratify their churches with some endeavours about the compilement of this work: which work seconded by a letter from the ministers in and about London unto me, when I was in Ireland many years ago, I was very glad of the motion, and laid it very seriously to heart, and conferred with some of my brethren about it that we might bring the work to some perfection. Doctor Downam the Bishop of Londonderry was a man whose studies were much bent that way: for which cause it was referred to him; and he readily did undertake the task to draw up a model or platform, according to which that system or body might be compiled, that the ministers who had written to be might be able to choose their tasks, and set themselves awork about it.

This model he promised to send unto me to revise it before it should be imparted to the foresaid ministers, that in our joint name it might be sent unto them. But he either for want of health, or some other impediments, did not expedite the work before his

---

[375] Durie himself spelt his own name in at least five different ways not including his renderings in other languages. I use the spelling 'Durie' as this was his most used spelling.

death, and when the troubles of Scotland did begin: which by reason of my Lord of Stratford's intermeddling had some reflection upon us in Ireland; and not long after I had been come over hither, he the Bishop of Londonderry being dead, the troubles of Ireland taking fire, at the proceedings of the then Parliament here, and the great distractions of this and the two nations increasing ever since, I could not do what was desired of me and what I heartedly desired might have been done, and wish yet may be done; for it will never be too late or unseasonable to set upon such an enterprise.

If therefore by your solicitation and pains you can oblige those that in the universities, or in and about this city are able and willing to undertake it, I think you will do a work very acceptable to all that are godly, and profitable to all the churches at home and abroad. Let me therefore entreat you to proceed, that whilst there is any appearance of doing good to our generation, we may not neglect the opportunity.

As for the model of the heads which you have shewed unto me;

First, I shall advice this, that the precognitions[376] may not be insisted upon largely, but as briefly and substantially as may be; and if some references to be made unto such authors as handle the heads of the pre-cognitions more at large, it may give satisfaction to such as will be more curious and desirous to see things amply handled.

Secondly, my advice is, that the work may be contracted to as few hands as may be; who may meet and confer together about it when they are perfecting their tasks.

Thirdly, I would not have the work too large and voluminous for several reasons, yet as full of matter as it can be: and where enlargement may be thought useful, references may be made to such authors as use them most effectually.

Lastly, concerning the cases of conscience which should be handled in this body, I think they might be brought in and inserted under every head of matter whereunto they belong.

---

[376] That which can be taken for granted in the understanding of the reader.

This is for the present that which I would suggest. I pray God direct and assist you and all those that go about it; and what I shall be able to do towards the encouragement of able workmen therein, you may be confident shall not be wanting from

Your loving friend
Ja. Armachanus

From my study
Decemb. 14, 1653

However, not only George Downam had finished his earthly testimony but many of Durie's team of over twenty years before had also died so that Ussher's plea that the work should be undertaken by as few hands as possible were now fewer than Ussher imagined and Durie was left to go it alone.

In 1654 Durie had completed his *Summarie Platform of the Heads of a Body of Practical Divinity* which his agent Hartlib distributed throughout the Continent. Dr George Horne, Professor of History at Leiden University, who had received a copy from Hartlib, including Ussher's letter, wrote back, saying:

Mr Durie's idea of practical divinity, hath pleased me as much as anything that ever you sent me. Believe me, there is not a more sovereign remedies than this, for the putting an end to the controversies and quarrels now between Protestants; nor fitter for the propagating of true piety, even amongst atheists and heretics, That great work of pacification, will never be brought to the desired end of settlement but by this means. The whole order and scope of this work do please me exceedingly. And (I pray you) what can hinder, your Joshua from imposing it on the world by his authority within a short time? England doth abound with men, that are most fit for this work, and as it were born to perform it. It were certainly much better, to have the cares, and hands of many men employed about such a work, as this, than in compiling of commentaries on scripture wherewith the world is already overwhelmed, and the churches groan under them as under a burden. But I will read over this whole tract more heedfully, and if anything come into my mind, which may conduce towards the building of this Temple of Jerusalem, I will carefully set it down. Although in this part, your English men do so excel, that the Christian world needs not to have it done by any else; So many godly souls having for these many years been preparing abundant matter for it; What is now to be done, but for some Solomon to call his workmen together, and build up a Temple, far more magnificent, then the ceremonial one was?

The result was that now Durie, Horne's 'Joshua', compiled his *The Earnest Breathings of the Forreign Protestants, Divines & Others: to the Ministers of these three Nations, for a Complete Body of Practicall Divinity* in 1658, the year Ussher died.[377] Besides, in the years covered by the Durie school's efforts to engage Ussher for the Body of Practical Divinity project, Ussher had been more than busy producing his major works *Britannicarum ecclesiarum antiquitates* (1639) and his *Annales veteris testamenti* (1650) which had afforded him no time for other major works.

On dealing with the controversy around whether or not Ussher authored the *Body of Divinity* allegedly ascribed to him by a Mr Downham, Charles Richard Elrington D.D. of Dublin wrote in his work *The Life of the Most Rev. James Usher D.D.* published in 1848:

> During the Primate's residence in Wales, a book was published under his name by a Mr Downham entitled: a *Body of Divinity, or the sum and substance of the Christian religion.* The Archbishop lost no time in writing to Downham, and sent him the following letter, firmly disavowing the work:
>
>> Sir, – you may be pleased to take notice, that the Catechisme you write of is none of mine, but transcribed out of Mr Cartwright's Catechisme and Mr Crook's and some other English divines, but drawn together in one method as a kind of common place book, where other men's judgments and reasons are strongly laid down,

---

[377] I used a copy found in the Bodleian Library, Oxford and was able to procure a photo copy.

though not approved in all places by the collector; besides that the collection (such that it is) being lent abroad to divers in scattered sheets, hath for a great part of it miscarried; the one half of it as I suppose (well-nigh) being no way to be recovered, so that so imperfect a thing copied verbatim out of others, and in diverse places dissonant from my own judgment, may not by any means be owned by me; But if it shall seem good of any industrious person to cut off what is weak and superfluous therein, and supply the wants thereof, and cast it into a new mould of his own framing, I shall be very well content that he make what use he pleaseth of any the materials therein, and set out the whole in his own name: and this is the resolution of
Your most assured friend,

Ja. Armachanus
May 13 1645

Elrington comments:

When the Primate thus positively declared that the book was in diverse places dissonant from his own judgment, and that it could not by any means be owned by him, it might have been supposed that it would never have been republished with his name or quoted as his work; yet the fact is far otherwise. Many editions have been published by those who were aware of this letter and yet affixed the Primate's name; and every advocate of supralapsarian doctrines quotes in his support the opinions of Archbishop Ussher, as put forth in his Body of Divinity. I understand that several persons have expressed their disappointment at my not having published the Body of Divinity among the works of the Archbishop. Had the authorship been a matter of doubtful evidence, there might be a plausible ground for such complaint, but there can be none for not publishing amongst the works of Archbishop Ussher what Archbishop Ussher declared was not his work.[378]

The 'Body' became a best-seller but on hearing that a second edition was to be printed in 1648 Ussher protested and wrote that the editor had used a paper 'collected long since out of sundry authors, and reduced into one common method' which had been used as a basis for the 'Body' without his permission. Ussher protested repeatedly that the authors used in the work sometimes did and sometimes did not teach his views. In the 'Life' of Ussher published in the 1670s, the anonymous author speaks of Ussher having to collect various materials from authors when he was twenty-one to be examined in the college chapel on his knowledge of them. This could be the origin and start of the anonymous 'Body' which those eager to profit from the name of Ussher sent into the world. At Uppsala it was still a common examination procedure for the student to prepare such 'compendia' or 'common place' collection as we called them. As I often outlined the views of authors with whom I was in strong disagreement, such as the Three Bs[379] who were all the fashion then, I would be horrified by the idea that my compendia could be taken for my concrete views and published over thirty years later as my work. Ussher protested too but the 'Body' went into edition after edition and left Ussher's protests behind.[380] However, various later editions of the 'Body' embroider this story to such an extent that Ussher is seen as using this student material to catechise the learned and even preparing Britain for the *Westminster Confession* though Ussher refused to have anything to do with it and did not attend a single meeting.

---

[378] Elrington pp. 248-250.

[379] Bart, Brunner and Bultmann.

[380] However, see Harrison Perkins' large essay 'Manuscript and Material Evidence for James Ussher's Authorship of *A Body of Divinity* (1645)', *Evangelical Quarterly*, 89.2 (2018, 133-161, which deals with most of the problems relating to a possible Ussher authorship where he has searched most of the appropriate nooks and crannies for pro and contra evidence. Though I disagree with him on a number of issues, his essay is a good starting point for those who wish to dig deeper. I am grateful to my friend of long standing Prof. Dr Crawford Gribben for this tip. In order to find the approval of an expert (Gribben wrote a most cautious and careful *Introduction* to a recent re-publication of the 'Body') I wrote to Crawford sending him a copy of this Appendix. He wrote back to say 'it sounds fine to me' and enclosed Perkins' (now Dr Perkins) essay. Prof. Gribben was Perkins' supervisor or 'Doktor Vater' as we Germans say.

Who then is the Mr Downham who allegedly published a work in Ussher's name which Ussher never authored? We know that George Downham whom Ussher had hoped would work with him on a possible *Body of Practical Divinity* died in 1634 but his younger brother John died in 1652 so the latter could possibly be associated with the publication of the work in question published in 1645. The connection between Ussher and John Downam is, however, scantily documented. John Downham's name was on the list of those close to Durie who canvassed Ussher for a *Body of Practical Divinity* which was obviously not forthcoming. But this does not entail any personal connection between the two men. Cromwell, much to the annoyance of John Milton who was for a free press, had curbed both the printing of books and newspaper publishing drastically and had set up a committee to sift out what he felt was unprofitable literature. Downam sat on this licensing committee, though he was not a member of the Assembly and might have thought that a book sent to him under the name of Ussher was fit for public reading and let it pass Cromwell's Roman Catholic-like *Index Librorum Prohibitorum* without asking too many questions. John Downam would have probably been familiar with Ussher's thoughts on a *Body of Practical Divinity* which he sent to his elder brother George and might have thought the manuscript he received was built on this initial sketch. Even so, Ussher told Downam that the work was not his and he should patch it up and put his own name as author on it as it was none of Ussher's.

This author is open to the question concerning whether certain writers have mixed up the titles 'Body of Divinity' with a 'Body of Practical Divinity'. The Durie school, in which I place Ussher, were for the latter but not the former, as they, with the exceptions of Hartlib and Comenius, rejected 'case studies', arguing that work on a synergised Practical Divinity had priority, then one could better understand any 'cases' studied afterwards.

In 1676, four years before his presumed death, Durie published what appears to be his last work, *Le Véritable Chrétien* (The True

Christian)[381] in which he pleaded with theologians to leave off Dogmantic Theology and take on Practical Divinity.[382]

---

[381] I have been unable to trace a copy of this work which is often cited. I have to comment concerning Dogmatic Theology and Practical Divinity from Joseph Minton Batten *John Dury: Advocate of Christian Union*, p. 357.
[382] I have this from Batten

Appendix III

Hetherington's Alternative History

Durie wrongly replaced by Henderson

Among Durie's numerous works on unity printed in 1641 are *A Memorial concerning Peace Ecclesiastical*: *To the king of England and the pastors and elders of the Kirk of Scotland meeting at St. Andrews* and *Petition to the Honourable House of the Commons in England now assembled in Parliament*. These documents led to Durie being proposed as a member of the planned Westminster Assembly because of his Continental Unionist activities and his strong pleas for a Practical Divinity as opposed to a Systematic Theology of case studies. The above petitions and writings and especially Durie's address to the General Assembly of the Scottish Kirk on unity, also help debunk the myth fostered by W. M. Hetherington in his *History of the Westminster Assembly* that, 'This truly magnificent, and also truly Christian idea, seems to have originated in the mind of that distinguished man, Alexander Henderson'.[383] Henderson, according to Hetherington, passed his ideas on to the Scottish Commissioners who then persuaded the Westminster Assembly to accept them and asked the Continental churches to join them. As evidence, Hetherington adds an appendix to his work entitled *Our Desires Concerning Unity in Religion, and*

---

[383] *History of the Westminster Assembly*, p. 363. See also pp. 362-364; 376-384.

Uniformity of Church Government, As a Special mean to Conserve Peace in His Majesty's Dominions. This work of allegedly 1641 he ascribes to Henderson, claiming it was sent to each foreign country in 1643 with a copy of the Solemn League and Covenant attached. This was two years after Durie appealed to the Assembly for support for his international project and ten years after Durie had appealed to the English, Scottish and foreign clergy for cooperation. It was also a decade after Scots-born Durie had first made overtures concerning his views directly to the Scottish Assembly. Durie had also spent very many years abroad campaigning for his ideas from 1628 onwards and probably a decade before judging by Durie's teen-age publications.[384]

History knows nothing of Hetherington's theory

Hetherington's view has no historical basis and ignores Durie's long and close connections with the Scottish Presbyterians, his grandfather and father being Scottish Presbyterian ministers of note. His grandfather of the same name was Knox's successor at Edinburgh. Hetherington presents Durie as first allying with Westminster's pleas for unity towards the end of 1643 when Henderson placed his ideas of unity before the Assembly of which Durie had recently become a member. However, *The Solemn League and Covenant* ratified in Parliament in February 1644 was not around when allegedly used as a basis for unity abroad by Henderson. Besides this political manifesto contends for a united British church in which all adults are forced to accept it or be severely punished. Such a Solemn League was only possible in a Tyranny or Dictatorship and was not applicable to the Continental churches. I see no evidence whatsoever pointing to Alexander Henderson following such a political programme masquerading under a religious varnish. Besides, though Henderson and his fellow Scottish Commissioners had been offered membership, they, including Henderson refused and thus had no voting rights. Durie was thus the only Scotsman at the Assembly with full voting rights and permission to vote on measures of Parliament.

Both Durie and Henderson were at the Assembly when the letters Hetherington mentions were allegedly sent abroad. By this time Durie's views were well known and supported by most of the Assembly

---

[384] Durie began publishing on the theme aged 18.

members and, as Antonia Fraser writes in her Cromwell biography, Durie 'exercised much influence in the Protectoral circle'. Indeed both the English and Scots Reformers and Puritans had been literally bombarded with Durie's pamphlets, letters and books on unity since the late 1620s and Durie had been officially supported in his work of unity both by Charles I and Cromwell and their Parliaments. So, too, Durie already had the backing of most European crowned heads and governments long before Assembly letters were sent out. Moreover, a good number of the Westminster Puritans, both English and Scottish, had supported Durie in his pan-European plan for unity and peace with their time, prayers, work and purses since 1631. The fact that both Durie and Hartlib had been lobbying Parliament concerning pan-European involvements for years led to the official invitation of the Educator Comenius of Prague by the Long Parliament in 1641 to help set up international pansophic schools and theological training colleges with ideas gathered by Hartlib, Durie and himself from all parts of Europe.

The document Hetherington quotes is not a circular letter appealing for mutual Protestant union but the view of an extreme intolerant faction. Nor does it reflect Cromwell's European policy in Europe as promoted via his favourite diplomats Durie and John Pell. Christopher Hill rightly says, 'As for the protestant interest, it was useful to be able to employ a man like John Dury, with an international reputation as a worker for protestant unity, as diplomatic representative to Sweden, Germany, Switzerland and the Netherlands.'[385] Durie's value was increased by his speaking at least five Continental languages fluently. Even Milton, the Minister for Foreign Languages could not manage that and Durie had even to translate by rule of Parliament Milton's political works into French. Henderson's alleged 'desires concerning unity' in the work attributed to him by Hetherington are non-apparent as the author castigates Episcopalianism and promotes a Hyper-Presbyterianism totally unknown outside of Scotland. This was the very opposite to Durie's approach. The Solemn League Presbyterians claimed according to Byfield's Westminster Assembly minutes that their views stemmed from the 'Presbyterians Calvin and Melanchthon', not realising that neither the one nor the other stood for Scottish Presbyterianism of the

---

[385] *God's Englishman*, p. 165.

Buchanan, Melville and Rutherford kind. So too, the doctrinal policy the Scottish Assembly had received from Geneva via Beza was totally different from Hetherington's description of Henderson's alleged 'Calvinism'. Indeed, Beza presented the Assembly with Bullinger's Confession as representative of Geneva's views, not Calvin's. Bullinger and his successor Rudolf Gwalther were opponents of the Presbyterian system and stern critics of the up and coming 'puritanism' that they fostered. Non-Presbyterians Calvin and Beza praised England's bishops and criticised the 'puritans' who, like Cartwright and Travers, had turned against them.

Hetherington denies the document he quotes was an effort by a Scottish minority to force their uniquely political and tyrannical idea of church government onto the English which appears to be the only objective interpretation possible. Furthermore, as Hetherington distrusted Presbyterian Adoniram Byfield's minutes, Byfield being the only Presbyterian Cromwell trusted, and believed it 'impractical' to consult the main Assembly records, we cannot take his presentation of the Assembly's work seriously.

Durie defends Henderson against evil reports
Moreover, it is risky hiding behind an alleged Henderson here and this staunch Scottish defender of the faith during the entire Covenanter and non-conformist debates in Scotland was constantly quoted by his enemies for expressing views which were never his and he found no backing whatsoever even in his own Edinburgh church. Forgeries concerning Henderson's teachings were numerous. At this time, he and Durie were royal chaplains to Charles I, and Henderson was granted large sums of money from the Bishops' Budget for use at his university and, unlike Durie, received a most substantial pension from the King. Henderson preached before Charles both in Scotland and England and in both countries Episcopalians opened their pulpits to him. This would suggest that Henderson was a supporter of the *status quo* under Charles I and far nearer Durie than Hetherington's display of Henderson's militant Presbyterianism.

Gunnar Westin, whose works first inspired me to take up Durie's ideas in the 1960's and David Mason in his excellent work on John

Milton and his times, produce far stronger evidence[386] to show Durie was the instigator of unity with the churches of foreign nations at the Assembly, not Henderson. Durie's own correspondence, preserved in the Swedish Archives show how he corresponded personally with Henderson sending him his plans for unity some *eight years* before the Westminster Assembly came into being. If Henderson were the author of the fierce, intolerant paper allegedly dated 1641 and from Henderson's pen, and over two years before his first addressing the Assembly, then this would have been a most violent reaction to Durie's and Cromwell's plans for unity and would in no way have fostered peace between the British and Continental Churches. And why would Henderson delay spreading such ideas abroad for several years? The unfounded position Hetherington takes has sadly become a nigh standard Presbyterian view which has helped erase the memory of Durie's great work from British church history and has marred Henderson's reputation no end.

Durie, however, wrote to Henderson from Hamburg in June 1643,[387] and from Rotterdam in December 1644 at some length, informing him of his support against the 'weeds' and 'aspersions' which wrongly accused Henderson. These people, and Durie hinted that they came from the outlawed Church of England, ought rather to support Henderson and not support the devil in sowing seeds of alienation. Durie advised Henderson to enter into correspondence with his critics and promised to send him materials which would help Henderson in his defence and further peace between the Churches.[388] The work Durie mentioned is possibly Durie's *A Large Epistle touching Peace, Unity and Charity* No. 57 in the *Hartlib Papers* which has been preserved in a scribe's hand with the letters to Henderson but which is undated. One interesting point in this 20 paged 'Epistle' is that the receiver had criticized Durie of all people for party mindedness because of a work Ussher had printed in Durie's name. Durie explained he had striven to present both sides but as his receiver was most partial to one side of the

---

[386] See Bibliography.
[387] *Hartlib Papers*, 1/17/1A-2B.
[388] *Hartlib Papers*, 1/18/1A-2B.

413

argument, an impartial presentation had annoyed him.[389] This shows, however, that Ussher and Durie had been working in close consultation.

Durie had continued to publish on church union and educational reform throughout 1642. He planned international theological colleges in London and Heidelberg under British supervision and a chain of schools throughout Britain based on his and Hartlib's 'Pansophical' system. Durie was praised repeatedly before Parliament as a man who (Hetheringtonites take note) 'well advanced the peace and unity of the Reformed churches' and linked with Bacon and Comenius as a 'pioneer of a new age'. However, the political unrest in Britain and the growing rebellion limited Durie's philanthropic and ecclesiastical endeavours greatly as monies were reserved for the war game that put a stop to the natural progress of reformation. Durie then published his *Motion Tending to the Public Good of this Age and Posteritory* which late nineteenth and early twentieth century Foster Watson called 'the best model'[390] for a child's education ever put forward in the seventeenth century'. I wonder why Watson left out the adults as Durie organized adult education as well as trade schools for school-leavers. Last century's J. M. Batten in his Durie dissertation was thus correct in calling Durie's *Motion Tending to the Public Good* 'a landmark in the history of English education'.[391]

---

[389] *Hartlib Papers*, 17/17/1A-20B.
[390] *Educational Review*, 'Dury's 'Public Good' and Education', vol. 1, p. 776.
[391] Batten, *John Dury – Advocate of Christian Reunion*, p. 168.

Bibliography

Adam, Gottfried: *Der Streit um die Prädestination im ausgehenden 16. Jahrhundert*, Neukirchener Verlag, 1970.

Anonymous: *A pack of old Puritans, maintaining the unlawfulness & inexpediency of subscribing the new engagement .... With mr. John Dury's considerations and just reproposals concerning it*, London, 1650, Bodleian Library.

Anonymous: *On the Death of that Grand Imposter Oliver Cromwell*, anon. 1660.

Anonymous: *An Account of the Last Houres of the late Renowned Oliver Lord Protector*, London, 1659. (Professedly by an eye-witness).

Anonymous: *Letters from Ireland, Relating the several great Success it hath pleased God to give unto the Parliaments Forces there, in the Taking of Drogheda, Trym, Dundalk etc.* printed by Parliament, 1649.

Ashley, Maurice: *Oliver Cromwell and the Puritan Revolution*, The English Universities Press, 1972.

Baker, J. Wayne: *Heinrich Bullinger and the Covenant: The Other Reformed Tradition*, Ohio 1980.

Bale, John, *Selected Works*, Parker Society, 1849.

Ball, John, *A Treatise of the Covenant of Grace*, facsimile reprint of 1645 edition, Peter and Rachel Reynolds, 2012.

Banks, John *A Critical Review of the Political Life of Oliver Cromwell*, John Banks, 2nd edit., London, undated, (17th C.?).

Barteleit, Sebastian, *Toleranz und Irenik: Politisch-Religiöse Grenzsetzungen im England der 1650er Jahre*, Mainz, 2003.

Batten, Joseph Minton: *John Dury: Advocate of Christian Union*, doctoral thesis, Chicago University, 1930.

Baxter, Richard et. al.. *The judgment and advice of the Assembly of the Associated Ministers of Worcester, Aug. 6th 1658 concerning the endeavours of ecclesiasticall peace, and the waies and means of Christian unity, which Mr John Durey doth present, sent unto him in the name, and by the appointment of the aforesaid Assembly*, 1658.

Beeke, Joel R., Election and Reprobation: Calvin on Equal Ultimacy, *BOT Magazine*, Issue 489, June 2004, pp. 8-19.

Berg, J. van den, and Wall, Ernestine van der, (eds), *Jewish-Christian Relations in the Seventeenth Century: Studies and Documents*, Kluver Academic Publishers, Dordrecht, undated, first 94 pages only. https://openaccess.leidenuniv.nl/bitstream/1887/.../1/3_908_005.pdf.

Blanke, Fritz and Leuschner, Immanuel, *Heinrich Bullinger: Vater der reformierten Kirche*, Theologischer Verlag Zürich, 1990.

Blanke, Fritz, *Der Junge Bullinger*, Zürich, 1942.

Bouvier, André, *Henri Bullinger, Réformateur et conseiller oecuménique*, Zürich-Neuchâtel, 1940.

Bowman, Jacob N.: *The Protestant Interest in Cromwell's Foreign Relations*, doctoral thesis, Heidelberg, 1900.

Braine, John: *Dr Durie's Defence of the Present Ministry*, John Braine, 1649, (Addressed to Cromwell's Parliament).

Brandes, Frederic H., John Dury and his Work for Germany, *Catholic Presbyterian*, July 1882 pp. 22-32, and August 1882 pp. 91-101.

Brauer, Karl, *Die Unionstätigkeit John Duries unter dem Protektorat Cromwells*, Marburg University, 1907.

Breslow, Marvin Arthur, *A Mirror of England: English Puritan Views of Foreign Nations 1618-1640*, Harvard University Press, 1970.

Bright, John: *A History of Israel*, SCM, 1960.

Bruce, John (ed), *The Calendar of State Papers, Domestic Series, of the Reign of Charles I*. vol. 4, 1629-1631; vol. 5, 1631-1633; vol. 6, 1633-1634; vol. 7, 1634-1635; vol. 8, 1635; vol. 9. 1635-1636; vol. 10, 1636-1637; vol. 11, 1637; vol. 12, 1637-1638.

Buchan, John, *Oliver Cromwell*, The Reprint Society, London, 1941.

Buchanan, George: *De Jure Regni aud Scotos or a Dialogue, concerning the due Privilege of Government in the Kingdom of Scotland*, London, Richard Baldwin 1689, EEBO.

Burton, Thomas, *Diary of Thomas Burton Esq. Member in the Parliaments of Oliver and Richard Cromwell from 1656 to 1659*, 4 vols, London, 1828.

Büsser, Fritz, *Calvins Urteil über sich selbst*, Zwingli Verlag, 1950.

Büsser, Fritz, *Die Prophezei: Humanismus und Reformation in Zürich*, Züricher Beiträge zur Reformationsgeschichte, Verlag Peter Lang, 1994.

Büsser, Fritz, *Heinrich Bullinger (1504-1575): Leben, Werk und Wirkung*, Band I, II, TVZ, 2004-2005.

Bulkeley, Peter: *The Gospel-Covenant or the Covenant of Grace Opened*, London, 1651.

Bullinger, Henry, *The Decades of Henry Bullinger: With new introductions by George Ella and Joel Beeke*, Grand Rapids, 2004.

Bullinger, Henry: Band 1, *Briefe der Jahre 1524-1531*, Zürich 1973.

Bullinger, Henry: Band 1, *Exegetische Schriften aus den Jahren 1525-26*, Zürich 1983.

Bullinger, Henry: *Briefe des Jahres 1539*, Zürich 2002.

Bullinger, Henry: *Briefe des Jahres 1540*, Zürich 2003.

Bullinger, Henry: *Der Widertoeufferen ursprung/fürgang etc.*, Zürich, 1561.

Bullinger, Henry: *Studiorum ratio*, 1. Teilband Text und Übersetzung; 2 Teilband Kommentar, Zürich, 1987.

Bullinger, Henry: *Unveröffentlichte Werke aus der Kappeler Zeit*, Zürich 1991.

Campi, Emidio et al (eds), *Heinrich Büllinger Schriften*, TVZ, 7 vols, 204.

Campi, Emidio and Opitz, Peter: *Henry Bullinger: Life-Thought-Influence*, Band 1, TVZ, 2004.

Campi, Emidio (ed.): *Heinrich Bullinger und seiner Zeit: Eine Vorlesungsreihe*, TVZ, 2004.

Carlyle, Thomas (ed), Oliver Cromwell's Letters and Speeches with Elucidations, (5 vols), Chapman and Hall, 1871.

Carr, J. A., *The Life and Times of James Ussher, Archbishop of Armagh*, London, 1895.

Carruthers, S. W., *The Everyday Work of the Westminster Assembly*, Philadelphia, 1943.

Chandler, S, *The History of Persecutions*, Longman etc., 1813. See especially Book IV, Of Persecution amongst Protestants, pp. 287-354.

Christoffel, R., *Huldrich Zwingli: Leben und Auserwählte Schriften*, Elberfeld, 1857.

Coenen, Lothar (ed.): *Teologisches Begriffslexikon zum Neuen Testament*, 2 vols, Brockhaus, 1983.

Calvin, John, Calvin's Calvinism, SGU, trans. Henry Cole, D.D., 1927.

Calvin, John, Institutes of Christian Religion (2 vols.), Eerdmans, 1979.

Cardwell, Edward, *Documentary Annals of the Reformed Church of England*, 2 vols, Oxford University, 1844.

Courvoisier, Jaques: *Zwingli: A Reformed Theologian*, The Epworth Press, 1963.

Cromwell, Oliver: *Cromwell's Letters to Foreign Princes and States*, London, 1700.

Cromwell, Oliver: Oliver Cromwell's letter to Landgrave William concerning Durie's work in uniting Lutherans and Reformed, Hessisches Staatsarkiv, Marburg.

Davenant, Bishop John et al., *Good Counsells for the Peace of Reformed Churches by some Reverend and Learned Bishops and other Divines*, Translated out of Latin, Oxford, 1641: containing,

The Opinion of some Famous Divines of the French Church.

The Opinion of the most Reverend Father in God James Usher, Lord Archbishop of Armagh and Primate of Ireland, with some other Reverend Bishops in Ireland, May 14, Anno 1634.

The Opinion of the Right Reverend Father in God John Davenant Bishop of Salisbury to his Learned and Worthy Friend Mr John Dury.

The Opinion of the Right Reverend Father in God Joseph Hall Bishop of Exeter.

The Opinion of the Right Reverend Father in God Thomas Morton Bishop of Durham, Concerning the Peace of the Church.

De Witt, J. R., *Jus Divinum: The Westminster Assembly and the Divine Right of Church Government*, J. H. Kok N. V. Kampen, 1969.

Duke, Alastair, *Calvinism in Europe 1540-1610*, Manchester University Press, 1997.

Durie, John (Johannes Duraeus): *A Summarie Platform of the Heads of a Body of Practical Divinity which the Ministers of the Protestant Churches abroad have sued for and which is farther enlarged in a Treatise intitled An Earnest Plea for Gospel-Communion, etc.*, 1654, London. Bodleian Library.

Durie, John: *An information concerning the present state of the Jewish nation in Europe and Judea: wherein the footsteps of Providence preparing a way for their conversion to Christ, and for their deliverance from captivity are discovered*, with Henry Jessey and Petrus Serrurier 1658, printed by R.W. for Thomas Brewster London. Bodleian Library.

Durie, John: *Certain Positions Concerning The Fundamentals of Christianity, Which bringe Salvation to all that entertain them.* 1656, Ref: 14/2/2/1A-6B, Hartlib Papers.

Durie, John: *Concerning the Question Whether it bee lawfull to admit Iewes to come into a Christian commonwealth*, Ref: 68/8/1A-2B, Hartlib Papers.

Durie, John: *Memo on the Conversion of the Jews.* Ref. 25/4/1A-4B, Hartlib Papers.

Durie, John: *The Earnest Breathings of Forreign Protestants, Divines and others: to the Ministers and other Able Christians of these three Nations, for a Compleat Body of Practical Divinity.* 1658, Bodleian Library.

Durie, John: *To the King's most Excellent Magesty: or to his Magesties Commisioner and to his Reverend and loving Brethren in Christ, the PASTORS and ELDERS of the Kirk, of Scotland met together at their generall Assembly appointed to be held at Saint Andrews in July Anno,* London. 1641, Bodleian Library.

Durie, John: *A memorial concerning PEACE Ecclesiastical amongst Protestants: which John Dury offered to Master Alexander Henderson, to bee sent or presented unto the General Assembly of the Church of Scotland.* Bodleian Library.

Durie, John: *The copy of a letter written to mr. Alexander Hinderson*, Lond. 1643, Bodleian Library.

Durie, John et. al.: *Good Covnsells for the Peace of Reformed Churches*, (John Dury; John Davenant; Thomas Morton; Joseph Hall; James Ussher), 1645 and 1654, Bodleian Library.

John Durie: *Jewes in America, or, Probabilities that the Americans are of that race. With the removall of some contrary reasonings, and earnest desires for effectuall endeavours to make them Christian*, printed by William Hunt. for Tho. Slater, and are to be sold at his shop at the signe of the Angel in Duck lane, London. 1650, Bodleian Library.

Durie, John et. al.: *An information concerning the present state of the Jewish nation in Europe and Judea: wherein the footsteps of Providence preparing a way for their conversion to Christ, and for their deliverance from captivity are discovered*, with Henry Jessey and Petrus Serrurier printed by R.W. for Thomas Brewster, London, 1658, Bodleian Library.

Egli, Emil et al.: *Huldreich Zwingli Sämtliche Werke*, Zürich 1983.

Ella, George M.: *John Gill and Justification from Eternity: A Tercentenary Appreciation 1697-1997*, Go Publications, 1998.

Ella, George M.: *John Gill and the Cause of God and Truth*, Go Publications, 1995.

Ella, George M., John Gill and the Charge of Hyper-Calvinism: A Vindication, *Baptist Quarterly*, October, 1995.

Ella, George: John Gill: Orthodox Dissenter, *New Focus*, June/July 1997.

Ella, George M.: The Life and Thought of John Gill, *New Focus*, Oct./Nov. 1997.

Ella, G. M., Henry Bullinger, *New Focus*, Part I, Vol. 7, No. 01, Part II, Vol. 7, No. 02, 2002 and Zürich University website, www.unizh.ch.

Ella, G. M., Henry Bullinger (1504-1575), Shepherd of the Churches, *The Banner of Sovereign Grace Truth*, Grand Rapids, Vol. 12, No. 5, May-June 2004.

Ella, George: *Law and Gospel in the Theology of Andrew Fuller* 2nd ed., Go Publications, 2011.

Ella, G. M., A Gospel Unworthy of Any Acceptation, *Focus*, No. 8, Winter 1993/94

Ella, G. M., John Gill and the Cause of God and Truth, Evangelical Times, April, 1994.

Ella, George M.: Archbishop James Usher, *New Focus*, Oct./Nov. 1998.

Ella, George M.: Bishop John Davenant and the Death of Christ: A Vindication, *New Focus*, Aug./Sept. 1997.

Ella, George M.: Walter Chantry and the New Law of Righteousness, *New Focus,* Dec./Jan. 2009.

Ella, George M.: Henry Bullinger and the Covenant of Grace, *New Focus,* April/May 2007.

Ella, George M.: New Covenant Theology by Tom Wells and Fred Zaspel, a Review Article, *New Focus*, Dec./Jan. 2007.

Ella, George M.: NCT: A Critical Evaluation, 1. A New Approach to the Law, *New Focus*, Feb/March 2007, Part 2. A New Approach to the Covenant of Grace, April/May, 2007, Part 3. The Offices of Christ, June/July 2007, Part 4. Attempts to Combat NCT, Aug./Sept. 2007, Part 5. The NCT Church, Oct./Nov. 2007.

Ella, George M.: The Works of Andrew Fuller, A Banner of Truth Facsimile Reprint. A Review Article, Part I, *New Focus* Feb./Mar. 2008, Part II, April/May 2008.

Ella, George M.: John Durie Part I, *New Focus*, Feb./Mar. 2009, Part II, April/May 2009, Part III, June/July, 2009.

Ella, George M.: John Durie: Practical Divinity, *New Focus*, Dec./Jan. 2011.

Ella, George M.: Covenant Theology As Seen by NCT, *New Focus*, April/May, 2011.

Ella, George M.: Oliver Cromwell: Rebel, Republican and Reformer Part I, *New Focus*, June/July, 2011, Part II, Aug./Sept. 2011.

Ella, George M.: *The Practical Divinity of Universal Learning: John Durie's Educational Pansophism*, (Dr. theol thesis), VKW, 2012. See especially Chapter Five on 'The Place of the Jews in Durie's Quest for Universal Learning'.

Ella, George M.: Heinrich Bullinger: Vater und Hirte der Reformation. *gudh. Zeitschrift für Theologie und Gesselschaft*, 2, 2018, Nr. 22/12.

Evelyn, John, *The Diary of John Evelyn*, London, 1559.

Faber, Eva-Maria, Zur Frage der Prädestination in der Theologie Johannes Calvins, *Theologische Zeitschrift der Universität Basle*, Jahrgang 56, 2000, pp. 50-68.

Fisher, Edward, *A Marrow of Modern Divinity in Two Parts*, with Notes by Thomas Boston, London, 1837.

Ford, Alan, *James Ussher: Theology, History and Politics in Early-Modern Ireland*, Oxford, 2007.

Fox, George and Naylor, James: *To thee Oliver Cromwell, into whose hands God hath committed the Sword of Justice*, London, 1653.

Fraser, Antonia, *Cromwell Our Chief of Men*, Book Club Associates, 1973.

Fritz Blanke and Immanuel Leuschner: *Heinrich Bullinger: Vater der Reformierten Kirche*, Zürich, 1990.

Fuller, A. G., *Life of the Rev. Andrew Fuller*, Religious Tract Society, Undated.

Fuller, Thomas Ekins, *A Memoir of the Life and Writings of A. Fuller*, J. Heaton & Son, 1863.

Fuller, Andrew: *The Works of Andrew Fuller*, Banner of Truth, 2007.

Gäbler, Ulrich et. al, *Heinrich Bulinger Werke, Briefe der Jahre 1524-1531*, TVZ, 1974.

Gäbler, Ulrich und Herkenrath, Erland (eds), *Heinrich Bullinger 1504-1575: Gesammelte Aufsätze zum 400. Todestag*, Band II., TVZ, 1975:.

Gäbler, Ulrich, *Huldrych Zwingli: His Life and Work*, Fortress Press, 1986.

Ganoczy, Alexandre, *The Young Calvin*, T. & T. Clark Ltd., 1988.

Gardiner, Samuel Rawson (ed.), *Documents relating to the proceedings against William Prynne, in 1634 and 1637*. With a biographical fragment by the late John Bruce, Printed for the Camden Society, 1877.

Gardiner, Samuel Rawson (ed.), *The Constitutional Documents of the Puritan Revolution 1625-1660*, Clarendon Press, 1906.

Gardiner, Samuel Rawson, *The History of the Commonwealth and Protectorate 1649-1660*, 2 vols, Longmans, Green, and Co., 1894.

Geneva, Ann, *Astrology and the Seventeenth Century Mind: William Lilly and the Language of the Stars*, Manchester University Press, 1995.

Gibson, Kenneth, John Dury's Apocalyptic Thought: A Reassessment, *Journal of Ecclesiastical History*, Vol. 61, No. 2, April 2010, pp. 299-313.

Gill, John: *Body of Divinity* (3 vols), Subscription, 1767.

Gill, John: *Doctrine of God's Everlasting Love to His Elect, Baptist Standard Bearer*, 1987.

Gill, John: *Expositions of the Old and New Testaments*, Baptist *Standard Bearer* 1989.

Gill, John: *Doctrine of Justification by the Righteousness of Christ*, London 1756.

Gill, John: *Sermons and Tracts*, 3 vols, Primitive Baptist Library, 1981.

Gill, John: *The Cause of God and Truth*, Baker Book House, 1980.

Gloede, Günter, Calvin: Weg und Werk, Leipzig, 1953.

Göransson, Sven: *Den Europeiska Konfessionspolitikens Upplösning 1654,-1660*, Uppsala, 1956.

Golding, Peter: *Covenant Theology*, Christian Focus Publications, 2008.

Göransson, Sven, *Den Europeiska Konfessionspolitikens Upplösning 1654-1660*, Uppsala/Wiesbaden, 1956.

Gribben, Crawford: Review of Henry Bullinger: Shepherd of the Churches, Evangelical Times, June, 2008.

Hanko, Herman: Heinrich Bullinger: Covenant Theologian, *Standard Bearer*, 1993, vol. 69 #19.

Harder, Leland (ed), *The Sources of Swiss Anabaptism*, Herald Press, 1985.

Harrison, Graham, *Dr. John Gill and His Teaching*, Evangelical Library, 1971.

Hartlib, Samuel (Compiler), *The Hartlib Papers, A Complete Text and Image Database of the Papers of Samuel Hartlib (c. 1600-1662)*, Sheffield University, 2 CDs, 2002.

Healey, Robert M., The Jew in Seventeenth-Century Protestant Thought, *Church History*, vol. 46, March 1877, No.1, pp. 63-79.

Heath, James: *Flagellium or The Life and Death, Birth and Burial of Oliver Cromwell The Late Usurper*, London, 1663.

Hetherington, W. M., *History of the Westminster Assembly*, Edinburgh, 1843.

Hill, Christopher, *God's Englishman: Oliver Cromwell and the English Revolution*, Book Club Edition, 1970.

Hill, Christopher, *The English Bible and the Seventeenth-Century Revolution*, Penguin Books, 1994.

Hof, W. J. op 't, De internationale invloed van het Puritanisme, from *Het Puritanisme: geschiedenis, theologie en invloed* / W. van 't Spijker, R. Bisschop, W.J. op 't Hof. ('s-Gravenhage, Boekencentrum, 2001), p. 271-384, Boekencentrum | Claves pietatis, 2007.06.15; versie 1.0, Onderzoeksarchief / Research Archive Nadere Reformatie, Nummer B01001994.

Holstun, James (ed.) Pamphlet Wars: Prose in the English Revolution, University of NY, 1992.

Hollweg, Walter, *Heinrich Bullingers Hausbuch*, Neukirchen, 1956.

Hyamson, A. M., *A History of the Jews in England*, Chatto & Windus, London, 1908.

Hyamson, Albert M., The lost tribes and the Return of the Jews to England, *Transactions of the Jewish Historical Society of England*, vol 5, 1903, pp. 114-147.

Johnson, Ronald A. P., 'For Such a Time as This': John Dury, Jean-Baptiste Stouppe, and Cromwellian Diplomacy, *Selected Annual proceedings of the Florida Conference of Historians*, 15, (2008) 95-101.

Jones, Guernsey, *The Diplomatic Relations between Cromwell and Charles X. Gustavus of Sweden*, inaugural dissertation for the degree of Doctor of Philosophy, submitted to the Philosophical Faculty of the University of Heidelberg, 1897.

Journal of the House of Commons, vol. 7, 1651-60, 1802.

Katz, David S. and Israel Jonathan I, (eds), *Sceptics, Millenarians and Jews*, Brill, Leiden, 1990.

Katz, David S., *Philosemitism and the Readmission of the Jews to England, 1603-1655*, Oxford, 1982.

Katz, David, S., *Philosemiticism and the Readmission of the Jews to England, 1603-1655*, Oxford, 19821.

Kendall, R.T., Calvin and English Calvinism to 1649, Paternoster Press, 1997.

Kevan, Ernest: *The Grace of Law*, Soli Deo Gloria, 2003 reprint.

Kirkby, A. H., Andrew Fuller: Evangelical Calvinist, *Baptist Quarterly*, XV, 1954, pp. 195-202.

Kirkby, A. H., The Theology of Andrew Fuller and its relation to Calvinism, Ph.D., Edin., 1956.

Knox, R. Buick, *James Ussher: Archbishop of Armagh*, University of Wales Press, 1967.

Köhler, Walther: *Huldrych Zwingli*, Hoehler & Amelang, Leipzig, 1943.

Lang, August, *Zwingli und Calvin*, Bielefeld and Leipzig, 1913.

Lasker, Daniel J., Karaism and Christian Hebraism: A New Document, *Renaissance Quarterly*, 59 (2006) pp. 1089-1116.

Lawson, Thomas, *Calvin: His Life and Times*, London, undated.

Levy, S., John Dury and the English Jewry, *Transactions of the Jewish Historical Society of England*, vol. 4, 1899-1901, London, pp. 76-82.

Lindeboom, Dr. J., Johannes Duraeus en Zijne Werkzaamheid in Dienst Van Cromwell's Politik, *Nederlands archief voor kerkgeschiedenis, Dutch Review of Church History*, vol. XVI, 1921, Leiden, pp. 241-268.

Locher, Gottfried W.: *Huldrych Zwingli in Neuer Sicht: Zehn Beiträge zur Theologie der Züricher Reformation*, Zwingli Verlag, Zürich/Stuttgart, 1969.

Locher, Gottfried, W.: Grundzüge der Theologie Huldrych Zwinglis im Vergleich mit derjenigen Martin Luthers und Johannes Calvins, *Zwingliana*, Zürich, Sonderdruck aus den *Zwingliana*, Heft 7 und 8, 1967.

McGrath, Alister E.: *Johann Calvin*, Benziger, 1991.

MacGregor, James, The Free Offer in the Westminster Confession, *BOTM*, 82-83, 1970, pp. 51-58.

Mandelbrote S, 'John Dury and the Practice of Irenism', in N. R. Aston (ED.), *Religious Changes in Europe (1650-1914)*, Essays for John McManners , Oxford, Clarendon Press, 1997, p. 41-58.

Mason, Archibald: Observations on the Public Covenant betwixt God and the Church, Glasgow, 1799.

May, Thomas, MP, *An Epitomy of English History, Wherein Arbitrary Government Is Display'd to the Life, In the illegal Transactions of the late Times under the Tyrannick Usurpation of Oliver Cromwell; being a Parallel to the Four years Reign of the late King James, Whose Government was Popery, Slavery, and Arbitrary Power*, London, 1690.

Members of the University of Oxford, *To the Supreame Authority the Parliament of the Commonwealth of England*, undated, Ref: 47/19/1A-6B, Hartlib Papers.

Menk, Gerhard, Die Hohe Schule Herborn, Der Deutsche Kalvinismus und die Westliche Welt, Sondredruck aus *Jahrbuch der Hessischen Kirchengeschichtlichen Vereinigung*, 35. Band, Hessisches Staatsarchiv, Marburg, 1984.

Metzler, Ed, *The Impact of Israel on Western Philosophy*, Baalschem Press, Herborn, 1993.

Milton, Antony, 'The Unchanged Peacemaker'? John Dury and the politics of Irenicism in England, 1628-1643. In Samuel Hartlib and Universal Reformation: studies in intellectual communication, ed. M. Greengrass, 95-117. Cambridge: Cambridge University Press, 1994.

Moore, Jonathan D., *English Hypothetical Universalism*, Eerdman's, 2007.

Müller, Patrik, *Heinrich Bullinger: Reformator*, Kirchenpolitiker, Historiker, TVZ, 2004.

Murray, John: *A Biblio-Theological Study*, Tyndale Press, 1954.

Murray, John: *The Covenant of Grace: A Biblico-Theological Study*, Tyndale Press, 1954.

Niesel, Wilhelm, *The Theology of Calvin*, Westminster Press, 1956.

Nuttall, G. F., Calvinism in Free Church History, *Baptist Quarterly*, 22 (8), 1968, pp. 418-428.

Opitz, Peter, *Heinrich Bullinger als Theologe: Eine Studie zu den 'Dekaden'*, TVZ, 2004.

Parker Society, *Decades*, 4 vols, 1849.

Parker Society, *Original Letters Relative to the English Reformation, 1537-1558*, 2 vols, 1847.

Parker Society, *Zürich Letters, First Series, 1558-1579*, 1842.

Parker Society, *Zürich Letters, Second Series, 1558-1602*, 1845.

Parker, T. H. L., Calvin's Doctrine of Justification, *EQ*, XXIV, 1952.

Paul, Robert S, *The Lord Protector: Religio and Politics in the Life of Oliver Cromwell*, Luterworth Press, 1955.

Peacey, Jason, *Politicians and Pamphleteers: Propaganda During the English Civil Wars and Interregnum*, Ashgate, 2004.

Pestalozzi, Carl, *Heinrich Bullinger. Leben und ausgewählte Schriften*, Eberfeld, 1858.

Pine, Leonard, Heinrich Bullinger. The Common Shepherd of All Christian Churches, *Zürich University website*, www. unizh.ch..

Popkin, Richard H., Hartlib, Dury and the Jews, in *Samuel Hartlib and Universal Reformation: Studies in Intellectual Communication*, Cambridge University Press, 1994, eds M. Greengrass, M. Leslie, and T. Raylor, 118-136.

Popkin, Richard Henry, James R. Jacob. Henry Stubbe, Radical Protestantism and the Early Enlightenment, review, *Journal of the History of Philosophy*, 24, 2, 1986.

Popkin, Richard Henry, The Fictional Jewish Council of 1650: A Great English Pipedream, *Hîstôrya yêhûdît*, Haifa, vol. 5, No. 2, Fall 1991, pp. 7-22.

Popkin, Richard Henry, The First College for Jewish Students, Revue des études juives, Peeters, Paris, 1984, pp. 351-364.

Popkin, Richard Henry, The Lost Tribes, the Caraites and the English Millenarians, *The Journal of Jewish Studies*, Oxford, 1986, Issue 37, 213-227.

Popkin, Richard Henry, Three English Tellings of the Sabbatai Zevi Story, Jewish History, vol. 8, Numbers 1-2.

Prestwich, Menna (ed), *International Calvinism 1541-1715*, Clarendon Press, 1986.

Popkin, Richard Henry, "The End of the Career of a Great 17th Century Millenarian - John Dury." In *Pietismus und Neuzeit*, ed. M. Brecht, 1988, 203-220.

Price, Seymour, Dr John Gill and the Confession of 1729, *Baptist Quarterly*, IV, 1928, pp. 366-371.

Reilly, Tom, *Cromwell: An Honourable Enemy*, Phoenix Press, London, 1999.

Reisinger, John and Seiver, Randy: *God's Righteous Kingdom Unrighteously Defended*, Sound of Grace, NY, undated.

Reisinger, John: *Abraham's Four Seeds*, New Covenant Media, 1998.

Reisinger, John: *But I Say Unto You ...*, Crowne Publications, 1989.

Reisinger, John: *Christ Lord and Lawgiver Over the Church*, New Covenant Media, 1998.

Robinson, Henry, *An answer to Mr. John Dury his letter which he writ from the Hague, to Mr. Thomas Goodwin. Mr. Philip Nye. Mr. Samuel Hartlib: Concerning the manner of the reformation of the church, and answering other matters of consequence. And King James his judgment concerning the Book of Common Prayer*, printed Anno Dom. London, 1644.

Ringgren, Helmer: *The Messiah in the Old Testament*, SCM Press, 1967.

Robinson; Olin C., The Legacy of John Gill, *Baptist Quarterly*, xxvi, 1971, pp. 111-125.

Rohr, John Von, *The Covenant of Grace in Puritan Thought*, Wipf & Stock, 1986.

Rutherford, Samuel: *Lex, Rex, or The Law and the Prince*, London, John Field, 1644.

Ryland Jun, John, *The Life and Death of the Rev. Andrew Fuller*, Button and Son, 1818.

Scougal, Harry J., *Die Pädagogischen Schriftern John Durys*, German doctoral thesis, Jena 1905.

Seiver, Randy: *In These Last Days*, New Covenant Media, 1998.

Seymour, R. E., John Gill. Baptist Theologian, 1697-1771, Ph. D., Edin., 1954.

Shaw, William A., *A History of the English Church During the Civil Wars and Under the Commonwealth*, 2 vols., Longmans, Green and Co., 1900.

Spalding, Ruth, *The Improbable Puritan: A Life of Bulstrode Whitelocke 1605-1675*, London, 1975.

Stähelin, Ernst, Johannes Calvin: Leben und ausgewählten Schriften, 2 vols, Elberfeld, 1863.

Staedtke, Joachim: *Johannes Calvin: Erkentnis und Gestaltung*, Göttingen, 1969.

Staedtke, Joachim, *Die Theologie des jungen Bullinger*, Zwingli Verlag, Zürich, 1962.

Stevens, W. Peter: *The Theology of Huldrych Zwingli*, Clarendon Press, 1983.

Stotz, P. (trans. and ed.) *Heinrich Bullinger Werke, Studiorum ratio: Studienanleitung*, Teil Band 2, Einleitung, Kommentar, Register, TVZ, 1987.

Stotz, P. (trans. and ed.), Heinrich Bullinger Werke, Studiorum ratio: Studienanleitung, Teil Band 1, Text und Uebersetzung, TVZ, 1987.

Suts, Johannes, *Heinrich Bullinger: Der Retter der Züricher Reformation*, Zürich, 1915.

Tatham, G. B., *The Puritans in Power*, CUP, 1913.

Terry, Charles Sanford, *Papers Relating to the Army of the Solemn League and Covenant 1643-1647*, 2 vols, 1917.

Trevor-Roper, Hugh, *The Crisis of the Seventeenth Century: Religion, the Reformation and Social Change* (Indianapolis: Liberty Fund, 2001).

Trenchard. Ernest H., 'Grace, Covenant and Law', *Evangelical Quarterly*, 1957/3, pp. 131-148.

Trevor-Roper, Hugh, *The Crisis of the Seventeenth Century: Religion, the Reformation and Social Change* (Indianapolis: Liberty Fund, 2001).

Tudur-Jones R., et al (eds), *Protestant Nonconformist Texts 1550-1700*, Vol. 1, Ashgate, Aldershot,1988.

Turnbull, G. H., Letters Written by John Dury in Sweden 1636-1638, *Kyrkohistorisk Årsskrift*, 49, 1949, pp. 204-251.

Valeris, Mark: 'New Divinity and the American Revolution and Bellamy's call to Armed Revolt', *William and Mary Quarterly*, vol. 46, no. 4, Oct 1989, pp. 741-69.

Van den Berg, J. and Van der Wall, E.G.E (eds): *Jewish-Christian Relations in the Seventeenth Century: Studies and Documents*, Kluwer Academic Publishers, Dordrecht, undated.

Venema, Cornelis P., *Heinrich Bullinger and the Doctrine of Predestination*, Baker Academic, 2002.

Vom Berg, H. G. And Hausammann S. (eds), *Heinrich Bullinger Werke, Exegetische Schriften aus den Jahren 1525-1526*, TVZ, 1983.

Vom Berg, H. G. et al (eds), *Heinrich Bullinger Werke, Unveröffentlichte Werke der Kappeler Zeit*. Theologica, TVZ, 1991.

Von Schulthess-Rechberg, Gustav: *Heinrich Bullinger der Nachfolger Zwinglis*, Halle, 1904.

Wall, van der, Ernestine, *A Precursor of Christ or a Jewish Impostor? Petrus Serrarius and Jean de Labadie on the Jewish Messianic Movement around Sabbatai Sevi*, openaccess.leidenuniv.nl/bitstream/ 1887/12129/1/3_908_17pdf. pp. 109-124.

Wall, van der, Ernestine, *The Dutch Hebraist Adam Boreel and the Mishnah Project: Six Unpublished Letters (Durie-Boreel)*, LIAS 16 (1989) 2, pp. 239-263, Leiden University.

Wall, van der, Ernestine, *Three Letters by Menasseh Ben Israel to John Durie* (original letters with commentary), *Nederlands Archief voer kerkegeschiedenis 65 (1985)*, Leiden, p.p. 46-53.

Walser, Peter, *Die Prädestination bei Heinrich Bullinger im Zusammenhang mit seiner Gotteslehre*, Zürich, 1957.

Weber, Otto: *Grundlagen der Dogmatik*, 2 vols, Neukirchener Verlag, 1983.

Wells, Tom and Zaspel, Fred: *New Covenant Theology*, New Covenant Media, 2002.

Wernle, D.P.: *Calvin und Basle bis zum Tode des Myconius 1535-1552*, Basle, 1909.

West, Jim et al: *From Zwingli to Amyraut: Exploring the Growth of European Reformed Traditions*, Vandenhoeck & Ruprecht, 2017.

Westin, Gunnar: *Svenska Kyrkan och De Protestantiska Enhetssträvandena under 1630- Talet*, Uppsala, 1934.

Westin, Gunnar *Negotiations about Church Unity, John Durie, Gustavus Adolphus and Axel Oxenstierna 1628-34*, including *John Durie, Documents and Letters*, Uppsala 1932.

White, B. R., John Gill in London 1719-1729, *Baptist Quarterly*, XXII, 1967, pp. 72-91.

Whitfield, H.; Ed. Calamy et al, *A Narrative of the Late Proceedings at Whitehall, Concerning the Jews*, London 1656. Reprinted in *Harleian Miscellany*, pp. 445-454, 1810.

Wies-Campagner, Elizabeth, Messianismus und die Entdeckung Amerikas: Menesse Ben Israel, *Internet Zeitschrift für Kulturwissenschaft*, 16, März 2005.

Wilcox, Peter, The Lectures of John Calvin and the Nature of his Audience, *Archiv für Reformationsgeschichte*, Jahrgang 87, pp.136-48.

Wilensky, M. L., 'Thomas Barlow's and John Dury's attitude towards the readmission of the Jews to England,' Part 1, The Jewish Quarterly Review 50 (1959): 167-175.

Wilensky, M. L. 'Thomas Barlow's and John Dury's attitude towards the readmission of the Jews to England, Part 2, *The Jewish Quarterly Review* 50, no. 3 (1960): 256-268.

Windsor, Graham, The Reunion Views of Archbishop Ussher and his Circle, *Churchman*, 77/3, 1963.

Witsius, Hermann, *The Economy of the Covenants Between God and Man* (2 vols), Reformation Heritage Books, 2010.

Woolsey, Andrew A., *Unity and Continuity in Covenantal Thought: A Study in the Reformed Tradition to the Westminster Assembly*, Reformation Heritage Books, 2012.

Zwingli, Huldrych: *Hauptschriften*, 9 vols, Volksausgabe, Zwingli-Verlag, Zürich, 1940.

Index Of Scripture Passages

Old Testament

Genesis

1:28-30	341fn	20:10	192fn
2:16	341fn	23:20ff	193
3:15	342fn	24:3, 7	193
8, 9	342fn	24:4-8	336
15:13	192fn	24:7, 8	147fn
16, 17	189	24:8	333
17:9	191	31:17	85
17:7	130	32:7	193
17:15	191fn	32:13	75, 339fn
17:18	191	34:27, 28	73
17:19	191fn		
17:23-26	189	**Leviticus**	
18:18	191fn	17:8ff	192fn
21:12	191	25:48, 49	298fn
21:18ff	189		
25:9ff	190	**Numbers**	
28:8ff	190	16:28-30	136fn
43:9	305fn	18:19	277
49:1-33	195fn	22-25	195fn
		25:13	332

Exodus

3:6	75, 339fn	**Deuteronomy**	
3:8	155fn	4:13	277
12:37, 38	155fn	5:14	192fn
19	193	6:5	348, 348fn

429

New Testament

Galatians cont'd

3:16	389
3:18	307fn
3:19-25	110, 111
3:23	117, 118
3:23-25	388, 389
3:24, 25	313fn
4:4	299fn, 301fn
5	113fn, 118

Ephesians

1	301
1:23	301fn
2:1ff	391
2:1-5	53, 63
2:3	279, 290
2:12	48fn, 277
2:15, 16	48, 392fn
3:21	150fn
4:4	382
4:20ff	286

Colossians

1:5	382
1:21	296
2:11-14	107
3:9	286

1 Thessalonians

4:13-17	382fn

1 Timothy

1	71fn
1:8	79
1:8, 9	101
1:13-16	323
1:15	386
2:5	296fn, 300fn

2 Timothy

1:1	320
1:5-11	314
1:9	285
2:12	265
2:19	264
3:7	108fn
3:14-17	149
3:16	71fn
3:16, 17	150, 233

Titus

1:2	285, 320, 383
1:4	323
2:13	383fn
3:7	264

Philemon

18, 19	304fn

Hebrews

2:13	305fn
2:17	334
2:18	299fn
3	340
3:1	334
4:14, 15	334
5:1	334
5:5	334
5:6, 10	335fn
6:12	308fn
6:20	335fn
7:1ff	179fn
7:1-25	335fn
7:11	336
7:20-22	304fn
8	76
8:6	296fn

Index Of Names And Places

443

Talmud	165, 170
Tartars	174
Taylor, Hudson	192
Theophilus	148
Thirty Years' War	34, 35, 242, 246, 257
Thorpe, William	367
Thurloe, John	36
Thyatira	369
Tigrinya	161, 164
Tiny Tim	145
Toplady, Augustus	55
Tossanus, Paul	353
Towneley	366
Trail, Robert	55
Travers, Walter	211, 352, 361
Turkey	157, 177, 342, 344
Twisse, William	22, 395
Tyndale, William	321, 337, 353, 358
Ugaritic	161, 163, 167
United Nations	178, 179
United States of America	173
Universal Learning	14, 166, 175, 242, 252, 259, 421
Uppsala	19, 31, 35, 38, 118, 159, 257, 374, 405
Ursinus, Zacharias	321
Uz	342
Vaterjude	165
Vaud	226
Vos, Gerhard	214, 228
Wakefield	366
Waldensians	221
Waldron, Samuel	12, 47-49, 52, 60, 62, 294
Wales	30, 403
Walker, George	241, 396
Ward, Samuel	258, 353, 395, 396
Warfield, Benjamin B.	33
Watson, Foster	414
Weber, Otto	295
Webster, Tom	23
Wejrud, Anders	257
Wells, Thomas	70, 71, 96, 135, 145, 149, 150, 153, 324, 351
Wenkel, David H.	385-393
Westin, Gunnar	31, 412
Westminster Abbey	32
Westminster Assembly	11, 28, 29, 32, 34, 203, 214, 215, 249, 257, 321, 357, 409, 411, 413

Magazines and Journals